MOTHER MIDNIGHT

Plate Number 1 of William Hogarth's *The Harlot's Progress.*
(From *Hogarth's Graphic Works*, comp. Ronald Paulson, Volume
2: The Engravings. Yale University Press, 1965. Used with
permission.)

MOTHER MIDNIGHT

Birth, Sex, and Fate in
Eighteenth-Century Fiction
(Defoe, Richardson, and Sterne)

Robert A. Erickson

AMS PRESS INC.
New York, N.Y.

Library of Congress Cataloging-in-Publication Data

Erickson, Robert A.
  Mother Midnight.

  (AMS studies in the eighteenth century, ISSN 0196-6561;
no. 10)
  Bibliography: p.
  Includes index.
  1. English fiction—18th century—History and criticism.
2. Fate and fatalism in literature. 3. Defoe, Daniel, 1661?-
1731. Fortunes and misfortunes of the famous Moll Flanders.
4. Richardson, Samuel, 1689-1761—Criticism and interpre-
tation. 5. Sterne, Laurence, 1713-1768. Life and opinions of
Tristram Shandy, gentleman. 6. Childbirth in literature. 7.
Sex role, in literature. 8. Women in literature.
I. Title. II. Series.
PR858.F35E75 1986   823'.5'09   85-48010
ISBN 0-404-61476-0

Manufactured in the United States of America

Liisalle

The Lord hath called me from the womb; from the bowels of my mother he hath made mention of my name (Isaiah)

He corseth . . . His burthe, hymself, his fate, and ek nature (Chaucer)

Birth, and copulation, and death. . . . That's all the facts when you come to brass tacks (T. S. Eliot)

This word is our eternal mother in whose body we are begotten and nourished (Boehme)

Comes the blind Fury with th' abhorréd shears, And slits the thin spun life (Milton)

A tailor made thee (Shakespeare)

Wyrd goeth as she will

Heav'n from all creatures hides the book of Fate (Pope)

I must penetrate into the last wrinkle of his soul . . . then I do not let him go until his fate is fulfilled (Ibsen)

Fate is unpenetrated causes. . . . The secret of the world is, the tie between person and event. Person makes event, and event person. . . . the copula is hidden. . . . We learn that the soul of Fate is the soul of us . . . but we have not eyes sharp enough to descry the thread that ties cause and effect (Emerson)

This is the chain I forged in life (Dickens)

emptiness is a great feminine secret . . . one is tempted to say that this constitutes the whole "mystery" of woman. Such a female is fate itself (Jung)

Contents

NOTES

Preface

This book is the first study of the role of "fate" in English fiction. I am not primarily concerned with developing a comprehensive definition of fate, nor with whatever we today may mean by the word or concept of fate, but with the representation of fate in four major eighteenth-century novels, Defoe's *Moll Flanders* (1722), Richardson's *Pamela* (1740) and *Clarissa Harlowe* (1747-48), and Sterne's *Tristram Shandy* (1759-67), as experienced in the context of seventeenth- and eighteenth-century representations and discussions of the midwife, the witch, the "cunning woman," the bawd, and the traditional figure of fate as spinner and sewer of men and women. Fate, up through the eighteenth century, is represented primarily under the dual aspects of, on the one hand, language, spoken or written, and on the other, the procreation and termination of human life. Everyone knows that the concept of fate has something to do with death, limitation, closure; among other things, this study shows that fate, as it appears in early English fiction and before, is also intimately associated with sexuality and birth, and thus has the effect of making both birth and sex "fatal" in ways which have yet to be explored.

The study originated with an image which grew in richness and depth: the controlling icon of the book is Mother Midnight, and I offer this work to anyone, not simply eighteenth-century specialists, for whom the name might have a certain fascination. Margaret Doody, in her fine study of Richardson, is right to remind us that "we pay too little attention to the nature of images in novels of the past: these images may have a significance now partly hidden from us. The iconography of images in prose fiction is worth our study." We might also pay more attention to names in fiction. The name "Mother Midnight" has a low and obscure origin. It was a cant term in the seventeenth and eighteenth centuries for a midwife, or a bawd, or both together in the same person. I first encountered the name in *Moll Flanders* and it reappears in the writings of Ned Ward and others. Much of this book is an unfolding of that name into the dark, multifaceted literary figure who exerts, in one guise or another, profound influence on what happens to the main characters in these four novels. I hasten to add that Mother Midnight is not, in my view, an archetype, nor are the roles of midwife, or witch, or bawd interchangeable, nor are they all necessarily working at the same time in one character. But I hope to show that there are enough similarities among the roles to give the figure a proper name, and to describe her function as that of an agent of fate.

The study covers roughly the period 1660 to 1760 in England from the genesis of three important books on midwifery by Sharp, Sermon, and Wolveridge (discussed in the Introduction) to the publication of the first volumes of *Tristram Shandy*. When I use the term "era" in the following pages, it is for this hundred year period, a coherent historical era which included the following important social developments which underlie this study: the rise of the novel, an event having much to do with women as both subjects and authors of fiction; the evolution of modern obstetrics; the growth of large-scale organized prostitution in London; the continued increase of cloth manufacturing and trade, involving large numbers of women, as England's dominant industry and one that affected everyone's life; a high rate not simply of infant but also of human mortality. Every age is an age of anxiety. The period 1720 to 1750, however, owing in part to the effects of influenza epidemics, violence, and the prodigious consumption of gin, might be called in England "the age of mortality"—only one out of four children born in London survived. As M. Dorothy George tells us, the "Bills of Mortality" for that period (which includes the publication dates of three of the four novels considered in this study) indicate that deaths far outnumbered births, and to at least one contemporary it seemed that "half the lodgings within the Bills of Mortality are fill'd with the *Coiners of false Love*." Besides social history, the study is concerned with an odd assortment of things, activities, and characters, with names, strings, threads, clothes, doors, houses, wombs, wallets, watches and books, curses, breathings, windings and turnings, midwives, thieves, bawds and whores.

Although much literary criticism has been written about "rebirth," very little has been written about birth itself and its impact on human experience as depicted in literature. It is true that there are not many explicit treatments in literature of childbirth, but the birth experience stands behind a multitude of images and metaphors of generation. And even to talk intelligibly about "rebirth" and "deliverance" (as I try to do with respect to Moll Flanders, Pamela, Clarissa, and Uncle Toby), it seemed to me that one must learn as much as one could about how the experience of birth was described and understood in the era. It became increasingly clear after examining the midwife literature that Mother Midnight, simply in her role as a midwife, was a figure of deep and intense human interest. A midwife in those days, and in ours, has many functions: she knows when labor has begun, she soothes and encourages the mother, she delivers the child and announces its sex; she cuts off and ties the navel cord, and introduces the mother to her child whom she unofficially names; in cases of emergency, she may baptize the child, and she takes care of and prepares the child for the mother's care. Her role is not simply that of passive auxiliary; she must also be a mistress of speech and "good words." The midwife stands between the woman in labor and the world. She operates at the source of life, mediating at the mystery of creation among the worlds of the unborn, of life, of death, and of all the figurative extensions of those worlds. She is a companion, an assistant, a handmaid. She is a useful medium for information about the role and image of women in the era, and about relations between the sexes.

It may be said that the fall into birth is the biological paradigm of the Fall
of Man, as is suggested in Donne's pun on "ruin" (*ruere*, to fall) in "An
Anatomy of the World (The First Anniversary)":

> We are born ruinous: poor mothers cry
> That children come not right, nor orderly,
> Except they headlong come and fall upon
> An ominous precipitation.
> How witty's ruin! how importunate
> Upon mankind! It labored to frustrate
> Even God's purpose . . . . (ll. 95-101)

But it may also be said that the birth labor is the paradigm for every creative
human act which results in an artifact, and that the midwife, although she
does not literally "make" anything, may be a type of the artisan (or artist—
literary, visual, political) who manipulates the issue of his creation out of its
peculiar matrix. The experience of characters as different as Achitophel in
Dryden's poem and Robinson Crusoe might be considered in the light of this
notion. In the eighteenth century the ubiquitous midwife appears in works
as diverse as the second book of *Gulliver's Travels* (where the infantile hero
is "delivered" from his safe Cartesian travelling-box by a monkey-nurse), and
Christopher Smart's "Index to Mankind," *The Midwife, or Old Woman's
Magazine* (1751). A little later Jane Austen will evoke associations with the
midwife-witch in subtle ways to delineate the evil of Emma Woodhouse's
project with Harriet Smith, and Dickens, with the dark housekeeper of
David Copperfield, Jane Murdstone (a direct, if mirthless, descendant of
Mrs. Jewkes in *Pamela*), black-browed Mrs. Sparsit and her "Staircase" in
Hard Times, and the marvelous "female functionary" of *Martin Chuzzlewit*,
Sairey Gamp ("who had a face for all occasions . . . and . . . went to a lying-in
or a laying-out with equal zest and relish"), extends the image of the midwife
as figure of fate in ever new and compelling directions.

Let me stress that the primary impulse of the book is exploratory and
speculative. I argue that a full examination of the hitherto neglected Mother
Midnight figure, in her historical and literary contexts, helps to further our
understanding of the four major English novels here discussed, particularly
the development of the main characters in these novels, and opens new lines
of inquiry and discussion of the novels and other literature as well. The
Introduction presents and develops the figure of Mother Midnight in all her
associations, with primary emphasis on her relation to fate. The individual
discussions of the novels are not full dress readings but are intended to
render, as comprehensively as possible, the full implications of the fate of
the main characters in relation to the Mother Midnight figure, to each other,
and to the characters' own sense of and expression of their individual fates.
In order to make the discussion of fate more intelligible I have at times

digressed onto other related subjects such as the significance of names, the role and power of the mother, the role and representation of women, the changing representation of Nature in the medical and "scientifick" literature of the era. The re-invention of Nature is a constant theme in English literature, and the Restoration and eighteenth century have their peculiar and influential variations on the theme, from Fainall's admonition to Mirabell (in *The Way of the World*), "Had you dissembled better, things might have continued in the state of nature," to Sterne's complex evocation of a kindly maternal Nature who simply cannot turn out a proper married man. The discussion of Clarissa's fate entails too a correspondingly full analysis of the Ovidian Lovelace, and of the influence in turn upon him of his adopted "family" of whores presided over by the "mother" of them all, Mrs. Sinclair. And in the heat of much recent debate over *Clarissa*, which has included Lovelace's elevation as a proto-Nietzschean superman (Warner) and Clarissa's as a proto-Freudian phallic heroine (Eagleton's rejoinder to Warner), it seemed to me necessary to affirm, in our pervasively deconstructive critical moment, some things the text is saying about Clarissa and Lovelace and their relationship. Finally, in a brief conclusion I comment on the three authors, discuss how their main characters relate to each other in terms of the meanings of fate we have explored, and offer further speculations, in the light of some more recent conceptions of fate, on the significance of fate to the study of these fictions.

The four novels, owing in part to their topical nature, are the kind of works of literature which allow to—and demand from—the reader an active role in their re-creation. I believe the reading of fiction should require of us the same care and creative engagement we bring to the study of poetry. The reader will encounter here many direct quotations from the texts of the novels and from contemporary sources. This allows one to perceive for oneself points of contact, in diction, idiom, style, and content, among varying linguistic contexts—literary and sub-literary—throughout the era.

This book began with ideas that led to two articles, "Mother Jewkes, Pamela, and the Midwives," *ELH: A Journal of English Literary History* 43 (1976), 500-516, and "Moll's Fate: Moll Flanders and 'Mother Midnight'" *Studies in Philology* (1979), 75-100. I am grateful to the editors of these journals for permission to reprint parts of the articles in much revised and augmented form. My Introduction and a chapter on *Tristram Shandy* cover a small portion of the ground first charted in "'The Books of Generation': Some Observations on the Style of the British Midwife Books, 1671-1764," which appeared in *Sexuality in Eighteenth-Century Britain*, ed. P.-G Boucé, Manchester University Press (1982), 74-94. Again I thank the editor and the publishers for permission to reprint.

Many people have assisted me in the long evolution of the book, not least my students in English 232. I wish to thank them for their perceptive responses to the eighteenth-century novels we have read and discussed together over the years, and I am thankful also to those people who have, at various stages of composition, made valuable suggestions or helped resolve difficulties, particularly Alan Bower, John Carroll, Liisa Erickson, Les Harrop, Endel Kallas, Patrick McCarthy, Melvyn New, Mark Rose, George Starr, and Everett Zimmerman. Special thanks are due to Christopher Lauer for introducing me in the early days to *The Midwife and the Witch*, and for other timely observations; to Patricia Want, librarian of the Royal College of Obstetricians and Gynaecologists, London, and to the staffs of the library of the Wellcome Institute for the History of Medicine, and of the British Library, London; to my long-time colleague, William Frost, for generous counsel and encouragement; to Iska Alter, a sympathetic and acute reader and editor; and to three of the best and most patient of typists, Louisa Dennis, Kristina Nash, and Linda Sanchez. Whatever deficiencies remain are my own. Much of the research for the book was carried out with the assistance of grants from the Research Committee of the Academic Senate of the University of California, Santa Barbara.

The introduction and the commentary on the four novels was written between 1975 and 1981. Several studies have appeared since 1979 which touch on some of the notions I develop: William Beatty Warner's *Reading Clarissa*, Terry Castle's *Clarissa's Ciphers*, Brian Easlea's *Science and Sexual Repression*, and Lennard Davis's *Factual Fictions*. I wish also to recognize another of these works, Arnold Weinstein's *Fictions of the Self, 1500-1800*, a brilliant re-evaluation of the emergence and character of European fiction.

Finally, I owe more than I can say to the person who is named in the Finnish dedication.

PART ONE:

INTRODUCTION:
"THE BIRTH OF FATE"

1. "Midwife": Word and Function

The sexual mores of an age can be deciphered tellingly, if never completely, by attention to certain controversial titles or appellations. This book is not about social history or medical history, but the following pages will, I hope, make clear that the midwife of the seventeenth and eighteenth centuries was, in life and in literature, a figure who carried with her a complex of possible associations linked to but going beyond her role in childbirth, and according to the *OED*, the word "midwife" itself, in its long evolution, conveys a fundamental duality of meaning, depending on how one interprets "mid," either as an adjective or as an adverbial preposition. A midwife may be either a woman *by whose means* the birth is effected, or a woman who is *with* the mother at the birth, as a companion. The *OED* finds the latter view the primary sense, "though analogies are wanting for this mode of formation." "Wife" here has the older sense of "woman," but the word "wife" too has a mysterious origin. We shall be considering several of the women characters in these novels (most notably Clarissa and Pamela) under the aspect of and in association with a house, and also in terms of error, wandering, winding, and with respect to the activities of sewing and clothing; the word "wife" is ascribed to both the Indo-European base *weik-*, a dwelling, and *weip-*, to twist, turn, wrap, in the sense "the hidden or veiled person" (*New World Dictionary*). Othello seems to be split in half before the prospect of what has become for him the malignant mystery of Desdemona when he rages,

> Sir, she can turn, and turn, and yet go on
> And turn again; and she can weep, sir, weep;
> And she's obedient . . . . O well painted passion! (IV,i,253-57)

The history of the word "midwife" reminds one of the no less tortuous legacy, down to our own day, of "housewife" and its phonetically reduced companion, "hussy," a light, worthless, or pert woman or girl (*OED*). It is a curious sidelight, in terms of professional appellations for men, that in the eighteenth century male-midwives in Britain (who were called man-midwives) were as much in search of a better title for themselves as women who work at home have been in ours. "Obstetrician" was eventually hit upon after "accoucheur," "midman," and even "Andro-Boethogynist" had been exhausted. With all or some of this in mind, it may not be too much to suggest that the word "midwife" constitutes a genuine linguistic enigma.

Our examination of the Mother Midnight figure in these novels will deal, in literal and figurative terms, with the dual function of the midwife as a person (usually a woman) who is *present with* another woman at the moment

3

of birth and who helps to *bring about* something significant with respect to that woman or her offspring. Moll Flanders' "Governess," "Mother Midnight" (so designated by Moll herself) is a midwife and a bawd who becomes Moll's confidante, delivers one of her children, and helps launch her career as a thief. Pamela's Mother Midnight, who demonstrates marked affinities with the midwife, the bawd, and the witch, is the mannish, vigilant, coarse-speaking Mrs. Jewkes, the "House-keeper" on Mr. B.'s estate charged by her master to keep Pamela confined and to discover her secret writings. "Mother" Sinclair, in *Clarissa*, is not literally a midwife but a bawd, and I will argue for her importance as a figure who exerts great influence not only on the protagonist herself but on Mrs. Sinclair's figurative son, Robert Lovelace. Other figurative midwives in that novel include Lovelace himself, several of his human implements, and the man who becomes Clarissa's "executor," John Belford. Finally, in *Tristram Shandy*, Sterne presents us with two midwives, one the traditional older motherly woman preferred by Mrs. Shandy in her lying-in, the other an example of the new breed of male "scientifick operator," Dr. Slop (preferred by her husband), who incorporates certain features of the traditional bawd. Most important, in all of these manifestations the Mother Midnight figure, whatever the source of her power, functions as an agent of fate, or in the role of fate, profoundly influencing the destiny of the protagonist while playing an intimate part in relation to that character's own richly delineated personal expression of her (or his) individual fate. Fate may be an inscrutable impersonal or supernatural force, or mere chance, but in eighteenth-century fiction fate usually operates from within a human form. Hence we shall be looking closely at Mother Midnight as a medium for unraveling the workings of fate in these novels, and at the character's own language of fate.

In this Introduction, the midwife will be considered first in her relation to birth and fate, then in her allied roles as witch or "cunning woman" with special powers of perception and influence, and finally as bawd with a proprietary relation to her house and to the women of her house.

2. Socrates, Fate, and the Midwife

One of the assumptions of this book is that certain conventional images of women (that is, as seen under the aspect of a beautiful house; as a good or bad midwife, or white or black witch; as an elegant whore or politic bawd) persist from the early English Renaissance up to the time of Defoe, Richardson, and Sterne, and that these writers could generally count on their readers being familiar with such images. Part of the pleasure in reading the new fiction then would lie in recognizing the images and reinterpreting them in new contexts. This applies as well to the modern reader. *Moll Flanders*, for example, may seem to be a rather flat, overcrowded narrative until one begins to gather some sense of the power inherent in the Governess figure and in her influence on Moll, and Pamela too, I think, comes more alive for us in her relations particularly to Mrs. Jewkes, and later in the narrative, to Lady Davers. There are more complicated and far-reaching expressions of traditional images of women in *Clarissa* and *Tristram Shandy*.

The London physician and nostrum-monger, William Sermon, an industrious plagiarist copying from the work of the French chirurgeon, James Guillimeau, first published in 1612, provides us in his *Ladies Companion* of 1671 with a convenient description of the roles of the complete midwife as useful for the works of Spenser and Shakespeare as it is for the eighteenth-century novel. Few better examples could be found, I believe, of the power of an image to survive from one age to the next. Sermon's midwife is as much alive for him in 1671 as she was for Guillimeau's English translator, and as she would be for Defoe:

> Among those that have practised Physick, were many that have applied themselves most of all to deliver women; and that they might be distinguished from others, they were frequently called cunning women . . . these last [midwives] took upon them three things, as Galen and others do witness. The First was, to make the match . . . and to joyn the husband with the wife; and likewise to pass Judgement whether they were fit and capable . . . to beget children . . . The Second was, to be present at the delivery of women, which work was committed to none but such that have had children, (as *Plato* saith) . . . neither did the said *Midwives* attempt this Art, til they were past Childbearing, because *Diana* (the Patroness of women in child-bed) was barren: and also a woman that beareth children is over-much troubled, so the more *unfit* to labour in such a great work. The Third thing was, to resolve to tell women whether they were with Child or not . . . ."[1]

The ultimate source of this description is Plato's *Theaetetus* where Socrates acknowledges that he himself is the son of "a fine strapping midwife"
and an authority on midwifery. He knows the midwives' art, but he keeps
this knowledge secret from all but a few of his adepts.[2] The midwives'
knowledge is the secret knowledge of women pertaining to the private parts,
generation, and birth. It is women's knowledge. And yet at the very beginning of the literature about midwifery we are faced with the complex irony of
a male voice speaking authoritatively—and perhaps even appropriating the
language—of the exclusively female experience of birth. Certainly this is an
important aspect of the innovative role of Socrates in Greek philosophy, but
more important for our purposes, we must ask the question, how does this
male voice speaking of female experience affect the subsequent depiction,
presentation, and response to birth on the part of male and female alike?
Socrates presents himself as a man who has learned the secret of his philosophic art from the secret knowledge of women, a master of philosophical
discourse who yet knows how to keep silent, and to manipulate silences.
This motif of linguistic mastery combined with the arts of silence and secrecy
will reappear throughout the present consideration of the midwife and her
figurative offspring, the novelists. The subject of secrets, particularly the
secret knowledge of women, is a potent area of interest in early English
fiction which has received little attention. Socrates goes on to compare his
own search for truth with the activities of a midwife, but he is also careful to
distinguish his practice from hers. (Sermon too, on the word of two ancient
authorities, observes that "Phanerota, the mother of Socrates, was a midwife.")[3] Socrates reminds Theaetetus (the name means "obtained of God")
that no midwife "attends other women while she's still conceiving and
bearing children herself,"[4] and authoritatively reviews for him the art of
midwifery: the recognition of pregnancy, the use of drugs and charms in
easing the pains of labor, knowledge of abortion, and skill in matchmaking
(which Socrates likens to the arts of planting and harvesting). Good midwives
avoid matchmaking, however, so as not to incur the charge of procuring.
Socrates calls himself a midwife to men's minds, and the greatest thing in his
art is to distinguish between false and true intellectual conceptions. "God
compels me to be a midwife, but has prevented me from giving birth."[5]
    A crucial characteristic of midwives, for Socrates and Sermon, is that they
are past childbearing, though midwives were expected to have borne children and to have been good mothers. Old, wise, experienced, they have
entered "the change of life," or menopause; because their own biological
lives are no longer affected by the reproductive cycle, they live a new life, at
once within and without the birthing experience. They are beyond
menstruation and generation; they are in a sense beyond time and thus have
a godlike status. They are a bit like Tiresias: having known what it is to be
sexually active women, they now share with men the knowledge that they

can never give birth. Although now barren themselves, they are consummately skilled at bringing forth fruit in others, and they can remake others through an uncanny power of influence over their lives. They are usually old women, full of experience and cunning in the art of predicting human consequences.

In these respects they are similar to the Greek Fates, or *Moirai*, conceived as three very old women who control the thread of man's destiny. (Sermon even ends his description by referring to the "three honest Midwives"—the Fates of their day, better known as the grave "Jury of Matrons"—who adjudge whether a female prisoner is pregnant and so may escape hanging.)[6] The Fates belonged (and still belong) primarily to folk beliefs stemming from the permanent preoccupations with birth, marriage, and death, and Fate is almost always represented as a woman: a mother, the Three Fates, the Norns, Dame Fortune, Dame Nature, the Weird Sisters, the Parcae, the Destinies, the Spinners, Lady Luck, Fate as the mother of birth and death.[7]

Mythographers of the era have much to say about the Fates. First of all, they are "the Daughters of *Erebus* [Darkness] and the *Night*";[8] of the "strange Goddesses" located in the "lower Regions of the Earth . . . . *Nox*, the Night, was she that had the greatest command"; "she was held to be the Mother of Love, Deceit, Old Age, Death, Sleep, Dreams, Complaint, Fear, Darkness."[9] Hence "Night," in mythological terms, is the mother of the emotional life as well as the Fates, and she is located within the greater mother, Earth: "The Earth was also worshipped under the Name of *Maia*, which signified a Nurse or Mother."[10] And "maia" is the Greek name for midwife.

Hesiod identified the Fates by name: Klotho (from *klothein*, to spin), the Spinner of the thread of life; Lachesis (from *lanchanein*, to obtain by lot or fate, happen), the Apportioner of the Length of the thread of life; and Atropos (from *a* and *trepein*, to turn; i.e., *not* to be turned), the Inflexible, represented as cutting the thread of life, for part of the meaning of fate is always termination, closure, boundary—the image of finality.[11] The mythographers supply further details:

> In the Palace of *Pluto*, the three Sisters, named *Parcae, Clotho, Lachesis*, and *Atropos*, did reside. These were the fatal Goddesses, or the Destinies, that did appoint unto every one the several adventures of his Life; what they had decreed according to the Judgement of the Gods could not be altered: They were more especially busied in handling the thread, and disposing of the course of Mens Lives. The youngest held the Distaff and did draw the Thread, the second in age did wind it about the Spindle, and the third old and decrepit did cut it off; and this was followed with the immediate death of the person living.[12]

Life is seen as a series of "adventures," and the Fates are distinguished by age. "*Lucian* sets them out in the Shape of Three poor old Women, having large Locks of Wool mixed with Daffodils on their Heads, one of which held a Distaff, the other a Wheel, and the third a Pair of Scissors, wherewith she cut off the Thread of Men's Life."[13] "They represent unto us all sorts of Time, past, present, and to come; and the birth, Growth, and end of all things is attributed to them."[14] The Fates control not only human destiny, but human time, a subject to be considered in more detail later. Danet gives us another, less familiar, image of fate:

> FATUM. *Fate, Destiny*. It was represented as of a Goddess, treading upon the Globe of the World, because all that is contained in it, is submitted to her Laws. She holds in her hand a Vessel, or the fatal Urn, wherein (as Poets say) all the names of mortal men were deposited. The Heathens complained in their Epitaphs, of the malice, envy and cruelty of the Fates, that were inflexible, and could not be moved with tears.[15]

Again, there are links between Fate and the world, or earth, a round globe whose image carries over to the womblike "Urn" containing all mortal names. Fate is the bearer of men's names, and she herself is androgynous: "It can't be objected that the *Latin* word *Fatum* is not of the feminine gender, and therefore the Destiny should not be represented by the figure of a Goddess, for we see that many Divinities, as *Venus*, the Moon, and *Bacchus* were accounted both male and female . . . the Gods were of both Sexes. And the Greeks themselves . . . called Destiny by a feminine name."[16] Though the feminine predominates, and the Fates are seen under a feminine aspect, they include the masculine. Another traditional way of representing this relationship is in the image of Fate as the woman who encloses man, the mother with the child in her womb, the mother (*mater*, matter) who bears the Word, *logos*, "Spirit." Fate always goes back to the body. Before the "Spirit"-voice of *Genesis* is the body of God rising out of the maternal chaos, and the God's mouth is the womb of words.

Danet fixes on the word *Fatum*, the neuter past participle of *fari*, to speak. As with those rich terms in the critical lexicon, myth, epic, logic, irony, and narrative, the source is a word for human speech. In the beginning is the fate; specifically, *fatum* is a prophetic declaration, an oracle. "Fate" to us means the power supposed to determine the outcome of events before they occur, or something inevitable, supposedly determined by this power, or simply that which happens to a person, one's fortune, or finally, the outcome itself, death or doom. The ancients, however, and poets and writers of the seventeenth and eighteenth centuries, tended to personalize, and humanize fate, to represent the power of impersonal or divine fate acting through a recognizably human figure. They also tended to emphasize the verbal or linguistic nature of fate, and the association of fate with the procreation (and termination) of human life. We shall look a little more closely at the linguistic emphasis first.

Gautruche counterbalances Danet's urn of fate with "the fatal Chest, where the Names of all the living upon Earth were registered,"[17] and Danet quotes Martianus Capella's designation of the Fates as "the Secretaries and Guardians of the library of Heaven";[18] William King calls the Fates "the Secretaries to the Gods."[19] The "Book of Fate" has a long and interesting poetic history. Tertullian's *fata scribunda* were Fates who apparently wrote the child's destiny. "Fame," "Rumour," "Report," "Reputation" and so on are all tied in one way or another to verbal fate, and these ties are all vital to the fiction of Defoe, Richardson, and Sterne. It should be noted also in connection with the idea of a "Book of Fate" that the old astrological notion of a person's fate being decided by the conjunction of the planets at one's birth was based on the assumption that the stars in the night sky are themselves the literal characters in a cosmic book of fate. Chaucer's Man of Law, alluding to the ill-fated "Sowdan" of his tale, brings birth, love, and death together in one stanza when he says

Paraventure in thilke large book
Which that men clepe the hevene ywriten was
With sterres, whan that he his birthe took,
That he for love sholde han his deeth, allas!
For in the sterres, clerer than is glas,
Is writen, God woot, whoso koude it rede,
The deeth of every man, withouten drede. (ll. 190-96)

Robert Burton says "that the heaven is God's instrument . . . a great book, whose letters are the stars (as one calls it), wherein are written many strange things for such as can read,"[20] and we still talk about events being "written in the stars."

We shall be concerned in the four novels with the unfolding verbal and textual nature of the lives of the main characters. If fate is in some sense the power which determines the outcome of events before they occur, a large component of that power, insofar as these novels are concerned, is linguistic, and resides in the generative process—analogous to the process of physical procreation—of the author creating his texts, and in that of his creatures creating their individual languages and helping to create the characters within their narratives. We may see fate-as-language working in these novels in either spoken or written form. "Fatum," "that which is uttered," is often prophetic, or predictive, of the character's own "fate," and of the fates of others.

The written aspect of fate is more complicated. It is first, of course, the words the character is imagined to have written with some editorial revision (as with Moll Flanders), or as imagined to have actually written completely by herself (Pamela, Clarissa) or by himself (Tristram, Lovelace). The four novels share this intense interest in the protagonist's relation to her *self* (or his self) in terms of the personal narrative each is presumed to be writing (which distinguishes them from Fielding's *Joseph Andrews* and *Tom Jones*). Each novel is a first person narrative, or a collection of first person narratives (as in *Clarissa*), or a first person narrative which includes other stories (as in *Tristram Shandy*). The characters spin webs of words which enmesh other characters and the writers themselves.

In the largest sense, we as persons in our individual worlds, and the characters in the worlds of these novels, are always "writing," whether we use words or not. We create our own "line" of life as our shape, gestures, movements impinge upon the consciousness of others. The way we impress ourselves upon the human world through the individual expression of our being is our "signature" upon the world. The characters in these novels are all highly expressive verbally and in other ways. For example, the Governess in *Moll Flanders* communicates much through her pregnant silences, and a series of silences is itself a language; Pamela can at times express more through the language of her clothing, and her gestures, and her "Fits," than through the powerful medium of her spoken and written words. The same principle applies, in a few other important instances, to Clarissa's gestures and to what she does *not* say, to Nancy Howe's representation of Solmes, to the language of Uncle Toby's fortifications, and to the brilliant language of Widow Wadman's eyes, and the mystery of her silent but potent presence.

Though the Fates' silence may at times be more audible than their spoken words, I would like to stress at this point not only the traditional linguistic power of fate, but also the "law" of fate. What the Fates say or do, and what their translators and representatives, the novelists and their characters utter, may have the force of a decree, of a sentence, of a definitive, binding legal judgment or verdict. What the characters say or write may be used against them, and what they say plays a large part in what happens to them. To a considerable extent, their language is their fate. What Terry Castle says of Clarissa applies to this discussion: "As we move through the great pattern of letters, utterance . . . seems to have an anticipatory, even affective force. With a kind of tragic fatality characters' speculations about the future invariably come true. Clarissa impresses on us, thus, an odd sensation of linguistic causality."[21] We must next consider, however briefly, the primal relationship between fate as language and fate as birth. Here again the midwife is a critical agent.

Hesiod's most important assertion about the Fates is that "they give man at their birth both evil and good to have."[22] William King stresses that "at the moment of the Birth of any Person, [the Parcae] decreed what should happen to him" (p. 158). H. J. Rose comments on the etymology of fate with a similar emphasis: "In Latin, the plural Fata . . . gave rise to a feminine singular . . . which still exists in the Italian and French words for "fairy" (*fata*, *fee*). A surer instinct led the Romans to identify their own spirits of birth, the Parcae (Paricae, from *parere*, to bring forth) with the Moirai."[23] Hence the fates are birth spirits in folklore, taking the form of old midwives, witches, nurses, or beldams. As Erich Neumann puts it, in what is still the most provocative modern discussion of the fate figure, "the Goddesses of destiny are always goddesses of birth, and . . . for women there is an essential connection between childbearing and death as well as between marriage and death."[24] Like the Norns of Scandinavian lore, the Moirai assist at the birth of a child, and at the moment of birth they determine the child's fate.

In midwife lore of the era, the moment of birth is the "critical Minute" at which the midwife senses the child is to come forth, and her procedures then may have a crucial bearing on the subsequent development of the child. She is thus in a very real sense the child's fate, and the moment of birth is one enveloped in utterance and speech. Mouth and tongue are the generative organ of language, and the breaking through, in speech, of thought into language is itself a risky kind of birth. The spoken word had, from the time of the Egyptians (and presumably earlier), been associated with the rituals of birth. In the birth scene through the ages there is the spectrum of, at one end, the inarticulate crying in pain of mother in labor and child after delivery ("we come crying hither") to, in primitive times and later, the midwives' incantations and charms, (some even written down and tied around the mother's belly or thighs), to the midwife's words of encouragement to the mother, and finally to the naming of the child at birth or shortly after, the christening ceremony. One's fate is then in a sense that which is spoken for one at birth, so that every person's name—and every name is a sign of inexhaustible meaning—constitutes an emblematic script for one's life. It might be said that the name is the link between the great ongoing mysteries of human regeneration and language. Over the whole birthing scene is the hubbub of women's voices, for birth (particularly in this era) was often a communal affair of women with, ideally, the mother's and the midwife's friends or "gossips" in festive and sympathetic attendance.[25] These are some of the ties between the fate figure and the midwife, and between language, fate, and birth. There is a further, related connection between the "fate" and the midwife which must here be stressed: they are both spinners and sewers of men.

3. "Cover'd in Our Mothers' Womb"

Sermon in his *Ladies Companion*, referring to the older women in attendance at labor, recalls "a common saying among the hearty good women . . .
to the Midwife, if it be a boy, make him good measure, but if a girl tye it
short."[26] This cryptic joke refers to the custom of tying the umbilical cord
longer or shorter at birth. The custom is described or alluded to in many
English midwife manuals printed before 1700, and in several afterwards.[27]
Now the complete midwife of the seventeenth century carried with her
certain indispensable tools of her trade, among which were a spool of "soft
thread" for tying the umbilical cord and "a sharp pair of scissors" for cutting it
off:[28]

> Many do observe, that the Navell [cord] must be tyed longer or shorter
> according to the difference of the Sex, allowing more measure to the
> Males; because (say they) it doth make their Tongues and privy Mem-
> bers longer, by which means they will speak the plainer, and become
> more serviceable to Ladies, (or to such as delight in long things). And
> that by tying it short or almost to the belly in Females, will cause their
> Tongues not to be so nimble, and their secret parts to be more strait, &
> c.[29]

Mrs. Jane Sharp, the first midwife in England to write an actual handbook
on midwifery, goes into more detail and offers some maternal clarifications:

> all *Midwives* have cause to be careful to cut the Navel string long
> enough, that when they tye it, the Yard may have free liberty to move
> and extend itself . . . *Miraldus* [ie, Antonius Mizaldus] bids cut the navel
> string long in both Sexes, for . . . if womens Navel-strings be cut too
> short, it will hinder their Child-bearing. . . . If Nature framed the child
> by the Navel-string in the womb, there is no small use of it afterward.[30]

For example: carrying a piece of the navel-string on one's person (or "wearing" it) was thought by some to prevent "convulsive fits" and to defend the
wearer from "the Devil" and "Witch-crafts." If the navel string touched the
ground, the child would not be able to hold his urine throughout life, and
the number of knots in the cord supposedly indicated the number of children the woman would have.[31] Mrs. Sharp is skeptical of most of these
claims, but she had good reason to believe that the umbilicus is of great
importance to life, "for by the Navel-string the Mother gives both vital and
natural blood to the Child." There is a blood tie between midwife and child
as well as mother and child. "The cutting of the Navel-string helps much, for

it keeps the blood and spirits in, after the Child is born. A Midwives skill is seen much if she can perform this rightly." If the child is weak, "you must gently put back part of the vital and natural blood into the childs body by the Navel," or if the child seems dead, "you must crush out six or seven drops of blood" from the severed cord, and put the blood in its mouth to drink.[32]

It is necessary to take such a close view of the cutting of the umbilicus because here the metaphor of the Fates controlling the thread of man's destiny becomes a literal fact of life. It was thought, more or less seriously by many physicians, midwives, "good women," and "gossips," that the midwife had within her power not only the life-blood of the child but the means to determine the sexual (and verbal) fate of men and women through her control of the length of the navel string, since this cord itself was part and parcel not only of one's sexual constitution, but of one's very being, as Mrs. Sharp asserts ("Nature framed the child by the Navel-string in the womb"). Thus the fatal shears of Atropos are, in seventeenth-century birth lore, as effectual at the beginning of life's thread as at its end.

The association of the old midwife with scissors, string, and sewing allies her, from the beginning, with the goddesses of fate who were all spinstresses ("Klothes" in Homer), whatever their particular role in the spinning process was thought to be. But beyond the midwife's link with sewing and her supposed control of sexual and verbal destiny is a deeper connection between spinning and man's fate. Neumann points out several examples, especially in representations of the "sewing" Madonna, of the mother who "spins" the child in her womb: "the woman must not only provide the clothing of man in the literal sense but also clothes him with the body she spins and weaves . . . . the [Virgin] mother becomes the spinning goddess of destiny; the child becomes the fabric of her body."[33] The body itself is a suit of clothes, sewn in the "tiring house" of the womb:

> What is our life? a play of passion;
> Our mirth the music of division;
> Our mother's wombs the tiring houses be
> Where we are dressed for this short comedy.[34]

Long before Swift's "Taylor God" and the "Clothes Philosophy" of *A Tale of a Tub*, the authors of the midwife manuals (who may themselves be targets of Swift's wide-ranging satire) rehearse, in their introductory lectures on anatomy, the notion that man's body consists of three layers or "coates" (an outer skin, a fleshy skin, and fat). These authors go on to discuss in detail the formation in the womb of the clothes-creature man, and the midwife herself functions as a "taylor-god" sewing the creature up after his delivery.

Following a long panegyric on the "excellency" of man, the English man-midwife James Wolveridge invites the reader to make with him "a

nearer indagnation [sic] and scrutiny into the formation of man . . . from the
first conception till the day of his birth."[35] The initial formation parallels the
hexaemeral creation, and incorporates a new image of the thread of life:
"Presently, from the first day until the sixth or seventh, there grow and arise
very many and very small fibers or hairs."[36] These eventually become the
chief organs, liver, heart, and brain. Wolveridge (quoting Psalm 139) notes
that the more seriously we weigh this marvellous formation, "and pry into
it," the more with the Psalmist, we shall admire our Creator by our creation,
and bless that God that hath cover'd us in our Mother's womb, and praising
him, say; We are fearfully and wonderfully made, marvellous are thy works
. . . . My substance was not hid from thee when I was made in secret; and
curiously wrought in the lowest parts of the Earth. Thine eyes did see my
substance yet being unperfect, and in thy Book all my members were
written.[37]

In some respects, this remarkable text, which is quoted more often in the
midwife literature than any other from Scripture and which shaped our
ancestors' understanding of their origins as creatures who are formed by God
and then recorded in God's book, could be taken as the paradigm for this
entire study. We shall be concerned in more detail later with the fundamental connection, in eighteenth-century imaginative literature, between
the arts of sewing and writing, but for now we may simply note that "cover'd"
in the womb means clothed there, though this account is sufficiently general
to suggest other metaphors of creation, like painting or building.[38] One may
compare Job 10:11: "Thou hast clothed me with skin and flesh, and hast
fenced me with bones and sinews," which combines images of sewing and
fortification; Psalm 22:9-10: "But thou art he that took me out of the womb
. . . Thou art my God from my mother's belly"; and Psalm 71:6: "thou art he
that took me out of my mother's bowels."[39] In Psalm 139, the Old Testament
God, supreme authority on all matters relating to women and birth, is seen
to have his own "Book" of generation, the prototype of all midwife books, a
counterpart of the Greek and Roman books of Fate, and the prototype as
well of the "Book of Nature" in its etymological sense as the power that
brings things to birth. Hence God, as the source and arbiter of fertility in
women and the first sewer and knitter-up of the skin, flesh, and bones of the
clothes-creature man, is the Judaic masculine counterpart of the feminine
spinning Greek fates and the original of the midwife who takes the child out
of the womb and, with her scissors and thread for tying off the umbilicus,
presents the child to the mother. By the seventeenth century, though an
inscrutable or unintelligible Fate or Fortune may intervene in the process so
far as human affairs are concerned ("binding Nature fast in fate," as Pope puts
it in "The Universal Prayer"), God is seen creating through his "Hand-
maiden," Nature. She is then the master-midwife overseeing the work of all

midwives, good and bad, on earth. Noting that the "Original of all . . .
proceeds from the first Command of the great Lord of Creation, *Increase
and Multiply*"—a favorite phrase of the midwives—and putting the words of
Job and David together, the author of *Aristotle's Master Piece* says "they
make up the most accurate System of Philosophy, respecting the Generation
of Man, that has ever been written."[40]

The workshop of God's animal creation is the "Womb," or "Matrix." By
"womb" was meant the uterus, or sometimes the whole female reproductive
tract, or even the "belly" or stomach. The importance of the womb's relation
to the overall development and psychology of woman is a commonplace in
the literature of generation and midwifery in the era, and literary criticism
hardly touches the subject. It is in any case a difficult one, partly because the
functions of the womb were thought to be so various. The most famous
physician of the seventeenth century, William Harvey, calls the womb "a
principal part, which doth easily draw the *Whole body* into consent with it.
No man . . . is ignorant, what grievous *Symptomes*, the Rising, Bearing
down, and Perversion, and Convulsion of the *Womb* do excite; what horrid
extravagancies of minde, what Phrensies, Melancholy Distempers, and Out-
ragiousness, the *praeternatural Diseases* of the womb do induce, as if the
affected Persons were inchanted."[41] The womb is the dark source of a
woman's "extravagancies of minde." It will be recalled that the Greek Fates
were thought to dwell in "the lower Regions of the Earth" with "*Nox*," the
source of man's emotional life;[42] God in Psalm 139 "Wrought" man "in the
lowest parts of the Earth," a metaphor for the womb. Hence the womb itself
is a dark matrix of fate, and the image keeps re-appearing in different guises
throughout the literature of the era.[43]

Certain midwife authors are fond of citing Hippocrates' dictum that "the
Womb is the Source of Six Hundred *Griefs*,"[44] but Harvey, the balanced
observer with the psychologist's eye and the love poet's joy in description
does not stop here; one notices also, he says,

> how many difficult *Diseases*, the depraved effluxion of the Terms, or the
> use of *Venus* much intermitted, and long desired do foment. Nor is it
> less known, how great an Alteration doth befall Virgins, when their
> Uterus doth enlarge [in puberty] . . . for they grow mature, and their
> complexion doth improve; their Breasts strut forth, they become more
> beautifull, their Eyes glisten, their Voice is more tunable, their Gate,
> Gesture, and Discourse, are more graceful than formerly . . . .[45]

The passage is worth keeping in mind as a "natural philosopher's" background to all the descriptions of young women in the four novels, but
especially to Moll Flanders' and Pamela's adolescence, and to Clarissa's
beauty in Lovelace's eyes.

The womb has always been a storehouse of metaphoric possibilities. For Plato and Aristotle, it is an animal within an animal,[46] capable of moving around within the lower part of the body; it has its own consciousness, is affected by smells, and in its disturbed state upsets the whole animal economy of the body. In the words of Aretaeus, the womb is "altogether erratic";[47] this medical doctrine helps to establish the stereotype of feminine error, flightiness, and changeability. The womb is "another house" within the woman,[48] with its own "port" and "gates," like a harbor; it is "a house for the infant to lie in" until it becomes his "prison." The womb is a well watered "field," or "good ground" which attracts seed, or it is a "famishing stomach," voracious, ravenous, a powerful gripping organ which holds first the "Yard," and later the infant within its "two hands"; its treatment of the infant is at first tender, but finally it helps to expel the child into the world. In these latter images, there is again a strong suggestion of the manipulatory motions of fate, especially the "hand of fate."

But the primary metaphor is still the womb which spins or sews the child in a series of wondrous layers or garments. Jane Sharp, whose observations on sexual anatomy have more the texture of the woolen manufacture than of the medical textbook, is again our guide. Her language is full of "seams," "wrinkles," "strings fast knit," "bridles," "coats," "woven networks," and allusions to "hollow weaving" and "Weaver's Shuttles." She has much to say about the inward and outward layers or "membranes" of the womb itself, and within the womb the two further outward and inward coats: "The first thing Nature makes for the child, is the *Amnios* or inward skin"; next comes "the outward or *Chorion* which . . . wraps the Infant round, and this membrane is like a soft Pillow for the Veins and Navel-arteries of the Child to lean upon . . . but the inward Coat which is wonderful soft and thin . . . is loose on each side . . . . These two Coats grow so close together that they seem to be but one garment."[49] Finally, in Mrs. Sharp's directions for governing the woman after childbirth and caring for the child, there emerges the midwife herself providing a new "chorion" for the child: "In the swaddling of it be sure that all parts be bound up in their due place and order gently, without any crookedness, or rugged foldings."[50] The image of the caring midwife in her motherly relation to the infant clothes-creature has its perversion in the image of the midwife-bawd who nurtures the female child up into the well-clothed whore whose whole being is laid at the disposal of men.

The next five chapters of this introduction emphasize in detail these dark sides of Mother Midnight, a "grave Matron" whose presence permeates large areas of the three novels of Defoe and Richardson discussed in this book, and who impinges, in her transformation into Dr. Slop and the old "motherly midwife," on most of what happens to Tristram Shandy.

4. The Midwife and the Witch

That the English midwife in the seventeenth century, particularly the country midwife, was at the bottom of the social ladder, no one would dispute. Jean Donnison points out that "the bulk of midwives," ill-educated and drawn from the lower classes, "were limited to lowly paid attendance on the Poor" and "were full of the ignorance which so often led to rash and fatal interference."[51] All the midwife authors, including Jane Sharp, inveigh against unskillful, officious, or meddling midwives whose ministrations to the woman in labor cause unnecessary pain and disrupt the natural process of labor. Willughby calls them "torturing midwives."[52] Perhaps some of these midwives thought that their labors must match those of the women under their care, but many, as Willughby testified, were dangerously ignorant of anatomy, believing, for example, that the child could be "stuck" to the mother's back.[53] Often midwives sought to help the birth by "forcibly stretching the reproductive parts, sometimes tying the reluctant woman to the obstetric chair, and in more obstinate cases, by tossing her in a blanket, rolling or rocking her, or other violent measures."[54]

Women with a reputation for such practices could incur other unsavory titles. Thomas Forbes was the first social historian of science to call specific attention to the interesting connection, in every day life and in legend, between the lowly midwife and her mysterious and ever-fascinating counterpart in popular culture, the English witch. "Ignorant, unskilled, poverty stricken, and avoided as she often was, it is small wonder that the midwife could be tempted, in spite of the teachings of the church, to indulge in superstitious practices or even in witchcraft."[55] Now witchcraft, in our time, has come to have a many-faceted and lurid kind of glamor, and it may be well to go back to George Lyman Kittredge's definition of what a witch was, at least to the English: "in considering the tenacity of the popular belief on this subject, we should never forget that the essence of witchcraft is *maleficium*. The hatred and terror which a witch evokes is due to her will and her power to inflict bodily injury . . . she is hunted down like a wolf because she is an enemy to mankind. Her heart is full of malignity."[56] Or so it was thought. The ignorance of the midwife was more than offset by the ignorance of popular belief, and the ignorance we impute to the midwife was not thought of as such by most ordinary people. Kittredge notes further that along with the belief in witchcraft "came another dogma, likewise of abysmal antiquity—the theory that all diseases are of supernatural origin," and "that madness may be caused by witchcraft is one of the most persistent of superstitions."[57]

It may be well at this point to enter another note of caution. Forbes does not suggest that all midwives were witches, nor do I wish to imply here or in what follows that midwives, witches, and bawds are all interchangeable functionaries. Neither does Kittredge, despite the vigor of his exposition, argue that witchcraft, superstition, and madness always went hand in hand. There are, however, obvious links between attitudes toward midwives and popular superstition right on into the eighteenth century, and in the following chapters I will attempt not only to delineate the features of Mother Midnight as she appears in the four novels under discussion, but also to allude, as a secondary concern, to the part played by superstition in the minds of major women characters, especially Moll Flanders, Pamela, and even the comparatively enlightened Clarissa.

With respect to witchcraft and midwifery, I am concerned here largely with the period from the English Middle Ages up to Jacobean times, and so far as the English novel is concerned, with the popular notions of how midwives and witches came together into a legendary composite figure during the seventeenth and early eighteenth centuries. This figure had a special name: she was "the cunning woman" or the "wise woman," as Sermon noted. (There were of course "cunning men" as well, but they did not, as a rule, deliver children.) The figure is especially compelling—and difficult to grasp—because she combines such potent contradictory images relating to the infliction of destruction and death, or to the promotion and enhancement of life. In her contradictory nature, she is reminiscent of the creator-destroyer god, whether seen under a patriarchal or a maternal aspect.

Keeping in mind that the main thing here is the *power* of the cunning woman, and how she chooses to use her powers, it may be convenient to separate the good and bad components of the figure as follows: on the dark side is all the power attributed to the ancient, malignant, "black witch," especially her capacity for inflicting crippling *verbal* abuse and calling up diabolic forces, through invective, spells, and so on, which may literally destroy the victim; the witch takes on the further terror of the torturing midwife—not considered ignorant but knowing in the arts of inducing pain—who has the helpless victims, mother and unborn child, in the power of her literal grasp. On the other side, there is the image of the good, mature, or aged midwife (or "white witch"), a woman beyond childbearing but intimate with all it implies, a "hearty good woman," merry, a "blesser" who can "unbind" the evil of the black witch and who has a beneficial effect on the individual person and the community. She too has strange power of speech, but to heal not to hurt. She lives in trusting accord with the great birth-giving power of Nature. As Nature is God's handmaid, the good midwife-witch is Nature's handmaid (Wolveridge's manual, for instance, is subtitled "The Expert Midwives Handmaid"); she knows, moreover, how to wait patiently upon Nature, and assist her gently when necessary. She knows how to promote organic and communal health; she can cure the ague and the pox, charm children so no harm will come to them, promote all the functions of the farm, from ensuring good milk and eggs to making the plough fruitful. She knows the ways of all animals and they are her familiars or friends. She has uncanny powers of discernment, can tell fortunes, find lost property, forecast the outcome of love affairs, match the proper man to the proper woman. Above all, she knows, or is thought to know, things beyond the ken of ordinary folk. The many similarities between the "cunning woman" and the midwife described by Sermon and Socrates are obvious enough. This is a comprehensive view of most of the aspects of the cunning woman. No character in the four novels has all of them and they are presented here simply as a diagrammatic point of reference. It is remark- able, though, that such a lowly figure in the economic scale could ever have called forth such a wealth of contradictory natural and preternatural detail.[58]

Perhaps these disparities are partially explained in that the function of birth takes on enormous religious significance in human culture, and that the midwife's calling was thought to be a sacred one, despite her low station. The Scottish man-midwife, James McMath, admonishes all midwives to "study a prudent, wary and religious Performance" of their practice, "that by a right presage and prognostick of the Event, the most worthy and admirable part of their Art, and as it were next to Divination, they may preserve entire, the Dignity of their Name and Office, so ancient and venerable."[59] But this sacred calling can easily become a wicked one, depending on the midwife's will, or the power of the will which directs her. The midwife's proper knowledge of ointments was thought to enable witches to fly and certain of their drugs were undoubtedly hallucinatory. The midwife of course had prime access to unbaptized children—and to the fetal membranes, placenta, or umbilical cords—used in witch's rites. The soul of the unbaptized child was thus lost to the devil.[60]

This much of the lore will suffice for introductory purposes until our encounter with Moll Flanders and her Governess, and with Pamela and her Mrs. Jewkes. To sum up in graphic form, the following is a contemporary description of one of the most notorious of all the equivocal "cunning women" in English legend, Mother Shipton, a picture of whom still graces one of the pubs in London's Camden Town. The description begins, appro- priately enough, with Mother Shipton's strange and unnatural birth:

> The usual time of Forty weeks being expired, her Mother, after many strange and horrible Torments which she underwent in her Travail, was at last Delivered (by the rare Skill and Industry of her Midwife). . . . they beheld the strange and unparallel'd Phisiognomy of the Child . . . misshapen . . . she was of an indifferent height, but very morose and big bon'd, her head very long, with very great goggling, but sharp and fiery Eyes, her Nose of an incredible unproportionable length, having in it many crooks and turnings, adorned with many strange Pimples of divers

colours . . . which like vapours of Brimstone gave . . . a lustre to her
affrighted spectators in the dead time of the Night . . . . Her cheeks were
of a black swarthy complexion, much like a mixture of black and yellow
Jaundices, wrinkled, shrivelled, and very hollow . . . . two of [her teeth]
. . . stood quite out of her Mouth, in imitation of the Tusks of a wild
Bore, or the Tooth of an Elephant, a thing so strange in an Infant, that no
age can parallel: Her Chin was of the same Complexion as her Face,
turning up towards her Mouth.

Not surprisingly, Mother Shipton's "father" was "the Devil . . . a great
Scholar, well read in all things, and much acquainted with the constitutions
of all sorts of persons."[61]

5. The Midwife and the Bawd

The comprehensive description of the complete midwife presented by Sermon (after Guillimeau) indicated that her first function was "to make the match." Ned Ward gives us a lively picture of a garrulous, tipsy midwife, Mother Midnight, speaking to the bridegroom at a wedding feast:

> I look upon my Master to be a likely Man, and one that can do Business.
> . . . I hope, Mr. Bridegroom, you are as well provided as my Husband
> was; I am sure your Nose promises as well . . . . I assure you all
> Physicians are of Opinion, that Maids are ripe at Fourteen, and Men at
> Seventeen . . . . O my Conscience, quoth Mother Midnight . . . *Marry*
> *your daughters betimes, or they will marry themselves,* Now you may
> think, that I say this to promote my own Trade; But ifecks I speak
> cordially for the publick Good . . . Now Son prove your self a Man; I'll
> warrant thee, Boy, thou hast a Maiden-head. But have a care of being
> too boisterous at first, you must crop the Flower gently, lest you pull up
> the whole Plant by the Roots.[62]

As Jean Donnison says, "the midwife had a long-standing and unsavoury reputation of another kind—that of a manager of sexual intrigues—'truest friend to lechers,' as the seventeenth-century poet Rochester put it."[63] In "The Character of a Towne-Misse," 1675, a country girl gets pregnant at thirteen by either the plowman or the squire; the latter dispatches her "to be disburthen'd at *London,* the goodliest Forrest in *England* to shelter a great *Belly*: There the *Bantling* was exposed to the Tuition of the *Parish* in a *Handbasket,* and the Charitable *Midwife* (who counts procuring in a civil way, a necessary part of her Office) soon brought her acquainted with a *Third Rate Gentlewoman,* who took her a lodging in a Garret."[64] The learned old woman of *The Whores Rhetorick,* 1683, recounts that after quitting "the warfare of *Venus*" she "turned Natures hand-maid, and a Midwife to love, which had often proved abortive, had not my importunate prayers and solicitations brought it alive into the world, to the infinite satisfaction of the loving pairs."[65] And John Dunton, the energetic and earnest crusader against London prostitution who combined piety and titillation long before Richardson in his monthly newspaper, *The Night-Walker,* advises

> a young Spark . . . to beware of that sort of People called *Procurers,*
> which is only a new Name for the *Odious and Wicked Bawds*; and of this
> Sort there are diverse Forms and Shapes; *viz.* Some of them are *Mid-*

wives, some are *Nurses*, a third sort are . . . *she-Hawkers*, who under
pretence of selling *Lace*, *Muslin*, *Gloves*, and other knacks for Women,
make it their Business, not only to debauch handsome Servant *Maids*,
but . . . make Assignations betwixt young Sparks, and *Change Women*,
Seamstresses, & c.[66]

Dunton introduces the important motif, to be noticed in much of what
follows, of prostitution masked under fine clothing.
Moll Flanders' Governess is a bawd as well as a midwife; Mrs. Jewkes in
Pamela is depicted, in the heroine's eyes, as a former bawd or "Procuress";
and Richardson's Mrs. Sinclair is the greatest representation of the bawd in
English literature. In addition, Moll Flanders calls herself a "Whore."
Whores are important characters in *Clarissa*, and Pamela herself has been
characterized as a "whore" not only by Henry Fielding in *Shamela* but by her
own husband-to-be-in the novel. For these reasons, and because of the scant
critical discussion of bawd and whore figures in English literature, the
following commentary is given in some detail. There are perhaps even more
links between midwives and bawds than between midwives and witches, but
it may be well first to observe the traditional picture of the bawd, one
comparable in many respects to Richard Head's vision of Mother Shipton. In
J. D. Breval's *The Lure of Venus*, 1733, a verse commentary in six cantos on
Hogarth's *The Harlot's Progress*, there is this description of the bawd (whom
he identifies as Mother Bentley) accosting the young girl newly arrived from
Yorkshire in the first plate:

> Up strait, a venerable Matron comes,
> Of size unweildy, with a waddling Pace.
> Frosted her Locks, and patch'd and prim'd her Face;
> Her Front deep furrow'd, and her Eyes on Flame,
> Like Cats by Night, and *Bentley* was her Name.
> This Load of Lust, this Lump of deadly Sin,
> First chucks the harmless Maid beneath her Chin,
> Then, like another SHIPTON, soon displays,
> What shall befall her in her later Days.[67]

6. Bawd, House, and Whore

The distinguishing features of the conventional bawd are constant, but subject to much individual embellishment: an old "Tradeswoman" and "Mother" always associated with darkness and the night, she is primarily a fat, large-boned, unwieldy lump of mortality with goggling, fiery or rheumy eyes which miss nothing, heavy black eyebrows, a prominent nose and chin and a myriad of furrows and wrinkles like an ancient garment or a worn-out piece of land. Robert Gould in 1683 gave this picture of the "Illustrious Bawd," Mother Bewley, weighed down to hell by her sins:

> Prest with the pond'rous guilt, at length she fell;
> And through the solid Centre, sunk to Hell:
> The murm'ring Fiends all hover'd round about,
> And in hoarse howls did the great Bawd salute;
> Amaz'd to see a sordid lump of Clay,
> Stain'd with more various bolder Crimes than they . . . .
> *Creswold*, and *Stratford*, the same path do tread;
> In Lust's black Volumes so profoundly read,
> That wheresoe're they die, we well may fear,
> The very tincture of the Crimes they bear,
> With strange infusion may inspire the dust,
> And in the Grave committ true acts of Lust.[68]

Here the ancient bawd is invested with the creative power—perversely analogous to that of the Father God in Genesis—of inspiring the dust with life and so promoting further acts of fornication even in the grave. The would-be whore of *The Whores Rhetorick*, Dorothea, sees Mother Creswell as a bawd who

> seemed so loaden with years as to be scarce able to support the burthen; she had very near as many furrows in her Face, as Hairs on her Head, her Eye-brows were thick and hoary, her eyes . . . sending forth a certain yellow matter . . . . there was an uninterrupted communication between her Mouth and Nose . . . her Breasts appeared like a pair of Bladders, without the least particle of Air within . . . . her Chin was acute and bending upwards . . . . her Legs, a pair of Broomsticks covered with Parchment . . . . Her nails were certainly visible . . . and so her tallons were laid open to every eye . . . . [and] those large characters time had imprinted in her face, as the marks of his impartial, but cruel hand."[69]

The London Bawd of 1711 offers perhaps the most detailed and all-embracing character or anatomy of this aged "Matron of Iniquity":

> A BAWD is the Refuse of an Old Whore . . . . She is one of Nature's
> Errata's and a true Daughter of *Eve*, who having first undone herself,
> tempts others to the same Destruction . . . She's a great preserver of
> Maiden-heads. . . . She's a great Enemy to all Enclosures, for whatever
> she has, she makes it common. She hates *Forty-One* as much as an *old
> Cavalier*, for at that age she was forced to leave off Whoring, and turn
> Bawd. . . . she's never *ripe* till she's *rotten*. She is never without store of
> *Hackney Jades*, which she will let *any one Ride*, that will *pay for their
> Hire*. She is the very Magazine of Taciturnity; for whatever she sees, she
> says nothing: it being a standard Maxim with her, *That they that cannot
> make Sport, should spoil none*. She has learnt so much Philosophy as to
> know that the Moon is a dark Body, which makes her like it much better
> than the Sun, being more suitable for her Business. Besides, she's still
> *changing Quarters*, now Waxing and then Waining, like her: Sometimes
> in the Full, and flush'd with store of customers; and at another time in
> the Wane, and beating Hemp in *Bridewell* . . . . she is such a cunning
> Angler, that she don't fear getting her Living by Hook or by Crook . . . .
> She's often *broke*, and as often *sets up again* . . . She sits continually at a
> Rack Rent, especially if her Landlord bears Office in the Parish, because
> he may Skreen her from the *Cart* and *Bridewell* . . . . She has an
> excellent Art in transforming Persons, and can easily turn a Sempstress
> into a waiting Gentlewoman. . . . He that hath past under her, hath past
> the Equinoctial; and he that escapes her, hath escaped a Rock which
> Thousands have been split upon to their Destruction.[70]

If the good midwife is the handmaid of Nature, the bawd is one of Nature's errors, but like the midwife, she is past childbearing. She is *always* a former whore. She is an emblem of fallen nature, like her mother Eve, and she seeks to spread her destruction to others. As "the Magazine of Taciturnity," she is a virtual storehouse of ways of keeping silent about all manners of evil which she sees but never speaks of, and never forgets. She has as much command of her rhetoric of studied silences appropriate to individual crimes as does the garrulous midwife of her rhetoric of bawdy. In this respect, "The London Bawd" prefigures Moll Flanders' Governess. Though the bawd-whore is an emblem of change, like the Moon, she is consistent and inflexible in her wicked practice, particularly in her transforming of naive young girls into hardened whores. She takes on the huge proportions of the Earth itself for those who pass "under her," or luckily escape her treacherous "rocks." The only thing missing from this portrait is a consideration of the bawd's house, our next concern.

There is a rich complex of traditions around the notion of woman as man's house, for woman's maternal role has always been linked with clothing and shelter. The popular seventeenth-century depiction of woman as a well-built and beautiful house goes back at least as far as Cornelius Agrippa (1486-1534), whose ingenious *De nobilitate and praecellentia foeminei sexus* was translated as *The Glory of Women* in 1652 and 1670. Agrippa, despite the patriarchal underpinning of his argument, was remarkable for his advocacy not of the doctrine of women's equality to man, but of her *preeminence* to him in the divine scheme of things. The most suggestive and memorable adaptation of Agrippa's doctrine in English is William Austin's *Haec Homo, Wherein the Excellency of the Creation of Woman is Described,* 1637.

The following passage is quoted for purposes of comparison to what follows in this part of the Introduction, and for particular application later to Richardson's portrayal of Clarissa. Austin first recounts the creation of woman by God, the "Skillful Architector":

> After he had framed and erected, he *builded, finished,* and *establisht* her: like a firme *edifice,* and beauteous house: as having perfectly finished her, and [in *her*] both heaven and earth . . . . The *Woman* therefore being . . . *builded* after the manner of a *house,* must have and retain some qualities of an house also . . . . when God hath framed a *Wife* for Man, he must dwell with her even untill he die, or till this beautiful building fall into the *Lords hands* before him . . . . AEdificatio . . . signifies, not only a *private house,* but a *Temple* . . . . a *wise Woman* (saith *Solomon* the *wise man*) buildeth her house: so that, she is both a *building,* and a *builder* too . . . shee is therefore so *largely* made, with so *many roomes* then the *masculine* building; because she must containe *another house* within her.[71]

There is much more to Austin's philosophy of the preeminence of woman than even this passage suggests, and the tradition has persisted down to our own day, but the obvious prevalence of theories of female inferiority and subordination to man, and of radical feminine evil, by far the more influential interpretations of the creation of Eve and the fall of man in Genesis, has obscured this tradition with its own dark version of the woman as house, a version which supplies most of the following examples of the bawd and her house, and the bawd's whore and her "tenement," which make up the subliterature of prostitution drawn upon by Defoe, Richardson, and even Sterne, in their fiction. This prevailing tradition is concisely depicted in the virulently antifeminist *A Discourse of Women, Showing their Imperfections Alphabetically,* 1662: "A woman is a creature so difficult to be known, that the most ingenuous spirit in the world knows not certainly to define her; she hath about her so many cabinets, such back-shops, so many secret holes, such cunning warehouses, that one knows not wherein to trust her."[72] It is remarkable that many of the images associated with the prostitute stem from definitions, generalizations, and characterizations of the attributes of women—not necessarily antifeminist in tone—such as this.

Many of the early midwife books refer to the two midwives in Exodus I who saved the Hebrew male children from destruction and who earned the approbation of the Lord, "who built them houses." Ignorant and poor though most seventeenth-century midwives were, the better sort, especially those in London, had their own houses, and some of them put these houses to questionable use. Moll Flanders' Governess is this kind of midwife. The "Dying Midwife's" advice to her daughter in the popular *Compleat Midwifes Practice* of 1656 contains this specific warning: "I charge thee Daughter, that in all thy life thou never receive a Woman into thy house to lye in; for that is but a kind of Panderism clothed in some pretence of charity . . . . to receive such persons into your house is but a means to encourage evil, as the receivers of stollen goods are a means to encourage thieves." The Midwife admits that when she started out in practice she took two such women into her house, "And I must needs say I had better have kept a herd of swine." The women suffered such fits of despair that the midwife could hardly help them to recover. "Such unrests as these ought not to enter into the breast of a Midwife, for her mind ought to be free and at peace. Beside, that a custom of laying Women of an ill life spoils the reputation of a Woman."[73] Thus the midwife echoes Socrates' advice in the *Theaetetus.*

Even today the words "bawdy" and "whore" are habitually linked to the word "house." In the era 1660 to 1760 the bawd and her house are almost synonymous, and the whore is trapped into the bawd's house, and eventually becomes a part of it. Father Poussin describes the typical scenario of the "Trading Madam," drawing upon Hogarth:

> There liv'd till about a Year ago, an elderly Woman, near *King-street, Westminster,* who was every Day very needful in the World, yet every Day did a world of Mischief; who kept a House of free Hospitality, but made Folks pay vastly dear for what they had . . . . she had always a Bible in her Hand at Home, and always a to-be-ruin'd Damsel Abroad; each Morning she took her Rounds to all the Inns, to see what Youth and Beauty the Country had sent to *London* to make their Fortunes; and when she found a Rural pretty Lass skip out of a Waggon, she drew her by smoothing Language to a private Box within . . . . This antiquated She-Captain of Satan's Regiment, would offer the poor innocent Creature an Apartment and all Accomodations in her House *gratis,* till she saw if she should like the Town.

The bawd skillfully weaves her way from her own "house of free Hospitality" to the "private Box" of an "Inn" and back to an "Apartment" offered to the girl in her House "*gratis.*"[74]

The London whore-turned-bawd not only excels in the "Art" of "transforming Persons," but she herself is a paragon of metamorphosis, and these changes are reflected in the various guises and "Denominations" of her house:

> "I have in my time run through Varieties of Changes . . . . The House which I now keep, is a House of Convenience for Gentlemen and Ladies; and goes under several Denominations: Some call it *The School of Venus*; others a *Vaulting School*; others the *Assignation House*: And some that are my Enemies, bestow upon it the Title of a *Bawdy-house*; but this title I never lay claim to, nor take pleasure in . . . for I value my Reputation more, than to put a bad commodity into any Man's Hand.[75]

The bawd's chief disguise is "Respectability," and her house must be indistinguishable from the stately facades of other houses in her street. Mother Creswell in *The Whores Rhetorick* tells Dorothea, "You must not be unprovided of the *Whole Duty of Man, Practice of Piety*, and such like helps to Devotion; as having been from the beginning a great pretender to Religion," and as the image of the bawd is transferred subtly to her "daughter" the whore, she goes on to describe "the most convenient habitation for a Trading Lady [as]—a small convenient House of her own, rather than . . . Lodgings. . . . [The] main inconveniency of Lodgings is, That in them it will be difficult to contrive several small Chambers, or dark place of refuge, just large enough to contain a Bed, which may be easily had in her own House." These "by-places" will become "dark Conventicles, for the entertainment of the Family of Love."[76] In time, Dorothea will become as accomplished as the whore in Tom Brown's *Works* who

> can convey one Man away from under [her] Petticoats to make room for another, with as much dexterity as the *German* Artist does his Balls, that the keenest Eye in Christendom shall not discern the Juggle, for a Woman ought to be made up of all Chinks and Crannies, that when a Man searches for any thing he should not find, she may shuffle about her secrets so, that the Devil can't discover them, or else she's fit only to make a Seamstress on, and can never be rightly qualified for Intriguing.[77]

The image of the crafty whore whose deceptively mobile "chinks and crannies" elude the male aggressor is offset by a surfeit of more conventional and stationary images of a woman's body as "Fortifications" for her virtue. These are too familiar to need repetition here, but the furthest extension (and reduction) of the whore to a house may be noted in the following examples. The salacious *Covent-Garden Magazine; or Amorous Repository. Calculated solely for the Entertainment of the Polite World, And the Finishing of a Young Gentleman's Education,* advertises a "nun" in Fenchurch Street who "displays as pretty a little tenement, and as delightful a woodland country round about as any one would wish to live in: the rent of which is just as much as she can get."[78] And the unquenchable Ned Ward recalls a whore who says the "Extasies of Joy" conjured up by a smooth-tongued bawd "have struck up such an unextinguishable Fire in my most Pleasurable Apartment, that I fear its past the Power of *Tunbridge* Waters . . . to stop the Flames from consuming the whole miserable Tenement."[79] In this is heard one of the first notes, to be amplified later, of the whore's self-contempt.

7. "The Art of Stitching"

Intimately connected with the motif of the woman as house is the perennial association of woman and the arts of spinning and sewing—metaphors central to the discussion of the midwife and the formation of the child in the womb. What follows is another major generalization about women, this time not from an ardent (and anonymous) antifeminist, but from the kindly William Alexander, who notes at the beginning of the second volume of his great *History of Women*, 1779, a compendium of lore, ancient and modern, "composed solely for the amusement and instruction of the Fair Sex," containing nearly every commonplace about women current in the era, that "the art of spinning, one of the most useful that ever was invented, is, by all antiquity, ascribed to women . . . . This, and the art of sewing . . . the fables and traditions of almost all nations ascribe to the fair sex." Furthermore, "If . . . the origin of clothing was neither altogether owing to necessity, nor to shame, then the cause . . . we suppose to have been a kind of innate principle, especially in the fair sex, prompting them to improve by art those charms bestowed on them by nature."[80] As the child is spun in the womb, woman, prompted by Nature, spins herself anew in the beautiful adornment of her body.

This tradition, like that of the woman as a house, also has its darker representation in the literature of prostitution. A major image associated with whores, and one of even greater significance than that of the house, is that of rich, expensive clothing: like the infant swaddled in the fabric of amnios and chorion in his wombhouse, the whore too is a creature of clothes. The preoccupation of women with clothes begins early for mother and daughter. It might be said that the tailor begins where the midwife leaves off. Father Poussin can find no "more ridiculous Custom, than to set up a *young Thing* scarce out of Leading-Strings, in the riches of *Silks* and *Linnens*, dish'd out like a Bride in the most delicious Manner, with *Lace*, *Essence* and *Ribbons*, as though she was going to be led to a Couch instead of a Cradle," and he laments "the boundless Pride and Extravagancy of others, in dressing out their Daughters of riper Years, so vastly beyond what their Circumstances are able to support, another chief Reason why our Stews are so plentifully supplied with *Women*."[81]

Much of Father Poussin's book is cribbed from Bernard Mandeville's *A Modest Defence of Publick Stews: or, an Essay upon Whoring*, 1724, where we learn that "young Girls are taught to hate a *Whore*, before they know what the Word means; and when they grow up, they find their worldly interest entirely depending upon the Reputation of their Chastity."[82] And as they grow up, "Impudence and Idleness soon gain Ascendancy over them, and then it is that a Wench of Fourteen, fancy's her self as fit for Man, and ripe for Joy as a Woman of Five and Twenty."[83] A young woman was considered nubile at fourteen.[84] Unfortunately, for many girls—before they "grow up" (these writers imply)—such early education about whores may help to explain "the strange Paradox; that a Girl, who cou'd never be brought to the use of her *Needle*, becomes of a sudden a wonderful Proficient in the art of *Stitching*."[85] "Stitching," "Stitching," "sewing," (and "sowing"), "basketmaking" or "basketweaving" are all metaphors for "the Ancient Science of Copulation" in the eighteenth century. The woman is both the material to be stitched by the aroused male and the expert in guiding the needle. The male is the mere instrument of her art, and together they sew and stitch a new person into being. The emphasis in the literature of prostitution, however, is not on human regeneration but on the old bawd's large-scale transformation of poor servant girls into better paid and finely dressed whores.

In *The Crafty Whore*, the mother of Thais, the prostitute, was "a Woman sufficiently tutor'd and experienced in Pandarisme" to dress her daughter in "pink colour satin slasht, and with very short sleeves," and lay "the most part of her patrimony on [Thais'] back, (as your Chambermaids use)."[86] An "Old Bawd" in Dunton's *Night-Walker* "was one of those that pretends to help Servant-Maids to Places . . . . (if I would be a Chambermaid [says a young whore] she could help me to a very good Place, where I should have *six pound a year, and fine Cloaths*.)"[87] These comments help to explain Father Poussin's observation that "The Town being overstock'd with *harlots*, is entirely owing to those numbers of Woman-Servants, incessantly pouring into it from all Corners of the Universe, and those Debaucheries practis'd upon 'em in almost all the Families that entertain them . . . . Many of 'em are as restless as a *New Equipage*, running from Place to Place, from Bawdy-House to Service again.[88] In anticipation of the ensuing discussion of Moll Flanders and Pamela, these passages illustrate the long established connections between poor servant girls, chambermaids, their needlework and apparel, and the context of prostitution.

This survey of images of the London harlot's progress from childhood onwards, seen through the eyes of male writers of the era, finds her now full grown. Probably the best historical account of prostitution in London in the late eighteenth century is the German traveler W. De Archenholtz's *Picture of England*, originally written in 1789. It is a late picture but, like Alexander's *History*, much of it applies to the England of Sterne, Richardson, and Defoe. De Archenholtz divides the estimated 50,000 prostitutes in London into different classes, the lowest sort living under the direction of an old bawd "who furnishes them with cloaths," and others living in furnished lodgings and their own houses. Many of these women of the higher class "possess those virtues we admire in the sex, youth, beauty, the graces, gentleness, education, principles, and even . . . . delightful modesty," but he stresses a feature common to all the prostitutes, high or low:

> enter into all the shops in the city, and ask who are their best customers . . . They will answer, that these unhappy creatures, who deny themselves every necessary of life in order to furnish their wardrobe, will often expend with them in an instant the whole gain of a week . . . . They are, in general, handsome and well clothed: their dress has the appearance of some taste . . . a stranger is apt to be embarrassed at first, and can scarce imagine that they are not gentlewomen. They are usually clad in gowns well adjusted to their shapes, and hats adorned with ribbands. There are some who even wear silk and sattin, when they are dressed . . . . England surpasses all the other nations of Europe in the luxury of dress and apparel . . . .[89]

Historically, the London whore of the eighteenth-century was so expensively arrayed that the unknowing could easily mistake her for a lady of quality, just as a bawd's house was impossible to distinguish, on the surface, from its respectable neighbors. It is not at all surprising, in the historical context of London prostitution, for Clarissa to be duped by the appearance of Mrs. Sinclair, her "nieces," and her house.

Mother Creswell of *The Whores Rhetorick* provides an authoritative summing up of the whore who incorporates the images of stately architecture and opulent dress in one figure: "Assure yourself, *Dorothea*, that nothing advances a Whores credit and reputation more than these external appearances of pomp and grandeur: as a stately and majestick deportment in her Looks, Gesture, Words, and Actions, does forcibly extort respect and veneration; so costly Cloaths, rich Furniture, do singularly advance her profit and advantage. The price of her vendibles does notably increase when they are dispensed in a splendid and magnificent Shop."[90] The literature of prostitution stresses over and over that, with the bawd's help, the whore makes herself into a rich, salable commodity, like the fine silk, lace, and satin she wears. She is a piece of merchandise, an "armful of good, wholesome British beauty" as a character in Foote's *The Minor* has it, who knows how to trade shrewdly on that beauty. Finally, the ancient convention of the motherly bawd instructing her "daughter," common in this literature, is taken up, with remarkable variations, by Defoe and Richardson.

Of the surviving handbooks on prostitution in that era, *The Whores Rhetorick* is perhaps the one most aware and perceptive of the whore's artificial sense of self and how she may best manipulate it. Again, Mother Creswell advises that a Whore

must be at least as dexterous in the vending her goods, as the Habber-
dasher at putting off his small-ware: and if she knew her own wealth, she
has in her Shop no less variety . . . for if he can cry Pins, Needles, Laces,
and Thimbles, and such like stuff; the Whore has likewise in her Magazine dainty words, sweet Kisses, pretty Smiles, and charming Looks
. . . . she has in her Cabinet, Rubies, Pearls, Emeralds, and the joy and
melody of the World . . . .[91]

Her alluring raiment is linked figuratively with the whore's command of
persuasive language, only partially verbal, and these features are embraced
in the house metaphor by way of her "Magazine" and "Cabinet." The passage
makes a good bridge to the third and last phase of the harlot's progress.

8. "The Arts of Pleasing"

At the start of his *History of Women*, which is in part a history of *attitudes* towards women, William Alexander notes that "Subjects of writing upon, like modes of dress, have their turns of being fashionable." In the medieval period it was the fashion to extol women's virtues and varnish over their vices:

> When this kind of gallantry, which taught every man to consider every woman as a kind of superior being, had wore itself out . . . the minds of men took an opposite direction . . . looking upon [women], either as the play-things of a sportive hour, or the mere instruments of animal pleasure. . . . In England, the libertinism of the court of Charles the Second first debauched the morals of almost all the women, and then taught the men to despise them for the want of what they themselves had robbed them of . . . . the earl of Rochester set the example . . . .[92]

Out of the fashion and philosophy of libertinism, Richardson was to create the greatest rake in eighteenth-century fiction, Robert Lovelace, modeled in part upon Rochester, just as the "pre-eminently bright" Clarissa's creation owed something to the older philosophy of female preeminence (linked with the medieval tradition Alexander discerned) in which woman's superiority began with her name: "Poor Adam from vile earth his name derives, / But Eve denoteth things inspir'd with lives." Woman also has a natural pre-eminence to man in the pristine, instructive power of her language:

> "Is't not from Mother, or the Nurse we draw
> And learn the Science of the speaking Law?
> 'Twas natures pleasure to accomodate
> Women with speeches most immaculate;
> So that in thousands you shall scarcely find
> One dumb or speechless of the Female kind."[93]

"A voice she hath most sweet and inchanting,"[94] or as William Austin put it, "the *voyce* was the very flower (or chiefest *grace*) of a good *forme*," and "from *their voice* men learne to frame *their owne*, to be understood of others. For in our infancy, we learne our language from them. Which men (therein not ingratefull) have justly termed our *Mother Tongue*."[95]

By William Alexander's time, it was the new fashion to see female "softness," beauty, chastity, and above all, "delicacy," contrasted with male "fairness," "constancy," courage, and bravery. "Women, in themselves, weak, timid, and defenceless," stood in need of male strength to protect them in body and mind. It is an axiom for Alexander that "there is nothing by which the happiness of individuals and society is so much promoted, as by constant efforts to please," and there follows this corollary: "It is by the arts of pleasing only, that women can attain to any degree of consequence or power." "This being the state of things between the sexes, nothing seems more plain, than that though men govern by law, women may almost always govern by the arts of gentleness and soft persuasion," that is, by the right use of her beauty, docility, and power of speech, Woman is not only an artist of adornment but of language.[96]

Once more, as in the case of the metaphor of the woman as house, and the perennial association of women with sewing and beautiful clothing, the definition of woman as chief practitioner of the "art of pleasing" has its dark parallel in the literature about whores. The third major image of the whore, and the one which takes precedence over the others, is the whore as seductive mistress of the arts of communicating with a man: "The Whores Rhetorick is nothing else, but the art to multiply insinuating words, and feigned pretenses to persuade, and move the minds of these men, who falling into their nets, do become the trophies of their victories . . . . A Whores language in the lascivious dialect, is ever to please the present lover." But to please him only in order to improve her own self-interest, at his expense, for "Interest is the subject of this art . . . . your avarice must be insatiable, you must therefore never fly an occasion of increasing your stock: and your whole life must be one continued act of dissimulation."[97] The whore then is a kind of female libertine, and the libertine a kind of male whore, with his own victims and trophies. But for the whore, "Interest" means money, not the self-gratification of the wealthy rake.

Like all women, the bawd says, "we are naturally inclined to weave fraudulent webs . . . but a Whore ought to exceed others of her sex in these undertakings . . . . she moves in a higher sphere, than the rest of Women . . . ." It becomes obvious that the bawd is contemptuous of the prevailing image of Women, whom she regards—*defines* by implication—as crudely deceptive, retiring, weak, and dependent creatures. The whore, by contrast, is an assertive artist with gestures and words:

> As you must not be stiff nor starched in your conversation, so neither in the ordering of your Body; remembering that *Venus* transformed herself once into an Eel, to leave a precedent for Young Ladies, not to degenerate from the first principles of this science, to be ambitious of perfection in the methods of dispensing pleasure. By this model you are Taught to circulate, to wind, to turn and to wriggle.[98]

Venus, whom at least one eighteenth-century mythographer classified as one of the Fates,[99] is a particularly appropriate model for the whore because she can take any shape.[100] It appears too that the "higher sphere" in which the whore moves is really the undulatory realm of the snake. Dorothea seems revolted: "This is a filthy motion," but Mother Creswell proceeds without interruption: "To stretch, to contract, to push forward, to retract, to raise upward, to bend down, and other delicious motions, that are acquired better by experiment than by any notional precepts." Even as an artist of language, the sphere of the whore's verbal motions is unintentionally debased by Mother Creswell, nor is the bawd complimentary toward the cultural attainments of the whore's clients: "You must be furnished with great variety of words, and even those that are most familiar and trivial, to enable you to entertain your lovers on all subjects." As an artist with words, the whore's speech mirrors the language of her body: she must "use ambiguous expressions, and for ornament sometimes, synonymous terms; to equivocate, vary and double . . . all which do extreamly enhance the value of your words."[101] That is, the whore is to become a poet of sexuality in her efforts to please men.

The accomplished harlot is then an artist of equivocal language, a protean actress, a soldier in the wars of Venus, a well bound book, an elegant horse, a beautiful suit of clothes, an expensively furnished "Shop," a mysterious sliding "Cabinet," a sexual magician—anything but a "Woman." "For that, Daughter, I must tell you: a Whore is a Whore, but a Whore is not a Woman; as being obliged to relinquish all those frailties that render the Sex weak and contemptible." On the face of it, the sophisticated whore of *The Whores Rhetorick* and its successors has attained a remarkably strong self-sufficiency and freedom from the stigma, "frailty thy name is woman." With the bawd's emphasis on wideness of experience, total awareness of the self in action, and unremitting dissimulation in the service of the whore's own "Interest," she has helped the whore to make herself into a new order of "cunning woman," but she must "take particular care, not to betray her self, at the same time deceiving her Lover, by procuring a Gentile outside, without equal care had in the furniture of the inner Chambers. Such a one may serve to please a Passengers eye, but can never be fit for habitation or use." The reader might now expect some sort of revelation about the inner life of this extraordinary creature. "When the Gallant is excited to strong desires by the agreeableness of exterior ornaments; it will be no small disappointment to him, and disparagement to the Lady, to find under such fair promises a course or dirty Smock . . . [or] ill smells . . . from Breath, under the Armes, or else-where . . ."[102] Mother Creswell's disturbing capacity for anti-climax is nowhere more evident than here.

As the house and clothing metaphors for the whore converge one more time, the whore and bawd (and their creators, the Italian author of *The Whores Rhetorick* and his English translator) give themselves away. For all her external accomplishments and the brilliant variety of her guises, the supreme whore is finally seen to be no more than a series of finely crafted surfaces; under her beautiful "exterior ornaments" she must be careful not to betray a dirty smock or a dirty smell. Her "inner Chambers" are empty of mind, opinions, and character, except insofar as these have been fashioned to appeal to her victims. Far from being her own woman, the whore as she is represented by the surviving literature of this era is ultimately defined and conditioned by the men who helped to bring her to birth, her literary midwives, her "victims" and her sustainers: "A Whore ought not to think of her own pleasure but how to gratifie her Bedfellow in his sensitive desires; She must mind her interest not her sport." And then there is the question of respect: "Men will be sure to respect those most, who set a high value on themselves, and their own goods."[103] The whore is thus the proponent of a philosophy of self-affirmation—and emancipation from the demeaning title of "woman"—which proclaims her economic self-worth, her "Interest."

9. "A strange Fate attends Our Sex"

It is always hazardous, of course, to generalize about the behavior and mores of an age from the limited evidence at our disposal, even where that evidence is unusually abundant. In the particular case of prostitution in seventeenth- and eighteenth-century England, the evidence is not full, but there is much in the literature of the era to suggest a prevailing moral view of women who lose their modesty, a view forcibly articulated by Mandeville and echoed by those who imitated him, that

> the Minds of Women are observ'd to be so much corrupted by the Loss of Chastity, *or rather by the Reproach they suffer upon that Loss,* that they seldom or never change that Course of Life for the better; and if they should, they can never recover that good Name, which is so absolutely necessary for their getting a Maintenance in any honest Way whatever . . . . Young Girls . . . when they grow up . . . find their worldly Interest entirely depending upon the Reputation of their Chastity.[104]

It would seem that a woman's sense of worth, in the eyes of society and in her own eyes, was conditioned from childhood in terms of the value of her chastity, and for the young lady, as well as for the whore, the subject of self-worth comes down to the question of "Interest," what Mandeville calls "artificial Chastity." Hence, with regard to self-interest, the prevailing morality for respectable women is the same as that for the whore.

But since the whore no longer has a "reputation of Chastity," she has no "Interest" in the eyes of the World and strives to create her own counter-"interest." That this is apparently a losing battle is conveyed in the poignant final words of Mother Creswell herself, who bravely tries to encourage Dorothea to renounce, in the quasi-religious terminology of eighteenth-century prostitution, not only her womanhood but her membership among the living:

> Agreeably to a young Female that is cloystered up in a Monastery, who has renounced the World, put on a new dress, new manners, new thoughts, and who is become (as the Lawyer has it) a person dead in Law, so you must now at your initiation in this profession devest your self of all Womanish conceits, abandoning that weakness and pusillanim- ity that renders many of our Sex, and more of your Trade, the object of men's charity and contempt: and to compleat the parallel, be sure to believe your person dead as to all Laws, except those prescribed by your own interest.[105]

But for the whore, in most cases in literature and in life, this interest was brittle, deceptive, and transitory. As melodramatic as it may still appear, the social fact seems to have been that when a woman crossed the line of Modesty, or was thought to have crossed it, she had virtually entered the land of the dead. Few there were strong enough, physically, psychologically, and fiscally, to thrive in that wilderness. The "Loss of Chastity," carefully defined by Mandeville as the "Reproach [women] suffer upon that loss," brought a kind of loss of the self which is variously represented, particularly in *Moll Flanders* and *Clarissa*, as a transformation of the protagonist effected in part under the influence of the Mother Midnight figure.

Mother Creswell saw weakness and pusillanimity in "many of our Sex, and *more of your Trade*," thus detaching herself for the moment from her Daughter, the whore. The whore's prevailing view of her own kind is that of the "crafty whore," Thais: "for though those of your profession are for the most part very beautifull and well-spoken, yet how depraved are our natures, how corrupt and rotten? how inconstant and deceitfull."[106] Mother Creswell had exhorted Dorothea to free herself from the weak image of Woman. Feeding this sense of feminine self-contempt was a variety of notions clustering around the principle that woman, not man, was her own worst enemy. In a gathering of "Bona-Roba's" met in the lodgings of one of their profession, a whore laments: "A strange Fate attends our Sex, we love the Men best, who have been the first cause of our Ruin, even tho' they neglect and condemn us . . . . 'Tis very true, Madam . . . you have hit upon our Female Weakness, which is rooted so deep in our Nature, that it would baffle the Wisdom of a *Solomon* to pluck it out."[107]

The sense of the whore's organic fate is unusually strong here. She is the victim of her *first* sexual encounter with a man, but deeper than that is the perception of an inherent and inexplicable predisposition peculiar to women (a "Female Weakness") to be victims of themselves. The Adam and Eve story qualifies this assertion: in the very act of sex after the Fall, woman is man's (and Yahweh's) victim. John 3:16 is counter-balanced by Genesis 3:16: "thy desire shall be to thy husband, and he shall rule [or. . .lord it. . .] over thee." It would appear, however, that the "strange Fate" is not man nor in man, but "rooted" by an umbilicus to maternal "Nature," womankind as her own mother, midwife, nurse, bawd, and betrayer. This dynamic seems to operate, as I shall try to show, behind Clarissa's tragic demise in the world as well as behind the frustrated tragicomic outcome of the Widow Wadman's overweening curiosity.

The inherent natural irony of the whore's situation was expressed in other ways. In addition to the all-too-common ravages of venereal disease, it was thought that too frequent repetition of the sexual act exhausted the strength of nature (an idea familiar to readers of Donne's poetry), and could thus be considered a form of self-murder. Whores were destroying themselves by the very practice of their profession, and they could not propagate because too frequent repetition was thought to prevent conception, or as the author of *Aristotle's Master Piece* puts it, "the Grass seldom grows in a Path that is commonly trodden in." The bawd was in the business of breaking young women into the trade by the services of hired "bullies," and women thus broken, or lost, were thought to desire the same fate for others: "I cannot help remarking," says one male observer, "that the Fair Sex are far more indebted for their ruin to female friends . . . than male foes. There is a lust in a woman who has once lost her reputation, to bring every other upon a level with herself, that her pride may not be hurt with reproach . . . . Thus has many a virtuous Young Female been debauched by Woman-kind."[108] It is Nature in reverse, a terrible process of maternal self-consumption especially applicable to the action of *Clarissa*.

The harlot's progress then, as pictured by Hogarth and described again and again by the predominantly male authors of the literature of prostitution, is one of physical and moral decline, a gradual process of stripping away the vain worth or "Interest" of a creature declared worthless by society and by herself when she lost her "Modesty." The last stage of this progress is summed up, along with several of the conventional images noted above, in these verses:

Each Day a *Head*, a *Smock* or *Suit of Cloaths*
In sad Succession to the *Broker's* goes . . .
At length their Suits obtain'd, her Clients fail,
Nor can her Person, or her Wit prevail.
All weary, to some fresher beauties stray,
Leaving the Wretch a whole Month's Rent to pay.
The cruel landlord joyful at her Fall,
Turns her away, and seizes on her All.
This unthought Blow, all Hopes of Joy defeats,
And gives a frightful Prospect of the *Streets*.
Where she must now the Midnight Sot regale
For Six-pence dry, and Six-pence spent in Ale.
Dejected thus, and overcome with Pain,
She seeks her last Resort in *Drury-Lane*;
Where rank Diseases on her Joys attend,
And only finds in Death a real Friend.[109]

Richardson stresses the speed of this disintegration in his concluding series of moralizing epitaphs on the characters in *Pamela*: "the abandon'd Prostitute, pursuing the wicked courses, into which, perhaps, she was at first *inadvertently* drawn, hurries herself into filthy Diseases, and an untimely Death; and, too probably, into everlasting Perdition afterwards."[110] The familiar images of Swift's great elegy, "A Beautiful Young Nymph going to Bed," and Hogarth's first "Progress" complete the picture.

10. Time, Space, and Birth

The main features of the midwife and her counterparts, the Fates, the witch, the "cunning woman," and the bawd-whore, a figure which I have called by her old proper name, Mother Midnight, are these. First, Mother Midnight is aged, past childbearing, and outside of the menstrual-reproductive cycle. She is beyond time, yet for this very reason, she seems to have a special relation to time. The Fates, for example, are sometimes pictured by age, from young, to middle-aged, to old and decrepit, with Atropos spinning or singing the past, Klotho the present, and Lachesis the future. We may define the Fates as a female god-like triad, the first trinity. The grouping into three reflects the major functions of spinning life into being, apportioning good or evil destiny, and taking life away. The midwife presides over birth; the midwife-bawd, in all her sexual transformations leading inexorably to death, presides over the coming together of the sexes in illicit copulation; the black midwife-witch promotes death, the white one enhances the powers of healing and the renewal of life.

More immediately, the Fates govern a particular moment in everyone's destiny, the moment of birth. The midwife's great skill is seen in her sensing of the critical moment when the birth begins, and bawds as well as lechers and rakes knew when a young woman's tender or yielding moment had arrived. Much eighteenth-century fiction and art is consciously constructed on a series of arrested dramatic moments in the progress of a protagonist, a female one in three of the four novels considered in this book. The chapters which follow are essentially considerations of some of these moments.

Mother Midnight, in all her guises, is always linked to darkness and Mother Night. There is an elaborate dark mythology of mother-daughter relationships running through the literature about prostitution and in *Moll Flanders* and *Clarissa*, particularly. Fate is the daughter of Night as the whore is daughter of the bawd, and the strumpet Fortune (to which Moll Flanders is allied) could as well be considered a daughter of Fate. Mother Midnight combines the images of Fortune and the three Fates in one multifaceted figure. She is the old woman of the night who incorporates as well the harlot daughter of her younger self.

Midwife, witch, and bawd are all active in the "heavy middle of the night." By any estimate, the hour of midnight has always been a critical one. It is a time of transition, the hour of change from old day to new day, from old year to new. It is a time of transformation, so that in Swift's mock romance, "the beautiful young nymph" turns back into her syphilitic self at "the midnight hour." Some variants of Mother Midnight, like the good maternal spirit of the oldest Cinderella prototype or the Mummy in Strindberg's complex and bizarre *Ghost Sonata*, are thought to control the critical moment of change in a character: to control time, stop it, reverse it, comprehend past, present, and future in an instant. Midnight is the perfect temporal metaphor for the bawd who ever changes "Quarters" like the moon and who possesses the "art of transforming persons."[111] The rape of Clarissa occurs at midnight.

Besides having an intimate relation to time, Mother Midnight has an equally important relation to space. As she presides over a critical moment so also she inhabits a secret inner space. She is the primal "housekeeper," a term relevant to the midwife and fate who know the secrets of the child's womb-house, to the midwife-bawd with her own mysterious "house," and to the whore who was even called a "housekeeper,"[112] metaphors vital to the discussion of the four novels. Moll Flanders is usually pictured within a shadowy enclosure or house in childhood and adolescence, then during the experience in her Governess's house in London, finally in her climactic ordeal in Newgate and within the convict ship. Pamela's most intense experience of life is lived out in the Lincolnshire house of Mr. B., overseen by the "Housekeeper," Mrs. Jewkes, whereas Clarissa's destiny is decided in the cunningly arranged London brothel of Mrs. Sinclair. The "house" of the Shandys is a literal and figurative presence all through *Tristram Shandy*, and it is in Widow Wadman's house that Uncle Toby undergoes his great revelation about women.

Mother Midnight hovers over a secret inner space in which something crucial happens to the main character, and in *Clarissa* her presence is enlarged into a figure of the fallen world. Fate, Fortune, and bawd are often pictured in relation to the globe of the earth. The three metaphors for the bawd-whore which emerged in the foregoing discussion, namely those of the secret house, rich clothing, and the artist of language, resonate throughout Richardson's fiction especially, and all share the motifs of attraction and concealment. House, clothing, and language all serve defensive, sheltering, or concealing purposes in life and in art, and Mother Midnight is a master manipulator of these allurements and defenses. This, combined with her secret knowledge relating to the sexes but especially to women and to everything connected with sexual reproduction—the secrets of the sexual parts and their pleasures, of copulation, conception, gestation and abortion, and birth—makes her a formidable worldly counterweight and antagonist to the heroine (or hero) within her enclosure. In the literature of midwifery, Mother Midnight's secret knowledge is expressed at one extreme in enigmatic charms and spells, or at the other in the most painstakingly lucid and precise instructions for delivery. She is praised as well for her gravity, taciturnity, and a self-command attributed also to the bawd. Above all then, Mother Midnight is an artist of speech and silence, who knows as well when *not* to speak as when to be most eloquent.

Mother Midnight makes an especially attractive figurative agent for the

literary artist whose imaginative powers are in close touch with the pain,
anxiety, and minutiae of ordinary living. Sterne, Richardson, and Defoe,
different as they are in so many other respects, have this kind of imaginative
kinship with each other. Each in his own way gives us a memorable evocation of life full of a thousand natural shocks and heartaches, particularly for
heroines (or a hero, in Sterne's case) who take upon themselves the joy and
the burden of writing out their mortality. In general, the women of these
novels, writers or not, constitute a "ground of being" which suffers and
sustains life. With this emphasis on suffering and renewal, the experience of
birth takes on more than ordinary significance. It is true that only three
women characters in the four novels to be considered actually give birth (the
prolific Moll Flanders, Pamela in the second part of her story, and Mrs.
Shandy), but the images of gestating, birthgiving, and travail (sometimes
spelled "travel"), recur throughout the novels in literal and complex figurative expressions.

It will be useful for the ensuing discussions to consider the act of birth, as
experienced by the one born, as essentially a journey of painful separation,
the cataclysmic prototype of all he or she will later suffer under the names of
dislocation, disorientation, confusion, frustration, toil, pain, anguish, fear,
alienation, doom—in a word, the trouble man is born to. The pain suffered
by mother and child in the act of birth is counteracted by pleasure in the
mother's reunion with her severed offspring in maternal care, but the
original wound of birth for both sets in motion an alternating process of
healing and tearing as the child grows up and the external world becomes, in
Otto Rank's words, "a substitute for the mother." In this view of life, the
birth trauma is the first great shock and separation, to be followed by a
partial healing, and then by many more shocks and healings until the final
separation from the world in death. Life is defined as a series of more or less
violent birth shocks leading to growth and new being, with the emphasis on
strong physical and emotional sensation, either of pain or pleasure. In the
four novels to be considered, the birth shocks, even those of a sexual nature,
are usually experienced as pain. Our coming into the world, then, is only the
first, traumatic stage in the journey of the birth process. As John Donne says
in *Deaths Duell*, his own funeral sermon, "*wee celebrate our own funeralls
with cries, even at our birth; as though our* threescore and ten years of life
were spent in our mothers labour." We are struggling to be born all our
lives, "passing through nature to eternity," and every gesture is a movement
away from (and back to) the original womb which always stands behind us,
the womb of our fate which continues to lay its threads upon us long after the
navel cord is tied and falls away. This journey is an elaboration of the
philosophy of birth espoused in the Wisdom literature of the Old Testament
and in the seventeenth- and eighteenth-century literature of generation.

PART TWO:

MOLL'S FATE

11. "Art and Dexterity"

How now, you secret, black, and midnight hags?
What is't you do?

(Macbeth, IV.i. 47-8)

The language of *Moll Flanders* is for the most part the same common English of Ned Ward, Tom Brown, and the authors and translators of the midwife manuals, treatises on mythography and witchcraft, feminist and anti-feminist handbooks, and works on prostitution discussed in the Introduction. At their crudest, all of these speakers have a tendency to equate wombs and wallets, bags and women. Ward's immoderate "Spy" once defined "*Woman* [as] a meer Receptacle" who should walk "Arse-upwards,"[1] and Moll Flanders herself says that "when a Woman is . . . left desolate and void of Council, she is just like A Bag of Money, or a Jewel dropt on the Highway."[2] But Moll has an analogous tendency to take the human part for the human whole. One of her colloquies with Mother Midnight, her Governess, sets off in the narrator (the prosperous old penitent who is telling the story) a reflection on the helplessness of children and their need of "an assisting Hand, whether of the Mother, or some Body else" (173). This hand must possess "Care and Skill" if the child is to survive—the midwife books and Moll Flanders share an insistent stress on human survival. As is typical of Moll (and perhaps of Defoe himself) when discussing human nature (here specifically the relationship betweeen mother and child), individual "Parts" take precedence over the whole. On the surface, the idea of motherhood is reduced to its salient components: the careful, skillful hand that keeps a child from becoming a "Fool" or a "Cripple" through neglect, with motherly "Affection" added as an extra ingredient. We shall be concerned later, in a more complicated form and with insistence on a different kind of survival, with a male perception of woman as a series of parts or a "collection of beauties" in discussing the relationship between Lovelace and Clarissa.

Yet Defoe's language for human functions, as colloquial and reductive as it may at times be, is a highly flexible and suggestive means of expression. Defoe insists upon "the infinite variety of this Book" in his "Preface," and as the "Story" insists, from many angles, upon the importance of Moll as a woman of Fate, the reader is reminded at the outset of our earlier examination of Fate and the midwife in Chapter 2. Moll, like other archetypal woman characters in fiction, is associated with the spinstress figure: she begins life as a seamstress and she resumes the work, although reluctantly, as an adult. (It should be noted that this is the only honest work she represents herself as doing between childhood and old age.) Her adopted name of Flanders recalls fine lace material. Her obsession with amassing quantities of fine clothes is a major expression of her lifelong desire to establish herself as a prosperous gentlewoman in the world. The ancient idea of human mortality (and morality) consisting of a series of layers of clothing, alternately being put on and put off, is expressed in more subtle ways in the novel by Moll's continual allusions to mental disorders, cases of conscience, and habits which alternately take effect and then wear off.

But it is the figurative correspondence in the novel between the arts of midwifery and thievery (as they are embodied in the Governess and her relationship to Moll) which I find the most compelling feature of Defoe's deceptive art in the novel, specifically, in his depiction of Moll as a woman of Fate in the dual sense that she is shaped by a fate-like figure and that she becomes a figure like fate. It is perhaps impossible to determine how consciously Defoe uses midwifery as a metaphor for, or an analogue to, theft, "the archetypal Augustan crime," as Pat Rogers puts it in *The Augustan Vision*. I have found no firm evidence in Defoe's other works of his possessing an uncommon knowledge of the subject. Still, an exploration of this correspondence, and its consequences, deepens our understandings of Moll's evolution into the master thief and powerful Mother she becomes by the end of her story.

If *Moll Flanders* is in many ways a searching examination of the meaning of Fate in the role of a "woman of the world" who becomes a criminal and finally a wealthy "Penitent" on her own plantation in Virginia, the one character in the novel who has the most decisive influence on her career as a thief is her Governess, Mrs. B—. In the Preface to *Moll Flanders*, Defoe tells us that "two of the most beautiful Parts" of the "Story" remain to be told. One of these is the "life" of Moll's Governess.[3] The present inquiry then is an attempt to restore some of the historical and literary particularity of Mother Midnight[4] as we trace Moll's development under the influence of this powerful and mysterious character. We shall see that a concern with Moll's relation to Mother Midnight also entails an analysis of Moll's "grand Secret," her "true Name" (159) and actual origin. The main endeavor here is not to *discover* Moll's "true Name" (i.e., the historical model for Moll) but to try to understand, with the help of Mother Midnight, who the real Moll Flanders is for Moll herself: that her own sense of her real name is relevant to her sense of who she is.[5]

Martin Price has said that "if there is any central motive in Defoe's novels, it is the pleasure in technical mastery: the fascination with how things get done, how Crusoe makes an earthenware pot or Moll Flanders dexterously makes off with a watch."[6] Closely allied with this pleasure in making and making off with is the manufactory impulse in much of Defoe's writing: an acute concern with the manual industry necessary for making and acquiring material goods. On almost every page of *Moll Flanders* there is a hand at work, literally or figuratively. Moll Flanders learns her most important technical skills under Mother Midnight's auspices ("it was to this wicked Creature that I ow'd all the Art and Dexterity I arriv'd to" [213]), and it is Mother Midnight's own unparalleled "Art and Dexterity" as a practicing midwife (in all its associations—as thief, as bawd, as procuress—the term suggests in the novel) which seals Moll's fate as a thief and fundamentally alters the course of her life.

12. "My True Name"

Moll "runs thro" many different names and appellations in the novel as she moves from one personal crisis to the next. She begins the world over and over again, usually under a new name, and she is as careful to record every new name (every new Fate), as she is to account for her goods in her well-known periodic Stock-taking. Many of her new names are open to connotations of promiscuity, and she sees herself from the start as "a poor desolate Girl without Friends . . . as was my Fate" (8). She seems always to need a friend or a guide, and often this friend is a woman.

At age eight Moll, "the little Gentlewoman" (14), begins her working life as a seamstress to avoid the horrors of "working House-Work" as a servant. Why, one might ask, is little Moll so afraid of working as a servant? She presents herself as an impressionable, sensitive child, more than ordinarily vulnerable to childhood fears. Not knowing the details of her early upbringing, she seems uncommonly afraid of being abandoned and perhaps submerged back into the obscure sink from which she was rescued. We see in the young Moll an exceptional little girl who wants to do her own work and not be ordered around by some frightful cookmaid.

At the death of her kind old Nurse, a foster mother to her, Moll, now fourteen, is almost frightened out of her wits at the prospect of being "turn'd out of Doors to the wide World" (16). As early as this, the "wide World" for Moll is a terrifying antagonist. After her sojourn as Mrs. *Betty* (the proverbial name for the loose servant girl) in the household of the two brothers, and her unhappy five-year marriage to Robin, she is again "left loose to the World" (59). She is soon drawn into a "World of wild Company" (60) where she becomes the "pretty Widow . . . that Name I got in a little time in Publick" (60). In her career as "Fortune" hunter (and as a self-styled figure of Fortune), "I was hurried on (by my Fancy to a Gentleman) to Ruin myself" (61)—the shadow of ruin and destruction haunts Moll's rhetoric until her reprieve from Newgate. She continues in "the Habit of a Widow" (though she is still legally married to her second husband, the linen-draper) and assumes the name of Mrs. Flanders (64).

Having married her third husband, Moll winds up on his "great Plantation" in the colony of Virginia. Here Moll's real mother discovers, after considerable effort, that Moll is "*her Daughter* born of her Body in *Newgate*; the same that had sav'd her from the Gallows by being in her Belly" (95) and who is now married to her son, Moll's half-brother. The whole process of this discovery is represented in terms of gestation and birth. While literally pregnant with her third child by her brother, the secret of her true relationship to him is such a load on Moll's mind that she cannot sleep (88). Moll says, "I liv'd with the greatest Pressure imaginable for three Year more" (89), "no good Issue came of it" (90), "I found the thing too far gone to conceal it much longer" (94), and finally, she says, her mother "us'd her utmost Skill . . . to get the main Secret out of me" (94). Her mother's "Opinion was that I should bury the whole thing entirely . . . and so let the whole matter remain a secret as close as Death" (97), a solution all too reminiscent of ways of disposing of unwanted children. In effect, Moll does dispose of the burden by transferring it to her husband. By *naming* the dreadful secret she brings it out in the open, gives it birth, rescues her own life, inflicts her husband with the knowledge of his incest and thus contributes materially to his two attempts at suicide.

We are never told Moll's married name in Virginia, but it is here, apparently for the only time in her life, that she reveals her maiden name to someone. Since this revelation to her real mother clinches her identity as the sister of her own husband, misery and ruin follow with almost Oresteian inevitability: "I know not by what ill Fate guided, every thing went wrong with us" (90). From that time on Moll reserves, like a Rosicrucian adept, "the grand Secret" of her true identity. Speaking of Jemy, her Lancashire husband, she says, "I . . . never broke my Resolution, which was not to let him ever know my true Name, who I was, or where to be found" (159). Not Jemy, not Mother Midnight, not even posterity knows Moll's "True Name," though it is, by her open admission, "well known in the Records, or Registers at *Newgate*, and in the *Old-Baily*" (7), if one knew how to find it.

We must pause briefly to reflect on this "True Name." The more one inquires into it, the more mysterious it becomes. Is it the name she was christened with in Newgate, still preserved (as Moll might suppose) in the records of illegitimate children born there? Is it her mother's maiden name, or was her mother married when she "pleaded her Belly" seven months before Moll was born? Or is the "True Name" recorded in the Old Bailey the last of the five married names (or any of the others) which she has acquired by the time of her induction into Newgate? When Moll was apprehended by the belligerent mercer as the "Gentlewoman" thief, mistakenly as it turned out, she was loath to identify herself so she told the justice in Bloomsbury her name was *Mary Flanders*. This seems to be at least one of her names "so well known among the People at *Hicks's Hall*, the *Old Baily*, and such Places," that no court would ever give damages to a "Person of such a Character" (248). Her "True Name" would seem to be her given and maiden names, but it is not likely that she would later give this name to the authorities.

In any case, Moll's true name—whatever it is—would seem to be the sign of her true identity, the person who she really is in her own eyes. The *real* Moll Flanders is the one with the name that can never be revealed, the innocent child, imprisoned in her womb-house, who ironically saved her mother from hanging and freed her for a new life ("the same that had sav'd her from the Gallows by being in her Belly" [95]), and who as a woman gave life to her one true love Jemy ("a Life that had given him a new Life" [299], as he tells her in Newgate). Moll seems to feel about her name as some women feel about their age, that to reveal it would be to lose a certain power. Moll's true name works for her as a talisman tied to the precious illusion of her original self, the innocent, life-bringing child. In some mysterious and nonrational way, she seems to know that keeping the secret of her true name will preserve her and help her to flourish in the world. And for us too there seems to be a further power in her *not* having a precise name but a resonant, inclusive, *generic* one. "Moll Flanders" has come to suggest a free, dangerous, and powerful kind of woman, one who comprises many.

13. Mother Midnight

We are introduced to Mother Midnight at about the midpoint of the narrative when Moll, pregnant and "very Melancholy" (161), returns to London after having parted with Jemy, her Lancashire husband. The old woman has an instantaneous good effect upon Moll: "Every word this Creature said was a Cordial to me, and put new Life and new Spirit into my very Heart; my Blood began to circulate immediately, and I was quite another Body; I eat my Victuals again . . . " (162). An experienced midwife was acquainted with the best cordials for lying-in women, and this midwife (who eventually delivers Moll's baby) seems, with her heartening words, to have delivered Moll herself anew into the world. From the point of view of seventeenth-century physiology, a baby's circulation began at birth, and we recall Mrs. Jane Sharp's detailed and urgent emphasis (in Chapter 3) on the importance of keeping "the blood and spirits in after the Child is born." Mother Midnight, in a figurative sense which will be developed and enlarged for much of the rest of the novel, is Moll's spiritual mother.[7]

Moll's response to Mother Midnight's life-giving ministrations is worth closer attention: "Every word . . . was a Cordial": Moll's old Governess is a "Mistress of her Tongue" as Moll is fond of saying, and as we have noted, the etymological nature of the classical Fate figure, who also presides over birth, is rooted in speech (see Chapter 2). When Moll speaks about her own "Blood" in the novel she always means her life-blood, her vital spirits, and just as *aurum potabile*, the famous gold cordial so often referred to in contemporary satirical contexts meant something magical, so the association of gold and life has an almost miraculous effect on Moll's spirits throughout the novel. She is not entirely capricious in writing on the window with the diamond ring of her third husband-to-be, *"But Money's Vertue; Gold is Fate"* (79).

If we consider for a moment Moll's relationship with gold in the first half of the novel, two scenes spring vividly to mind. In the first, a young girl of seventeen or eighteen in the "Pride of [her] Beauty" and freshly awakened sexual desire pores for hours upon the "Handful of Gold" the elder brother at Colchester had put in her hand. The gold is a dream vehicle for her reverie, a mirror for her desire, her imagination, and her sexual vitality all involved together: "Never poor vain Creature was so wrapt up with every part of the Story" (26). In the second, a more worldly Moll throws her own six guineas from a drawer onto the bed and her wealthy lover Sir Walter Cleave[8] (117) has her bring him his private drawer containing 200 guineas:

> He took the Drawer, and taking my Hand, made me put it in, and take a
> whole handful; I was backward at that, but he held my Hand hard in his

Hand, and put it into the Drawer, and made me take out as many
Guineas almost as I could well take up at once.

WHEN I had done so, he made me put them into my Lap, and took
my little Drawer, and pour'd out all my own Money among his, and bad
me get me gone, and carry it all Home into my own Chamber.

I RELATE this Story the more particularly because of the good
Humour there was in it, and to show the temper with which we Con-
vers'd (112).

For Defoe's Moll, a modern Wife of Bath who will marry five husbands (and
be married to four of them at once) this is all jolly good fun, a good joke. She
and her Bath lover are laughing all through the mock-marriage (his taking
her hand) and physical consummation through gold. Their gold act seems
almost to outweigh for Moll the sex act it mimics.[9] Furthermore, the pouring
Guineas are almost liquid here. For Moll, gold and all valuables are the
external sign of the life blood and active good spirits within her. Gold is the
life-blood of the world, and of *her* world. Moll's most striking and deeply felt
metaphor for personal economic disaster is fused with her own life-blood.
Just before meeting Sir Walter, she finds her expensive way of living had
"sunk [her] exceedingly . . . so spending upon the main Stock was but a
certain kind of *bleeding to Death*" (106). And she recalls that at the lowest
point of her economic decline, just before she became a thief, she wept
continually over her dismal circumstances, "and as it were only bleeding to
Death, without the least hope or prospect of help from God or Man" (190).

To return to Moll's first meeting with Mother Midnight. We are soon
acquainted with the old midwife's practical philosophy of life: at the heart of
the matter, for her as for Moll, is bare unaccommodated money, "the thing
indeed, without which nothing can be done in these Cases" (163). Where-
upon she offers her famous three "Bills" of ascending order of expense, and
Moll, smiling, chooses the short form. The whole tenor of their conversation
is that of two women who understand each other. They speak the same
language, despite Moll's ambivalent feelings about the "wicked Practice" of
this "eminent Lady," into whose hands Moll first admits she "put" herself,
and then says she "fell" (166-68). Moll reveals that Mother Midnight, like so
many of her sisterhood in the seventeenth and eighteenth centuries, is not
merely a midwife. "This grave Matron had several sorts of Practise," one of
which was to run a lying-in hospital for whores and unwed mothers and
another to sell babies procured from "private Labours" (168).[10] Ned Ward
tells of a pimp who gained two to three hundred pounds from such
transactions,[11] probably an inflated figure, but there is no doubt that infants
could, in the right hands, be valuable merchandise. This passage gives the
first hint of Mother Midnight's traffic in stolen goods. We also learn, though
very indirectly in words redolent of Moll's moral confusion under the in-

fluence of this woman, that Mother Midnight is a bawd who does not seem to operate an actual brothel.

She is called "the Governess" by the "Ladies of Pleasure" in her house (169), and Moll henceforth adopts that name for her, a name which defines their relationship until shortly before Moll's capture as a thief. When the time for Moll's lying-in arrives, the "Governess did her part as a Midwife with the greatest Art and Dexterity imaginable, and far beyond all that ever I had had any Experience of before" (171). Since this is Moll's tenth lying-in, we may accept her occasional hyperbole as, at least in this case, genuinely meant. Mother Midnight is a true non-pareil in her profession, and Moll seems more attracted by the woman's technical mastery than repelled by her "wicked Practice."

While on the one hand Moll is being delivered of her brave but un-welcome burden, she is being relieved of concern on the other by the convenient suicide of the wife of her banker, whom she is now free to marry. At this point Moll begins, distantly, "to open [her] Case" about the Lancashire marriage to her friendly Governess, whose "Care of Moll in her confinement" has been so great "that if she had been [her] own Mother it could not have been better" (171-72). Indeed the midwife reminds one of Moll's mother in several respects: they are both born storytellers with shady pasts, they instruct Moll in the lore of the underworld, and each has a remarkable facility for extracting Moll's secrets. This aspect of what the two mothers have in common requires further examination.

When Mother Midnight is first described, in the Preface, she is referred to as a "Midwife, and a Midwife-keeper, *as they are call'd*" (5). Sermon remarks that at the time of delivery the woman should "send for her Midwife and keeper," that is, her midwife companion.[12] But a good midwife was also considered an excellent keeper of secrets: Mother Midnight says "it was her business to Conceal every thing" (172) and she importunes Moll continually to reveal what is troubling her. Her importunity recalls that of Moll's brother and mother in Virginia when they "labour with" Moll to get "the Main Secret" out of her. Mother Midnight is a professional secret keeper; her livelihood, like that of the London bawd in Chapter 5 who was "the very Magazine of Taciturnity," depends on her withholding of knowledge: "*she told me to* unfold my self to her, was telling it to no Body; that she was silent as Death" (172). It is not easy for a woman so wrapped up in deception as Moll to unfold herself to anyone, but Mother Midnight characterizes herself as "no Body," an impersonal silent presence who can nevertheless be of help to Moll. Moll concludes that "she had such a bewitching Eloquence, and so great a power of Perswasion, that there was no concealing any thing from her" (172). So Moll resolves to "unbosome" herself and discloses to her the history of her Lancashire marriage and the nature of the "good Offer" she has received from her faithful Citizen (172).

Mother Midnight suggests, "in so many Words," that the child Moll has just borne must be "remov'd," and this touches off the brief disquisition, on the part of the old narrator, imagining herself back into the troubled frame of mind of her former self, about motherhood and the proper upbringing of children. Moll freely represents to her Governess, "who I had now learn'd to call Mother," the "dark Thoughts" she is having about giving up her little boy (174). As Moll's mind darkens with genuine concern for the child, Mother Midnight, "hardened" as to any "Religious" consideration in the case, "impenetrable" as to "Affection," and amoral, pretends to match her mood, and, becoming "graver," establishes a new direction for their thoughts by reminding Moll of the "careful" and "tender" handling she received from her expert midwife in her recent lying-in. With Moll under Mother Midnight's capable hands, the two women have just shared the physical and emotional intimacy of the birth experience and now they are talking about the most efficient way of abandoning the child. Moll was abandoned by her real mother, rediscovered her in Virginia, learned the horrible secret of her own incest and incestual motherhood, and escaped back to England. Now she has entrusted herself into the hands of a woman who has taken as good care of her as if she had been "her own Child" and whom she calls "Mother." This person then says, "Well my Dear . . . and when you are gone, what are you to me? and what would it be to me if you were to be Hang'd?" (174). Long before Moll is to face the actual prospect of being hanged, Mother Midnight forecasts that eventuality. The old narrator Moll—who is a wise counterpart of the Governess here—knows that this encounter of the younger Moll with Mother Midnight is crucial to her future and dwells with increasing emotional intensity on the interview. Moll must sense that she has been through something like the fearful intimacy of this encounter in her relationship with her actual mother, and what more horrible revelation does Mother Midnight have for her than her own mother had? What more horrible knowledge than the story of Moll's death?

One of the most influential of early eighteenth-century midwives notes that "the Midwife . . . has need of Sagacity, to discern the different Tempers of Women; for a great many, like Children, are to be treated with Gentleness . . . and sometimes with Severity are to be school'd to do what they ought."[13] Combining tenderness and sinister insinuation in a gesture suggestive of the expert midwife's mastery of the "Touch" (the external and internal palpations by which she determines the readiness of her patient to deliver), "the old Beldam" whispers, "Are you sure, you was Nurs'd up by your own Mother? and yet you look fat, and fair Child . . . and with that she stroak'd me over the Face; never be concern'd Child, *says she*, going on in her drolling way . . . I employ the best, and the honestest Nurses that can be had . . . we want neither Care nor Skill" (174).[14] The Governess has *already* delivered Moll of her unwanted child and knows the secret of its origin. Now she seems to be in possession of a far more important secret—for Moll, the "grand Secret"—the knowledge of Moll's true origin and identity, and perhaps even her destiny.

Mother Midnight seems to know more about Moll than even her own mother knew, or than Moll knows herself, and the touch over Moll's face seems at once to herald and to seal Moll's confirmation of that secret. But Moll is silent; she trembles and looks pale. After the midwife's literal "touching" of Moll, in labor and here, Moll's inward exclamation, "She touch'd me to the Quick" (175),[15] expresses in the deepest possible sense for the narrator and Defoe Mother Midnight's significance for Moll. In completely naturalistic terms, the old midwife in this passage becomes for Moll a figure of "impenetrable" darkness (at once intimately, maternally familiar and yet uncaring, impersonal, alien), a figure of almost godlike ambivalence and omniscience. She exhibits the powers assigned to the Greek Fates in seeming to know at once Moll's past ("Are you sure, you was Nurs'd up by your own Mother?"), her present ("yet you look fat, and fair Child"), and her future ("what would it be to me if you are to be Hang'd?"). She seems to know as much about Moll as the old narrator does. In her encounter with this old woman, Moll has come into intimate personal contact with her own past, present, and future—a sense of her total fate—and by the conclusion of the interview she seems to know that her fate is linked with Mother Midnight inexorably.

As Moll seems to grow up anew under the tutelage of her adopted mother, she stands before her now like the vulnerable little girl in Colchester terrified of being abandoned by her old Nurse and wonders if "this Creature cannot be a Witch, or have any Conversation with a Spirit that can inform her what was done with me before I was able to know it myself" (175). Perhaps the old folktales of the witch who demands possession of a child in exchange for her services and the other witch who fattens up children before eating them lie behind Moll's present relationship to Mother Midnight, for her fear would be reinforced by the proverbial superstitious identification of the midwife and the witch. The midwife-witch, as we have seen (Chapter 4), was thought to possess uncanny powers of prophecy, a gift which Defoe and Moll both attribute to Satan's ministers.[16] Mother Midnight passes over Moll's disorder, but Moll's repetition of "Mother" in addressing the old woman after her fright, and her upsurge of relief at the Governess' assurance that Moll's "Child shall be used well" (176), indicate that Moll is now securely bonded to her new mother at the expense of her more humane impulses: "O Mother, *says I*," in an echo of Othello with Iago, "If you can do so, you will engage me to you for ever." Mother Midnight has become Moll's "ill Fate."

14. Midwife-Thief

Moll practices two main careers in her search for a respectable monetary establishment in life: the first revolves upon the use of her sex, the second upon her dexterity as a thief.[17] At the outset of both of these careers she is framed for an indelible instant in an open doorway, each an entry into a new life. Defoe's language for describing Moll's commencement, apprenticeship, and career as a professional thief bears remarkable resemblance to the rhetoric and lore of the noble "Art of Midwifery," a resemblance which makes her transition from the life of sexual intrigue to the life of a thief seem the most natural thing in the world.

Moll had five years of ease and content with her banker husband but his untimely death, like "a sudden Blow from an almost invisible Hand . . . turn'd [her] out into the World" (189) in worse economic straits than she has yet experienced. Tom Brown's "Contemplative Traveller" once observes that "while I behold this Town of *London* . . . I fancy I behold a Prodigious Animal."[18] The world has by this time become for Moll a huge unpredictable labyrinthine antagonist, dominated by powerful commercial and legal forces, which has always defeated her and which she must now outwit and over-come. Grass time is done ("it was past the flourishing time with me" [189]), her faithful Citizen is dead, bodily "Ruins" have succeeded the "Ruin" she once feared as "a Whore to one Brother, and a Wife to the other" (31), and Moll is "the most dejected, disconsolate Creature alive" (189-90). The sexual games of her life and the "politick Schemes" (67) of marriage, in all their variety of manipulation and intrigue (which occupy slightly more than the first half of the novel) now give way to a new kind of game which Moll learns to play with even greater relish than the ones of her lustier years.

The vital impulse is the same in Moll's first sexual encounter and her first theft, in which the Devil, as tempter and prompter, plays a part. At the beginning of both scenes Moll has had a "smooth Story" to tell, in the first case, of life in a "Family Noted . . . for Vertue and Sobriety" (19), in the second, of "an uninterrupted course of Ease and Content" with a "Husband . . . Quiet, Sensible, Sober . . . Virtuous" (188-90). In the first scene the Tempter enters in the guise of the Elder Brother who is skilled at laying traps: the Elder Brother well knows "how to catch a Woman in his Net," baiting "his Hook" and laying it in Moll's way (19-20). So too in the later scene, a more literal Devil, as Moll tells it, "carried me out and laid his Bait" (191). Both scenes are framed just inside a doorway, the first in the work room of the Elder Brother's sisters (who are absent), the second in an apothecary's shop, whose two attendants have turned their backs. In the first scene, the Brother clasps and kisses her and his "Words," Moll says, "fir'd my Blood, all my Spirits flew about my Heart . . . and my Heart spoke as plain as a Voice, that I lik'd it . . . it was . . . a Surprise . . . my Head run upon strange Things" and "my vanity was elevated to the last Degree"; in the very next encounter they kiss again, and "tir'd with that kind of Work, we sat down" (21-23). In the scene of the theft the Devil's prompting is "like a Voice spoken to me over my Shoulder"; "I felt not the Ground, I stept on . . . I was tyr'd and out of Breath, I was forc'd to sit down . . . my Blood was all in a Fire . . . I was under such a Surprize that I . . . knew not . . . what to do" (191-92).

The Devil's effect upon Moll is not much different from the Devil's workings with women in seventeenth-century literature. The best known example is Milton's Satan who, through a dream, manipulates the senses of a highly suggestible Eve and elevates her to a new level of vanity and pride, preparing the ground for his later temptation in daylight. Milton's presentation of the whole process of the temptation is subtly orgasmic. For Defoe the sequence is more mundane, but characteristically lively. As Moll sums it up, "Thus the Devil who began, by the help of an irresistable Poverty, to push me into this Wickedness, brought me on to a height beyond the common Rate, even when my Necessities were not so great" (202). "I that was once in the Devil's Clutches, was held fast there as with a Charm" (203).

As active as Moll's Devil is, however, in pushing her into her career as a thief, Mother Midnight, as an external confidante and Governess allied with Satan's internal promptings, is far more interesting and important. What the Devil instigates the midwife fosters and brings to maturity. The spiritual presence of the old woman of the night seems to hover over Moll's first thefts. For much of the story, Mother Midnight *is* Moll's fate. She stands in relation to Moll at the end of the first half of the novel as Newgate stands to Moll near the end of the second half—as the dark, powerful medium to a new life. Moll becomes "quite another Body" after first meeting Mother Midnight, and the old midwife is there to deliver and dispose of Moll's unwanted son just as she will later dispose of the goods Moll steals; she will provide Moll's "School-Mistress" in thievery just as she will later provide the minister who delivers Moll from Newgate.

Moll first steals from an apothecary's shop. Midwives and apothecaries were linked professionally. The "little Bundle wrapt in a white Cloth" (191) and lying upon a "Stool" is reminiscent of a new-born baby placed upon or near the itinerant midwife's stool. The bundle turns out to contain (among other things) "a Suit of Child-bed Linnen in it, very good and almost new, the Lace very fine" (192), an item listed in Mother Midnight's third bill of particulars.

Moll's second sally into the new world of crime has often been cited as a vivid example of Defoe's art but with very little commentary on its excellence:

one Evening . . . the Devil put a Snare in my way of a dreadful Nature
indeed, and such a one as I have never had before or since; going thro'
Aldersgate-street there was a pretty little Child had been at a Dancing-
School, and was going home, all alone, and my Prompter, like a true
Devil, set me upon this innocent Creature; I talk'd to it, and it prattl'd to
me again, and I took it by the Hand and led it a long till I came to a pav'd
Alley that goes into *Bartholomew Close*, and I led it in there; the Child
said that was not its way home; I said, yes, my Dear it is, I'll show you
the way home; the Child had a little Necklace on of Gold Beads, and I
had my Eye upon that, and in the dark of the Alley I stoop'd pretending
to mend the Child's Clog that was loose, and took off her Necklace and
the Child never felt it, and so led the Child on again: Here, I say, the
Devil put me upon killing the Child in the dark Alley, that it might not
Cry; but the very thought frighted me so that I was ready to drop down,
but I turn'd the Child about and bad it go back again for that was not its
way home; the Child said so she would, and I went thro' into *Bartholomew Close*, and then turn'd round to another Passage that goes into
Long-lane, so away into *Charterhouse-Yard* and out into *St. John's
street*, then crossing into *Smithfield*, went down *Chick-lane* and into
Field-lane to *Holbourn-bridge*, when mixing with the Crowd of People
usually passing there, it was not possible to have been found out . . .
(193-94).

The most disturbing thing about this passage is that the little girl is in danger
of her life. She has been practicing postures in a dancing school, and Moll
(taking her own instructions almost puppet-fashion from the Devil) takes
over for the dancing mistress. With the compulsive, slow-motion quality of a
dream, Moll leads the girl into a "dark Alley" that enters a "close," or dead
end street, and there performs with her a chilling minuet: "I talk'd to it, and
it prattle'd . . . I took it by the Hand and led it a long." As in a dream, all that
Moll can see is the necklace which she must have and the child becomes a
mere instrument for that transaction. "The Necklace . . . of Gold Beads . . .
might have been formerly the Mother's, for it was too big for the Child's
wear" (194-95). Moll very adroitly delivers the child (and by implication the
child's mother) of the cumbersome necklace and is then seized with her fatal
impulse. For the moment Moll, on that evening, in that dark alley, is
invested with all the terrible power over life and death of Mother Midnight
herself. She is terrified by that power, but her presence of mind allows her
to save the child and the necklace at once.[19]
    Most of the authors of the midwife manuals, whatever their verbal attain-
ments, take great pains to make their important instructions concerning
delivery as precise and lucid as possible. Defoe's language for Moll's thefts
has this same charged, minute, intense quality, as if he, through Moll, were

giving vital directions to the reader. The foregoing passage is vivid as well because the scene it describes is densely suggestive. It evokes the shadows of an underworld, images of snares, traps, lurking thieves, closed-in and claustrophobic blind alleys, midwives who murder children that they "might not cry," and a whole labyrinth of crooked lanes (actually one of the most sordid and disreputable parts of the London of 1720)[20] into which Moll recedes before mixing with the crowd of people.

I have so far been drawing merely analogical connections between Moll's thefts and the lore of midwifery. It is interesting that Defoe now chooses to reintroduce Mother Midnight into Moll's narrative. A businesswoman who made a good living in the illegitimate baby market would probably also provide a good market for Moll's stolen goods, and indeed her old Governess, though fallen (like Moll) on hard times, still "stood upon her Legs" as a "*Pawn broker*" and fence (197). The manipulative side of Moll and her adopted mother is readily apparent in Moll's anticipation of their new life together and her farewell to the old life of sexual intrigue:

> I Now began to think this necessary Woman might help me a little in my low Condition to some Business, for I would gladly have turn'd my Hand to any honest Employment if I could have got it; but here she was deficient; honest Business did not come within her reach; if I had been younger, perhaps she might have helped me to a Spark, but my Thoughts were off of that kind of Livelihood, as being quite out of the way after 50, which was my Case, and so I told her (198).

Like Plato's and Sermon's midwives, Moll is past childbearing and ready for a new career. But her new career of thievery need not be any less exciting than her old one of sexual politics. Mother Midnight suggests a "School-Mistress" in crime for Moll: "I trembled at that Proposal," but the Governess soon "conquer'd all my Modesty" (201). It must take a certain boldness to become a midwife or a thief, and as Moll embarks on this dangerous new profession, Defoe explicitly establishes the midwife-thief parallel. Moll, old in years but "young in the Business" of crime, is apprenticed, "Just as a Deputy attends a Midwife without any Pay" (201),[21] to a hardened younger female thief ("no Woman ever arriv'd to the Perfection of that Art, so as to do it like her" [201]). Moll is an apt pupil. She had been good with her hands since the age of ten, when she was Assistant to her first Nurse (and mother surrogate) in Colchester: "I was very nimble at my Work, and had a good Hand with my Needle" (14-15). Had not the Mayoress of Colchester herself one day pronounced, after a close examination, that little Moll had "a Gentlewoman's Hand" (13)? In the first half of the book Moll has learned the ruses, deceptions, and stratagems of sexual intrigue from a variety of expert school-mistresses, particularly the Captain's widow ("I told her . . . I would give up myself wholly to her Directions" [77]), her landlady in Bath ("a cunning Creature" and prototype of Mother Midnight [110]), and the "she Devil" (143) of Lancashire, a "*go-between*" (149) who deceives her about the rich "Irishman," Jemy. Moll is thus more than ready for the intrigues of thievery.

The first victim (or "Prize") for a "Deputy Midwife"-thief would be, appropriately enough, a pregnant woman expensively attired:

> At length she put me to Practise, she had shewn me her Art, and I had several times unhook'd a Watch from her own side with great dexterity; at last she show'd me a Prize, and this was a young Lady big with Child who had a charming Watch, the thing was to be done as she came out of Church; she goes on one side of the Lady, and pretends, just as she came to the Steps, to fall, and fell against the Lady with so much violence as put her into a great fright, and both cry'd out terribly; in the very moment that she jostl'd the Lady, I had hold of the Watch, and holding it the right way, the start she gave drew the Hook out and she never felt it; I made off immediately and left my Schoolmistress to come out of her pretended Fright gradually, and the Lady too; and presently the Watch was miss'd; ay, *says my Comrade*, then it was those Rogues that thrust me down, I warrant ye; I wonder the Gentlewoman did not miss her Watch before, then we might have taken them.
>
> She humour'd the thing so well that no Body suspected her, and I was got home a full Hour before her: This was my first Adventure in Company; the Watch was indeed a very fine one, and had a great may Trinkets about it, and my Governess allow'd us 20£. for it, of which I had half, and thus I was enter'd a compleat Thief, harden'd to a Pitch above all the Reflections of Conscience or Modesty, and to a Degree which I must acknowledge I never thought possible in me (201-02).

The woman cries out, perhaps, because she thinks first of her baby, and Moll, holding the watch "the right way," lets nature do the work for her: "the start she gave drew the Hook out and she never felt it." As Sermon says, "Nature surpasseth all" in the art of midwifery,[22] and Moll's "Schoolmistress," like a "mild, gentle" midwife, "humours" the "Gentlewoman" after the "delivery," helping "the Lady too" to come out of her "Fright gradually." Like Sermon's "Lady's Companion," the schoolmistress is able "to speak many fair words . . . to deceive the apprehensive woman" in order to allay her fear. (Of course Sermon is speaking of a "commendable deceipt . . . done for the good of the person in distress.")[23] It may be said of Moll and her tutor, as of male midwives, that they "have advanced their *Dexterity* by degrees, and are now come to the length of discharging [their] Office by *Slight of Hand* only . . . ."[24]

The language for Moll's smooth delivery stands in precise contrast to the horror, expressed in many of the midwife manuals, of incompetent midwives extracting dead (and sometime living) children with the aid of hooks and other instruments. But the most significant contrast here, to Moll's mind, is that between an infant and a watch. From our point of view, the adjectives for describing babies and watches in the novel are almost interchangeable ("pretty," "brave," "fine," "good," "charming"), both entities are small and delicate (possessing faces and hands) and are often decorated, and both may be considered emblems of mortality. (Moll's innocent little dancing student in the dark alley combined some of these attributes.) But from Moll's point of view at this crucial stage in her life, gold watches are far more interesting and valuable objects than infants. She has had enough of producing children, unwanted, unpredictable burdens as they are to the vulnerable mother. Watches now take their place, but the excitement of producing *them* is far preferable to Moll because the technical mastery (or "Dexterity") involved in the activity enhances her illusion of "artistic" control over a life which has been all too often at the mercy of manipulators of both sexes. Her new skills are attained in part as an over-reaction to her previous all-too-frequent incompetence as a woman on her own in the world.[25]

Moll soon serves out her apprenticeship as a midwife-thief and becomes a "compleat Thief" (202), working on her own. Her description of her new role could apply just as accurately to the compleat midwife: "I pass'd with [my Governess] from this time for a very dexterous Manager in the nicest Cases" (211). Midwives from Sermon to Dawkes repeatedly refer to their dexterity as managers of labor, to nice and critical points in examination and delivery, and to nice and difficult cases of labor which they have successfully resolved. In the famous gold-watch passage, Moll gives a post-operative analysis of her narrow escape which reveals further refinements of her new trade:

I was so frighted, that I ventur'd no more at Gold Watches a great while; there was indeed a great many concurring Circumstances in this Adventure, which assisted to my Escape; but the chief was, that the Woman whose Watch I had pull'd at was a Fool; that is to say, she was Ignorant of the nature of the Attempt, which one would have thought she should not have been, seeing she was wise enough to fasten her Watch, so, that it could not be slipt up; but she was in such a Fright, that she had no thought about her proper for the Discovery; for she, when she felt the pull scream'd out, and push'd herself forward, and put all the People about her into disorder, but said not a Word of her Watch, or of a *Pick-pocket*, for at least two Minutes time; which was time enough for me, and to spare; for as I had cried out behind her, *as I have said*, and bore myself back in the Crowd as she bore forward; there were several People, at least seven or eight, the Throng being still moving on,

> that were got between me and her in that time, and then I crying out *a*
> *Pick-pocket*, rather sooner than she, or at least as soon, she might as well
> be the Person suspected as I, and the People were confus'd in their
> Enquiry; whereas, had she with a Presence of Mind needful on such an
> Occasion, as soon as she felt the Pull, not skream'd out as she did, but
> turn'd immediately round, and seiz'd the next Body that was behind her,
> she had infallibly taken me (212).[26]

The precision of this is remarkable. Moll's timing cannot be improved upon.
In those critical two minutes, recorded as if Moll were timing herself by her
own gold watch, she is able to get away. She is here working alone, without a
partner, and she has learned to manipulate the crowd, and extricate herself
from it, as cleverly as she ever lifted a gold watch.[27] In fact, extricating
herself with art and dexterity from dangerous situations now seems to take
precedence over extracting precious articles from others.

In growing up all over again as a thief, Moll attains her majority after
amassing twenty-one gold watches, and her disclaimer that after the above
incident "I ventur'd no more at Gold Watches" is as much an admission that
they are no longer so interesting to her as it is a sign of caution. Moll's
growth in crime is paralleled by a similar aging of the objects or victims of
her thefts. We have followed Moll's career from her first theft of a bundle
(containing "Child-bed Linnen") resembling a new-born infant to the safe
delivery of a necklace from a little girl (who is herself delivered from a dark
alley) to the theft of a "charming Watch" from the side of a "Lady big with
Child." The overall chronology of Moll's life progresses from the largely
passive role of bearing children in intrigue, to the active game of stealing
watches, to the predominating joy of bearing herself alive from ever-
increasing peril. She will shortly amass "near 500*l*. . . . in ready Money"
(221) and could retire comfortably, but she goes on. It is not the lust for gain
which drives her. Thievery is now a career subsidiary to the art of eluding
capture—and Newgate.

The old Moll, the narrator, draws back after the gold watch passage to
give a fuller historical dimension to her story, paying homage to the greatest
professional (and personal) influence on her life with "a short Touch" (appropriate term for a midwife) at the "History" of her Governess, who

> led me as it were by the Hand, and gave me such Directions, and I so
> well follow'd them, that I grew the greatest Artist of my time, and
> work'd myself out of every Danger with such Dexterity, that when
> several more of my Comrades run themselves into *Newgate* presently,
> and by that time they had been Half a Year at the Trade, I had now
> Practis'd upwards of five Year, and the People at *Newgate*, did not so

much as know me; they had heard much of me indeed, and often expected me there; but I always got off, tho' many times in the extreamest Danger (214).

The Governess, she says a little later,

listened & did what she said

> told me she would never recommend any Partner to me again, for she always found . . . that I had the best luck when I ventur'd by my self. . . . I got out of [Danger] with more Dexterity than when I was entangled with the dull Measures of other People who had perhaps less forecast, and were more rash and impatient than I; for tho' I had as much Courage to venture as any of them, yet I . . . had more Presence of Mind when I was to bring my self off (220).

Moll now sounds like the pretentious male-midwife instructors who deprecate "rash, hasty, and passionate" practitioners: "these people do commonly want that other, almost inseparable Talent, a good and prudent Deportment . . . let [them] spin and card (the properest Employment for them!),"[28] and the one Moll knew but detested. Moll has attained a level of competence equivalent perhaps to "Men" who, according to Maubray, are "commonly endued with greater *Presence of Mind* . . . than common *Midwives.*"[29]

Whatever knowledge of the lore of midwifery Defoe may have possessed, the analogues between midwifery and thievery we have observed tend to give Moll's life as a thief fresh significance and urgency. Defoe is at one with his creature as Moll offers her hard-earned "Directions" to the reader, for if there is any motive more central in Defoe's novels than the pleasure in technical mastery, it is the pleasure in *telling* how this mastery was achieved and how it operates. Moll/Defoe's descriptions of her thefts have no less importance for her than the descriptions of proper delivery have for the midwives because both trades, at least as they were practiced in the early eighteenth century, were life-and-death occupations, and were considered "Arts." By 1720 men had gradually gained pre-eminence over women as self-styled professional midwives; the lowly "Trade" of midwifery had evolved, in the hands of male practitioners, into what they deemed a true "Art." Maubray (to choose just one example) refers to men as "the more Skillful and Judicious Practiser[s] of this Art," and he goes on elsewhere, in what must be the most self-flattering preface in the literature of midwifery, to "expound the Truth of Things; and reveal the *Mysteries* of our great Art."[30]

Moll is not so pompous as Maubray, but in her own way she is just as proud of herself. The midwife parallels to Moll's career as a thief call attention to her role as a *woman*—a woman of the world who, in a society and economy dominated by men, surpasses women *and* men in her proficiency and "Fame" as a thief. The parallels reinforce the sense of a woman's life-giving skill with her hands (a skill of which Moll becomes complete master), but it is Moll's own life ("many times in the extremest Danger") which is being quickened, enhanced, and preserved by these skills. She becomes in effect the expert midwife-thief to herself, stealing herself from danger time after time and living to tell about it. She not only survives, but survives in her "long Race of Crime" with a "Name" as the greatest "Artist" of her time (214). Moll's triumph is that she becomes autonomous and self-perpetuating, a genuine mythic heroine. And as in all myths, but most significantly in the more primitive and vital ones, whether they emanate from a people or from one man (like Defoe's charging unbroken narratives), Moll's proper name, the name given her at birth by her real mother and everyone's first Fate, is intimately connected with her destiny and essential self. For as triumphant as Moll becomes as an artist, that is not who she really is in her own eyes.[31]

15. Mother Newgate

As Moll grows more and more skillful at manipulating the London street crowds to her advantage, another crowd of her "Comrades" who first "run themselves" and then are "catch'd and hurried to *Newgate*" (214), is growing in numbers and power to do her harm. This envious and angry crowd of thieves claims her for their own: "These were they that gave me the name of *Moll Flanders*: For it was no more of Affinity with my real Name, or with any of the Names I had ever gone by, than black is of Kin to white, except that once . . . I call'd my self Mrs. *Flanders* . . . but that these Rogues never knew" (214). This is a crucial distinction for Moll. None of the names she has ever gone by, since childhood, was her "real Name." That name is separate and inviolable. But she is now christened by Newgate as certainly as she was born there, and she can be "Impeached" by Newgate as well—naming her in this way will seal her destruction. Moll emphasizes that her real name is no more "of Kin" to "Moll" ("almost a generic name for a female criminal," as McKillop notes[32]), than white is to black. Her real name, like the original identity she wishes to preserve, is unique, not generic; it is white, innocent, and pure, despite the virtual blood kinship she has with Newgate through her mother's line.

Though Moll seems only dimly aware of the fact, Mother Midnight, her real mother, her mother's mother and a "Kinswoman of hers who . . . was . . . Condemn'd to be Hang'd but . . . got Respite by pleading her Belly afterwards in the Prison" (87), are all intimately tied to Newgate.[33] This ancient prison is the mother of them all. It functions as an inescapable womb of fate. The more famous Moll becomes as a thief, the larger looms the prison behind her and seems to draw her to itself. From this point until her reprieve, Newgate, her birthplace and her spiritual home, will come to exert more influence on Moll than any of the other mother (or fate) figures in her life, even Mother Midnight. At the height of Moll's success as a thief, "the old Gentlewoman began to talk of leaving off while we were well," but an unknown "Fate," allied to Moll's "Success" and her "Name [now] famous as any Thief of my sort ever had been at *Newgate*" (262), guides her on. This fate is the consummate paradox of Newgate, a teeming mob held together in one place; the ultimate extension of both the London bawd's house of iniquity, and of the bawd herself; a dread microcosm of Moll's old antagonist, the World; "an Emblem of Hell itself" (274): "To conclude, the Place that had so long expected me, and which with so much Art and Success I had so long avoided" (273). When Moll arrives there she says "it seem'd to me that I was hurried on by an inevitable and unseen Fate to this Day of Misery . . . . I was now to give satisfaction to Justice with my Blood . . . . These things pour'd themselves in upon my thoughts in a confus'd manner, and left me overwhelm'd with Melancholly and Despair" (274). Moll the expert manipulator of crowds is now seen, ironically, to have been part of that same crowd of hapless comrades rushing towards the vortex of Newgate. Her language dissolves in the image of drowning in her own blood.

At her lowest point in Newgate, Moll is reduced to the condition of all the other poor wretches. Like the picaro, she has become her surroundings: "I degenerated into Stone . . . I became as naturally pleas'd and easie with the Place, as if indeed I had been Born there" (278), meaning, apparently, as if she did indeed *belong* there, with the spoken emphasis on "had." Moll's sense of herself has centered all along on the notion of her being an *exceptional* person, but that uniqueness was always expressed and qualified in equivocal terms. She was not like the other little orphan girls in that she abhorred the thought of working "Housework." As a remarkable and sought-after "little Gentlewoman" she unknowingly modeled herself on a woman of ill fame. She had the advantage of a young gentlewoman's education, and was superior in beauty and voice to the daughters of the Colchester house-hold, but she became a "Whore"—not a common whore of course, but a special kind of one, "a Wife to one Brother and a Whore to the other." This pattern continued in her career as a "Widow bewitch'd" (64), as "a Woman of Fortune, tho' I was a Woman without a Fortune" (106), as a "happy but unhappy" (120) mistress who then became involved with a man who had "*a Wife* and *no Wife*" (133). Finally, she became a thief, but she developed into an exceptional one, the best "Artist" of her time, and a unique kind of survivor. Now after her leveling experience in Newgate, Moll must begin life all over again; this time, however, she begins as the end product of all her previous roles. She is still exceptional, but it may be said that she will no longer be one thing and its opposite, no longer the equivocal creature she was.

Moll undergoes at least a partial moral regeneration when she can move from the state of "stupid and senseless" inactivity by way of raving madness to an overwhelming sense of grief, not for herself but for Jemy when she sees him in the pressyard. Her meeting with the "Minister" sent to her by Mother Midnight is a pious reenactment of her former dark interview with the Governess concerning motherhood, but the secret of Moll's wicked life will now be known only to God and herself. The minister here effaces himself in the service of God as Mother Midnight had before characterized herself as "no Body," a secret-keeper as silent as death. Moll opens her soul to the minister (who might well be a stand-in for Defoe himself) and experiences the joys and comforts of true repentence, mirroring but going beyond the "new Life" and new circulation of her blood she felt upon meeting Mother Midnight for the first time: "So swift did Thoughts circu-late" that she could have then gone freely to execution without any uneasi-ness (289). Her new penitent thoughts have, at least for the moment, taken the place of gold as an expression of her deepest vitality, the force of her life-blood.

16. "A new Foundation"

Whether we believe in the sincerity of Moll's repentance in prison or not, there is no question that after Newgate she is a more confident and capable woman of the world. The other Newgate, the colony in the "New World," Virginia, now draws her, but instead of the pressure of a malign fate impelling her actions ("my own Fate pushing me on" [104]), there is now "Providence" (326). More than ever, her Mother Midnight, now extremely old, mirrors her experience in Newgate and after (the old woman too undergoes a virtual conversion, by way of a grave illness); she is still practical and helpful, ever faithful, a true friend, but she is now demythologized: no longer is there any sense of the fatal power she had over Moll as her Governess. In fact, their roles are now reversed: Moll is the director, her Governess the child. Referring to Mother Midnight in a conversation with Moll on the eve of her departure, the Boatswain says she "cryes after you like a Child" (309). Even her husband and co-partner Jemy, a prototype of the great man in Fielding's sense, "was as much at a loss as a Child what to do with himself, or with what he had, but by Directions" (311), that is, Moll's directions. Moll is as much the actress now as ever, pretending to be poorer than she really is on the ship, but she is now in control of her fate. Indeed she has *become* her fate because she is now her own governess. She has finally arrived at the level of practical competence and wisdom of the world which she always admired in her old Governess. Moll becomes her own Mother Midnight. At the same time, her new self is a regenerated version of the innocent child (associated with her "True Name") who brings fresh life to a new world.[34] She and Jemy are set to "begin the World upon a new Foundation" (303): they will "live as new People in a new World" (304); as Moll sums it up, after an inventory of the stolen goods which make up her dowry as an incipient planter and colonist: "In the Sixty first Year of my Age, I launch'd out into a new World" (312).

In her early sixties, she can even afford, emotionally and fiscally, to become a real mother for the first time. When she sees the handsome and prosperous young Humphry, her son by her own brother, she experiences the final agony of childbirth: "It was a wretched thing for a Mother thus to see her own Son . . . and durst not make herself known to him . . . I thought all my Entrails turn'd within me, that my very Bowels mov'd" (322). This may seem "contrived and meretricious"[35] to us from our perspective on Moll's hapless career as a mother, but for her in the immediate moment of recognition it is a genuine emotion, and a love approaching veneration.[36] She may now claim the material legacy her own mother left her, having survived the legacy of Newgate. Moll's mother had fallen into bad company in her London youth, became both *Whore* and *Thief*, wound up pregnant in Newgate, bore Moll in prison and was then transported to Virginia where she fell into a good family, married her master, presumably repented of her wicked past, and "improv'd the Plantations" after his death "to such a degree . . . that most of the Estate was of her getting, not her Husband's for she had been a Widow upwards of sixteen Year" (88). Obviously Moll is her mother's daughter. Her life recapitulates her mother's in several crucial respects (as whore, thief, convict, transported felon, penitent, planter, and widow), just as it does Mother Midnight's.

Her real mother and her spiritual mother have bequeathed to Moll an impressive legacy as a wealthy and respectable planter and director of plantations in the new world, but our experience of Moll's ancient alter ego, Mother Midnight, would not be complete without noticing her last gift to her disciple. The cargo Moll ordered the Governess to send from England "arriv'd safe, and in good Condition, with three Women Servants, lusty Wenches, which my old Governess had pick'd up for me . . . one of which'd happen'd to come double, having been got with Child by one of the Seamen in the Ship . . . before the Ship got so far as *Gravesend*; so she brought us a stout Boy, about 7 months after her Landing" (340). The Governess and erstwhile Fate still plies her trade as a midwife-bawd even at a distance, and the three wenches are three young fates who will "begin the World," like Moll, all over again.

PART THREE:

PAMELA'S BOOK OF FATE

17. "A little Volume of Letters, in a common Style"

> . . . go flea dogs and read romances! - I'll go to
> bed to my maid.
>
> (Petulant in The Way of the World)

At the age of sixty-four, eight years before his death, Samuel Richardson recalled his earliest experiences as a writer, and these memories are rendered with peculiar fullness and vividness of detail. The old man remembers "a bashful and not forward Boy" of thirteen, the "Favorite" of the young women of the neighborhood who would "borrow" him to read to them and their mothers as they did their needlework:

> three of these young Women, unknown to each other, having an high Opinion of my Taciturnity, revealed to me their Love Secrets, in order to induce me to give them Copies to write after, or correct, for Answers to their Lovers Letters: Nor did any one of them ever know, that I was the Secretary to the others. I have been directed to chide, & even repulse, when an Offence was either taken or given, at the very time that the Heart of the Chider or Repulser was open before me, overflowing with Esteem & Affection; & the fair Repulser dreading to be taken at her Word; directing this Word, or that Expression, to be softened or changed . . . . I recollect that I was early noted for having Invention,

and several boys, his schoolfellows, would often ask him to tell them stories. One of them "was for putting me to write a History" which turned out to be about "a Servant-Man preferred by a fine young Lady (for his Goodness) to a Lord, who was a Libertine."[1] In this *soi-disant* paradigm of Richardson the novelist (copyist, reader, letter-writer, editor, and storyteller), the boy Richardson (surrounded by women, old and young, quietly sewing) was a little medium between the sexes, a precocious Socrates, a secretary to the Fates, a small "Magazine of Taciturnity" recalling, in this regard, the London bawd herself. He knew when and when not to speak. He knew how to write model love letters, and how to keep secrets. He devised stories for boys based in part, presumably, on the love knowledge he gained from young women. He understood from an early age, or he came to understand, that language can be manipulated to reveal the lover's deepest wish while seeming to conceal it. He had the benefit of hearing from the young women and their mothers on these matters.

Thus Richardson's imagination had a brief adolescent flowering before his long professional career as a printer. His experience as apprentice and successful printer was to give him a knowledge and depth of appreciation of the *literalness* of the English language unique among the great English writers, but it was not until he was fifty years old that his imagination would again burst forth, and in circumstances reminiscent of his first writing efforts. He notes further to Stinstra that two booksellers (successors to the boy who put him upon writing the "History" of the good servant) entreated him to write "a little Volume of Letters, in a common Style," on subjects that might be of use to country readers who could not write for themselves; he "yielded to their importunity," as he tells Aaron Hill in an earlier letter,[2] and while writing "two or three letters to instruct handsome Girls" going out to service, he remembered an innkeeper's old neighborhood story (about a young gentlemen who married his mother's beautiful waiting maid) told to him by a friend twenty-five years before, "And hence sprung Pamela."[3] The book began as a model letter and rapidly grew into a two-volume novel. As is well known, Richardson began writing the novel in secret up in his "little Closet," but soon had the company every night of his "worthy-hearted wife" and a young lady—Elizabeth Midwinter—who was then living with them, and who in some ways, perhaps in her appearance and speech, may have been a model for Pamela. "Have you any more of Pamela, Mr. R? We are come to hear a little more of Pamela,' &c."[4] Richardson was back in the comfortable and liberating milieu of his earlier writing experiments, in the company of a young woman and an older one (a mother, his second wife) sampling his "Pamela," sympathetically, we may suppose, giving encouragement and making observations of their own, and certainly "pleased with the Observations they put [him] upon making,"[5] as he had said of the earlier experience. (One is reminded of the communal, mutually supportive eighteenth-century birth setting described at the end of Chapter 2.) Hence Mrs. Richardson and Miss Midwinter collaborated with him—in their womanly ways—in the creation of Pamela over the following intense three months of its composition.

Richardson tells Hill what he was trying to do in *Pamela*: "I thought the story, if written in an easy and natural manner, suitably to the simplicity of it, might possibly introduce a new species of writing, that might possibly turn young people into a course of reading different from the pomp and parade of romance-writing . . . . I therefore gave way to enlargement: and so Pamela became as you see her."[6] However accurately this pronouncement reflects Richardson's actual intentions before and during the writing of *Pamela*, it is important for what it implies about the language and style of the novel. Far from abandoning a concern for decorum, Richardson as the inventor of a new species of writing is intensely concerned with creating and sustaining "an easy and natural manner, suitably to the simplicity" of the story. In the first place, he wants to be read, and to be read by younger, mostly female readers. He believes that by representing as faithfully as possible the diction, idiom, and speech patterns of an extremely bright and well read adolescent waiting maid of the early eighteenth century, he will secure and keep those readers, aware as he proceeds, perhaps, that he has contrived a language for his heroine which is inadequate to the full expression of her complex emotional life. But he is willing to run that risk because language can take on an emotional life of its own. Of course we have no way of knowing precisely how accurate Richardson's representation of actual speech is, but if Pamela's language lacks subtlety, it abounds with fervor and intelligence.

Pamela's lamentation, however sincerely felt, over "her miserable hard Fate"[7] sounds to us stilted and hollow, whereas the wonderful liveliness and urgency of colloquial quarrel, badinage, innuendo, and hyperbole—from *both* of them—in her exchanges with B. make *Pamela*—even today—a joy to read aloud. (I am thinking particularly of the early exchange in letter XV [40-42]). Pamela uses the word Fate often and in different contexts. As with *Moll Flanders*, the word and the idea will have more significance for readers of the novel when seen in the light of its associations as sketched in the Introduction. The reader may be frustrated by the formulaic repetition of many of Pamela's girlish utterances (part of her "easy natural manner" because she is drawing—as we all do in colloquial speech—on ready-made phrases), but one also feels, at least in about two-thirds of the novel, a remarkable consistency and vibrancy in her speech, the activity of, in B.'s words, "an open, frank and generous Mind" which is nonetheless unsure of itself at times and even self-deceived. And in that other third of the novel, roughly between the time of her declaring her love for B. and her encounter with Lady Davers, we might ask what has happened to Pamela to make her sound so different.

Since the motifs of the child sewn in the womb, and woman as spinner and creature of clothes are important concerns of this study (see especially Chapters 3 and 7), we begin our inquiry with Pamela's relationship to sewing, clothing, and writing as a necessary preliminary to examining in detail her encounter with her Mother Midnight, Mrs. Jewkes, and the resolution of her "hard Fate."

18. The Needle and the Pen

> I am no enemy to the distaff; but the woman who writes a book, breaks
> not thereby the rank she holds in the world. The pen is almost as pretty
> an implement in a woman's fingers, as a needle . . . . were I to chuse the
> attitude that I would have one of the dearest of my lady-correspondents
> drawn in, it should be with a pen in her hand, in the act of writing . . . .[8]

From the beginning, Pamela's whole being revolves around her experience of Mr. B. and her expression of what that experience means to her. This expression is given to us in two main forms, directly through her writing (one long letter home, written at intervals, to her parents) and indirectly through the clothing which she wears and sews. In curious and fascinating ways, her clothing becomes a form of communication with B., and her writing becomes a form of clothing concealed from him. Eventually, not long before Pamela becomes Mrs. B., the formal motifs of writing and clothing come together.

Pamela is extraordinarily expressive whether she is using her needle or her pen, and whatever she writes or sews seems instinct with her own physical and emotional self. "Don't wonder to see the Paper so blotted" with her tears, she says to her parents in Letter I, and this first letter introduces most of the major concerns in the novel. We have first of all an immediate indication of Pamela's divided mind ("I have great Trouble, and some Comfort, to acquaint you with") and we sense a fragmented and vacillating self divided between the poor little servant girl and the genteel personal waiting maid to the deceased Lady B. The insecure child-woman is also the cherished favorite who has learned some of the accomplishments of a lady ("Qualifications above [her] Degree") [25]), and Pamela's special relation to her benefactress is now to be transferred, in part, to her son. B. says to her, "*Pamela* . . . for my dear Mother's sake, I will be a Friend to you, and you shall take care of my Linen" (25).[9] Pamela is to take care of B.'s underclothing, and she will have a peculiar concern for and care of his clothing—and he for hers—from this point on. We might say, in a formulation dear to Defoe, that Pamela is a servant and not a servant. Her parents understand this all too well. We learn from them that Lady B. "for Three Years past has always been giving [Pamela] Cloaths and Linen" (27). They know, with Father Poussin, Mandeville, and Dunton (see Chapter 7), that fine clothing can corrupt maidenly innocence, especially that of chambermaids; in Pamela's father's words: "our chief Trouble is, and indeed a very great one, for fear you should be brought to any thing dishonest or wicked, by being set so above yourself . . . what avails all this, if you are to be ruin'd and undone!" (27)

In the first quarter of the novel, interspersed with Pamela's vivid recollec-
tions of B.'s attempts on her virtue and her repulses of him, there is a
subdued but no less significant game of give and take going on between them
over clothes. Pamela's care of B.'s linen is countered by his giving her his
mother's fine clothing, including stays (a laced underbodice) and "silk Stockens"; Pamela is a little "inwardly ashamed" about this transaction, but B.
says, "Don't blush, *Pamela*: Dost think I don't know pretty Maids wear
Shoes and Stockens?" (31). He gives her fine clothing and she works "all
Hours with [her] Needle, upon his Linen . . . and [is] besides about
flowering him a Waistcoat" (34). She cannot return home to her parents till
she has put the linen in order (46) and B. will have her stay until she finishes
the waistcoat (49): "O! I forgot to say, that I would stay to finish the
Waistcoat; I never did a prettier Piece of Work; and I am up early and late to
get it finish'd; for I long to come to you" (51). Both impulses, of staying and
leaving, seem genuine, but there is more urgency in her elaborating the
waistcoat, Penelope-like. She loves sewing it, creating it for him—this is part
of her expressive artistry. Hence she clothes him as he clothes her; each will
enhance the other's image. Despite all the violence of their spoken exchanges, they are deeply attracted to each other and this attraction is spelled
out by the mute language of their bodies, the "fine Shapes" adorned by
apparel they have devised for each other's wearing or approval. As B.
reclothes her in the image of his beautiful mother, so Pamela clothes him in a
gorgeous undercoat to be worn around his heart.

With her very first letter, B. is Pamela's first, imperious, and fascinated
reader: "Why, *Pamela*, you write a very pretty Hand and spell tolerably too"
(26), as he takes the letter before she can hide it in her bosom. From the
start, Pamela's beauty is mirrored for B. in her handwriting, and the gesture
of Pamela trying to hide her letter and B. taking it away from her to read it,
prefigures the pattern of their "correspondence" through the entire first half
of the novel. For a long time, B. secretly reads her letters and forms his
opinion of her through her behavior and even more important, through what
she writes. We as readers are in something like B.'s privileged position.
Anyone opening the novel *Pamela* at any point and reading it is at once put
into the quasi-illicit position of reading someone else's mail, of observing,
like voyeurs, the secret acts of Pamela and B. B. and the reader have an
uneasy fictional alliance all through the novel, as if observing the phenomenon of Pamela from opposite sides of the scene.

Most of the novel is built on the fiction of Pamela remembering and
faithfully transcribing dialogues between herself and B., and between herself and B.'s servants and acquaintances. As one who did needlework and
looked after the linen of the household, a large part of Pamela's job would be
to take out copies with her needle and repair the linen. Pamela is a duplica-
tor, an expert copyist with her needle and with her pen. She keeps on

making one transcript of reality after another in her letters home, and these letters become the fabric of her life, figuratively and later, literally, as they become her underclothing. The letters are the phenomenal, superficial, and yet essential *Pamela*. These we must accept as the true record of her experience with B., even when Pamela seems to be deceiving herself, or when she seems not to be in touch with her true feelings toward B., or when we wish that B. could write a little more on his own behalf, and not always be perceived through the screen of Pamela's consciousness.

So much for how the two motifs of mutual clothing and B. as Pamela's reader are established. Now, ostensibly, in order to ease her transition back to the old life of poverty with her parents, Pamela puts in practice a "Project" (the first of many in her dealings with B. and later with his agent, Mrs. Jewkes) of fashioning a dress of "good sad-colour'd Stuff" consisting of "a Gown and two Petticoats . . . two pretty enough round-ear'd Caps, a little Straw Hat . . . two Pair of ordinary blue Worsted Hose, that make a smartish Appearance, with white Clocks . . . two Yards of black Ribbon for my Shift Sleeves, and to serve as a Necklace" (52-53). This "sad" outfit has a remarkable history in the first half of the novel. Pamela knows very well as she looks in the glass (60) that this new dress enhances her beauty, but she prefers to take pride in her ingenuity and resourcefulness as she descends the staircase with "Ease, Innocence and Resignation" (60).

B. does not at first recognize her in the new garb, and then pretends she must be "Pamela's Sister." She is forced to proclaim her real identity —"I am *Pamela* . . . Indeed I am *Pamela, her own self!*"(61) when he threatens to kiss this sister. The new dress in fact plays a part in inciting B. to his attempt on Pamela that same night after she undresses for bed. The new clothing presents a new Pamela to B.'s eyes, just as her letters home give him a new view of her. The sad outfit and the responses to it are a kind of displaced Pamela, preceding the gradual "displacement" of herself into her letter-history.

And on the level of enhancing each other's image, B. shortly after this— almost as if trying to outdo the effect on him of her sad outfit—models before Pamela (who is alone with him in the room) his new "Birth-day Suit" to honor the king and celebrate his rumored promotion to the peerage. "How are these Cloaths made? Do they fit me!—I am no Judge, said I . . . but I think they look very fine" (71).

One may reasonably wonder why it is Pamela stays so long in the house with B. if she really wants to leave for home. Considering the enormous social power with which Richardson invests B. in the novel, the main reason is that Pamela cannot leave without her master's permission. One of the less obvious reasons for his not giving it is Mrs. Jervis. This kindly, motherly housekeeper is working quietly out of earshot promoting Pamela's interest with B. and mollifying his anger. She also stage manages the important scene in which Pamela, preparing for her leave-taking, divides up her clothing into three bundles as B. watches in secret from behind a curtained closet (78). The three bundles are like the three caskets of folktale lore, and Pamela's expressive, allusion-making mind—fed with Puritan doctrine and her reading in "reflection"—seethes with more analogies to the spiritual life than that of a gifted Dissenting preacher.

The first parcel consists of the clothes and linen her good lady gave her, the second one of "the Presents of [her] dear virtuousMaster," and the third parcel is of course "poor *Pamela*'s Bundle, and a little one it is, to the other" (79). She enumerates its contents, which include the making of the sad-outfit. As in fairy tales, the least showy bundle is the best one. It stands for the good, virtuous Pamela. Hence Pamela, in this scene, soothes her mind and orders her experience by making external, in a self-dramatizing little game, the three major influences in her life, namely Lady B., B. himself, and the attitude toward herself and her virtue fostered by her parents, which she sustains. She deliberately contrasts the "second wicked Bundle"—the "Price of her Shame" if she had been ruined, the potential prostitute-self represented by fine silk clothing—with the third, which has come to represent her "Innocence," the "Pride of [her] life," and the "Companion of [her] Poverty"(80). (The "sweet Companion [her] Innocence" mentioned in an earlier scene takes objective form here in the third parcel.) These three parcels are dumb presentiments of the bundles and parcels of Pamela's writing which she will sort out, conceal, send away, or sew around her body in the great crisis of her life at B.'s Lincolnshire estate. Bundles two and three are like signposts indicating the two possible directions of Pamela's life, the road to ruin and the road to the preservation of her virtue and her true self, for in her mind the two are identical. But by having linked an unbecoming pride with a prior scene of self-display Richardson raises doubts here too about the honesty of her present self-embracing pride.

We turn back now to the chief form of Pamela's expressiveness, her writing, and B.'s role as her closest and most deeply affected reader. Pamela's self which had been expressed in her clothing gives way to her writing self, but both of these stem from the same potent creative nature. Indeed, the novel is in part a parable of the creative eighteenth-century woman transforming herself from weaver into writer. The motifs of sewing and writing are brought together explicitly and comically at one point when B., irritated, pretends to wonder why Pamela has still not left his house. She says she has not yet finished the waistcoat: "You might . . . have finish'd that long enough ago . . . . Indeed . . . I have work'd early and late upon it; there is a great deal of Work in it! Work in it! said he; yes, you mind your Pen more than your Needle; I don't want such idle Sluts to stay in my House" (55). But

Pamela at this point is minding her pen and her needle with almost equal assiduity. Later, when the tormented B., who is far more unstable and oscillating a figure than his adolescent maidservant, finally decides to declare his love for her, he does so, appropriately enough, in his library, the one room in the Bedfordshire estate which Pamela describes in detail. It is "a noble Apartment," full of rich appointments. Characteristic of his time, his class, and his temperament, B. begins by declaring he will no longer think of her as his "Servant"; then he says he "cannot but love" her. He will now consider her as his "sweet-fac'd Girl" who is also a writer:

> I have seen more of your Letters than you imagine, (This surpriz'd me!)
> and am quite overcome with your charming manner of Writing, so free,
> so easy, and so much above your Sex; and all put together, makes me, as
> I tell you, love you to Extravagance (83).

He suggests that his reading of her over an extended period has made him love her more deeply than he would have done otherwise. She knew a long time before that one of her letters was missing, and she suspected he had been reading them. It can be surmised that part of her writing mind was and still is at work for him. After this declaration, she finds her "poor Heart giving way!" He now treats her with more respect because of her writings whereas before he had often contemptuously dismissed them, or pretended to dismiss them, as exposés of himself and his family. Still, Pamela cannot believe him. "Strange, damn'd Fate! says he, that when I speak so solemnly, I can't be believed!" (84). The condemnatory words he had before used for her he now uses for his "Fate." It is his fate not to be believed, but by his erratic and self-contradictory words and actions, he has earned this fate.

On a deeper level, Pamela has become his fate in the sense that what she means to him is shaping his behavior. All along she has been operating within the great social and personal power B. has over her, but his power is largely *external*. B.'s progress with Pamela could be described as a continual effort to know her, first physically and then emotionally. He can shift her from one county to another as if she were the "Tennis ball of Fortune," but unless he touches her heart, her innermost emotional center—secret even to herself—he cannot win her. And Pamela, despite her vast social inferiority to him, has power over him *internally* without either of them knowing the full extent of it, but it is enough to make him hers on her terms. By this point in the novel then, the great social and personal power of B. is no longer in his own power. As Mrs. Jervis had said, B. dotes upon Pamela, and "it is not in his Power to help it" (65).

After the library scene, B. is physically off the stage of the novel for sixty pages, but his presence and dark influence are continually felt. For much of her Lincolnshire captivity, the richest and most dramatic section of the novel

(94-209), Pamela will not be able to perform for him in person in her fetching clothes and attitudes. She will express herself instead solely through her writing and in her conduct toward the people at the new house, but her writing will itself become a new secret form of clothing. The physical form of this writing in its relation to Pamela's "person" is so important to Richardson (and to her) that he has her take extraordinary pains to account for it at every stage of its development. And he makes our inquiry more convenient (and intriguing) by explicitly noting three main stages or chapters of Pamela's Lincolnshire journal (corresponding to the ordering and objectifying impulse which produced the three bundles of clothes earlier), which we may designate as (1) "the Sunflower Correspondence" (94-128), (2) the "Rosebush" papers (128-150), and (3) the "Petticoat" Papers, in two parcels (parcel I, 150-164; parcel II, 164-189).

19. The Sunflower Correspondence

"It has Witchcraft in every Page of it; but it is the Witchcraft of Passion
and Meaning"

(Aaron Hill on *Pamela*, 17 December 1740).

Pamela's confinement at B.'s Lincolnshire estate precedes her marriage
to him, and the idea of Fate, linked in her mind to uncertainty, to plotting,
and to the treachery of a bawd who will preside over her forcible rape,
permeates the heroine's consciousness throughout this period. When she
becomes fully aware that B., instead of having his coachman Robin take her
back home to her parents, has instead abducted her some eighty miles north
to his estate in Lincolnshire, Pamela sets the keynote for her "Journal" with,
"Let me write and bewail my miserable hard Fate" (94). She has the deep
sense here of being the victim of a plot, nothing less, in fact, than a
kidnapping.

Even before her arrival at the estate, she had had forebodings of trouble
when the "Face of the Country" (98) was nothing like what she remembered
and having stopped at a farmhouse and "laying Middle and both Ends
together" (98) she soon perceived "all [her] Plot cut out" (100) on her "way to
the Place [B.] has allotted for [her] Abode for a few Weeks" (99). The familiar
ground of Bedfordshire has been cut out from under her, and a new plot—
both as a piece of ground and as as a pattern for her life—has been sub-
stituted by her "wicked Master." The word "plot" will reflect almost all of its
main senses as B. and Pamela wage a battle of plot and counterplot whose
stakes are the heroine's exalted Virtue, more important to her than her life.

Pamela's guard during her confinement is B.'s loyal "House-keeper"[10] at
the Lincolnshire estate, Mrs. Jewkes, Richardson's Mother Midnight in this
novel, a "cunning woman"—in Pamela's eyes—of considerable skill and
watchful foresight. In Richardson's version of the popular myth of the
persecuted country maiden, Mrs. Jewkes makes a natural antagonist to the
chaste but sexually awakened Pamela, and in terms of her function in this
novel, a figure comparable to Defoe's governess-midwife-bawd who initiates
Moll Flanders into her new life of crime. Like that Mother Midnight, Mrs.
Jewkes plays several critical roles with respect to the woman in her charge.
The housekeeper makes much of the "Letter of Instructions" (103) her
master has given her, and she moves with assurance all over the great house
and its grounds. She is keeper of the keys and guardian of the gates of the
house;[11] she will be Pamela's constant companion and her bed-fellow (104);
she is determined to see everything this "great Writer" writes (105); she will
promote the developing relationship between Pamela and Parson Williams
to her master's advantage; above all, she will do everything in her power to

prepare the girl against the time when Mr. B. "will require her at [her] Hands" (172). Mrs. Jewkes must, therefore, keep Pamela safe and under constant surveillance, control her, and finally, after a period of confinement, deliver her up to Mr. B., and assist at the consummation.

"Let me tell you," says Pamela to those parents who now seem so infinitely far away from her, "what has befallen me; and yet, How shall you receive it? For I have now no honest *John* to carry my Letters to you" (95). She has not yet been enlightened about the perfidy of "honest John," who showed all her letters to B. before delivering them to her parents, so that B. and her parents have been reading "Pamela" in unwitting complicity from the start. Then as if sensing her "rough-natured Governess" (96) over her shoulder, she says " I am likely to be watch'd in all my Steps, till my hard Fate ripens his wicked Projects for my Ruin" (95). If B. is the author of Pamela's fate, moving her at his whim from county to county and "allotting" her her new abode, rough Mrs. Jewkes is the agent who makes it a particularly hard one, and who presides over its ripening toward ruin. As the episode progresses, the sense of something ugly coming to birth is repeated: John Arnold says, "your Undoing has been long hatching" (111), Pamela too fears *something* must be hatching (139), and wild stories about B.'s man-servant may introduce "some Plot now hatching" (157). Pamela faces an apparently overwhelming threat. She has no counter-project, no counter-plot at this point, but she will keep on with her writing: "I will every Day now write my sad State; and some way, perhaps, may be open'd to send the melancholy Scribble to you" (95). Implied in this and other related passages are two lines of organic development: a malignant, constricting, ruinous one attributed to B. and Mrs. Jewkes; and a healthy one struggling toward openness and freedom attributed to Pamela the writer.

For psychological reasons unknown to Richardson or to us, but which seem exactly right under the circumstances, Pamela's first instincts of self-preservation take the form of "planting," figuratively and then literally. For fear of being searched, she hides the pens, ink, and paper ("above forty Sheets" given to her by the old servant Longman [96]) all over the house, interleaving sheets of paper "among [her] Linen" (105), thinking that "something . . . might happen to open a Way for [her] Deliverance, by these or some other Means" (105). The shrewd care she once lavished upon wrapping the money sent home to her parents so "that it mayn't chink" (26) has here given way to the careful packing and concealing of her pen, ink, and paper. Already she senses in this scattering and hiding process a means towards her deliverance, and her exclamation of "O the Pride . . . I shall have, if I can secure my Innocence" echoes the self-satisfaction of "O the pleasure of descending with Ease, Innocence and Resignation" in the sad outfit scene (60).

With the advent of "sensible, sober young" Williams (105), the resident clergyman at the estate, she begins to exercise her planting powers more

purposefully: "Sir, I see two Tiles upon that Parsley-bed; cannot one cover
them with Mould, with a Note between them, on Occasion?—A good Hint,
said he; let that Sun-flower by the Back-door of the Garden be the Place; I
have a Key to that; for it is my nearest way to the Town" (113).[12] After she
whispers this scheme of the secret post-box[13] to Williams, and he obligingly
designates the "Sun-flower" by the back garden door as the sign-post, she
hugs herself at the thought, as she had formerly hugged her "third Parcel" at
the thought of how it stood as a "Witness of her Honesty" and a symbol of her
self-preservation in innocence. She soon receives her first letter from Williams at the "dear Place" (116,119): "I popt down, and whipt my Fingers
under the upper Tile, and pulled out a little Letter, without Direction, and
thrust it in my Bosom, trembling for Joy" (117). In this clandestine communication with Mr. Williams, carried out with the maid only a few yards
away from her, Pamela experiences something like sexual pleasure, but
pleasure divorced from any actual physical contact with a man, which is of
course, in her unmarried state, her greatest abhorrence. That she associates
such contact with defilement and death is clear enough from her responses
to B. during and after the scenes of attempted rape. Pamela seems most alive
when she is acting defensively, at one or more removes from physical
sexuality through the use of her considerable verbal powers, either speaking
or writing. She was reared by her parents to suppress any kind of direct
sexual response, and the business here with Williams, while it incorporates a
kind of displaced sexual intercourse and intense, secret emotional excitement, also recalls the trials of separated lovers in the Pyramus and Thisbe
legend and the ruse of the duplicated key for the garden encounters in
Chaucer's "Merchant's Tale" and its bawdy analogues.

Pamela continues to commit her urgent messages for Williams "to the
happy Tiles, and to the Bosom of that Earth," from which she hopes her
"Deliverance will take Root, and bring forth such Fruit, as may turn to her
inexpressible Joy" (115). Once, while angling with her jaileress, Pamela
catches a carp which she likens to her unhappy self and then frees. While
Mrs. Jewkes tries her luck, Pamela, who has somewhere managed to find a
few "Horse-beans" says, "I will plant Life then . . . while you are destroying
it . . . I'll go and stick them into one of the Borders [near the sunflower] . . .
and I will call them my Garden" (120). The success, under the very nose of
the watchful Jewkes, of her postal activities in this veritable victory garden of
tiles, sunflower, and beans, allows Pamela to establish, for her harsh antagonist and for the reader, the rules of a game of life against death. It is at
this point that the role of Mrs. Jewkes *vis à vis* Pamela becomes most
compelling.

In spite of Pamela's penchant for exaggeration in her fearful state, it is
almost certain that she is right in implying early on that Mrs. Jewkes was a
bawd before she came to work for B., and Richardson indirectly character-

izes her as such. Pamela says "she was an Inn-keeper's House-keeper before she came to my Master; and those Sort of Creatures don't want Confidence" (102). She laments further that she is "got into the Hands of a wicked Procuress . . . a Woman that seems to delight in Filthiness!" (102). Like the London bawd whose established practice it was to wait at inn doors for unsuspecting girls from the country and lure them into her service (as pictured in the first plate of Hogarth's *The Harlot's Progress*), "who should be at the Inn" that Robin first puts up at but "the wicked Mrs. *Jewkes* expecting me, and her Sister-in-law was the Mistress of it . . . *Jewkes! Jewkes!* thought I, I have heard of that Name; I don't like it" (101) as in the nursery rime logic of "I do not like thee, Dr. Fell . . . " Mrs. Jewkes first accosts Pamela with disgusting familiarity, teasing the girl "with her Impertinence and bold Way," even offering to kiss her. "I don't like this Sort of Carriage, Mrs. *Jewkes*; it is not like two Persons of one Sex" (102). At the outset, Mrs. Jewkes acts in an unwomanly or mannish way with Pamela. The girl can have no trust or confidence in her as one woman with another.

Pamela sees and characterizes Mrs. Jewkes as a shrewd, experienced woman of exceptional "cunning," practiced in the arts of illicit love, and Pamela herself is seen by Mr. B. and Mrs. Jewkes as a "little Witch" with her own strong component of cunning (see the discussion of "cunning women" in Chapter 4). The relationship between Pamela and Mrs. Jewkes could be described as a contest between two cunning women, an older and a younger witch, each intent upon detecting the secrets of the other. "I believe this little Slut has the Power of Witchcraft, if ever there was a Witch; for she inchants all that come near her" (55). In this early observation, Mr. B. is by no means giving merely a lover's rhetorical estimate of the character of his bewitching maidservant.

Besides having the uncanny power of ubiquity ("This Creature's always in my way, I think! . . . D—n you! . . . for a little Witch!" [48]), Pamela continually displays, for Mr. B. in her Bedfordshire period, the "Perverseness and Folly" (45) not only of a "little Witch" (62) but of a "Gypsey" (40), an "Equivocator" (40), an artful "Hypocrite" (45), "a strange Medley of Inconsistence" (76), whose oft-noted diminutiveness and apparent duplicity suggests the figure of the "chamber-maid" as defined by Roland Barthes in his essay on Michelet's *La Sorcière* (1862). For Michelet the period 1400 to 1800 was the third "great historical state" of the evolution of the witch (termed "diminutive . . . slender and oblique, delicate and cunning") derived "from the knowing little girl (doll, perverse toy), pernicious in that she is double, divided, contradictory, uniting in equivocation the innocence of her age and the knowledge of an adult." The witch always "participates substantially in a physical site, interior (objects) or landscape," ranging from the domestic hearth ("the terminal point of rape") to "the cabinet, the alcove, the professional locus of the chambermaid . . . the disgraced category of the

intimate, the stifled."[14] Pamela as a captive in her Lincolnshire surroundings, a setting "that looks made for Solitude and Mischief" (102), shifts
back and forth between an oppressive interior of closets and a garden
landscape which appears grotesque and forbidding to her until she begins to
establish a sense of trust with Mr. B.

The intense personal drama enacted by Mrs. Jewkes and her charge
during Pamela's confinement at Lincolnshire evokes a sense of the ancient
hostilities and wiles of rival practitioners of cunning as well as the immediate
urgency of female plot and counter-plot. Just before the success of her
horsebean plot (in both its senses), Pamela, thinking of her Sunflower
scheme, exclaims:

> How nobly my Plot succeeds! But I begin to be afraid my Writings may
> be discover'd; for they grow large! I stitch them hitherto in my Under-
> coat, next my Linen. But if this Brute should search me!—I must try to
> please her, and then she won't (120).

As earlier she had interleaved her writing paper with her linen, Pamela now
stitches her writings to her underclothes. The motifs of sewing and writing
come together vividly at this point in a new form of concealment which
moves ever closer to her genitals. Her writings enable her to defend her
physical virtue from the assaults of B. and Mrs. Jewkes. Her tangible
writings thus defend her virtue and preserve it by keeping a record of her
continued purity. The writings themselves finally come to stand for that
virtue.

At Bedfordshire, her sad clothing, fashioned in secret, had been a mute
form of communication with her master; now her writing becomes a secret
form of clothing for her continued correspondence with Williams. This
growing body of letters, moreover, is the natural outcome of their secret
correspondence; it is their symbolic yet tangible offspring and must be
preserved from the clutches of Jewkes and eventually from the eyes of the
tyrannical B. The "Sun-flower Correspondence" (128), though "a most
tedious Parcel of Stuff, of [Pamela's] *Oppressions . . . Distresses . . . Fears*"
(133), is nonetheless a precious little Pamela, and when the papers are "safe,
in [Williams's] Hands" (128), their progenitor sighs, "I am deliver'd . . . from
the Fear of their being found, if I should be search'd, or discover'd" (128).
With Pamela's sewing and writing of the ever-growing "Pacquet," and her
obvious relief at having safely delivered it to her parents, one is reminded of
the Virgin Madonna whose child is sewn in the womb, and the traditions of
the spinning womb and the infant as a creature of clothes in the midwife
books. In another sense, her secret penmanship and needlework make her
an an innocent yet comic exponent of the "art of stitching" (as discussed in
Chapter 7). The "large Parcel" survives its journey back to Pamela's parents

despite Williams's beating at the hands of two ruffians (135) hired by Mrs. Jewkes expressly to discover those papers (149).

So ends Pamela's first great victory over Mrs. Jewkes, but she will not relax her guard. Though her adversary seems more civil than usual after this triumph, Pamela is convinced that "she is horrid cunning and is not a bit less watchful. I laid a Trap to get at her Instructions, which she carries in the Bosom of her Stays, but it has not succeeded" (130). We never learn what this trap was, but we are made aware that just as Pamela tries to conceal her secret papers stitched to her underclothes, so Mrs. Jewkes hides her instructions in an equally inaccessible place on her own body. The older and the younger woman thus keep their special writings secret from each other like deep bodily mysteries. "You are Beauty to the Bone," muses "the strange Wretch" at Pamela's not eating enough "to keep Life and Soul together" (117),[15] and the girl's cautious reserve at Mrs. Jewkes's announcement of the match (131) that is to be made between Pamela and Mr. Williams elicits this astonished gesture of admiration from her adversary: "Mrs. *Jewkes* held up her Eyes and Hands, and said, Such Art, such Caution, such Cunning for thy Years!" (132). Well may she recognize a potent rival spirit and a challenge to her own powers of detection: "You have an excellent Head-piece for your Years; but may-be I am as cunning as you" (138). "She is so officious to bring on the Affair between us," thinks Pamela, "that being a cunning, artful Woman, I know not what to make of it" (135). She begins the sentence as if speaking of a bawd and ends it with unintended ambiguity. Her paranoia and childhood superstition almost convince the girl, however, that "there is Witchcraft in this House," and that a "nasty grim Bull . . . with fiery Saucer Eyes," a kind of familiar of her hated keeper, is watching her every movement when she goes out of doors: "I believe in my Heart, Mrs. *Jewkes* has got this Bull of her Side" (136). Indeed, "double Witchcraft" (137) seems to be at work, for one day she spots two bulls coming at her: "Here is the Spirit of my Master in one . . . and Mrs. *Jewkes*'s in the other" (137). These of course turn out to be innocent cows, but Pamela's fear of Mrs. Jewkes has been heightened by what she knows of a witch's power. Conversely, Mrs. Jewkes's respect for Pamela's power of intrigue is not diminished: "I despair of getting out of you any thing you han't a mind I should know, my little cunning Dear" (138).

20. Mother Jewkes and the Rosebush Papers

With the Sunflower Correspondence and its fruits, Pamela's own "Book of Generation" and "Deliverance" may be said to begin, and Mrs. Jewkes, in her single-minded determination to get at the secret writings she suspects Pamela to be hiding from her, recalls the corollary function of almost every eighteenth-century bawd, a practical readiness in the art of midwifery and knowledge of the secrets of abortion.[16]

We know that Mrs. Jewkes practices medicine. She may be an "inhuman Tygress" (155), a "Brute of a Woman" (148), a "horrid Creature" (155) and so on to Pamela, but after the girl injures her head in a futile effort to escape the Lincolnshire estate, she has to concede that "if this Woman has any good Quality, it is, it seems, in a Readiness and Skill to manage in Cases, where sudden Misfortunes happen in a Family" (156). A "Family Plaister" is prepared and Mrs. Jewkes takes "a good deal of Care" to assist Pamela in her recovery. It is important too that shortly after Pamela cures B. of his illness by simply returning to him after her abortive departure from the Lincolnshire estate ("Mrs. *Jewkes* . . . this lovely Creature is my Doctor, as her Absence was my Disease" [220]), the housekeeper, with some pique, reminds him of her own ministrations on his behalf ("I hope you are not the worse for my Care, and my Doctoring you!" [233-34]). Hence managing in cases of family misfortune covers a multitude of ills, including those of the master, as these two medical rivals attest.

Pamela's emphasis, however, is not on Mrs. Jewkes's healing management but on the cruelty of her treatment of the prisoner in her care, and when Mrs. Jewkes accosts Pamela in the woodhouse after the unsuccessful escape attempt the governess seems almost to concede the victory of a witch stronger than herself:

> The wicked Woman, as she entered the woodhouse said, Where is she?—Plague of her Spells, and her Witchcrafts! She shall dearly repent of this Trick, if my Name be *Jewkes*; and coming to me, took hold of my Arm so roughly, and gave me such a Pull, as made me squeal out, (my Shoulder being bruis'd on that Side) and drew me on my Face. O Cruel Creature! said I, if you knew what I had suffer'd, it would move you to pity me! . . .
>
> The Coachman *Robin* seem'd to be sorry for me too, and said, with Sobs, What a Scene is here! Don't you see she is all bloody in her Head, and cannot stir?—Curse of her Contrivances! said the horrid Creature; she has frighted me out of my Wits, I'm sure. How the D—l came you here?— (155)

As the rough governess hauls her squealing charge back into harsh present reality, the image of the midwife re-emerges with chilling brutality from the background of cunning witchcraft associated with both women. Despite her condition of prostrate vulnerability before Mrs. Jewkes, the vitality for others Pamela represents in the face of her deadly tormentor is illuminated at her discovery by the joyful maid, Nan: "you, Madam! . . . Now . . . you'll make us all alive again!" (155). Pamela has, on her own reckoning, been saved from "a worse Enemy" than either Mr. B. or Mrs. Jewkes—"the Weakness and Presumption . . . of her own Mind" (150) when she seriously contemplated suicide.

Mrs. Jewkes's performance in the woodhouse scene and elsewhere, and the sensation of torture which she wrings from Pamela on other occasions (104, 131), would bring to mind for Richardson's contemporaries, especially his women readers, characteristics of the torturing midwife (mentioned in Chapter 4) an all-too-common social evil inveighed against by nearly every writer of midwife manuals in the seventeenth and eighteenth centuries:

> I have heard simple women much to commend haling, torturing mid-wives, and to account them good and expert in their callings. For that, in the woman's labour, they took great paines to deliver them, and that the sweat did run down their faces, in performing of their work to deliver their women.[17]

The true character of the torturing midwife may be inferred from this list of negative attributes:

> She ought not to be too *Fat* or *Gross*, but especially not to have thick or fleshy *Hands* and *Arms*, or large Bon'd Wrists; which (of Necessity) must occasion racking *Pains* to the tender *labouring Woman* . . . . Neither ought she to be a Self-indulger . . . nor a *Light, Dissolute,* or *Daring* Person; . . . Neither ought *she* to be a *Tipler* or *Drunkard,* nor a *Tatler* or *Vagabond.* . . . [18]

Says Pamela of Mrs. Jewkes,

> Now I will give you a Picture of this Wretch! She is a broad, squat, pursy, fat Thing, quite ugly, if any thing God made can be ugly; about forty Years old. She has a huge Hand, and an Arm as thick as my Waist, I believe. Her Nose is flat and crooked, and her Brows grow over her Eyes; a dead, spiteful, grey, goggling Eye, to be sure, she has. And her Face is flat and broad; and as to Colour, looks like as if it had been pickled a Month in Salt-petre: I dare say she drinks!—She has a hoarse man-like Voice, and is as thick as she's long; and yet looks so deadly

strong, that I am afraid she would dash me at her Foot in an Instant, if I
was to vex her. —So that with a Heart more ugly than her Face, she
frightens me sadly; and I am undone, to be sure, if God does not protect
me; for she is very, very wicked—indeed she is. (107)[19]

Almost as if to convince herself of Mrs. Jewkes's superlative wickedness ("to
be sure"), Pamela consciously paints a vivid picture of her own fears and
spite in a portrait which nonetheless recalls consistently repeated features in
the traditional physiognomy not only of the torturing midwife, but also of the
witch, the bawd, and the seventeenth- and eighteenth-century Fate figure
(see Chapters 2, 4, and 5 particularly). First of all, Mrs. Jewkes's nose, while
not of the labyrinthine audacity of Mother Shipton's with its "many crooks
and turnings," is nevertheless "flat and crooked" and her Cyclopean "dead,
spiteful, grey goggling Eye" recalls the "very great goggling, but sharp and
fiery Eyes" of Head's more virulent witch.[20] Like Gould's Mother Bewley,
whose "Eye-brows were thick and hoary," Mrs. Jewkes's "Brows grow over
her Eyes."[21] This element in the portrait is as old as Hesiod's "dark-browed
Night," the mother of the "ruthless, avenging Fates." Mrs. Jewkes's "hoarse
man-like Voice," and her earlier unwomanly overtures to Pamela, recall
Danet's remarking of the "male and female" nature of the Greek Fates and
the masculine features associated with witches from the time of Reginald
Scot. Mrs. Jewkes is about forty, past the conventional period of childbearing, and the age at which midwives (as we have seen) and bawds were
thought to be most active in their professions ("the London Bawd . . . hates
Forty-One as much as an *Old Cavalier*, for at that age she was forced to . . .
turn Bawd"). Above all, the traditional picture of "Mother Midnight," and
Pamela's picture of Mrs. Jewkes, both stress the unnatural power and *weight*
of this implacable figure. Hateful Mother Shipton is "of an indifferent height,
but very morose and big-bon'd"; Mother Bewley is so pressed down with the
"pond'rous guilt" of her manifold sins that she breaks through the "solid
Centre" of the earth on her way to hell; Mother Bentley is a "Load of Lust," a
"Lump of deadly Sin," "of size unwieldy, with a waddling Pace." Mrs.
Jewkes offers to return the heroine's confiscated shoes if she will take a walk
with her in the garden—"To *waddle* with me, rather," thinks Pamela (107).
Her adversary is a "broad, squat, pursy, fat Thing," with huge hands and
arms, and she is "deadly strong." In Pamela's eyes Mrs. Jewkes is like a great
animated corpse with horrible staring vitality and a deadly physical power
unnatural for a woman. She combines powers of life and death into the sheer
weight of a fatal presence which terrifies the girl. We may imagine Mrs.
Jewkes to have been one of those midwives "that tread so hard on the Floor,
as to make the Room *shake*, and so disturb Lying-in Women."[22] This early
stress on Mrs. Jewkes's weight and invasive power prepares us for her
performance in the final rape scene (176).

"None should come into this Number," continues Dawkes, the man-midwife, "who have abandon'd all *Discretion* and *Modesty*; whose Discourse is compounded of *lascivious* and *immodest* Speeches . . . No *morose*, nor *churlish*, *cruel* or *profligate* Persons. . . . "[23] A clear indication that Pamela is not the asexual being she has sometimes been taken for is her quickness to apprehend Mrs. Jewkes's slightest risqué remark. The housekeeper talks like a "*London* Prostitute" (158) with her "wicked Jest, unbecoming the Mouth of a Woman, about Planting, &c."[24] (122) and her sexual puns: "I'll send him word to come to satisfy you, if you will!" (114).[25]

But Mrs. Jewkes's bawdy joviality can turn inexplicably into protracted ill temper, just as Pamela's own moods shift wildly from manic excitement when she thinks about escape, to the listless depression of self-doubt. And again, the sense of her own fate haunts her: "Alack-a-day! what a Fate is this! I have not the Courage to go, neither can I think to stay. But I must resolve" (136). Her fate at this moment signifies paralysis. For all her apparent intrepidity, there is a self-doubting side to Pamela—a radical sense of her own weakness and unworthiness—which appears most obviously (and drearily) in the long prelude to her marriage after returning to B., but which is evident now too: "O why are poor foolish Maidens try'd with such Dangers, when they have such weak Minds to grapple with them" (137). She is repeating eighteenth-century assumptions (detailed in Chapter 8)' about female weakness of resolve and she genuinely believes they apply to her case. It is a measure of Pamela's true heroism that she is able to summon the mental resolve to overcome this acquired sense of female imbecility and passivity.

In her deepest depression and fear as Mrs. Jewkes's prisoner, Pamela tells Williams in a letter, "my presaging Mind bodes horrid Mischiefs!—Every thing looks dark around me; and this Woman's impenetrable Sullen-ness and Silence . . . bids me fear the worst" (141). The worst is spelled out in B.'s letter for Jewkes which Pamela receives by mistake: "Well, I think I now *hate her* perfectly; and tho' I will do nothing to her *myself*, yet I can bear . . . to see any thing, even what *she most fears*, be *done to her*; and then she may be turned loose to her evil Destiny, and echo to the Woods and Groves her piteous Lamentations for the loss of her fantastical Innocence. . . . I will be with you, and decide *her Fate*, and put an End to your Trouble" (144-45). We can imagine Pamela underlining these hard things as if they were already happening to her. The girl is most terrified by the thought that B. will employ the Swiss man-servant Colbrand, "a Giant of a Man" (147) who is under Mrs. Jewkes's authority, to decide her fate ("I was quite mortified . . . about that fearful *Colbrand*, and what he [i.e., B.] could *see done* to *me*" [145]). We noted (in Chapter 9) that London bawds often kept hired bullies whose particular task it was to break young women into the trade of prostitution.[26] Pamela's "presaging Mind" seems to move from viewing her fate as paralysis to associating the treatment here described with the "hard Fate" B. has in store for her. It is the hard genital fate of rape.

Considering the specific nature of her fear, one can perhaps better understand Pamela's outrage at Mrs. Jewkes's sexual innuendo and jokes, especially her amused response to Pamela's nightmare of Colbrand and her master "both coming to [her] Bed-side, with the worst Designs" (148)[27]: "All I fear'd was but a Dream . . . and when it was over, and I was well awake, I should laugh at it as such" (148). Mrs. Jewkes on more than one occasion reminds Pamela that a better bedfellow than she is waiting in the wings for the girl (139, 169), and that Pamela herself will make "a fine Bedfellow . . . for [her] Master" (158). This last witticism takes on harsher overtones in the Hogarthian scene where Mr. B., in order to show Mrs. Jewkes, the expert appraiser, that even "so young a Sorceress" as Pamela is "most beautiful in [her] Tears" (162), spins her around before a hand-mirror and concedes that even now he might forgive the "intriguing little Slut" were it not for her correspondence with Williams:

> O, said the Sycophant [Jewkes], you are very good, Sir, very forgiving, indeed!—But come, added the profligate Wretch, I hope you will be so good, as to take her to your Bosom; and that, by to-morrow Morning, you'll bring her to a better Sense of her Duty! "Could any thing, in Womanhood, be so vile!" (163).

In her own implicit apprehension of the idea that "a strange Fate attends our Sex," Pamela senses in Mrs. Jewkes an enemy greater even than B., because the woman Jewkes betrays her own sex. This theme becomes more complex and important in *Clarissa*.

The voice of the "Female Physician" continues: "She [the midwife] ought to be Watchful, Diligent, and Expert in all Cases . . . so that no *Opportunity* in the beginning of the Labour be lost."[28] The "dead, spiteful, grey, goggling eye" of Mrs. Jewkes is multiplied, as the journal progresses, into a veritable "*Argus*" (113);[29] "my Master writes me, that I must have all my Eyes about me; for, tho' you are as innocent as a Dove, yet you're as cunning as a Serpent" (125).[30] She is always on the alert for improving that "critical *Minute*,"[31] dear to the authorities in midwifery, when her charge seems most likely to divulge her burden: "I . . . am sure you have . . . more Paper, than I am aware of: and I had intended to romage you, if my Master had not come down" (173). Mrs. Jewkes even improves upon the rhetoric of midwifery with her own terminology. Hoping to allay Pamela's suspicions of Mr. B. concerning Williams's proposal, she concludes, "my *Watchments* are now over, by my Master's Direction" (138). But Pamela, alert to her adversary's every linguistic nuance, mistrusts: "she did this to pump me. . . . Why, Mrs. *Jewkes* . . . is all this fishing about for something, where there is nothing, if there be an End of your *Watchments*, as you call them? Nothing, said she, but Womanish Curiosity, I'll assure you; for one is naturally led to find out Matters, where there is such Privacy intended" (138). Aaron Hill, despite his excesses, spoke for many readers when he confessed to Richardson, "I can never escape Mrs. *Jewkes*: who often keeps me awake in the Night" (18).

Mrs. Jewkes's commitment to Mr. B. will not allow her to do anything inconsistent with her "Duty and Trust": "I glory in my Fidelity to my Master" (147), she asserts. Her devotion to duty recalls the "sacred Work" of the midwife's office,[32] but, as we have seen, Mrs. Jewkes cannot always be counted on to keep her temper with a prisoner whom she terms "as slippery as an Eel" (161). The midwife-physicians offered this advice for dealing with a recalcitrant patient:

> . . . if the [labouring woman] will not follow *Advice*, and *Necessity* require, the *Midwife* ought to reprimand and put her smartly in mind of her *Duty*; yet always in such a manner, however, as to encourage her with the *Hopes* of a happy and speedy *Delivery* . . . so she [the midwife] ought to be *Faithful* and *Silent*; always on her *Guard* to conceal those Things, which ought not to be spoken of.[33]

Despite her frequent outbursts, the faithful Mrs. Jewkes earnestly reminds Pamela of the happy and speedy deliverance that awaits her if she will only consent to Mr. B.'s desires: "I should rather be out of my Pain, than live in continual Frights and Apprehensions, as you do" (125).

Mrs. Jewkes's drinking, her Lesbian overtures, her sexual jokes, and her extreme vigilance are all annoying enough to Pamela, but it is the deadly power of the midwife's hand, the symbol of her art and authority, that the girl most fears: "I dread her huge Paw most sadly" (121). There is a whole linguistic network of manual phrases associated with the officious Jewkes from Pamela's first falling into "the Hands of a Woman that seems to delight in Filthiness" (102) to the sorrowful moment when "this merciless Woman" seizes Pamela's Rosebush Papers (197), the parcel of writings which succeeded the Sunflower Correspondence and which Pamela had buried under a rosebush in the garden for safe keeping (150) and later removed (194). Mrs. Jewkes's seizure of the Rosebush Papers (and "rosebush" has sexual overtones here and later) is the midwife's greatest triumph, counterbalancing Pamela's victory in conveying the Sunflower packet to her parents by way of Parson Williams. Richardson places Mrs. Jewkes on the stairs, a characteristic locus for the busy housekeeper who is "up and down, so much" (129), as she makes her presentation to Mr. B.:

> "my Master being coming up, she went to him upon the Stairs, and gave him my Papers. There, Sir, said she; you always said Mrs. *Pamela* was a great Writer, but I never could get at any thing of hers before" (198).

Amid variations on an anguished litany of "O what vile Hands am I put into!" (158, 170, 102), Pamela imprints Mrs. Jewkes in the reader's imagination as a domineering, managing, ensnaring, clutching, striking antagonist, one who literally has power to pick her up and "dash [her] at her Foot in an Instant" (107). Thus we have Mrs. Jewkes in the following offensive postures: she "waddled up to me; and . . . held [me] by my Arm, half out of Breath" (116); "Why, *Jezebel*,[34] said I . . . would you ruin me by Force?—Upon this she gave me a deadly Slap upon my Shoulder" (116); "I'll warrant I can take such a thin Body as you are under my Arm, and carry you in, if you won't walk. You don't know my Strength" (117); "I doubted not her taking hold of [Williams's] joyful Indiscretion" (132); "she curses and storms at me like a Trooper, and can hardly keep her Hands off me" (158); "the barbarous Creature struck at me with her horrid Fist" (159); she "lifted me up upon my Knees; for I trembled so, I could not stand . . . She gave me a Push, and went away in a violent Passion" (160-61). Finally, as prelude to Mr. B.'s final attempted rape,

> She came to me, and took me in her huge Arms as if I was a Feather; said she, I do this to shew you, what a poor Resistance you can make against me, if I pleased to exert myself; and so, Lambkin, don't say to your Wolf, I *won't* come to-bed!—And set me down, and tapped me on the Neck: Ah! said she, thou art a pretty Creature, it's true; but so obstinate! so full of Spirit! If thy Strength was but answerable to that, thou wouldst run away with us all, and this great House too on thy Back! but undress, undress, I tell you. (170)

Pamela's prophetic allegory of the "strange Tribunal" in which she as "the poor Sheep, in the Fable . . . was try'd before the Vultur [Mr. B.], on the Accusation of the Wolf [Mrs. Jewkes]!" (162) here comes to frightening life. Leaving aside for the moment the problem of Mr. B.'s vacillations, nowhere in the novel are the lupine Jewkes's own ambivalent feelings toward the heroine—of tenderness, angry frustration, respect, and lust—more urgently expressed. This cunning woman also intuits, with her magnificent image of a gigantic Pamela carrying the house and all away on her back, that the heroine indeed has them all captive within the strange power of her spirit. Ultimately, they are all merely characters in Pamela's own predominating "Fable."[35]

21. Pamela's "Fits"

When Pamela buried the Rosebush Papers during the night of her attempted escape, she also remembered to fling into the pond her "Upper-Petticoat" (149), her "Neck-handkerchief, and a round ear'd Cap, with a Knot" (150) to appear as if she had drowned herself and thus get a great way off. The clothes she discards are remnants of the old sad outfit which gained so much attention from B. and others at the Bedfordshire estate. Here again the motifs of writing, clothing, and unclothing in Pamela's experience coincide: she hides her papers, then hides her clothes in hopes that they will be discovered, but the fact that she throws away the clothes she was once so proud of suggests that she is trying to get rid of her proud, vain self. This impulse is consciously reinforced by her reflection at the pondside on "all the lurking Vileness of [her] Heart" and (in a premonition of Clarissa's self-reproaches) her having perhaps "too much prided [herself] in a vain Dependence on [her] own foolish Contrivances" (153). But for Pamela, pride too is double-edged. Where does the healthy, candid pride of her declaring herself a "free Person" to her master "and not . . . a sordid Slave, who is to be threatened and frightened into a Compliance, that . . . would be otherwise abhorr'd by her" (126)—certainly one of Pamela's finest moments—where does this shade off into the presumptive pride of self-delusion? Or are both kinds of pride always intertwined? It must be admitted that much of Pamela's vitality and interest as a character in a fiction derives from her proud and ingenious battle of wits with Mr. B. and Mrs. Jewkes, and when the battle is over she is a far less vital (and even more pathetic) figure because she seems to have given away much of her autonomy. She chooses to give her will to B. This chapter and the next are concerned with how this change in the relationship between Pamela and Mr. B. comes about.

Toward the end of her imprisonment and distress at the Lincolnshire estate, Pamela undergoes two trials, one the "worst Tryal, and . . . fearfullest danger" she ever suffered, when Mr. B., disguised as a maidservant, made his final desperate assault upon her virtue, and the other the mock-trial of Pamela which follows some days later, when Mr. B. sets himself up as literary critic, prosecuting attorney, and judge to deliberate upon the putative agreement between Pamela's conduct and her *account* of her conduct in the segments of her journal which B. has been reading. We can learn much about the Pamela who eventually becomes Mrs. B. by examining these two trials in some detail.

The scene of B.'s final attempted rape of Pamela brings together nearly all the elements of Pamela's experience during B.'s harrowing courtship of her. Again the very lines of her writing tremble with her fears—the appearance of the words on the page mirrors her mental state. Again B. conceals his

intentions, this time pretending to take a trip to Stamford to sort out the
Williams affair, but if she does not sign and seal his articles for keeping her in
a trial marriage, she knows the sexual "Fate that awaits her" (172). Again,
Pamela puts on an unwitting performance for the hidden B., this time
unconsciously justifying herself to him as she tells Mrs. Jewkes the "little
History" of her life. "All this time we were undressing ourselves" (173), says
Pamela, as her wicked Master sits in the "Elbow-chair" attired in Nan's
"Gown and Petticoat . . . her Apron over his Face and Shoulders." B.'s
petticoat ruse becomes an unintended requital of Pamela's at the pondside.

We then have Richardson's most sensational exhibition of Mrs. Jewkes's
manual dexterity where her maneuvers, and those of the apparent maid,
seem to parody those employed by the old-fashioned midwife and her
assistants during labor; after speaking of the "two women . . . on each side of
the bed" who are to lift up "women in Labour" with swaths, Sermon specifies

> two more to take them by the hands, thereby to crush them when their
> throws come; and the other hand they must lay upon the top of their
> shoulder that they may not rise too much upward . . . . Sometimes the
> Midwife, &c. may gently press the upper parts of the belly, and by
> degrees stroke the Child downward; the which pressing down with
> discretion, will hasten and facilitate the delivery.[36]

> Mrs. *Jewkes*, by this time, was got to-bed, on the further Side, as she
> used to be; and, to make room for the Maid, when she should awake, I
> got into Bed, and lay close to her. . . . Here, said the wicked Woman,
> put your Arm under mine . . . So I did; and the abominable Designer
> held my Hand with her Right-hand, as my Right-arm was under her
> Left. . . . What Words shall I find, my dear Mother, (for my Father
> should not see this shocking Part) to describe the rest, and my Confu-
> sion, when the guilty Wretch took my Left-arm, and laid it under his
> Neck, as the vile Procuress held my Right; and then he clasp'd me round
> my Waist! . . . . I scream'd out in such a manner, as never any body
> heard the like. . . . (175-76)

Here Pamela is at least as vulnerable as a woman in labor. Out of the same
kind of exaggerated modesty that prevented men from assisting in delivery
until the seventeenth century, she chooses to exclude her father from seeing
"this shocking Part." This is a matter for mother and daughter only.

In this scene, the heroine undergoes a terrifying physical and emotional
ordeal at the hands of a mannish midwife-procuress and a master, whom she
loves and holds in awe, dressed up as a maid like herself. As Mr. B.
fulminates like the jealous God of the Old Testament, Mrs. Jewkes displays

the no-nonsense discipline of a surgeon's assistant at a routine operation ("What you do, Sir, do; don't stand dilly-dallying.") "Sure never poor Soul was in such Agonies as" Pamela, screaming and convulsing in a combined nightmare of the Crucifixion ("O God! my God! this Time, this one Time! deliver me from this Distress!" [176]) and the Last Judgment ("his Voice broke upon me like a Clap of Thunder. Now Pamela, said he, is the dreadful Time of Reckoning come, that I have threaten'd" [176]). Pamela says she was "taken with the Fit," survived "a deplorable State of Death," and came back to life again. In eighteenth-century medical terms, this would seem to be a peculiar kind of fit of the "Hysterick Passion."

Ilza Veith points out in her masterly historical survey of the disease that "the basic concept of hysteria remained unchanged for two thousand years. The essence of this concept was that hysteria was a physical disorder," and this disorder in women was generally thought to emanate from the disordered uterus.[37] The English physicians Bernard Mandeville and George Cheyne (who was Richardson's personal physician) provide some of the conventional medical wisdom against which we may evaluate Richardson's representation of Pamela's fits. Mandeville wants to show that the "Soul" (the "immortal Substance") "is without doubt the same" in men and women, but "Women are not of that robust Constitution as Men are. . . . Grief, Joy, Anger, Fear, and the Rest of the Passions make greater impressions upon them, and sooner discompose their Bodies." Women's "frame, tho less firm [than men's] is more delicate, and themselves more capable both of Pleasure and of Pain, tho' endued with less constancy of bearing the excess of either"; they often "exceed Men in Sprightliness of Fancy, quickness of Thought and offhand Wit."[38] Cheyne echoes these notions in his account of the "English Malady" (i.e., nervous diseases) which afflict both men and women, but particularly *those of the liveliest and quickest natural Parts, whose Faculties are the brightest and most spiritual, and whose Genius is most keen and penetrating, and particularly where there is the most delicate Sensation and Taste, both of Pleasure and Pain.*[39] Mandeville distinguishes two classes of hysteric women: those of the first class are afflicted with chronic disorder of nerves, frequent fits, and symptoms of indigestion, "but then there are others; that being to all appearances in perfect health, upon some accident of Grief, Passion, Surprize, . . . are thrown into Convulsive Fits; these Women as soon as the Fits are off are well again, and almost sure, that they'll never have any more, unless some new Violence disturbs them afresh."[40] Pamela has three attacks of such fits all of which are precipitated by Mr. B., the last two while Pamela is lying in bed, first with Mrs. Jervis, later with Mrs. Jewkes who says to the hesitant B., "And will you, Sir . . . for a Fit or two, give up such an Opportunity as this?—I thought you had known the Sex better.—She is now, you see, quite well again!" (177).

But B.'s concern for Pamela's danger in the present case is genuine enough. In the earlier crisis Pamela had "been in Fit after Fit" for three hours (67); B. now says, "I never saw a Fit so strong and violent, in my Life . . . what I saw you in before was nothing to it" (178). In medical language which reiterates the notion of the human body as a physical mechanism—a motif of considerable interest in *Tristram Shandy*—Cheyne goes into more physiological detail about what causes convulsive disorders: "It is well known, that whatever will prick, wound, tear, or violently stimulate the Solids [i.e., a solid part of the body], will thereby produce *Spasms, Convulsions,* and violent *Contractions* [which] . . . may be communicated further and further over the whole *Machine*; and . . . propagated through . . . whatever Part . . . the . . . Stimulation happens to be made in; but most readily where there is the greatest Collection of *Nerves.*" The greatest collection of nerves in the human body (excluding the brain) was thought to be in the genital region. Cheyne then specifically compares this process to the mechanism of childbirth, as it was generally understood in the eighteenth century. The convulsive action continues "till the offending Matter is by such violent Action or Motion worked off, or removed: in the same Manner as the *Foetus*, by its Motion or Pressure, raises these *Throws* and *Convulsions* in the Mother, that bring it into the World." Other similar afflictions, like "Gravel" and "Wind," stimulate this "Struggle of Nature to throw them out, which are commonly call'd *Hysterick Fits.*"[41]

We must note that Cheyne is here thinking of stimulants like "any *irritating, acrid,* or *sharp* humours or Steam," but in the great rape scene of *Pamela*, Richardson seems to be identifying the irritating agents which Pamela must "work off" as Mr. B. and the unwomanly Mrs. Jewkes. Pamela's three fits are triggered by Mr. B. touching her "Bosom." Several times in the novel up to this point, Pamela has characterized her bosom, and the "Bosom of the Earth," as warm, round, secret places which will nurture her writings and make them grow toward her "Deliverance." Her bosom is an inviolate place, a euphemism for her womb and her modesty. In the first rape scene, Pamela says, "I found his Hand in my Bosom, and when my Fright let me know it, I was ready to die" (67). She seems anaesthesized by fear in her delayed finding—not feeling—of his hand. In the second scene, "he put his Hand in my Bosom. With Struggling, Fright, Terror, I fainted away quite . . . so that they both, from the cold Sweats that I was in, thought me dying" (176). Even a brief survey of the abundant literature of hysteria from Richardson's time to Freud's and Janet's will produce interesting parallels to Pamela's symptoms.[42]

All of this serves to show that Pamela is delivered in this scene in two main senses: on the medical level, she "throws out" (Cheyne's term) her tormentors in a hysteric parody of labor and in the process mitigates the virulence of the irritating agents. Hence, in their bizarre machinations over the prostrate Pamela—a figurative act of midwifery— Mr. B. and his wicked accomplice are assisting, unwittingly, in the one last deliverance for which the heroine so urgently implores God. And on the religious level, Pamela is resurrected from a "deplorable State of Death" in a specific though muted parallel with Christ's crucifixion and resurrection. Pamela, in her own version of the Pauline paradox of strength through weakness, has "Reason to bless God, who, by disabling me in my Faculties, enabled me to preserve my Innocence; and when all my Strength would have signified nothing, magnify'd himself in my Weakness!" (177).

Out of the materials then of midwifery, bawdry, and eighteenth-century medical notions of hysteria, Richardson fashions in the rape scene a rich and indelible portrait of Pamela's terror of and victory over her antagonists, and the author indirectly shows himself to be a better psychologist than his own eminent physician, for he represents Pamela's fits to be psychological—not merely physical—in origin. They are the most bizarre expression of the language of fate as gesture in the novel, where the pattern of "Fit after Fit" acts as an external defense of her chastity, corresponding to the internal defenses of the gradually augmented petticoat of letters around the heroine's loins, the subject of the next chapter.

We have seen how Pamela has already undergone one symbolic childbirth in delivering the secret Sunflower Correspondence safely back to her aged parents. By preserving her writings, which tell of the preservation of her virtue, she is also preserving her parents. From their first letter onward, they themselves make this connection by implying that their life is in her hands: "the Loss of our dear Child's Virtue, would be a Grief that we could not bear, and would bring our grey Hairs to the Grave at once" (27). Pamela's overwhelming fear of the loss of her virtue is not simply for the loss of the only life she deems worth living, but for that of her parents as well.

What is born now out of the final rape scene is Pamela's virtue one last time and also a changed Mr. B. It is as if after having caused Pamela's near death in the strongest and most violent paroxysm he has ever witnessed, something seems to have gone out of him. (The effect is similar to the Marquis Walter's finally crying "This is ynogh, Grisilde myn," in Chaucer's *Clerk's Tale*.)[43] Like a surgeon (in the eighteenth century or now) visiting his patient the morning after a near-miss operation, "he sat himself," Pamela says, "on the side of the Bed, and asked kindly how I did?—Begg'd me to be compos'd; said I still look'd a little wildly. . . . What a Change does this shew!" (178), but of course she cannot yet trust him. B. will never again attempt the worst, and although his reformation under Pamela's largely unknowing influence is well under way, he still has much to learn about his future wife.

22. The Petticoat Papers

Instead of gaining Pamela's approval of his "Articles" in "the dreadful Time of Reckoning," B. finds himself now more than ever the victim of his "Love and Folly" (181). It becomes clearer too that Pamela's "little History" while undressing for bed "half disarmed" his "Resolutions" for the intended rape. B. may have been a fairly experienced would-be libertine at the age of twenty-five, but he was by no means the hardened artist of rape that so many of his fellow eighteenth-century aristocratic rakes aspired to be. As he begins now to talk to Pamela more fully and candidly of her effect on him, he seems to gain a new sense of her beyond her role as a "charming Creature." He treats the discussion as if it were a legal case, and makes her an "Adviser in this Matter; tho' not perhaps [his] definitive Judge" (184) as the legal metaphor begins gradually to displace the medical one in their relationship. The unwonted gentleness of "this Treatment" begins to open Pamela's "most guarded Thoughts" (184). She cannot declare her love for him, and B. becomes her psychologist in a further examination of whether or not she might really love Williams: "if I thought you had a secret Whispering in your Soul, that had not yet come up to a Wish, for any other Man breathing, I should not forgive myself to persist in my Affection for you" (185).

Richardson shrewdly sets this conversation between them (and an important later one) on the "Grass Slope by the Pond-side" (185) where Pamela had earlier talked with Mrs. Jewkes and Williams just after arranging the terms of the Sunflower Correspondence. The pond where she almost drowned herself now becomes the site of a new understanding with her gradually regenerated master. We must picture Pamela and Mr. B. arriving at their new relationship outside of the great house and its imprisoning interiors in a daylight setting of splendid natural openness and beauty, the large garden of the estate. Pamela and her creative counter-plotting is linked, until her marriage, with flowers and nature, from her first flowering of B.'s waistcoat, through the parsley bed and sunflower business, to the rosebush affair (150), to the wildflower pointed out by the gypsy (196), and finally to the "Fruits of her Pen" (201) in the second great trial scene. Pamela is regenerated for B. from water and the earth. She plants her words, her chief aids and weapons—"And what is left me but Words" (182) she tells B. plaintively after the rape scene—and they grow into an intricate web which captivates and ultimately captures him.

As we move back into the closed and threatening atmosphere of the house, the remarkable thing is that this web is not only a figurative one but a literal, carefully woven patchwork, which functions as a snare for both Pamela and B. Though Mrs. Jewkes seizes Pamela's Rosebush Papers and gives them to B., Pamela still carries with her the continuation of her journal, "sew'd in my Under-coat, about my Hips" (198). B. resumes the legal metaphor for his relation with Pamela and his role as her most attentive reader with, "So, *Pamela*, we have seized it seems, your treasonable Papers? . . . you are a great Plotter; but I have not read them yet" (199). She implores him not to read them, and she reminds him that she always thought herself "right to endeavour to make [her] Escape from this forced and illegal Restraint" (200). The Rosebush Papers (128-50) contain Williams's proposal of marriage to her and her model letter refusing him, as well as her account of the sustained warfare with Mrs. Jewkes, the mixed-up letters from B., and the sketch of Colbrand.

The next morning, having read these letters, B. comes down to the parlor holding "the Papers in his Hand . . . . Now, *Pamela*, you come upon your Trial" (200). The ensuing mock-trial of Pamela works in the novel as a formal, subtle, and ceremonious re-enactment of Pamela's "worst Tryal" in the great rape scene, as B.'s opening words echo the thunderous ultimatum of "Now, *Pamela* . . . is the dreadful Time of Reckoning come" (176). All through the novel, at first clumsily and unfeelingly, now more cleverly, B. has been trying to penetrate the mystery of this "charming Creature" to see her as she really is. He started with the mystery of her person in the sense of her physical appearance, a young woman adorned by attractive clothes which set off and at the same time concealed a beautiful body. In the first trial, the voyeur B. for the first time saw Pamela completely naked as she recounted her "little History." There are no more secrets for him there.

But B.'s interest in her now goes far beyond sexual curiosity. As the "little History" prefaced the first "Time of Reckoning," so the Rosebush Papers introduce the second trial, as B. now tries to read the emotional heart of Pamela, specifically to discover whether or not she has indicated a preference for Williams. His evidence is the Rosebush Papers; he suggests that Pamela and the Parson exchanged love letters, and that Pamela's apparent refusal was only a coy inducement to make Williams the more eager. "Well, Sir, . . . that is your Comment; but it does not appear so in the Text. Smartly said! . . . where a D——l, gottest thou, at these Years, all this Knowledge; and then thou hast a Memory, as I see by your Papers, that nothing escapes it" (200). For Pamela now, the text is everything, and the text (*textus*, fabric) includes the Rosebush Papers in B.'s hands as well as the hidden elaborate tissue of letters she has painstakingly sewn into the petticoats "about [her] Hips"—her Petticoat Papers. The motif of sewing and writing (and the traditional images of the spinning womb and the woman as book) here reach their most complex and complete extensions in the novel. Pamela has literally become her own book, a living monument to herself, her own contemporaneous minute history. She has almost completely displaced herself into her writings, and the writings, a facsimile of herself, have become the real Pamela, an artifact and a gift for B. Pamela is now *Pamela*, the book of her fate.

To us she may seem like an elaborate metaphysical (or metalinguistic) joke. This lovely sixteen-year old waiting maid standing before her master with reams of letters sewn into her underclothes is a vivid eighteenth-century metaphor—without a particular reference to Christ—of the word made flesh. The papers, beyond being a metaphoric legal text, have for Pamela almost the significance of sacred writ, for they preserve the truth of her experience as a vulnerable free person whose soul is of more value than that of a princess. Pamela's virtue has from the first been linked to her "immortal substance," her soul. But she may now be in more danger from B. than formerly because she finds herself giving way before his gentler and kinder approach, even if it is, as she suspects, only a change in tactics. She presents herself before B., however, in the posture advocated by St. Paul: "Wherefore take unto you the whole armour of God, that ye may be able to withstand in the evil day, and having done all, to stand. Stand therefore, having your loins girt about with truth, and having on the breastplate of righteousness" (Ephesians 6:13-14). The papers preserve her virtue, but they are also a record of her real attitude toward Mr. B., who is not now in the position of voyeur but of commentator on Pamela's text. His fascination with the mystery of her body and person-as-appearance has given way to the deeper mystery of the person in the text—sidestepping the most difficult problem of all, that of the living person herself—and he realizes that his knowledge of the text is fragmentary: "Where are the Accounts . . . previous to these here in my Hand? My Father has them, Sir" (200-201). These accounts are the Sunflower Correspondence with Williams, another version of Pamela and her virtue which sustains her parents, but which offered no consolation to the parson who delivered it and loved her. Pamela now inadvertently (it is implied) opens the door to B.'s further apprehension of the text ("as you have seen all my *former* Letters . . . you *might* see *all the rest*" [201]), and he asks to see the succeeding parts of the journal which he assumes she must have continued keeping beyond the papers in his hand. Pamela is now caught, but she allowed herself to be, and with B.'s recognition that he is in an acute sense the co-author of Pamela's papers and has some right to them, we see that the earlier dynamic of enhancing each other's image through clothing has now deepened into one of mutual author-ship and romantic entrapment.

B. knows that he can now move toward a mutuality of response with Pamela by means of the journal. First, he says he would be greatly obliged if she would show him the papers voluntarily (201). Then he compliments her on the beauty of her manner of writing, an extension for him of her physical beauty. "And as I have furnished you with the Subject, I have a Title to see the Fruits of your Pen" (201). If the Sunflower Correspondence produced a little Pamela, far more significant are the fruits of this collaboration. B. implies that he has a proprietary, almost paternal interest in this subsequent correspondence. "Besides . . . there is such a pretty Air of Romance, as you relate them, in your Plot, and my Plots, that I shall be better directed in what manner to wind up the Catastrophe of the pretty Novel" (201). And this, in effect, is exactly what he does. In terms of conventional social relationship, B. as Pamela's master has always been her "Original," in the sense of her "originator" (OED); shortly after B. returns to his estate on "the 36th day" of Pamela's imprisonment, he remarks bitterly: "I find you cannot forget your Original, but must prefer my Menials to me," and Pamela replies abjectly, "And I never shall, I hope, forget my Original" (161). Richardson will now allow Mr. B.—apparently with the author's blessing and approval— to become the virtual author of both Pamela and *Pamela* when this born gentlewoman permits him to refashion her into a "lady," the "pretty" and docile Mrs. B. who will, like an eighteenth-century marionette, perform and conform almost perfectly to what he wants in a wife.

B. the "keen Fox-hunter" goes on the track of Pamela's new writings: "as to those Writings of yours, that follow your fine Plot, I *must* see them" (202). The significance of the word "plot" has evolved in the novel from pattern to conspiracy to story line as B. finds himself caught up and entranced in the overall plot of Pamela's "Romance." He now uses the same language for her writings that he once used for her: "they are "bewitching Chit-Chat," "pretty Impertinence," "your sawsy Journal" (203). The coming together of B. and Pamela through the displaced interaction of commentary on a written text could never have happened through the medium of physical sex. What follows between them is a disturbing rape of the text: "tell me where it is you hide your Written-Papers . . . I *will* see them. . . . Are they in your Pocket? . . . Are they not . . . about your Stays?" She offers to "go up to them" and let him see "to the End of the sad Story. . . . I'll see them all . . . down to this Time . . . it is my Opinion they are about you; and I never undrest a Girl in my Life; but I will now begin to strip my pretty *Pamela* (203-04)." The whole written record of his earlier attempted rape girdles her loins at the very instant he threatens to strip her in a rape she has now almost encouraged. He begins to unpin her "Handkerchief . . . let me see them uncurtail'd. . . . I will, Sir.—On your Honour? Yes, Sir" (204). The "sad Story" has replaced the old sad outfit, and his power over her external being is on the verge of being immeasurably increased because her inner virtue, her honesty ("I am poor and lowly, and am not intitled to call it *Honour*" [187]), and her implied love for him revealed by her "forward Heart" at the very end of the Petticoat Papers (188), have all now become externalized in the text, which he will seize.

It is a poignant moment. Pamela goes upstairs and with great anxiety unpins and unsews her writings from the petticoat, in effect undoing herself. (One is reminded again, unfortunately, of "Swift's Beautiful Young Nymph" at the midnight hour.) Pamela continues, "I went to my Closet, and there I sat me down, and could not bear the Thoughts of giving up my Papers. Besides, I must all undress me in a manner to untack them" (204). This anxiously reluctant surrender of her Petticoat Papers recalls the anguished acknowledgement of her true identity in the scene when she first wore her sad outfit. Pamela is in a psychological crisis, a true dilemma. By keeping her journal going she has kept her story going, regenerating herself with this secret history girded round her loins; it has given order to her life and a measure of control over her chaotic and vulnerable experience with B. Now she has been coerced into giving it up, trusting B. to take a large measure of control over her future. She is dwindling into a wife. Although she still has power to extricate the story from herself, she finds now that she will not, or cannot, extricate herself from the story—that is, from the power of B.'s essential inward collaboration in her story, his novel now.

Pamela's two bundles of Petticoat Papers carry the history of her "Confinement" (178) down to "*Wednesday*, the 41st" day, corresponding to the forty days the Israelites wandered in the Wilderness and to the traditional forty weeks, or nine to ten months of pregnancy. During B.'s year-long courtship of her, she has almost completely transcribed herself into the various bundles of her journal. Now she is down to the last two of them: each describes the mock-death of Pamela (the "drowning" in parcel one; the rape attempt in two), and each builds towards a climactic scene with B. (the "strange Tribunal" in one, the reconciliation by the pond in two). Pamela has escaped the "hard Fate" B. had planned for her, has preserved her physical virtue through God's grace, and has preserved it in a fixed form in her journal. She has made an artifact of her virtue (and of herself) in the Petticoat Papers. Because B. seems to recognize that her former papers have told the truth ("I have only writ Truth" [206]) and because he understands the true worth of her transcribed self, she will now trust him to read the rest; nevertheless she remains reluctant—and coy. She tries to dole out the two parcels—perhaps he will be satisfied with volume one only. Finally she voluntarily resigns herself to put her fate in his hands again; this time, however, her fate, recorded in the Petticoat Papers, exists in a form she can accept:

> So I took out my Papers; and said, Here, Sir, they are. But, if you please to return them, without breaking the Seal, it will be very generous: And I will take it for a great Favour, and a good Omen.
>
> He broke the Seal instantly, and open'd them. So much for your omen, said he (207).

PART FOUR:

CLARISSA AND
"THE WOMB OF FATE"

23. Clarissa's Progress

"Women to be generally thought a trifling Part of the Creation."—May those who think so, never be blest with the Possession, or Conversation, of a good, a virtuous, a sensible Woman!—You must see that the Tendency of all I have written is to exalt the Sex

(Richardson to Lady Bradshaigh, 15 Dec. 1748)

The dying Clarissa gives into the hands of John Belford, a man she has come to trust despite his being Robert Lovelace's closest friend, the responsibility of executing her will and preserving her literary remains. Belford tells his friend,

> You cannot imagine how proud I am of this trust. I am afraid I shall too soon come into the execution of it. As she is always writing, what a melancholy pleasure will the perusal and disposition of her papers afford me! Such a sweetness of temper, so much patience and resignation, as she seems to be mistress of; yet writing of and in the midst of *present* distresses! How *much more* lively and affecting, for that reason, must her style be, her mind tortured by the pangs of uncertainty (the events then hidden in the womb of fate), *than* the dry narrative, unanimated style of a person relating difficulties and dangers surmounted; the relater perfectly at ease; and if himself unmoved by his own story, not likely greatly to affect the reader . . . . I am just returned from visiting the lady, and thanking her in person for the honour she has done me; and assuring her, if called to the sacred trust, of the utmost fidelity and exactness (IV,81).[1]

Belford will undertake the "sacred trust"; he will collect and safeguard "her own story" already preserved in the life-like style of her letters written to the moment. Clarissa undertakes an act of communion with Belford. She gives him her life story and says, in effect, take good care of it; you are a good man, I trust you; these letters are my true self, the truth of my experience with Lovelace; they are for all to see. Belford is her literary midwife; he knows what the "womb of fate" brought forth to her, and he is responsible for delivering and preserving her account and estimate of that painful burden of experience. In this extraordinary elegiac paragraph, well worth pondering as the keynote and epitome of the entire novel, we gain not only an acute sense of Clarissa's tortured sufferings during the fatal five months of her experience with Lovelace after leaving her father's house, but also Richardson's own view, expressed through Belford, of his narrative method. For Richardson, Belford is Clarissa's last, best reader in the novel, and he and all subsequent readers share the melancholy aesthetic pleasure of contemplating her tragic story from the distance of posterity.

Looked at simply as a species of narrative, *Clarissa* might be called the first great mystery novel. The crime it documents is the crime of rape, a murder of the spirit as well as a physical outrage. Nancy Howe, Clarissa's closest friend, first penetrates and exposes the mystery of deception which Lovelace creates for the heroine, but Miss Howe's discoveries are not made in good enough time or with good enough fortune to save her friend. A larger but related concern in the novel is the "mystery of iniquity," a favorite phrase of seventeenth- and eighteenth- century divines; Richardson in his own way raises Lear's question: "Is there any cause in nature that makes these hard hearts?" (III.vi.76). Implicit in this question is both the political struggle within the Harlowe family and the whole psychology of love and intrigue motivating Lovelace, who is deeply involved with his own family of bawds and whores, for if *Clarissa* is anything, it is a "family tragedy" in the most immediate and in the largest implications of that term. The third and most important concern of the novel is with the mystery of fate, the central issue of tragedy. In *Clarissa*, Richardson has written a tragic epic poem in prose which some have called a "Christian tragedy."[2] Focusing on the idea of fate with its close ties to the metaphor of birth, I would like to explore some of the tragic, epic, and Christian elements of the novel in an attempt to understand Belford's sense of what is sacred in Clarissa. The Clarissa who emerges from this marathon of novels is part Christian heroine, part saint, and part Old Testament angel. Like Milton in *Paradise Lost*, though without his learning and with far different technique and purpose, Richardson adapts the materials of Scripture, the pagan classics (especially Ovid), seventeenth-century representations of women, and a good deal else, to fashion a new kind of epic, one that substitutes a struggle between the sexes for the traditional masculine warfare of classical epic, and to create his own autonomous religious myth of a young English woman translated and exalted, in the eyes of Belford and the reader, into a figure of godlike power.

In the beginning, Clarissa is an extraordinarily beautiful, creative, bright and accomplished English country girl of eighteen whose deepest feelings of affection are for women: her mother, her friend Anna Howe (Nancy), her nurse, Mrs. Norton, and her maid, Hannah Burton. She stands in awe and pity of her gloomy father, she is disappointed with her foolish and headstrong brother, and she can see through her doting uncles. She is on a higher plane of trust with her women friends; she is distrustful of men. And yet she agrees to correspond with Lovelace. Their correspondence apparently began not long before Nancy's reference to the disarming of James Harlowe which begins the novel on January 10. Lovelace had insisted that Clarissa "direct the subjects" of the account of his Grand Tour which Uncle John Harvey had requested of him, and Clarissa willingly obliged.

A word must here be said about the eighteenth-century conception of delicacy in the feminine code. William Alexander notes that

> Of all the virtues which adorn the female character, and enable the sex to steal imperceptibly into the heart, none are more conspicuous than that unaffected simplicity and shyness of manners which we distinguish by the name of delicacy. . . . delicacy is the sentinel that is placed over female virtue, and that sentinel once overcome, chastity is more than half conquered . . . . delicacy is a virtue planted by the hand of nature in the female mind.

It is "an innate principle of the female mind" and "an outwork of chastity."[3] Although Clarissa inherits this inborn delicacy from her mother, by means of her reading and in the exemplary conduct of her life she has consciously refined her extraordinary sensitivity to notions of decorum, modesty, and shame. Now correspondence between a man and a woman had, in the canons of delicacy, a special significance which is not lost on Lovelace. He once notes jokingly to Belford that his cousin Charlotte Montague (Belford's future wife), "in a whim of delicacy, is displeased that I send the enclosed letter to you—that her handwriting, forsooth! should go into the hands of a single man! There's encouragement for thee, Belford! This is a certain sign that thou mayst have her if thou wilt" (IV,237). At another point, Lovelace, with ingratiating seriousness (and faulty etymology) tells Clarissa that he "loved familiar letter-writing . . . above all the species of writing: it was writing from the heart . . . as the very word, *correspondence* implied. Not the heart only; the *soul* was in it" (II,431).

As early as January 5, Clarissa's mother tacitly approves of her daughter's secret renewed correspondence with Lovelace in hopes of preventing future mischief between him and the Harlowe family (I,19-20). This secret correspondence is carried out through a post-box of loose stones in part of the garden wall not far from the "green lane" where Clarissa later initiates and keeps up her parallel secret correspondence with Nancy Howe. Clarissa feels guilty about these furtive procedures: "I should abhor these clandestine correspondencies were they not forced upon me. They have so mean, so low an appearance to myself, that I think I ought not to expect that you should take part in them" (I,39). Already she is worried about implicating her dearest friend in her own distress, but Nancy tellingly accuses her of harboring Lovelace in her heart as a secret lover, a secret she thinks her friend is not yet fully aware of:

> By your insisting that he should keep this correspondence private, it
> appears that there is *one secret* which you do not wish the world should
> know; and *he* is master of that secret. He is indeed *himself*, as I may say,
> that secret! What an intimacy does this beget for the lover! How is it
> distancing the parent! (I,45).

Clarissa, whose sense of delicacy surpasses even Charlotte's (or Nancy's), is
aware of the seriousness of her friend's charge, but she believes she is not
really in love with Lovelace.[4] Later (after responding with genuine tenderness and concern for him in his self-induced illness) she will virtually admit
to Nancy that her heart had deceived her (II,439). This admission is as close
as she can come to acknowledging that part of her feels a sexual attraction to
Lovelace, a feeling (or passion) inadmissible as love, and one which must be
suppressed. If Clarissa is "in love"—as she would like to use the term—with
anyone in the novel, it would seem to be with Anna Howe. She wants to
keep her correspondence with Lovelace secret in order, she believes, to
restrain him from resenting the indignities he later receives from the Harlowe family. He counts to his advantage on her delicate intention to influence and modify his behavior for the better, as he counts on her love of
writing—it is her favorite pastime or game—and in him he knows she has a
match.

For both Clarissa and Lovelace, writing (and reading) is their most
characteristic act: Clarissa "loves to write," and her "conversation by person
and by letter" with Anna Howe is "the principal pleasure of her life" (I,38);
Nancy informs her that Lovelace "delights in writing," and Clarissa marvels
at the diligence and self-discipline that even Lovelace must be master of to
write as he does. This clandestine writing and reading relationship, which
Clarissa enters to oblige her uncle (and perhaps herself, secretly) and continues with her delicate mother's connivance and equivocal encouragement
is the means which plants Lovelace (like a dark counterpart to her "delicacy")
ineradicably into her life, whether she wishes him there or not, so that
Nancy warns, "You are drawn in by a perverse fate. . . . Has not your man
himself had natural philosophy enough to observe already to your Aunt
Hervey, that love takes the deepest root in the steadiest minds?" (I,46). The
secret correspondence, or utterance, between Clarissa and Lovelace, is that
perverse fate, and Nancy has the perspicacity to observe long before Clarissa
does, that Lovelace is the natural philosopher of love and women. Her
prescience is borne out much later when she laments that she "knew it to be
a dangerous thing for two single persons of different sexes to enter into this
familiarity and correspondence with each other; since, as to the latter, must
not a person be capable of premeditated art who can sit down to write, and
not write from the heart?" (III, 8), as Lovelace can do at will.

Belford sees Clarissa's fate under the aspect of a womb ("the events then hidden in the womb of fate"). The line has an epic ring, and one would expect the literary Belford to have derived it from something like Dryden's *Aeneid*. But the phrase "womb of fate" is not in Dryden (nor in Pope, Milton, Spenser, Shakespeare, or the Bible).[5] This peculiarly Richardsonian phrase is the focal image for fate in this novel, and an attempt to suggest its meaning will help illuminate *Clarissa* as a tragic prose epic. One of the main contentions of this discussion is that the tragedy of *Clarissa* stems in large part from the presence and pressure behind and within Clarissa and Lovelace of two influential mother figures, Charlotte Harlowe, Clarissa's actual mother, and Mother Sinclair, the London bawd to whose house Lovelace brings Clarissa and where the climactic rape is performed. Mrs. Sinclair is Mother Midnight to both Lovelace and Clarissa.

The metaphor of birth in relation to the fate of the protagonist is as complicated for Clarissa (if not so explicit) as it is for Tristram Shandy. From the inception of her first correspondence with Lovelace, sometime around the middle of December, to the time of Clarissa's death (September 7), is a full nine months.[6] This is the period of gestation for Clarissa's new identity; it is a time of "soul-making," to borrow Keats's phrase, during which Clarissa's spiritual essence, preserved in her letters, takes increasingly full and independent form as her physical self dwindles away in an accelerated aging process. In her remarkable posthumous letter to her father, Clarissa describes "the last unhappy eight months" of this gestation period as a "weaning time." To "wean" is to make a child accustomed to food other than mother's milk, or to withdraw someone gradually from—or deprive them of—one way of life by substituting another. Clarissa comes to see this happening to her through God's grace. Her soul is weaned from a superficially attractive world and new-made for another realm of the spirit through a series of Job-like afflictions: "had I escaped the snares by which I was entangled, I might have wanted those exercises which I look upon now as so many mercies dispensed to wean me betimes from a world that presented itself to me with prospects too alluring" (IV,360). These alluring prospects, as Clarissa understands fully at the end of her life, are only the glittering veneer of a corrupt world ("the world showing me early, even at my first rushing into it, its true and ugly face" [IV,21]); such prospects were embodied, for the most part, in Lovelace and his two families, the respectable one including Lord M., Lady Betty, Lady Sarah, and the disguised one made up of the various whores, female and male, who work for him. Mother Sinclair and her family (which includes Lovelace), are the chief agents of this weaning process who provide the snares which make possible the grueling spiritual exercises for which Clarissa learns to be grateful. In the end, she achieves, as part of her prize, a triumph over the world.

Birth and weaning are both separations leading to the child's increased independence. If, as I have argued, the experience of birth is essentially an act of violent separation from one state of growth to another, the gestation and weaning of Clarissa's soul proceeds in a series of emotionally and physically painful separations or births. In the first of these, Richardson dwells (with strong overtones of the original birth experience) on the protracted and passionate separation, early in the novel (March 4) of Clarissa from her mother, her last hope within the family of salvation from the odious Solmes. The second separation is Lovelace's abduction of her from her father's house and from polite society and the subsequent banishment of every vestige of Clarissa's memory from Harlowe Place as conveyed in her sister's letter containing her father's curse. Clarissa herself marks April 10th, the day she left her father's house, as the true date of her death, and so inscribes it on her coffin. The severing process continues in the death of Clarissa's honor, through rape, which takes place in Mrs. Sinclair's inner house in London (midnight, June 12), under the figurative aspect of a case in midwifery. After this final torment, Clarissa enters her "last stage" of life, knowing she will die and preparing herself, by means of spiritual exercises, for that awful moment. Then follow her two escapes from Sinclair's house and from Lovelace, the second of which is successful (June 28); Clarissa's painful delivery of the burden of her own story (that is, the narrative, written for Anna Howe and preserved by Belford, of what really happened to her after Lovelace brought her back from Hampstead to Mrs. Sinclair's to complete the rape); the ecstatic separation of Clarissa's soul from this world on September 7; and finally the strange and dramatic separation, or resurrection, of the now sacred Clarissa from the human world as evidenced in her eleven posthumous letters to Belford, Lovelace, and the members of her family. We shall follow Clarissa's fate by looking primarily at the separations from her mother, from her honor, and from her human story.

24. Mother and Daughter

"it is the most cruel of fates, for a woman to be forced to have a man whom her heart despises"

Nancy Howe (II,317)

The major movement of the first two-thirds of the novel is the tragic descent of the heroine into a gradually contracting isolation, accompanied by disgrace and mortification. Clarissa has much to bear. Like her tragic prototype, Job, she endures wave after wave of suffering—not, as in Job's case, a sudden initial succession of disasters ("while he was yet speaking, there came another," and so forth) but in many misfortunes, some crowded together in a series of trials, others drawn out over a protracted present, a present stretched out to almost intolerable limits:

> Indeed, my dearest love (permit me to be very serious) I am afraid I am singled out (either for my own faults, or the faults of my family, or perhaps for the faults of both) to be a very unhappy creature!—*signally* unhappy! For see you not how irresistibly the waves of affliction come tumbling down upon me? (I,419).

These afflictions are irresistible; she is caught up in forces she cannot control. Lovelace, in one of his deepest moments late in the novel, describes his own grief as "sharper pointed than most other men's; and, like what Dolly Welby once told me, describing the parturient throes, if there were not lucid intervals, if they did not come and go, there would be no bearing them" (IV,263). Besides indicating to us Lovelace's acute interest in childbirth, this remark sums up the experience of the heroine though, characteristically, Lovelace seems not to be aware of its application to her. As everyone in the eighteenth century knew, "That sex is made to bear pain. It is a curse that the first of it entailed upon all her succeeding daughters, when she brought the curse upon us all" (III,450-51). Even women accepted this appraisement of their lot, mindful of God's original curse upon Eve in Genesis 3:16: "I will greatly multiply thy sorrow and thy conception; in sorrow thou shalt bring forth children; and thy desire shall be to thy husband, and he shall rule over thee."[7]

Clarissa sees her mother as the extreme exemplar of the woman as bearer, and she is critical: "had she been of a temper that would have borne less, she would have had ten times less to bear than she has had" (I,22). Clarissa recognizes the true power of a mother not only to bear and nurture, but by the proper exercise of her authority, to extinguish family feuds "in their but yet beginnings" (I,22). Her mother unfortunately is too passive to perform her proper function; she is the family "bearer"—she "bears with" the family feuds, she "bears" insulting behavior, she even "bears" the will of the family to Clarissa in the form of news and an ultimatum: it has been absolutely determined that her obedient daughter must marry Roger Solmes. Charlotte Harlowe's role, as she sees it, is to extract from Clarissa her promise to marry the man she detests above all others. The whole laborious action of the novel can be seen in another way as an effort to extract something from the heroine; in the first part of the story, it is this promise to the family; and in the remainder of the tale, the forfeit of her honor to Lovelace and his family of whores.

Charlotte Harlowe visits her daughter in seven increasingly more agonized conferences, trying to persuade her to accept Solmes. These visitations are like birth throes for both women. Richardson once said that "a child never can make its Parent Amends for her Pains in Childbirth, in Dentition, and for the Anxiousness and Sleepless Nights throughout every stage of her Infantile Life—on to Adolescency."[8] He was acutely aware of a woman's pains in childbirth and with her subsequent cares. He believed sincerely, and reiterated in his letters, that a child should obey her parents even when they do not deserve to be obeyed; "Clarissa might have been excused, if anybody," but she was guilty of the "Error, of Corresponding with Lovelace against Prohibition, tho' at first doing it on Motives not illaudable." Her "too timid Mother" however, who "tamely deserted the just Cause of her Child,"[9] was most to blame. It is as if Mrs. Harlowe must now "bear" her willful daughter all over again, and for Clarissa it is the ordeal of final separation from a mother to whom she is still deeply attached. They begin with tears for each other and few words:

> O my mamma! was all I could say; and I clasped my arms round her neck, and my face sunk into her bosom.
> My child! My child! restrain, said she, your powers of moving! I dare not else trust myself with you. And my tears trickled down her bosom as hers bedewed my neck (I,70).

Clarissa is the child again at the maternal bosom. At first she simply wants to be reunited with her mother but there is also the suggestion that Clarissa has innocent powers of persuasion which her mother can hardly resist. The two women have much in common. Both have a reputation for fine talents, for practical intelligence, for glowing beauty, for sweet and kind dispositions. Clarissa even looks like her mother, far more so than does Arabella. Most important, both mother and daughter have an inclination to preserve peace and decorum at considerable cost to themselves, the mother in putting up with the plots of other family members, Clarissa in putting up with Lovelace's correspondence and later with his relentless pursuit. As Nancy Howe tells her, "You are your mother's girl, think what you will" (I,40).

The interviews develop into a poignant duel between two women who love each other, and again (as with Pamela's relationships with both Mrs. Jewkes and Lady Davers) Richardson demonstrates his remarkable talent for representing an older and a younger woman in verbal conflict, a conflict always accompanied by much physical agitation and dramatic gesture. Clarissa throws herself across her mother's chair seat or at her feet, she clasps her, she weeps. The gestures are all suggestive of the ones Lovelace himself will use in his long "seduction progress." Clarissa in her innocent, gentle, yet desperate way, is trying to seduce her mother into giving up her unnatural and abhorrent scheme of pleading for Solmes or, as Richardson suggests (as delicately as possible), of procuring her daughter for a loveless marriage of family convenience.[10] It is Clarissa's fate to be forced to deal with a disguised bawd long before she meets Mother Sinclair. Then in a gesture of apparent openness and vulnerability, Clarissa tells her mother that she too can bear much, and implores her mother to tell her what is to become of her, as if her mother were the oracle of her fate:

> I could hold no longer; but threw myself at her feet: O my dearest mamma! Let me know all I am to suffer: let me know what I am to be! I *will* bear it, if I *can* bear it: but your displeasure I cannot bear!
>
> Leave me, leave me, Clary Harlowe! No kneeling!—limbs so supple; will so stubborn! Rise, I tell you (I,90).

Clarissa at this moment is still the child under the direction of her mother. For most of the novel the shape of her life is directed first by her parents (as instructed by James Harlowe, Jr.) and then by Lovelace. Compare his words with Mrs. Harlowe's when, after the fire scare, Clarissa implores him to spare her, and the "penetrated" rake, like the pagan god he fancies himself to be, confers new life upon her: "Rise then, my angel! Rise, and be what you are, and all you wish to be!" (II,504).

But Clarissa nobly resists the urgent pressure of these forces in an attempt to find her own way, and finally succeeds. What she really wants, very simply, is to be free to direct her own life. She recognizes her mother's great potential influence on her destiny, perhaps even stronger on the immediate personal level than her father's because she knows her mother just might, if she exerted herself, prevail over him. Clarissa seems to know that a mother has a unique knowledge of life. Most of us have only one experience of birth ("I've been born and once is enough," in the words of Eliot's Sweeney), but a woman who bears children carries not only the experience of her own birth but that of others, and a corresponding responsibility for the lives of others. Her body knows the meaning of birth as delivered and as deliverer. She is the transmitter of life, a link in an unbroken chain. "You have given me life, madam . . . O do not . . . make all the remainder of it miserable!", Clarissa pleads (I,98). Earlier she had said:

> But what then can I plead for a palliation to *myself* of my mother's sufferings on my account? Perhaps this consideration will carry some force with it—that *her* difficulties cannot last long; only till this great struggle shall be one way or other determined—whereas *my* unhappiness, if I comply, will (from an aversion not to be overcome) be for life (I,94).

Clarissa thinks that her mother has the power to give her daughter misery or happiness *for life* in the affair of Solmes. Richardson's original title for the novel, "The Lady's Legacy," has much more resonance than one might think at first. Charlotte Harlowe misuses the power she has assumed as a mother, she fails her extraordinary daughter, and she bequeaths her a legacy of indecision which contributes to Clarissa's downfall. Mrs. Harlowe's behavior under Clarissa's "powers of moving" foreshadows the heroine's own struggles, propelled by affection, revulsion, and regret into a state of charming paralysis under the relentless blandishments and teasing proposals of Lovelace:

> I never beheld so sweet a confusion. . . . Then. . . . struggling to free herself from my clasping arms: How now, sir! said she, with a cheek more indignantly glowing and eyes of a fiercer lustre. I gave way to her angry struggle; but, absolutely overcome by so charming a display of innocent confusion, I caught hold of her hand as she was flying from me (II,141).

Compare Clarissa to her mother:

> Yet tear not yourself from me! (wrapping my arms about her as I kneeled; she struggling to get from me; my face lifted up to hers with eyes running over, that spoke not my heart if they were not all humility and reverence) you must not, must not, tear yourself from me! (for still the dear lady struggled, and looked this way and that in a sweet disorder, as if she knew not what to do.)—I will neither rise nor leave you, nor let you go till you say you are not angry with me (I,90).

In these vivid pictures of the "sweet disorder" of an older woman torn between emotions of innate tenderness and assumed anger, profoundly aware that this task is the wrong task, and the sweet confusion of the younger woman knowing that she has taken a wrong step with a man who has abused her good faith, who appears to be proposing marriage and withholding that proposal at the same time, we glimpse Clarissa in her mother, and her mother in Clarissa. Furthermore, Clarissa insists that she will not let her mother go until she be "not angry" with her, as Lovelace will insist on Clarissa's giving him her "pardon" before he will leave her in the fire scene.

After the seventh interview, Charlotte Harlowe has had enough for the present: "I am tired out with your obstinacy. . . I must separate myself from you, if you will not comply. You do not remember that your father will take you up, where I leave you" (I,102). James Harlowe, Senior, is by this time merely his son's puppet, and Clarissa soon learns that she is "to be delivered up to [her] brother" (I,110). So begins her first extended confinement, one of many, initially at the hands of her family, then with Lovelace, and finally with the London law, during her protracted "weaning time" from the world.

25. Lovelace, Ovid, and "the Sex"

Two great eighteenth-century concerns are brought to bear in Clarissa's brief but profound experience of the world: the themes of confinement and flight and, particularly, the significance of rape, and their combined effect on the integrity of the self. The rape of Clarissa is not simply a single act. Everything builds up to the climactic violation by Lovelace (with the instigation and assistance of Mrs. Sinclair and the harlots), but until that event the heroine is subjected to one assault after another, the two most damaging of which are the abduction from the garden of her father's house, and his subsequent curse upon her. Before examining the rapes and confinements of the heroine, it will be necessary to take a closer look at Lovelace and his relation to women.

Robert Lovelace is a libertine and, as Anna Howe observed, a penetrating student of "natural philosophy" as it relates to the origin of women's love for men (I,46). As Clarissa is a woman of great natural gifts and native elegance, so too has Lovelace remarkable natural endowments, a strong constitution, exceptional masculine beauty, and a consuming interest in the natural world. His view of nature and of women has much in common with two of his Shakespearean forebears: like Iago, his talk about women is full of metaphors and analogies from the animal world, and like Edmund's, his estimate of human nature is essentially Hobbesian,

> Thrust Nature back with a pitchfork, it will return (II,99).
> There is more of the savage in human nature than we are commonly aware of (II,245).
> Have I not said that human nature is a rogue? (III,101).
> I love, thou knowest, to trace human nature, and more particularly female nature, through its most secret recesses (III,139).

Much of Lovelace's correspondence with Belford is a running commentary—often an ironic discourse as from master to disciple, from natural scientist to pupil, from connoisseur to neophyte—on the nature of "the Sex" and his predominant concern with it.[11] Lovelace seems to say that little boys in their often cruel preoccupations with living things, eventually graduate to the status of libertines, for whom the Sex is the prime subject in the natural world: "Whatever our hearts are in, our heads will follow. Begin with spiders, with flies, with what we will, girl is the centre of gravity, and we all naturally tend to it" (II,23). Woman draws the libertine to herself. She is the center of his universe. Lovelace the schoolmaster goes on to his favorite image of birds for women in the famous passage that prefigures Clarissa's fate under his persecutions:

> I will illustrate what I have said by the simile of a bird new-caught. We
> begin, when boys, with birds, and when grown up, go on to women. . . .
> Hast thou not observed the charming gradations by which the ensnared
> volatile has been brought to bear with its new condition? . . . with
> difficulty, drawing back its head, it gasps for breath. . . . at last . . . it lays
> itself down and pants at the bottom of the cage, seeming to bemoan its
> cruel fate and forfeited liberty. . . . Now let me tell thee, that I have
> known a bird actually starve itself, and die with grief. . . . (for a bird is all
> soul), and of consequence has as much feeling as the human creature
> (II, 245-47).

Lovelace as a philosopher is an amateur natural scientist. Woman is a
species of fauna which has not received proper scientific attention, and he
will carry out a series of operations, or empirical investigations, upon the
Sex. Because woman is a subject for inquiry, experiment, and manipulation,
the natural philosopher of women, in Lovelace's sense, must also be a
libertine: intrigue is the libertine's business and the scientist's proving
ground; Lovelace must be free to pursue both his inquiry and his intrigue,
for they go hand in hand. He is fascinated by the process of this pursuit, and
with the power of directing and controlling experiments upon the Sex.
Implicit in the libertine-philosopher's view of life (and this view is reflected
in varying degrees from Bolingbroke to Wilkes) is the perception of woman
in her natural state as something less than man, less than human, almost a
different order of being. The fascination of the eighteenth-century natural
philosopher with nature and her verifiable and predictable laws had a
counterpart in the fascination of the rake with the sex and its predictable
laws, for women, like nature, were to be subdued and controlled for man's
benefit and pleasure. Even Johnson's young scholar in *The Vanity of Human
Wishes* would hope to "indulge the generous heat, Till captive Science yields
her last retreat" (ll. 143-4).

The rake's science was also his religion, with its own creed, natural
maxims like axioms of eighteenth-century natural science. This secular, or
irreligious, religion had its root in the natural love philosophy of the pagan
classics, especially in Ovid, and particularly in his *Art of Love* and *Amores*.
The controlling metaphor of the art of love is that of warfare: *femina* for Ovid
and "the Sex" for the libertine-rake are deceitful, delicious enemies who
must be overcome by cunning and deceit. The Ovidian male lover, the
prototype for Lovelace, is a master liar and Protean shape changer where
women are concerned: "wise Men shift their Sails with every Wind;/As
changeful Proteus varied oft his Shape,"[12] and Ovid, like Lovelace the
"namefather," "Invent[s] new Names of things unknown before" (487).

Ovid is the master instructor in the school of love: "In *Cupid*'s School,
whoe're would take Degree, / Must learn his Rudiments, by reading me"

(480), and the chief of his "Rules and Principles of love," "First then believe, all Women may be won; / Attempt with Confidence, the Work is done" (489) is also Lovelace's: "Importunity and opportunity no woman is proof against, especially from a persevering lover . . . " (II,35).[13] Lovelace refines upon this basic assumption with a more heroic military one: "Has it not been a constant maxim with us, that the greater *merit* on the woman's side, the nobler the victory on the man's?" (II,253). For Ovid,

> Love is a kind of warfare; avaunt, ye laggards! these banners are not for timid men to guard. Night, storm, long journeys, cruel pains, all kinds of toil are in this dainty camp. Oft will you put up with rain from melting clouds of heaven, oft will you lie cold on the bare ground.[14]

This is Lovelace's highly particularized (and "Metamorphic") account of his obligatory difficulties with Clarissa:

> O Jack! what a night had I in the bleak coppice adjoining to her father's paddock! My linen and wig frozen; my limbs absolutely numbed; my fingers only sensible of so much warmth as enabled me to hold a pen; and that obtained by rubbing the skin off, and by beating with my hands my shivering sides. Kneeling on the hoar moss on one knee, writing on the other, if the stiff scrawl could be called writing. My feet, by the time I had done, seeming to have taken root, and actually unable to support me for some minutes! Love and rage kept then my heart in motion [and only love and rage could do it], or how much more than I *did* suffer must I have suffered? (II,493).

But a more characteristic scene, for Lovelace and for Ovid, is the brothel: "I sing the Brothels loose and unconfin'd' / Th' unpunishable Pleasures of the Kind; / Which all alike, for Love, or Money find" (481). For both lovers, the attack begins with letters in "the familiar Style": "By Letters, not by Words, thy Love begin . . . / In a familiar Style your thoughts convey; / And Write such things, as Present you would say" (494-95). As Lovelace's initial correspondence indicates, the Ovidian lover's first object is to get the woman of his desires to *read* him, "For she who Reads, in time will Answer too; / Things must be left, by just degrees to grow" (496). Once this is gained, all manner of promises, lies, and fabrications are justified:

> *Jove* sits above, forgiving with a smile,
> The Perjuries that easy Maids beguile. . . .
> But 'tis a Venial Sin to cheat the Fair;
> All Men have Liberty of Conscience there. . . .
> Thus justly Women suffer by Deceit;
> Their Practice authorises us to cheat (501).

If you would have a woman do one thing, you must always propose another. The sex! the very sex! . . . they lay a man under a necessity to deal doubly with them! [II,101] . . . Do not the poets of two thousand years and upwards tell us that Jupiter laughs at the perjuries of lovers? (III,145).

Toward the end of the novel, just prior to his great satiric vision of the female world as a new vanity fair, Lovelace consoles himself with the notion that in his dealings with Clarissa he was at least consistent and conscientious within the framework of "a libertine's creed": "after all, what have I done more than prosecute the maxims by which thou and I and every rake are governed" (III,316). Even Belford, at least early in the novel, saw women (with the exception of Clarissa) as fair game for libertines, "Neither are gratitude and honour motives to be mentioned in a woman's favour to men such as we are, who consider all those of the sex as fair prize over whom we can obtain a power" (II,158). Later Belford tries feebly to console Clarissa and rescue Lovelace in her estimation as an ingenuous man if not an honorable one by appealing once again to the socially sanctioned, if deplorable, creed of libertinism: "the *premeditated* design he seems to have had, not against you, *as* you; but as against the *sex*; over whom . . . it is the villainous aim of all libertines to triumph" (IV,77). For Lovelace, the Sex is essentially a race apart, almost a different species from man, a subordinate one which does not even possess a soul:

> We have held that women have no souls. I am a very Jew in this point, and willing to believe they have not. And if so, to whom shall I be accountable for what I do to them? Nay, if souls they have, as there is no sex in ethereals, nor *need* of any, what plea can a lady hold of injuries done her in her lady-*state* when there is an end of her lady-*ship*? (II,474).

"A bird is all soul," but women have none.[15] Late in the novel, after the rape, he tries to palliate his aunts with, "Forgive me, ladies, for saying that till I knew *her*, I questioned a soul in a sex, created, as I was willing to suppose, only for temporary purposes" (III,407). Even the name "woman" is too vulgar to apply to "this very fine creature": "my conscience would not let me call her a *woman*; nor use to her so vulgar a phrase" (III,127). (In this, Lovelace recalls Mother Creswell in Chapter 8.) But Clarissa, "charming creature" with a soul though she may be, is still a woman, and all women are basically the same: "the most charming woman on earth, were she an empress, can excel the meanest in the customary visibles only. Such is the equality of the dispensation, to the prince and the peasant, in this prime gift, WOMAN" (II,142).[16]

No one would dispute that the English eighteenth century was an age of virulent prejudice and xenophobia, and the prejudices about women—in spite of England's reputation as "a Paradise for wives"—were as deep-seated and as vivid as those about the French, the Dutch, or the Italians. Lovelace mirrors and focuses the libertine view, and we must do him the courtesy of taking him at his word. Following is a selection of his all inclusive maxims on the Sex, concluding with his picture of the ideal wife. All the observations, despite their lighthearted charm, humor, and wit (and here Lovelace is at times a Pope in prose), depict women as creatures of mischief, excess, vanity, and irrational predictability:

> These women, Jack, have been the occasion of all manner of mischief from the beginning! . . . at that moment I cast my eye full on my ewe lamb (II,221).

> Then for the sex's curiosity, it is but remembering, in order to guard against it, that the name of their common mother was Eve (II,21).

> Women, Jack, tacitly acknowledge the inferiority of their sex, in the pride they take to behold a kneeling lover at their feet (III,74).

> Like so many musical instruments, touch but a single wire, and the dear souls are sensible all over (III,63).

> Nor are women ever angry at bottom for being disobeyed through excess of love. They like an uncontrollable passion. They like to have every favour ravished from them; and to be eaten and drunk quite up by a voracious lover. Don't I know the sex? (II,209).

> How greedily do the sex swallow praise! (II,21).

> [The women] seemed pleased with my ardour. Women, whether wives, maids, or widows, love ardours (III,49).

> They love to have their sex, and its favours, appear of importance to us (III,60).

> Jealousy of itself, to female minds, accounts for a thousand un-accountablenesses (III,52).

> All women are cowards at bottom: only violent where they *may* (III,304).

> The sex love us mettled fellows at their hearts (III,83).

Women often, for their own sakes, will keep the *last secret* (III,131).

Yet, sweet dears, half the female world ready to run away with a rake, *because* he is a rake; and for no *other* reason (II,472).

But the whole sex love plotting—and plotters too, Jack (III,68).

Women, Jack. . .have a high opinion of what they can do for us (III,133).

What *once* a woman hopes, in love matters, she *always* hopes, while there is room for hope (III,510).

Even Belford is not immune from these formulations: "The women followed her in. 'Tis a strange sex! Nothing is too shocking for them to look upon, or see acted, that has but novelty and curiosity in it" (IV,256).

In the few times when Lovelace allows himself to think seriously about the state of shackles, his fantasy of the ideal wife embodies, not surprisingly, the image of the perfect sensual servant and concubine to whom he stands as a god:

> I cannot bear this. I would have the woman whom I honour with my name, if ever I confer this honour upon any, forego even her *superior duties* for me. I would have her look after me when I go out, as far as she can see me, as my Rosebud after her Johnny; and meet me at my return with rapture. I would be the subject of her dreams, as well as of her waking thoughts. I would have her think every moment lost, that is not passed with me: sing to me, read to me, play to me when I pleased; no joy so great as in obeying me. When I should be inclined to love, overwhelm me with it; when to be serious or solitary, if apprehensive of intrusion, retiring at a nod; approaching me only if I smiled encouragement: steal into my presence with silence; out of it, if not noticed, on tiptoe. Be a *lady easy* to all my pleasures, and valuing those most who most contributed to them; only sighing in private, that it was not *herself* at the time. Thus of old did the contending wives of the honest patriarchs; each recommending her handmaid to her lord, as she thought it would oblige him, and looking upon the genial product as her own.
>
> The gentle Waller says, *Women are born to be controlled.* Gentle as he was, he knew that. A tyrant husband makes a dutiful wife. And why do the sex love rakes, but because they know how to direct their uncertain wills, and manage them? (II,416).

26. Lovelace and Richardson

Lovelace's urge to generalize about the behavior of women is also reflected in the observations of his own creator, whose opinions, as revealed in Richardson's letters, are worth noting at this point. Extreme caution is required here because the opinion of the man and the representation of the artist are at times two different things, and more particularly, Richardson is writing to his correspondents (most of whom are female) after having created Lovelace. Because he enjoys at times playing the advocate for his own attractive devil, one never knows to what rhetorical extent he is playing with and off the attitudes of his creature for the benefit of his individual correspondent. Still, there is an uneasy similarity between Richardson's opinions about women and Lovelace's.[17] We proceed chronologically. Richardson informs Aaron Hill, without irony, that "All Women flatter themselves, that even the Man whom they know to have been base to *others*, will not, cannot, be so to *them*; and this from Vanity, as well as good Opinion of the Man they prefer."[18] In his most humorously combative and ironic vein (that is, when he sounds most like Lovelace), Richardson expounds his views to his favorite correspondent, Lady Bradshaigh, "the daughter of [his] mind":

> But, such is the nature of woman, if she be not a vixen indeed, that if the man sets out right with her; if he lets her early know that he is her lord, and that she is but his vassal; and that he has a stronger sense of his prerogative than of her merit and beauty; she will succumb: and, after a few struggles, a few tears, will make him a more humble, a more passive wife, for his insolent bravery, and high opinion of himself.[19]

This is not mere banter, for he then proceeds to echo not only Lovelace but the odious Solmes:

> I am sorry to say it, but I have too often observed, that fear, as well as love, is necessary, on the lady's part, to make wedlock happy; and it will generally do it, if the man sets out with asserting his power and her dependence. And now will your Ladyship rise upon me! I expect it. And yet you have yourself allowed the case to be thus, with regard to this husband and his wife.
>
> The struggle would be only at first: and if a man would be obstinate, a woman would be convinced, or seem to be so, and very possibly think the man more a man for his tyranny, and value herself when he condescended to praise, or smile upon her.[20]

Richardson was not averse to discussing, with Lady Bradshaigh, his own marriage, and Mrs. Richardson, in his eyes, emerges as a forerunner of Mrs. Shandy:

> I have as good a wife as man need to wish for. I believe your Ladyship thinks so.—Yet—shall I say, O Madam! women love not King Logs!—The dear creature, without intending contradiction, is a mistress of it. She is so good as to think me, among men, a tolerably sensible one; but that is only in general; for, if we come to particulars, she will always put me right, by the superiority of her own understanding. But I am even with her very often. And how, do you ask, Madam? why, by giving up my will to her's; and then the honest soul is puzzled what (in a doubtful case) to resolve upon. And, in mere pity to her puzzlings, I have let her know my wishes; and then, at once, she resolves, by doing the very contrary to what she thinks them to be.[21]

When he next goes on to give a fairly conventional account of the differences between the two sexes, his comments on women have an uncanny similarity in diction to Lovelace's final satiric view of the female vanity fair:

> Tell me sincerely, which do you think, upon the whole, men or women, have the greatest trials of patience, and which bears them the best? You mean, you say, from one sex to the other only?—What a question is here. Which? why women, to be sure. Man is an animal that must bustle in the world, go abroad, converse, fight battles, encounter other dangers of seas, winds, and I know not what, in order to protect, provide for, maintain, in ease and plenty, women. Bravery, anger, fierceness, occasionally, are made familiar to them. They buffet, and are buffeted by the world; are impatient and uncontrolable. They talk of honour, and run their heads against stone walls, to make good their pretensions to it; and often quarrel with one another, and fight duels, upon any other silly thing that happens to raise their choler; with their shadows, if you please.
>
> While women are meek, passive, good creatures, who, used to stay at home, set their maids at work, and, formerly themselves—get their houses in order, to receive, comfort, oblige, give joy to, their fierce, fighting, bustling, active protectors, providers, maintainers—divert him with pretty pug's tricks, tell him soft tales of love, and of who and who's together, and what has been done in his absence—bring to him little master, so like his own dear papa, and little pretty miss, a soft, sweet, smiling soul, with her sampler in her hand, so like what her meek mamma was at her years! And with these differences in education,

nature, employments, your Ladyship asks, whether the man or the
woman bears more from each other? Has the more patience? Dearest
lady! how can you be so severe upon your own sex, yet seem to persuade
yourself that you are defending them?[22]

Lovelace's comments on patriarchal marriage may be compared with the
following:

Polygamy is a doctrine that I am very far from countenancing; but
yet, in an argumentative way, I do say, that the law of nature, and the
first command (increase and multiply), more than allow of it; and the law
of God no where forbids it. Throughout the Old Testament, we find it
constantly practised. Enough, however, of this subject; though a great
deal more might be said . . . .

Bone of our bone, and flesh of our flesh—Why truly, so women
are—But, as the best things, corrupted, become the worst, your Ladyship would have a difficulty, if put to it, to prove, that the offspring
cannot be worse, when bad, than the parent.[23]

To Sarah Chapone he argues further for the subordination of woman to man:

It is certain that the Woman's Subordination was laid upon her as a
Punishment. And why?—*Because Adam was not deceived*, says the
Apostle; *but the Woman being deceived, was in the Transgression*. . . .

But . . . you say, 'How comes it to pass, *then*, that it should be
thought improper for a woman at *any Age* to be independent?' I have
enumerated upwards of Twenty Reasons to Miss Mulso, why Women,
for their *own* Sakes, shou'd not wish to be so. Subordination, Madam, is
not a Punishment but to perverse or arrogant Spirits. This Part of the
Curse was not, to [such] better spirits a very heavy one; the other part of
it [the curse], *In Sorrow shalt thou bring forth Children*, was much
more heavy. Clarissa says, 'Condescension is not Meanness. There is a
Glory in yielding that hardly any violent Spirit can judge of.' And I am
not convinced, 'that it is *not* for the Ease and Advantage of the Governed
to submit.'[24]

And finally, in this brief survey, let us consider Richardson's last general
observation (at the age of sixty-five) on women and "the two Sexes," with a
final tribute to the wise grandmother, Mrs. Shirley, in *Grandison*:

Indeed, my good Lady B, one too generally finds, in the Writings of
even ingenious men, that they take up their Characters of Women too
easily, and either on general opinions, or particular acquaintances.

Shakespeare knew them best of all our writers, in my humble opinion.
He knew them better than they knew themselves; for, pardon me for
saying, that we must not always go to women for *general* knowlege of the
Sex. Ask me now with disdain, my dear Lady B, if *I* pretend to know
them? No, I say—I only guess at them: And yet I think them not such
mysteries as some suppose. A tolerable knowlege of men will lead us to a
tolerable knowlege of women. *Mrs. Shirley* has said well, where she says
that the two Sexes are too much considered as different species. He or
she who aims to understand nature, and soars not above Simplicity, is
most likely to understand the human heart best in either Sex; especially
if he can make allowance for different modes of education, constitution,
and situation. . . . [25]

What seems clear in all these opinions is that despite his hatred of his
villain's actions toward Clarissa, there is much of Richardson's own wisdom
about women underlying his creature's expressed attitudes. It should be
stressed that though the author of *Clarissa* was by no means a modern
feminist, he genuinely loved the company of women and often put himself in
the role of women. He thought that women were the "better part of creation," but their own worst enemies, often obscuring their own genius and
goodness. Drawing upon the traditional representation of women's capacity
for heroism expressed through suffering, he was above all intent on creating
in Clarissa a female character who, though subject to mortal frailties, becomes a more heroic figure in her suffering martyrdom than the male heroes
of epic. In his old age, Richardson seems to reject Lovelace and adopts the
position of his own wise creature, grandmother Shirley, a transcendence of
the view of man and woman as perennially locked into sexual combat and the
struggle for dominance, and a view which seems to be shared, as we shall
see, with Sterne's Tristram.

27. Clarissa as Subject

Let us turn again to Lovelace and his remarkable collocations of what women mean to him: "My predominant passion is *girl*, not *gold* [II,20] . . . All my vice is women, and the love of plots and intrigues" (IV,36). Within that larger "passion" is the ultimate individual subject, "the divine Clarissa Harlowe." In his very first letter he explains to Belford, in a passage which may tell us something about Richardson the inventor of Pamela and Clarissa as well as about Lovelace the "goddess-maker," how he came to have his present notions about love. "What was it," he asks (and the meaning of "it" here, like the meaning of Bottom's dream, is not at all clear):

> egad, Jack, I can hardly tell what it was—but a vehement aspiration after a novelty, I think—those confounded poets, with their serenely-celestial descriptions, did as much with me as the lady: they fired my imagination, and set me upon a desire to become a goddess-maker . . . I must create beauty, and place it where nobody else could find it: and many a time have I been at a loss of a *subject*, when my new-created goddess has been kinder than it was proper for my plaintive sonnet that she should be (I,145-46).

For Lovelace, the meaning of "*girl*," "woman," "the Sex," obviously goes beyond sex, beyond love, beyond "plots and intrigues," beyond even his expertise as a natural philosopher of women. From the beginning of his pursuit of the Sex he was fired by "those confounded poets," most notably Ovid and his progeny of the English Renaissance and Restoration. Lovelace fancies himself as a poet of sexual intrigue who has at last found his true love, a divine novelty, "the inexhaustible subject" (II,491): "Indeed, I never had a more illustrious subject to exercise my pen upon" (I,510). The simple question, "What does Lovelace want of Clarissa?", is not easy to answer. We might start by saying, simply enough, that he wants to make her his own. When he gets her in his power, he will put the whole sex on trial in testing her virtue by her own judgment and his principles (II,37). His principal view is to "awaken the *woman* in her," to have her without marriage (II,42; cf. III,200). As his fantasy of the ideal wife indicates, he seems to want to make this beautiful, proud, intelligent, highly verbal young woman over into a dependent, willing, humbled exponent of all the "arts of pleasing" a man which were discussed in Chapter 8 as the attributes of the accomplished whore. Lovelace wants to reinvent Clarissa as his own love goddess and at the same time take his revenge on her family and on the Sex. And no matter what he does to her, or with her (short of taking her life), there is always the last act of marriage which would wipe all his sins away.

But Clarissa is first and foremost Lovelace's subject in almost every dependent sense of the noun given in the *OED*. She is bound to him, in his view, as a subordinate is to a superior, as a thing over which a right is exercised, as a piece of property; as the subject matter of an art or science; as a thing affording matter for action: a ground, motive, or cause, as that which may be acted or operated upon; as one who is subject to something injurious; as a person who undergoes medical or surgical treatment; as a person upon whom an experiment is made; as that which forms the matter of thought, or inquiry; a topic, theme; as an object of study for pedagogic purposes; as the theme of a literary composition; as an object, or figure chosen by an artist for representation. Lovelace defines Clarissa's (and woman's) subjective status this way: "She never was in a state of *independency*; nor is it fit a woman should, of any age, or in any state of life" (III,24).

Now Clarissa is also Richardson's great subject, and the author and his marvelously autonomous alter ego, the Ovidian Lovelace, carry on a kind of literary rivalry in their mutual rendering of their goddess. Much of the interest of the novel stems from the tension generated by these two discrepant yet supplementary visions of the heroine. It would seem that Richardson, imitating the conventional Christian paradigm of God permitting the devil's widest scope of activity, will allow Lovelace as much autonomy as his English master of the epic form, Milton, allows his Satan, believing, again conventionally, that the forces of evil will ultimately destroy themselves. Richardson the artist sees a different Clarissa from the one Lovelace sees, yet Richardson accomodates and goes beyond Lovelace's vision. With great care, Richardson delineates his heroine through her own letters and through Nancy's long before he allows Lovelace to "exercise [his] pen" upon her.

For Richardson then, in contrast to Lovelace, Clarissa starts out as a modern Eve without an Adam. She lives her first eighteen years in what for her is a virtual paradise. Clarissa herself, after the abduction, draws the parallel: "But here, sir, like the first pair (I, at least, driven out of my paradise), are we recriminating?" (I,502). Clarissa carefully tends the garden of Harlowe Place, and she herself is at home within an ordered and harmonious natural world. She keeps bantams and pheasants; she knows the ways of the dairy maid with her own Dairyhouse estate; she is an expert at "domestic management" (IV,506). She has a summer house, her own special creative bower like Eve's "nuptial Bower" (adorned with the handiwork of the feminine artist in tune with a feminine Nature). Richardson the editor describes the house:

> The *ivy summer-house* (or *ivy bower*, as it was sometimes called in the family) was a place, that from a girl, this young lady delighted in. She used, in the summer months, frequently to sit and work, and read and

write and draw and (when permitted) to breakfast, and dine, and sometimes to sup in it; especially when Miss Howe, who had an equal liking
to it, was her visitor guest.

She describes it in another letter (which appears not) as pointing to a
pretty variegated landscape of wood, water, and hilly country; which had
pleased her so much, that she had drawn it; the piece hanging up in her
parlour among some of her other drawings (I,445n).

Clarissa shares this private place with the one love of her life, Nancy Howe.
Hence Clarissa's paradise before her fall is essentially one of feminine
harmony independent of masculine influence or encroachment. Richardson
stresses the naturalness of Clarissa in her private garden world. Aaron Hill
first recognized this in his picture of his friend as a gardener tending a
splendid natural creation:

I send you back Letters XI. and XXI. of your still growing, as well as
lengthening, beauty. She is infinitely pleasing, and so sweetly natural in
her movement, that you could not make her seem too tall, though you
should stretch her out to as much vastness as the fame of Virgil . . . it is
in the first stages (if at all) that you must look for lopping-places. All your
after-growths are sacred, to the smallest twig; and can admit no cutting,
without downright violation.[26]

After establishing this sense of Clarissa's naturalness, her superior moral
qualities and *inner* worth, and her quiet, creative feminine space independent from the masculine world (though sustained, until her confinement, by her father's largesse and good opinion, never forgetting what she
owes him for this)—and showing in overwhelming detail how her freedom is
threatened by the rapacious Harlowes—Richardson finally allows Lovelace,
after the abduction, to describe her person, her *outward* image. It can be
said that Richardson the artist, all through the novel, is more concerned with
representing (through the letters of Clarissa, Anna Howe, and Belford) the
inner beauty and moral qualities of the person Clarissa, while Lovelace the
artist is more concerned with her outward beauty of person and gesture.
Thus Lovelace continues the evocation of the natural Miltonic Eve by noting
Clarissa's "native elegance" and the "wantoning . . . wavy ringlets of her
shining hair" (I,511), while at the same time recalling the Elizabethan love
poets and the heterodox Christian-humanist tradition, going back to Cornelius Agrippa, of "the Excellence and Preheminence" of women over men:
Clarissa flashes upon Lovelace "all at once in a flood of of brightness"; "I
never in my life beheld a skin so *illustriously* fair"; "this lady is all glowing,
all charming flesh and blood; yet so clear that every meandering vein is to be
seen in all the lovely parts of her which custom permits to be visible" (I,511).

Agrippa, and his English disciple William Austin, stress too the brightness of women: the female was made "best" in "glory"; "In [her] the fulness of the earth resides, Nay Heavens brightness in her face abides";[27] "Her Breasts . . . seem two sphears of Snow, or swelling Mountainets of Delight; long Arms, little Hands, [are] interwoven with a curious Labyrinth of Azure Veins";[28] "God not only made her body an *epitome* of the *Earth*, for proportion, but her face as an *epitome* of *Heaven* for beauty: which like some cleare glass (or *mirror*) being turned upwards toward heaven, presents it selfe wholly full of heavenly figures."[29] Lovelace notes "the fire of [Clarissa's] starry eyes," and the "sky-blue" ribbon in her headdress. She epitomizes the earth for him with "the charming umbrage" of her "pale primrose-coloured paduasoy, the cuffs and robings curiously embroidered by the fingers of this ever-charming Arachne, in a running pattern of violets and their leaves."[30] He dwells on the precious moment of her nearness to him: "How near, how sweetly near, the throbbing partners!" (I,512). Richardson allows his eloquent villain to express and pervert all this beauty to his own pagan vision, for the description edges over into an Ovidian evocation of rape and terror reminiscent of the Apollo-Daphne story.[31]

In Ovid's account, Daphne is a true daughter of nature enjoying the recesses of the woods and, as a rival of the virgin Phoebe, averse to love and to all the suitors urged on her by her father. Phoebus, the victim of Cupid, is consumed with love for her: "He marvels at her fingers, hands, and wrists, and her arms, bare to the shoulder, and what is hid he deems still lovelier." The maiden Daphne is "even in her desertion seeming fair . . . a light air flung her locks streaming behind her. Her beauty was enhanced by flight."[32] The last sentence is the quintessential Ovidian touch, and one of Lovelace's favorite views of Clarissa is her beauty enhanced by fear. Indeed, as we shall see later, his appreciation of her is always enhanced by her distress. He too marvels at the hair, dress, fingers and hands of his beloved, and he admires the Daphne-like "high health and vigor" Clarissa enjoys, for "she loves to use herself hardily" in her outdoor pursuits. Ovid's Apollo and Richardson's Lovelace are both hastened on "the wings of love," both compare their loves to "Lambs" and "Doves," both pursue them through a wilderness, and both lose them at last, the physical attractiveness of Daphne and Clarissa rapidly "changed and destroyed," yet transformed into a new kind of beauty.

Richardson and Lovelace play Christian and pagan allusions (Eve, Daphne, Arachne) off against their individual "Clarissas," allusions which figure forth her wandering destiny (her error), a motif reinforced by Lovelace's wavy, meandering, running images of hair, body, and dress. Eve and Arachne both exhibit an overweening pride in their own unique accomplishments, an error which Clarissa comes to see as the fatal impulse of her own downfall. But it would be simplistic to say that Clarissa has a tragic flaw. The legacy of indecision from her mother is intertwined with her credulity and her pride in her own good nature and right judgment, and these short-comings work against her finding worldly happiness. Lovelace's fascination with the running quality of Clarissa's dress and demeanor reflects a similar impulse in him, but his is the impulsive, persevering, ever forward-moving passion of the "seduction progress":

> Such a passion as this keeps love in a continual fervour; makes it all alive (II,187).

> More truly delightful to me the seduction progress than the crowning act: for that's a vapour, a bubble! (II,337).

Lovelace's first great verbal portrait of Clarissa's person (a term which we shall return to) is also a picture of his own passion for intrigue. We can see even at this early stage that he is more in love with this "all alive" state of his being than he is with Clarissa the woman, and in this respect he bears a noteworthy parallel to Moll Flanders' experience. She too (until she settles down with Jemy) is more in love with intrigue, sexual or criminal, than with the objects of the intrigue, men or money. Both Lovelace and Moll are thieves of the intangible, he of a woman's honor, she of time and "Fame." Lovelace looks at Clarissa and sees a beautiful labyrinth of unexplored possibilities, "ever charming," ever-in-motion, the inspiration for a well-laid plot. He puts it all quite succinctly much later in the novel:

> The charming *roundabouts*; to come the *nearest way home*; the doubts; the apprehensions; the heartachings, the meditated triumphs—these are the joys that make the blessing dear. For all the rest, what is it? What but to find an angel in imagination dwindled down to a woman in fact? (III,248).

It is the "woman in fact," the day-to-day person, whom Lovelace cannot abide. He must have passion, and the passion which sustains and impels his progress of intrigue is what Lovelace calls love. The secular religion of libertinism has its perversion of I Corinthians 13 by way of the art of courtly love:

> *Yet the woman who resents not initiatory freedoms must be lost.* For love is an encroacher. Love never goes backward. Love is always aspir-ing. Always *must* aspire. Nothing but the highest act of love can satisfy an indulged love (II,475).

Love, "when once got deep into the heart," is self-propagating. It is autono-mous, relentless, persevering, vengeful—it makes its own laws.

28. "Credulity" and "a strange Fatality"

> Wish me good speed,
> For I am going into a wilderness
> Where I shall find nor path nor friendly clue
> To be my guide.
>
> *The Duchess of Malfi*, I.ii.

Belford says that Lovelace is "a man who has no regard to his word or oath
to the sex" (II,159), and Lovelace himself believes that "*CREDULITY* is the
god of love's *prime minister*; and they never are asunder" (II,65). Hence
Lovelace's language to women is pure fiction. He will treat them as characters in his own fiction, or as readers of his fiction. He may have as many keys
as he will to the Harlowe's garden door, but credulity is Lovelace's real key
with Clarissa. In the first major rape episode in the novel, his abduction of
Clarissa from her garden world which has now become a prison ("a rape
worthy of a Jupiter!" [I,175]), Lovelace can count on her unsuspecting nature
(linked to her obligingness), a characteristic of almost all "good" characters in
eighteenth-century fiction. But although Clarissa is not simply a naive girl,
no one—not even a nineteen-year-old country girl with the suspicious
imagination of a Pamela—would have anticipated the comprehensive "plot-
proof" intricacy of Lovelace's overall stratagem. Therefore, the question of
Clarissa's credulity is a difficult one. Johnson's familiar maxim, "there is
always something which she prefers to the truth," is telling but too harsh. In
another of those significant "editor's" footnotes, Richardson quotes from a
letter of Clarissa's ("not inserted") describing the haunted coppice just
beyond the garden door, the place where Clarissa and Lovelace have their
interview and from which he tricks her, with Leman's help, into running off
with him. The place stands in dismal counterpoise to the "*ivy summerhouse*,"

> a spot where a man having been found hanging some years ago, it was
> used to be thought of by us when children, and by the maidservants,
> with a degree of terror (it being actually the habitation of owls, ravens,
> and other ominous birds) as haunted by ghosts, goblins, spectres. The
> genuine result of country loneliness and ignorance; notions which, early
> propagated, are apt to leave impressions even upon minds grown strong
> enough at the same time to despise the like credulous follies in others
> (I,446-47).

Obviously this coppice haunted Clarissa's consciousness, and she reveals
that the superstitious impression, a credulous folly, took hold of even her
strong mind. Hence Clarissa, though far more sophisticated and learned

than Pamela, her predecessor from the country, shares with her certain country notions.

A deeper indication of Clarissa's sense of the inexplicable concerns the awareness of her own destiny.[33] We have noted before, in trying to assess the full implications of her suffering, her strong belief that she is being singled out for her own faults or those of her family "to be a very unhappy creature (I,419). Earlier she had lamented:

> Oh, my dear! how wise have I endeavoured to be! how anxious to choose and to avoid everything, *precautiously*, as I may say, that might make me happy or unhappy; yet all my wisdom now, by a strange fatality, likely to become foolishness! (I,291).

> Something is working against me, I doubt. What an uneasy state is suspense! When a naked sword, too, seems hanging over one's head! (I,292).

And nearer to the fatal appointment with Lovelace, the assertion:

> And is there, after all, no way to escape one great evil, but by plunging myself into another? What an ill-fated creature am I? Pray for me . . . My mind is at present so much disturbed, that I hardly can pray for myself (I,424).

Clarissa, like the characters in the first act of *Macbeth*, is taken with the word "strange" to describe her plight. "A strange fatality" is altering her life; she and her family are "in a strange situation"; she has "strange forebodings":

> such a strange situation as we are in. *Strange* I may well call it; for don't you see, my dear, that we seem all to be *impelled*, as it were, by a perverse fate which none of us is able to resist? And yet all arising (with a strong appearance of self-punishment) from ourselves? Do not my parents see the hopeful children, from whom they expected a perpetuity of worldly happiness to their branching family, now grown up to answer the *till* now distant hope, setting their angry faces against each other, pulling up by the roots, as I may say, that hope which was ready to be carried into a probable certainty? (I,419).

The natural garden images associated with Clarissa also incorporate her entire family in that recognition of a strange, perverse, but wholly inevitable, natural, fate. Her word for Lovelace is "strange" ("A strange diligence in this man!" [I,446]), while his for her is "charming." Both words are highly charged, preternatural, fateful. The discussion in Chapters 2 and 10 stressed the linguistic, binding nature of fate—fate as the power of the word. Clarissa and Lovelace, by their repetitive, almost incantatory use of these words for each other, seem to be actively shaping each other's destiny through language; in a complex extension of the mutual authoring and ensnarement enacted between Pamela and B., they are naming, forming, recreating each other—*for* each other—through the powerful medium of their superb literary imaginations.

Nancy Howe had recognized "the perverse fate" long before, as we have noticed, and she pointed out further that "love takes the deepest root in the steadiest minds? The deuce take his sly penetration . . . " (I,46). Lovelace also tells us that love is "like some self-propagating plants or roots which have taken strong hold in the earth" (III,411). Clarissa attempts to articulate what it feels like to be impelled by a perverse fate—it is "working against her," she is being plunged into new evils—a fate arising out of the characters themselves, which tears up the "roots" of their own "branching" posterity. She is not aware that Lovelace, through his ineradicable diligence in love and his secret influence in the family—like a hidden nemesis—nourishes the Harlowes' natural propensity for tearing up their own roots and hopes. It is almost as if Clarissa is being punished for the sins of the Harlowes. Clarissa's sense of being impelled by something resistless and self-punishing has clear affinities with Lovelace's own account of the relentless and vengeful nature of the love that drives him. Throughout the novel, there seems to be a correlation between love and fate as deep, inexorable, driving forces within the experience of both Lovelace and Clarissa growing from an impulse to shape their experience in words. Lovelace's "love" becomes Clarissa's "perverse fate." A mysterious literary alchemy works between them: "a strange diligence" in this man and an intense preoccupation with her own fate help to shape Clarissa's "strange situation," but she does not know this, only feels it. Clarissa has an enormous apprehensive anxiety for sensing the pressure of events thickening around her now that Lovelace is her fate.

When he has gotten her to London, that great hiding-place and emblem of the world, he exults: "Am I *already* lord of the destiny of a Clarissa Harlowe?" (II,33). Clarissa now sees fate in two ways: as a violent impelling force ("I, who had, by a perverse fate, been thrown into his company" [II,26]) and as her lot (that word of foreboding used by Aunt Hervey [II,164]), the unique portion of life which was given to her alone and which was intimately bound to Lovelace:

> I find I must be *his*, whether I will or not. . . . the man who has drawn me into all this evil I must be thrown upon! . . . . *my fate too visibly in his power.* . . . let me collect all my fortitude and endeavour to stand

those shafts of angry Providence which it will not permit me to shun!
That whatever the trials may be which I am destined to undergo, I may
not behave unworthily in them, but come out amended by them (II, 166-
68).

Immediately after this courageous look into the future gives her a strong new
sense of resolution, Clarissa is prostrated by her father's curse, a further
shock to her credulity and to her will, and an even more powerful verbal
definition of her fate than any she has yet received from Lovelace.

29. "A Father's Curse"

The abduction from the garden then is Lovelace's first great assault upon and conquest over Clarissa, but her family is not quite through with her yet. As her mother had said, "your father will take you up, where I leave you" (I,102). Perhaps the most desolating theme in all literature is the calculated destruction of an innocent person. In *Clarissa*, we are witnesses to that destruction over a long period of our time, and it is wrought not only by Lovelace and his women, but also by Clarissa's closest kin. Just as Lovelace is unquestionably relentless and persevering, so too are Arabella and James, Jr. Sister Arabella is now the bearer of news (Charlotte the mother has faded into the kind of non-being that Dickens will indelibly recreate in Mrs. Gradgrind), and if the definition of rape can be extended beyond the historical meanings of abduction or sexual assault, to include the verbal stripping and degradation of one person by another, then Arabella, in her terrible letter, rapes Clarissa with the full approbation of the rest of the family, and particularly at the fervent desire and decree of her father.

We have examined Clarissa's credulity. Rational, discriminating, and delicate as her judgment is, she nevertheless shows great sensitivity to the subjective or irrational, to stories of supernatural terror, to an impending sense of her own doom, to the metaphysical power of language and religious symbols, to the weight of a father's curse:

> O my best, my *only* friend! Now indeed is my heart broken! It has received a blow it never will recover. Think not of corresponding with a wretch who now seems absolutely devoted. How can it be otherwise, if a parent's curses have the weight I always attributed to them, and have heard so many instances in confirmation of that weight! Yes, my dear Miss Howe, superadded to all my afflictions, I have the consequences of a father's curse to struggle with! How shall I support this reflection! My past and my present situation so much authorizing my apprehensions! (II,169).

"I am in the depth of vapourish despondency. . . . this dreadful letter *has unhinged my whole frame*" (II,169, 176); the healthy Clarissa, in discussing her spare diet, once specifically compared herself to a house, noting that "a well built house required but little repairs" (IV,503). The descent of the heroine is at this point like the collapse of a house, and Clarissa fears that even her best friend is in danger from someone utterly doomed. With much subtlety, as the letter bearing the curse indicates, Richardson evokes two popular traditions, that of a woman's original name and that of a woman as a well-built house, in his chronicle of the destruction of Clarissa Harlowe. The reader is referred to William Austin's description of God's creation of woman in Chapter 6. Concerning a woman's name, Austin also notes: "it is plaine, that the ancient *Iewes*, from the beginning, gave great respect to *names* . . . . The *first* [name: woman, Isha] was the *last name* [Adam] gave to any thing before his *fall*: And the *last* [name: Eva] was the *first name*, he gave to any thing *after his fall*. So that in his *felicity his last care*, and in his *misery, his first care* was for the *woman*." The name "woman" was given with great consideration "ere he could finde so *apt a name*, and so full of *mysterie* to adorn her." Eva has two names, a mortal one, "Isha," and an immortal one, "Eva," old and new: "*Isha* shall be translated into *Eva.*"[34] Such a description of woman was part of common tradition even before Austin wrote it down and persists to this day as part of women's wisdom. Austin was not only attempting to portray the ideal good woman but also to defend women against the tide of antifeminism in his own time as Richardson, in his far more original way, was trying to do in his.

Arabella Harlowe, modeled on the wicked sister in folk tale, and from the beginning, Clarissa's spiteful antagonist, first attacks the name: "Sister that was!—For I know not what name you are *permitted* or *choose* to go by." Then follows a rendition of the father's curse on her mortal and immortal selves ("that you may meet your punishment, both *here* and *hereafter*, by means of the very wretch in whom you have chosen to place your wicked confidence"), as if he were blotting out her mortal and immortal names. Her "clothes will not be sent":

> Your drawings and your pieces are all taken down; as is also your own whole-length picture, in the Vandyke taste, from your late parlour; they are taken down and thrown into your closet, which will be nailed up, as if it were not a part of the house, there to perish together; for who can bear to see them? Yet how did they use to be shown to everybody: the former for the magnifying of your dainty finger-works; the latter for the imputed dignity (dignity now in the dust!) of your boasted figure; and this by those fond parents whom you have run away from with so *much*, and yet with so *little* contrivance! (II,170).

One of Clarissa's great joys as a child and as a young woman was drawing and painting, as we have noted, in her summerhouse or ivy bower, her creative place, her retreat. She was mirrored in her father's house by beautiful and expensive portraits. Her pictures, made by her and of her, her rooms ("late" parlor and closet), her extensions, her spaces, her images, belonging to her and of her being, charged with sentiment, all symbolic manifestations of her—like Pamela, Clarissa is more in love with the symbolic than the actual—all of these are now "nailed up" in a resounding crucifixion, banished, left to perish. With an exulting sneer, Arabella intensifies the sense of sexual assault by degrading to "the dust" her envied sister's "boasted figure." Clarissa's being in the Harlowe family is erased, name, image, memory: "My brother vows revenge upon your libertine—for the family's sake he vows it; not for yours! For he will treat you, he declares, like a common creature, if ever he sees you; and doubts not that this will be your fate." "My brother," no longer Clarissa's, will not recognize her. She is faceless (defaced like Milton's fallen Eve), one of the common creatures, used and discarded, begging in the London streets. Clarissa's father, sister, and brother expect her to become a London whore, and in Mandeville's sense of the reproach women suffer upon the imputed loss of their chastity (described and illustrated in Chapter 9), that is precisely what happens to her. Then follows a solemn litany appropriate to this rite of family ex-communication:

> My Uncle Harlowe renounces you for ever.
> So does my Uncle Antony.
> So does my Aunt Hervey.
> So do I, base unworthy creature! the disgrace of a good family, and the
> property of an infamous rake, as questionless you will soon find yourself,
> if you are not already.

And a final brutal reminder of how her two mothers, the natural one and the spiritual one, have cut themselves off from her in joint self-reproach, shame, and disgust: "Your worthy Norton is ashamed of you, and mingles her tears with your mother's, both reproaching themselves for their shares in you and in so fruitless an education" (II,171). Clarissa says, for the first time, after reading, absorbing, incorporating this letter, that "now indeed is [her] heart broken." This is the first mortal blow to her heart, and she is not speaking figuratively, as we shall see later. She is not able to transcribe the letter. Writing it out in her own hand would somehow authenticate it and one of her strongest desires, from here to the end of her story, is to have the curse lifted. Even more than the burden of Lovelace's physical weight during the rape and the persecuting weight and wear of his love and terror tactics, it is the weight of this paternal curse that finally severs her from life in the world: "O my dear Mrs. Norton, what a weight must a father's curse have upon a heart so apprehensive as mine!" (III,340).

30. Sinclair, "the true mother of your mind"

Having captured or kidnapped Clarissa in a rape worthy of Jupiter, the pagan Lovelace gives full rein to his Ovidian fantasies: he is Jupiter, Achilles, Tiresias. He is every role—Proteus himself, but Proteus united with the Ovidian Apollo. Apollo, like his father Jupiter, was an imaginative shapeshifter, a master of disguises (often impersonating women); driven by burning love, and ill-fated passion, he was a cunning, ruthless rapist and murderer of women; as the "eye of the world," the Sun god, he was the master of prophecy and the future, a kind of male amalgam of the Fates ("What shall be, / Or is, or ever was, in Fate, I see")[35] speaking through selected prophets and sibyls. At the center (or omphalos) of the earth, he is allied with an old Pythian prophetess, his oracle. He is the god of poets ("Mine is th' invention of the charming Lyre; / Sweet notes, and Heav'nly numbers I inspire" [396]). For Lovelace, too, "man is the woman's sun; woman is the man's earth" (II,403); he is also a poet and "goddess-maker"; his Pythia is "the old dragon," Mrs. Sinclair, his prophetic voices her harlots, his temple her house, his center London, a place which Nancy naively thinks will be advantageous to her friend: "There, as in the centre, you will be in the way of hearing from everybody and sending to anybody" (II,105), and even Clarissa desires lodgings "in the heart of it" (II,111).

Lovelace, impelled ever forward by his rapacious energy for love and intrigue, plots the future and records the past in his ever-vivid present. He lives for the present in order to anticipate and arrange the future. He is always anticipating, "encroaching," as Clarissa puts it. If he can become all things, he can direct all things. He is the consummate stage-director of life.[36] His love of intrigue fuses with his directorial ambitions, which place him in the role of a general commanding troops, but his are a troupe of actors fighting under his directives in the Ovidian wars of love. Although Lovelace is over and over again seen as the "general," he is more aptly the director general. After he engineers the "rape" of Clarissa from Harlowe Place with the aid of a cunning actor and double-agent, Joseph Leman (whose instructions from his master read like detailed stage directions), Lovelace provides more instruction for his rake friends (and colleagues) at their carefully staged first meeting with his goddess. After noting that he has "suited their parts to their capacities" (II,215), he cautions,

> And let me add, that you must attend to every minute circumstance whether you think there be a reason in it, or not. Deep, like golden ore, frequently lies my meaning, and richly worth digging for. The hint of *least* moment, as *you* may imagine it, is often pregnant with events of the *greatest*. Be implicit. Am I not your general? (II,218).

Ever so delicately, Lovelace, like a master midwife of human affairs, presumes to preside over the mystery of the "womb of fate." "I have more contrivances still in embryo" (II,413), he declares. The Apollonian director, like the Ovidian expert in love, knows the secrets of nature. He works closely with nature, cautioning his actors to "be implicit," to be natural, never to overdo it, as he refines upon Hamlet's speech to his players. Be delicate and unaffected, for Clarissa's sake. He rejoices in the simplicity of his contrivances; they are "all pure nature" (II,491). As he prepares to show Clarissa off to his four friends, we see how Lovelace's favorite roles of Jupiter, Apollo, master-general of intrigue and revenge, infinitely patient and persistent stage manager of actuality, supreme natural philosopher of women, poet and all-seeing fate, come together:

> So generous a spirit as mine is cannot enjoy its happiness without communication. If I raise not your envy and admiration both at once, but half-joy will be the joy of having such a charming fly entangled in my web. She therefore must comply. And thou must come. And then will I show thee the pride and glory of the Harlowe family, my implacable enemies; and thou shalt join with me in my triumph over them all.
>
> I know not what may still be the perverse beauty's fate: I want thee, therefore, to see and admire her while she is serene and full of hope: before her apprehensions are realized, if realized they are to be; and if evil apprehensions of me she really has: before her beamy eyes have lost their lustre: while yet her charming face is surrounded with all its virgin glories; and before the plough of disappointment has thrown up furrows of distress upon every lovely feature (II,214).

This is the furthest development of Lovelace as the objective naturalist, gloating but restrained, now in full possession of the prime subject of his career, Clarissa Harlowe, the most charming specimen of the entire female sex, preserved in the display showcase of Mrs. Sinclair's inner house for the admiration, edification, and envy of Lovelace's talented but far less accomplished colleagues in libertinism. Lovelace muses on the fate of his perverse beauty "before her apprehensions are realized," and seems to know that the "plough of disappointment"—the exact Ovidian image for his notion of the superiority of male craft to silly female passivity—will soon do its work. Clarissa is to write in her will that if Lovelace "insist upon viewing *her dead* whom he *ONCE* before saw in a manner dead, let his gay curiosity be gratified" (IV,416). What Lovelace cannot foresee is that Clarissa's hope will not be extinguished, but translated.

Lovelace then switches from naturalist to satirist to present for his friends' entertainment the image of Clarissa's opposite, "the mother," Mrs. Sinclair. Belford is later to inform Lovelace, in one of the most telling (and cutting) lines in the novel, that this woman is "the true mother of your mind" (IV,445). We are meant to be struck by the names of the two women most important to Lovelace, "Clarissa" and "Sinclair," the most bright goodness set against lurid evil. Both women are uneasy with each other. Sinclair seems to sense the extraordinary goodness of Lovelace's prize; Clarissa just senses something very much wrong with the awkward old landlady. We should visualize them as Hogarth might have represented them, figures of vivid brightness and darkness, set close to each other but separate and apart, highly particularized and charged with the dramatic moment of their first meeting. However, it is Mrs. Sinclair's relation with Lovelace, rather than with Clarissa, that I would like to stress.

We know little of Lovelace's biological mother in the novel except that she raised him without discipline: "*Why, why did my mother bring me up to bear no control?*" (IV,442). And we know nothing of his father. This reinforces our sense of Lovelace as almost self-begotten of woman, with overtones of Milton's Satan, hence all the more ready for arrogating to himself any role of god or man. Yet Lovelace comes of a powerful and respected family, and Lord M., the superannuated but good-hearted rake, full of proverbial wisdom, stands to him as a father to a son. Lovelace, who will use his respected family to his advantage, has amused satirical contempt for them all. The true family of his desires and fantasies is the adopted one of "Mother Sinclair" and her "nieces,"[37] the harlots. Sinclair of course is not her real name—it is her mother's maiden name (II,215) and thus the old procuress cannot be traced; it is a secret name, a password for General Lovelace's army ("Remember the name! *Sinclair* . . . She has no other" [II,115]). (One is reminded of Moll Flanders' powerful and secret "true Name.") Lovelace has been intimate enough with Mrs. Sinclair to know her mother's maiden name. She is Richardson's revision of Milton's Sin, gatekeeper to the house of Hell. The relationship between Lovelace and this woman is one of the most crucial in the novel because the master rake, who prides himself on his independence, has been under her tuition, and in league with her daughters, for a long time. Lovelace's fictional family of Sinclair is a kind of matriarchy of prostitution comprised of Mrs. Sinclair, her own "daughters" (her husband's "nieces," maiden gentlewomen), and her sister, a fellow bawd. Lovelace prides himself on being a "namefather," on changing the names and rearranging the titles of the women and men in his troupe of deceivers, but he chooses for his "mother" (or Richardson has him choose) a name that conveys maiden autonomy, power through the mother's line, and Sinclair's power eventually ensnares even him.

As in the case of Defoe, much of the conventional background for Richardson's depiction of his Mother Midnight in this novel is derived from such commentaries as those of Ned Ward, Tom Brown, and other social satirists who could draw upon typical and wide-ranging scriptural associations of the prostitute and her house, like the following from Proverbs 7:27, for example: "her house is the way to hell, going down to the chambers of death." If Clarissa's decline can be seen under the aspect of a country house whose beautiful rooms have been stripped and boarded up, the widow Sinclair is even more profoundly identified with her house, and both mother and house are linked with a host of infernal and underworld associations. Ned Ward and his physician friend, upon arriving at the infamous "Widows Coffeehouse," "blunder'd thro' the long dark Entry of an Ancient Fabrick, groping our way like Subteranean Labourers in the Caverns of a Colepit" until they encounter the "old Weather-beaten Cerberus herself." She seems as ancient and decrepit as her dwelling place. The house is further characterized and humanized as an "Antiquated Sodom" suffering "a trembling in the Fabrick," like an "Earthquake," which gives an "Ague to the whole House."[38] Tom Brown gives an even more detailed picture of the proprietress of his "Coffeehouse" (English "bawdy-houses are fain to go in disguise"), a "receptacle of sinners" into which he and his friend fall after amusing themselves in the "spiritual bawdy house" of a Quaker's meeting:

> We were no sooner entered, but such a ton of female fat saluted us that the very sight was an amusement. The reverend matron of the place saluted us very civilly, tho' with this very odd appearance; her face was broader than the full moon, and as shining, but it was with sweat or pomatum, no light; her grey, or rather silver, locks were covered most curiously with powder, whose straggling hairs reached almost down to her eye-brows; something of a forehead there was, but all drawn over with the footsteps of wrinkles, which the fat had driven thence, and so they looked like seams of wounds which, mingled with pock-holes made an agreeable mixture over her face. This, with those and the large scars, was incapable of being clean; so that the dirt, and sallow complexion, gave her a phiz most surprising. Her neck looked like rolls of collared pig, and her bubbies like a quagmire, ready to over-run the brink, or like a hasty-pudding o'er-looking the dish. An ell and three quarters could not measure her from side to side, and she was no longer from head to foot than from hip to hip; she was spherical like a globe; but, I must needs say, very complaisant.[39]

This is the geography of the ancient bawd; she is a world unto herself and a hideous emblem of this world, a treacherous "quagmire." She is a parody of the earth, and a parody of life. Like Mrs. Jewkes in Pamela's terrified eyes, she is a fat animated corpse.

We shall return to this exemplum of old mortality in discussing Sinclair's death, but for now Brown extends the image from Proverbs to explain to his friend that this place, the bawdyhouse, "is the picture of the very celebrated

parts of hell. The great awkward lady of this place is called a bawd, who is
generally a worn-out whore of twenty or thirty years standing, and she deals
in damnation, and so is truly a factor for the devil."[40] It was commonplace to
see the bawd as a factor or agent for the devil. Lovelace is Richardson's
version of a Miltonic Satan with a pagan-Ovidian background of cruelty and
revenge, codified into art, directed toward the subsidiary species of woman.
The bawd herself often appears as a collection of classical tags, most of which
derive from Hades, and she (like Lovelace) also has her satanic associations
with witchcraft. The following remarks about widows from a popular early
eighteenth-century "arraignment of lewd woman" brings together many of
the current suspicions about widows which provide a further contemporary
perspective on Sinclair and other "widows":

> Widows . . . are come to that Perfection in the Art of Wickedness, that
> the next Step they take, is to become incarnate Devils, for there's no
> Creature else that can come near 'em. . . . in their latter End [they] turn
> Witches, and make a Compact with the Devil: For there are more old
> Widows that turn Witches, than of any other sort whatsoever. . . . As for
> Bawds, they are the Refuge and Sink of all Human Nature; who haveing
> passed thro' all the Degrees of Wickedness with their own Bodies and
> finding they are incapable of acting any further Wickedness themselves,
> do (when they are grown old) become the Devil's Factors, and tempt
> others to do that which they are unable to perform; and thereby do what
> in 'em lies to take the Devil's Work out of his Hands, their whole
> Business being to involve others in the same Damnations with
> themselves.[41]

The bawd may be the devil's agent, but her *Practice of Piety* is always on
display (Brown's bawd "has generally *The Practice of Piety* in her window,"[42]
and Ward describes an old cobbler laying aside his work "with as much
Cheerfulness as an old Whore does *The Practice of Piety*, upon the Reception of a Visitant")[43] and the Bible is always prominently displayed "at the
corner of a long Table." (Ward's "Reverend Doctress of Debauchery" has "a
large old Bible open, with her Spectacles upon one of *St. Pauls Epistles*,"[44]
and Brown's Mother Creswell, the most famous bawd of the Restoration,
made sure, in her words, that "a church-bible always lay open upon my hall
table, and every room in my house was furnished with the *Practice of Piety*,
and other good books for the edification of my family.")[45]
    Richardson outdoes the school of Ward and Brown by having his own
vicious satirist, James Harlowe, Jr., send his lost sister only "*Drexelius on
Eternity*, the good old *Practice of Piety*, and a *Francis Spira*," when she
requests her books. "My brother's wit, I suppose. He thinks he does well to
point out death and despair to me," she muses, unaware of the full scope of

her brother's wit (II,256). It is further characteristic of Richardson's (and Lovelace's) delicacy that *The Practice of Piety* is not found in the library chosen for Clarissa in Mrs. Sinclair's house (II,194). Except for his famous picture of the death of Sinclair toward the end of the novel, Richardson does not indulge in set-pieces like those of Brown for portraying his bawd, but he obviously had them in mind for elaborating his subtle yet powerful portrait of a "bawd of figure," in Brown's phrase, "who make[s] a pretty hand of it among the ladies, and men of figure," and who can "furnish a convenient apartment for lovers to dispute in,"[46] an apt phrase for the setting of Clarissa's and Lovelace's verbal, and intensely sexual, duels.

It seems appropriate that we should be introduced to Mrs. Sinclair's house before we meet her in the flesh, so to speak. The house, ostensibly located on Dover Street but not actually there, is described by one Thomas Doleman (the name evokes a Richardsonian Charon of doom) in a letter rich in comic overtones and underlined ironies dictated to him by Lovelace. Thus the house, like the description of it, is from the beginning shrouded in layers of deception—it cannot be located precisely—and it is the clue by which Nancy Howe unravels Lovelace's whole mystery in the crucial letter which Clarissa never sees:

You may have good accommodations in Dover Street, at a widow's, the relict of an officer in the guards, who dying soon after he had purchased his commission (to which he had a good title by service, and which cost him most part of what he had), she *was obliged to let lodgings.*

This may possibly be an objection. But she is very careful, she says, that she takes no lodgers but of *figure* and *reputation.* She rents two good houses, distant from each other, only joined by a *large handsome passage.* The *inner house* is the genteelest, and and is very elegantly furnished; but you may have the use of a very handsome parlour in the *outer house* if you choose to look into the street.

A little garden belongs to the inner house, in which the old gentle-woman has displayed a true female fancy; having crammed it with vases, flower-pots, and figures without number.

As these lodgings seemed to me the most likely to please you, I was more particular in my inquiries about them. The apartments she has to let are in the inner house: they are a dining-room, two neat parlours, a withdrawing-room, two or three handsome bed-chambers—one with a pretty light closet in it, which looks into the little garden; all furnished in taste.

A *dignified clergyman,* his *wife,* and *maiden daughter*, were the last who lived in them. They have but lately quitted them on his being presented to a considerable church preferment in Ireland. The gentlewoman says that he took the lodgings but for *three months* certain;

but liked them and her *usage* so well that he continued in them *two years*; and left them with regret, though on so good an account. She bragged that this was the way of all the lodgers she ever had, who stayed with her *four times as long as they at first intended*.

I had some knowledge of the colonel, who was always looked upon as a man of honour. His relict I never saw before. I think she has a *masculine air*, and is a *little forbidding at first*; but when I saw her behaviour to two agreeable *maiden gentlewomen*, her husband's nieces, whom for that reason she calls *doubly* hers, and heard their praises of *her*, I could impute her very bulk to good humour; since we seldom see your sour peevish people plump. She lives *reputably*, and is, as I find, *aforehand* in the world (II,110).[47]

Mrs. Sinclair's house is actually two houses, an outer house and an inner one, joined by a "large handsome passage." Lovelace like a Jovian father-lover to his bright captive, chose the house carefully for Clarissa and designed the description of it to appeal to her inmost desires for privacy and her own light creative space ("I shall make good use of the light closet in my apartment , if I stay here any time" [II,192]). The inner house, its garden "crammed" with objects of a "true female fancy" reminds us of Clarissa's ivy bower, her private summerhouse where she could remove herself from the family dwelling and be alone and happy, or enjoying her friendship with Nancy. At a deeper level, the house is a paradigm of the Sex—the house as a woman—with a very respectable-looking outer structure and an inner chamber or womb, with Lovelace's presence permeating the entire inhabitation. His key strategic area, where he can monitor all activity with regard to his prize, is the "passage-way," and he is constantly moving back and forth (or "occasionally passing to and fro," as he puts it) between one house and the other in his attentions to Clarissa. The house may belong to Mrs. Sinclair but it gives scope to Lovelace's invention and acts as a facade for his maneuvers. Still, the house *is* Mrs. Sinclair's and Lovelace feels her influence: "things already appear with a very different face *now I have got her here*. Already have our mother and her daughters been about me: 'Charming lady . . . What majesty in her person! *You owe us such a lady*'" (II,189).

Mrs. Sinclair has two "maiden gentlewomen" with her, Sally Martin and Polly Horton, the two whores most active, besides Sinclair herself, in instigating the final rape of Clarissa. In the observations of Tom Brown and Ned Ward, the cartoon prototypes of Richardson's whores also come in pairs:

> Then enter two tawdry whores, brisk, gay, and awkward, with sickly, smiling countenances, slatternly dress, and dirty shoes. The familiar doxies threw themselves immediately each in one of our laps, hands about our necks, and lips to lips, before we knew where we were; But

the bawd finding we did not like the ladies, tipped the wink. . . . [48] who should bolt down Stairs from *Fools Paradise* above, but a couple of Mortal Angels as nimble as Squirrels, with Looks as Sharp, and Eyes as Piercing as a Tygers, who I suppose, after rumpling their Feathers in a hot Engagement, had staid to rectifie their disorder'd Plumes, and make ready for a fresh Encounter. [49]

Clarissa too is struck by the eyes of the women of the house. This is Dorcas, chosen to be Clarissa's servant: "what I like least of all in her, she has a strange sly eye. I never saw such an eye—half confident, I think. But, indeed, Mrs. Sinclair herself . . . has an odd winking eye" (II,193). Clarissa's innocent eyes come to predominate, however: "[Lovelace] by stealth, as it were, cast glances sometimes at them, which they returned; and on my ocular notice their eyes fell, as I may say, under my eye, as if they could not stand its examination" (II,202). This emphasis on the power of Clarissa's "eye-beams," in contrast to the rapacious or knowing or lecherous eyes of the whores, achieves a climax in her unmanning of Tomlinson. Lovelace recalls, "He told me, that just then he thought he felt a sudden flash from her eye, an *eye-beam* as he called it, dart through his shivering reins; and he could not help trembling" (III,112). Lovelace uses "reins" here in the Biblical sense of the "loins," the seat of emotion, strength, or procreative power. If Clarissa has this kind of effect on the ordinarily smooth and unflappable rogue Tomlinson, it is not surprising that even Lovelace (who confesses to having felt such flashes) must eventually resort to drugging her in order to accomplish the rape.

Although Richardson is deliberately sparing in his allusions to the actual business procedures of London prostitution and to Lovelace's working relationship with Sinclair and her women, we can discern this much: Lovelace complains several times that "these women are continually at me"; that before Clarissa became his sole pursuit, they obliged him with "the flower and first fruits of their garden" (II,190). After Polly and Sally had been conquered by Lovelace, both were eventually admitted as "quarter-partners" in Sinclair's business (IV,546). Apparently new virgins in the "garden" were given first to Lovelace. Belford is our authority on "the abandoned people in the house who keep [Lovelace] up to a resolution against [Clarissa]" (II,487). If, in his view, Mrs. Sinclair's *trade . . .* is to break the resisting spirit" (II,489), then the "free liver" and "sensualist" Lovelace, in terms of his relation to Sinclair and prostitution, might be described more accurately as a more sophisticated "bully," and breaking naive young women into the trade would be simply another facet of what it means to be a natural philosopher/libertine subduing the Sex. (We recall Pamela's fears with respect to Colbrand and Jewkes.) Thinking of how angry the women are with Clarissa's and Nancy Howe's aspersions upon them,

Lovelace muses, "I had a good mind to give Miss Howe to them in full property" (II,364), and he even goes so far as to fantasize, "What pleasure should I have in breaking such a spirit!" (II,369).

Without a sense of partnership and property in the new and flourishing enterprise of prostitution in eighteenth-century London, we are apt to miss the import of Mrs. Sinclair and the women reminding Lovelace that he *owes* them such a lady as Clarissa. If he does not marry her, they believe that Lovelace, as an active associate in their organization, is under an obligation eventually to transfer his interest in the property of Clarissa over to them for training as a new employee. Belford mourns, "O Lovelace, Lovelace, how many dreadful stories could this horrid woman tell the sex! And shall that of a Clarissa swell the guilty list?" (II,489).

Lovelace lives under the eyes of Clarissa and the whores, but when he is with the latter in London, reality wears a whore's face. His individual passion for intrigue is allied with the ruined women's passion for including the "best of her sex" in their disgrace. Lovelace the conqueror and "name-father," the perennial "first discoverer," is under the influence of his own creatures. The master of creating someone else's reality is actually controlled in mysterious ways by the women he has ruined, by their milieu, by their maxims, and by their hold on his masculine self-image.[50] He often asks how he will look in rakish annals if he does not persist with his scheme to conquer Clarissa and cohabit with her, but it is how he will look in the women's eyes that seems to be his underlying concern. Lovelace is caught in the folds of his own Pythia, and Mrs. Sinclair, in her vast reach, includes them all. As early as the Doleman letter, we have a sense of her chief physical characteristics. Like all eighteenth-century bawds, she is fat, and her "very bulk" combines both a "true female fancy" and a "masculine air." As mother, woman, and man, she is beyond gender: her daughters are numerous; she is an eminent London personage—"*aforehand* in the world."

Tom Brown's remarkable description of the London bawd has given the main outlines for Mother Sinclair, and Richardson, in the voice of Lovelace to Belford, has only to elaborate, in a much richer context, on the basic image:

> you will be ready to laugh out, as I have often much ado to forbear, at the puritanical behaviour of the mother before this lady. Not an oath, not a curse, nor the least free word, escapes her lips. She minces in her gait. She prims up her horse-mouth. Her voice, which, when she pleases, is the voice of thunder, is sunk into an humble whine. Her stiff hams, that have not been bent to a civility for ten years past, are now limbered into curtsies three-deep at every word. Her fat arms are crossed before her; and she can hardly be prevailed upon to sit in the presence of my goddess (II,214).[51]

From curses to curtsies. Brown's bawd was afflicted with rolls of fat like a "collared pig," Richardson's Sinclair has "stiff hams"; other animal associations further accentuate the widow's kinship with the witch and her familiar animals. Brown saw a "reverend matron," Lovelace sees "puritanical behaviour."

The eighteenth-century bawd is almost always presented in a religious, or pseudo-religious, light; her house is a temple, her whores are priestesses and "infernal nymphs" (II,518) from classical mythology. Throughout history prostitution has reflected the dominant religions of varying cultures, and we shall perhaps always be ignorant of the full effect of sacred prostitution on the rise of ancient religions. Richardson's bawd is the matriarch of her own demonic religion (albeit one with the trappings of Christianity), and she has the power of damnation. Mrs. Sinclair's establishment is referred to as "Mother *Damnable*'s park" (II,522)[52] by one of the men in the street after Clarissa's first escape, and everyone in Hertfordshire knew that "Squire Lovelace was a *damnation rogue*" (III,161). Mother Sinclair once almost calls Lovelace her son ("excuse me, *so*—excuse me, sir [confound the old wretch! she had like to have said *son!*]" [III,286]). In his remarkable and intricate dream of a happy ending with Clarissa, Lovelace turns into the "grave matron," "Mother H.," a famous London bawd (III,250). The point of the dream seems to be that Lovelace and Sinclair are two interchangeable sides of the same demonic phenomenon, two interchangeable halves of the same vicious circle, or serpent, feeding from and nourishing each other.

31. "Grandmother-Wisdom"

For Lovelace, this continent of iniquities named Mrs. Sinclair is both *the* mother and *his* mother; he is her "damnation rogue," and she has taught him much. One of his great female subjects is women's wisdom, that is, worldly wisdom relating to birth, sexual relations, and marriage, much of which is derived from his association with Sinclair and her ilk. Of naive girls from the country like Clarissa, Lovelace says: "nothing but *experience* can enable them to disappoint us, and teach them grandmother-wisdom!" (II,113). Lovelace has this wisdom, and more. If Mrs. Sinclair combines masculine and feminine features, her "son" follows suit. Lovelace identifies intensely with women:

> Indeed I am bashful still with regard to this lady—bashful, yet know the sex so well! But that indeed is the *reason* that I know it so well (II,55).

> I, who, as to my will, and impatience, and so forth, am of the true *lady-make*, and can as little bear control and disappointment as the best of them! (II,386).

Lovelace's fascination with women is owing in part to his apprehension of the feminine within him. His own powers of identification with the Sex increase his knowledge of women and his authority with them. But this knowledge leads to his eventual thralldom to the women below, as he himself perceives in a rare moment of confession after the rape:

> I was under the power of fascination from these accursed Circes; who, pretending to know their own sex, would have it that there is in every woman a yielding, or a weak-resisting moment to be met with: . . . if neither love nor terror should enable me to hit that lucky moment, when, by help of their cursed arts, she was *once overcome*, she would be for *ever overcome*: appealing to all my experience, to all my knowledge of the sex, for a justification of their assertion (III,318).[53]

Again the Ovidian element surfaces in Lovelace's experience of himself. He calls the women "Circes," witchlike experts on potions, because of their malign influence on him and because drugs were used to render Clarissa insensible for the final attack. Much comes to a head in this passage. First, it is the culmination of the theme of Lovelace as a libertine authority on women and women's wisdom—"grandmother wisdom"—aphorisms shared by older women, grandmothers or not, by the hearty good women who attend at lyings-in and, in a darker form, by the London midwife-bawds of Lovelace's acquaintance. We catch more than a glimpse of Lovelace's practice in dealing with women who become pregnant by him in the following concise account, written by one who is knowledgeable about animal husbandry, for Joseph Leman:

> I was ever nice in my loves. These were the rules I laid down to myself on my entrance into active life: To set the mother above want, if her friends were cruel, and if I could not get her an husband worthy of her; to shun common women—a piece of justice I owed to innocent ladies, as well as to myself; to marry off a former mistress, if possible, before I took to a new one; to maintain a lady handsomely in her lying-in; to provide for the little one, if it lived, according to the degree of its mother; to go into mourning for the mother if she died. And the promise of this was great comfort to the pretty dears as they grew near their times (II, 148).

Beyond the philosophical underpinnings of Lovelace's libertine's creed discussed in Chapter 25, the "active life" meant the mature stage of new conquests in the advancement of knowledge of the sex, focusing in his case on the sole and supreme prize, Clarissa Harlowe. Though he is on intimate, day-to-day terms with the women of Mrs. Sinclair's establishment, Lovelace does not engage their services for his own pleasure and they resent it. The social fact that they are no longer ladies makes them all the more desirous of assisting in Clarissa's downfall. The active libertine who lives by strict rules of conduct, Lovelace must provide a midwife and attendants "to maintain a lady handsomely in her lying in." Moll Flanders had one Mother Midnight; Lovelace needs many.

He displays the wisdom he has gleaned from such sources in several unobtrusive ways. At one point prior to the rape, he refers to Hickman, Nancy Howe's intended, as a "male virgin," and offers a piece of his own libertine psychology:

> Now women, Jack, like not novices. *Two maidenheads meeting together in wedlock, the first child must be a fool*, is their common aphorism. They are pleased with a love of the sex that is founded in the *knowledge of it* . . . though those ardours are generally owing more to the *devil* within him, than to the witch *without* him (III, 81-82).

In his histrionic exploits among the good women of Hampstead to retrieve the escaped Clarissa, Lovelace is understandably impressed with the reserved young Miss Rawlins who, like Richardson from a boy, is possessed of all manner of female secrets:

> Again I enjoined strict secrecy . . . which was promised by the widows
> [Mrs. Moore and Mrs. Bevis], as well for themselves as for Miss Rawlins;
> of whose taciturnity they gave me such an account, as showed me that
> she was *secret-keeper-general* to all the women of fashion at Hampstead
> . . . . What a world of mischief . . . must Miss Rawlins know! What a
> Pandora's box must her bosom be! . . . I would engage to open it
> (III, 154-155).

And yet Lovelace can tell Belford that even Miss Rawlins would be easy prey
if he were so inclined: "I'll get her for thee with a *wet finger*, as the saying
is!" (III, 92). Lovelace may be intimate with women's language but, characteristically, he also despises it, as he despises women in general:

> But as to thy opinion, and the two women's at Smith's, that her heart is
> broken; that is the true women's language: I wonder how *thou* camest
> into it: thou who hast seen and heard of so many *female deaths* and
> *revivals* (III, 471-72).

One of Lovelace's favorite justifications for his deception of Clarissa is an
appeal to the advice of the poets (Ovid and his progeny) and grandmothers of
all ages: All's fair in love and war, and men were deceivers ever. Poetic
wisdom and grandmother wisdom coincide:

> As to the manner of endeavouring to obtain her, by falsification of
> oaths, vows, and the like—do not the poets of two thousand years and
> upwards tell us that Jupiter laughs at the perjuries of lovers? And let me
> add to what I have heretofore mentioned on that head, a question or
> two.
> Do not the mothers, the aunts, the grandmothers, the governesses of
> the pretty innocents, always, from their very cradles to riper years,
> preach to them the deceitfulness of men? That they are not to regard
> their oaths, vows, promises? What a parcel of fibbers would all these
> reverend matrons be, if there were not now and then a pretty credulous
> rogue taken in for a justification of their preachments, and to serve as a
> beacon lighted up for the benefit of the rest? (III, 145).

The term "reverend matron" was of course applied by Tom Brown to his
great "ton of female fat" and was a common designation for a bawd.
    The other bit of grandmother wisdom Lovelace recalls in his confession is
one we have encountered before, in the discussion of Mrs. Jewkes, but then
in the context of birth and midwifery: just as midwives' lore held that there
was a critical moment at which the experienced midwife would know when
her charge was ready to deliver, so the bawds hold "that there is in every

woman a yielding, or a weak-resisting moment to be met with" (III,318), when she may be conquered.[54] And if Lovelace cannot hit that "lucky moment" by means of "love or terror," they will help him out with their wicked arts, that is, with potions like laudanum. Ever since Lovelace entered their house with his prize, the women have been after him, like cruel Furies, to despoil her, and thereby to make her one of them. The whole procedure is a much more intricately developed version of Mrs. Jewkes's instigation of B. Lovelace's women work on him as untiringly, as persistently, and as vehemently as he works on Clarissa. Eventually he succumbs to his own worst self, that self which is a bawd, as the transformative dream of Lovelace turning into Mother H. suggested.[55] Humbled and despised by Clarissa, his angelic superior from above (literally, in the upper chambers of her inner house), goaded and badgered by the fiendlike "women below," Lovelace's plight, a typical Richardsonian rendering of the old Christian-humanist picture of man dangling midway between the angels and the beasts, is perhaps best revealed in the following tragic soliloquy, a poignant and vain denial of the machine self he will become under the prodding of the women:

> She now seems to despise me; Miss Howe declares that she really does despise me. To be *despised by a WIFE!* What a thought is that! To be *excelled by a WIFE* too, in every part of praiseworthy knowledge! To *take lessons*, to *take instructions*, from a *WIFE! More* than despise me, she herself has taken time to consider whether she does not *hate* me: *I hate you*, Lovelace, *with my whole heart*, said she to me but yesterday! *My soul is above thee, man! Urge me not to tell thee how sincerely I think my soul above thee!* How poor indeed was I then, even in my own heart! So *visible* a superiority, to so proud a spirit as mine! And *here* from below, from *BELOW* indeed! from these *women!* I am so goaded on.
>
> Yet 'tis poor too, to think myself a machine in the hands of such wretches. I am *no* machine. Lovelace, thou art base to thyself, but to *suppose* thyself a machine (II,399-400).

32. "A person so sweetly elegant and lovely!"

Clarissa before the fire scene is closer to being happy than at any other time in Lovelace's presence, but her happiness is that of the victim of Swiftian (and Lovelacian) satire, "the possession of being well deceived." The women now think she is ready. It is the critical moment. Lovelace reflects,

> They again urge me, since it is so difficult to make *night* my friend, to an attempt in the *day* . . . and ridicule me for making it necessary for a lady to be undressed. *It was not always so with me*, poor old man! Sally told me; saucily flinging her handkerchief in my face (II,471).

Despite what the women say, however, Lovelace stresses *midnight*: "night, *mid*night, is necessary, Belford" (II,376). That is the hour of his fire stratagem, to which he now refers (the scare actually occurs at 2 a.m.), and it is the hour of the finally successful rape itself. But it is also a time of meditation, as in Milton's phrase, "Or let my lamp at midnight hour, / Be seen in some high lonely Tow'r." Clarissa loves the night, or at least she used to before Lovelace altered her life. Though intent on describing her contrivances to blind her jaileress, she seems to mean it when she says, "Sometimes solitude is of all things my wish; and the awful silence of the night, the spangled element, and the rising and setting sun, how promotive of contemplation!" (I,348). She does most of her writing at night; at night the self seems to dissolve with the outlines of all other familiar things; at night she can at least be alone. Midnight too has peculiar Christian connotations: "at midnight, there was a cry made, Behold the bridegroom cometh" (Matthew 26:6), or as Milton elaborates in a remarkable sonnet which has almost premonitory relevance to Clarissa:

> Lady that in the prime of earliest youth,
>   Wisely hast shunn'd the broad way and the green,
>   And with those few art eminently seen
>   That labor up the Hill of Heav'nly Truth,
> The better part with *Mary* and with *Ruth*
>   Chosen thou hast; and they that overween,
>   And at thy growing virtues fret their spleen,
>   No anger find in thee, but pity and truth.
> Thy care is fixt and zealously attends
>   To fill thy odorous Lamp with deeds of light,
>   And Hope that reaps not shame. Therefore be sure

Thou, when the Bridegroom with his feastful friends
    Passes to bliss at the mid-hour of night,
    Hast gain'd thy entrance, Virgin wise and pure.

Clarissa is that virgin wise and pure, or would like to be, as she would like to be one of those five virgins who were ready with filled lamps to go to the marriage feast at midnight, but she is surrounded by enemies who fret their spleen at her virtue and seek her downfall.

As he moves ever closer to Clarissa's rape, Lovelace uses tactics of increasing terror, and as a terrorist in love-intrigue, his stratagem is simply to have a fire started on the floor above in order to scare her out of her room in *deshabille*, then "take her before her apprehension, before her eloquence, is awake—" (II,499). In this design he has the full assistance of the women. He writes to Belford at 11 o'clock Wednesday night: "So near to execution my plot . . . I have time for a few lines preparative to what is to happen in an hour or two; and I love to write to the *moment*" (II,498). This is no epistolary awkwardness on Richardson's part. For Lovelace in this *moment*, the anticipation, the plotting, the writing, the taking, all coincide. Recording the event is as alive as performing it, is an integral part of performing it, is perhaps even more meaningful for him than the event itself. "My beloved's destiny or my own may depend upon the issue of the next two hours," but he worries about fear taking *him* "in a cowardly minute" (II,499). He is genuinely afraid of Clarissa's fully awakened, conscious resentment and eloquence, for her greatest power is the clarity and force of her aroused moral intelligence.

The motif of rape as an extended act including all of Lovelace's attempts leading up to and including the final one, is presented as a process of trying to take Clarissa at moments of her ever more reduced or disabled consciousness, and his conscience seems to suffer a parallel diminution of force. He tries to explain that "heroes have their fits of *fear* . . . and virtuous women, all but my Clarissa, their moment *critical*" (II,499). He is a hero like Milton's Satan who has to resort more and more to the meanest tricks of seduction to effect his aims; everything that Lovelace knows of sexual intrigue, of the lore of midwives and bawds, or of "grandmother wisdom," is distilled in that phrase, the "moment *critical.*" The whole cluster of associations bound up with the fate of Clarissa and Lovelace comes together around the moment of intended conquest, as it does around the critical moments of birth and death. And this will indeed be the critical moment in Clarissa's destiny, for after this attempt her self-deluding, beautifully devised dream (sustained both by her hopeful imagination and by Lovelace's arts) of reconciliation with her friends and of Lovelace's reformation, is shattered. She escapes from Mrs. Sinclair knowing beyond fallible intuition (and without benefit of Nancy's researches), the true nature of the house and of its women

(III,113,130). And yet she is drawn back to the house and the rape is accomplished. This is where Clarissa meets her mortal fate and transcends it. Convincing us of the plausibility of this movement backwards is one of Richardson's finest achievements in the novel. From the fire scene to the rape and its aftermath, the interplay of Lovelace's perception of Clarissa as a person, and her perception of him, is at the heart of the tragedy.

For Lovelace, Clarissa is the most brilliant example of that subspecies of the Sex known as "the fine woman":

> I think a fine woman too rich a jewel to hang about a poor man's neck (II,25).

> but then is not a fine woman the noblest trifle that ever was or could be obtained by man? (II,426).

> These women . . . [are] the greatest triflers in the creation, to fancy themselves the most important beings in it . . . thou seest how women, and women's words, fill my mind (III,104).

In this sequence of observations, all leading up to the rape, we have a clear sense of Lovelace's appraisal of woman's—even a Clarissa's—value. A fine woman is a creature primarily of great beauty of figure and appearance, of good if not noble education and breeding (III,28), who possesses an excellent taste in clothes and bodily adornment. We saw Lovelace's careful and admiring description, after the abduction, of almost every article of Clarissa's clothing, and his Ovidian appreciation of the parts thus adorned and concealed. A fine woman has great worldly value for Lovelace—she is a jewel too rich for a poor man, and yet still a trifle, though the noblest one of all, to someone of his station and admittedly unique attainments. The physical qualities of Clarissa as fine woman are manifested in—and Lovelace's choice of the article instead of the possessive is telling—"the mantled cheek, the downcast eye, the silent, yet trembling lip, and the heaving bosom, a sweet collection of heightened beauties" (II,33). Of these individual attributes, her breasts are of special attraction to him, as later when she is sullen and angry, "her lovely bosom swelling, and the more charmingly protuberant for the erectness of her mien" (II,375).[56] Lovelace has just hinted at marriage shortly after the abduction. Clarissa is in some confusion and embarrassment, and again we recall the image of her mother, in similar distress at the pleadings of her daughter. Lovelace exults at her *heightened* beauties; he loves to see her in moments of arousal, usually colored by confusion, indignation, or fear. He always sees her as a *collection* of attributes, a string or series of beauties, almost never as an individual, in terms of an actual self or being as a person.

The fire scene itself brings Lovelace's perceptions of her into detailed and vivid focus. Clarissa, after the alarm, appears to him "with nothing on but an under-petticoat, her lovely bosom half open" (II,501); then follows a detailed tableau of her "sweet discomposure" after he seizes the scissors from her, leading up to her impassioned plea, "I conjure you not to make me abhor myself! not to make me vile in my own eyes!" and his "kissing (*with passion indeed*) . . . her inimitable neck, her lips, her cheeks, her forehead, and her streaming eyes, as this assemblage of beauties offered itself at once to my ravished sight" (II,503). The "sweet collection of beauties" is now aroused and in desperate motion. It is almost as if Lovelace prefers to arouse and experiment with this kind of terrorized passion in the fine woman instead of even attempting to arouse her willing ardor. He must always have her at a disadvantage, in distress or in fear, to appreciate her separate parts and how beautifully they are assembled. Lovelace loves to see her frightened surprise: "It delights me to think how she will start and tremble when I first pop upon her" (III,21) in her Hampstead retreat, and even when she is calling out to the "Good people" in the street from Mrs. Sinclair's window, surely one of the most excruciating scenes in the novel, Lovelace admires her all the more for the beauty of her rage and terror: "I caught her in my arms and lifted her from the window. But being afraid of hurting the charming creature (charming in her very rage), she slid through my arms on the floor" (III,268). He treats her like a dangerous animal and she behaves, when the spirit leaves her, like a rag doll. Mrs. Sinclair, the valiant successor to Mrs. Jewkes, vociferates: "What ado's here about nothing! I never knew such work in my life, between a chicken of a gentleman and a tiger of a lady!" (III,268). Lovelace admits, "Oh, what additional charms, as I now reflect, did her struggles give to every feature, every limb, of a person so sweetly elegant and lovely!" (II,505).

His use of the word "person" here sums up his sense of Clarissa as a fine specimen of the Sex. In the foregoing passages from the fire scene, Clarissa the person exists for Lovelace predominantly as the "living body of a human being" with or without clothing and adornment as presented to the sight (*OED*,III,4), much as Milton's Belial exists only in his phenomenal appearances: "a fairer person lost not Heav'n." "I think, sir, ladies should not be deceived. I think a promise to a lady would be as binding as to any other person, at the least . . . I would always keep my word, sir, whether to man or woman" (III,489), so says Nancy Howe's Hickman, in simple and dignified contrast to Lovelace. Lovelace unquestionably appreciates Clarissa's intelligence, her moral acuity, her unique dignity, and ultimately, her steadiness: "How came the dear soul (clothed as it is with such a silken vesture) by all its steadiness? Was it necessary that the active gloom of such a tyrant of a *father* should commix with such a passive sweetness of a will-less *mother*, to produce a constancy, an equanimity, a steadiness, in the *daughter*, which

never woman before could boast of?" (III,151). All of these attributes—
wonderful as they appear to be—are always expressed as just that—
attributes, parts, beautiful fragments, usually enumerated in a series, and
usually highly visible in this "dear soul . . . clothed with . . . a silken
vesture." Even her intelligence is here just another visual attribute for him.
Thus he describes Nancy Howe as a "first beauty among beauties when her
sweeter friend with such an assemblage of serene gracefulness, of natural
elegance, of native sweetness, yet conscious, though not arrogant dignity,
every feature glowing with intelligence is not in company" (III,170). Clarissa
is simply a steadier, more elegant, sweet, and fine-turned version of the
"fine, strapping Bona Roba, in the Chartres taste, but well-limbed, clear-
complexioned, and Turkish-eyed; thou the first man with her . . . " (IV,444),
whom Lovelace recommends, in one of his last letters, to the bearlike
Belford.[57]

   But beyond his undoubted carnal interest in her, Lovelace is entranced
with "Clarissa" as a marvelous aesthetic process. She is his living work of art,
there for his manipulation and pleasure, and if her steadiness, that special
and unique intractability which distinguishes her from the mutable substance of all her sex, infuriates and amazes him, it also serves to incite him to
greater efforts. She becomes the beautiful reflection of his own frenzied love
of the intricate chase-progress, a game that can end only with the loss of his
quarry, his subject.[58] As this quarry, Clarissa reflects the very *raison d'être*
of the "goddess-maker." The key words for his experience of her repeated
over and over are "charms" and "charming": she is his glowing angel—magic,
preternatural, constant, eloquent, brilliant—she conjures him like a witch,
but a good witch, enthralls and maddens him—but his overriding preoccupation with her as the goddess of his own making takes him ever farther
away from Clarissa the person (as another victim of his own perceptions,
Othello, is taken away from Desdemona) and finally kills her.

33. The Rape of Clarissa: Two Views

In the middle of the fire scene, beseeching Lovelace on her knees to spare her, Clarissa pleads, "Let not my father's curse thus dreadfully operate" (II,504). The dreadful paternal curse (that she meet her punishment in this life and the next by means of Lovelace), her imaginary picture of her father on *his* knees imploring her to have Solmes, her deep sense that the curse is somehow shaping her own destiny with Lovelace, and her desire after the rape to have the second part of the curse remitted, all operate upon Clarissa until nearly the very end of her life. We saw that the original curse was a shattering blow to her: combined with her sister's vindictive letter, it threw her more deeply into Lovelace's power, made her vulnerable to his further attacks, and prepared the way for Lovelace's assaults and final, literal rape. The curse is ultimately a prophecy, an oracle whose heavy weight she must live with.

The movement of the novel from the fire scene and Clarissa's escape from Sinclair's house through her return to the house and her response to the rape encompasses the highest reach of Richardson's art. He has Lovelace narrate much of this movement in a variety of styles (as comic dramatist, master of dialogue, satirist, historian, forger of letters and marriage licenses, all intermixed with quotations from Butler, Dryden, and Milton). This narrative includes his account of her being discovered at Hampstead and lured back to Sinclair's for the rape, her delirium afterwards, her detention there as he plans another more violent assault, her overawing of him and the women in a mock trial scene, and her second escape (III,20-205,213-321). Clarissa, then, in letters to Nancy Howe, Mrs. Norton, Lady Betty Lawrence, and others, attempts to reconstruct what really happened to her from the time she was persuaded to leave Hampstead until her delirium, relating to Nancy Howe at length, and without the reader feeling the slightest sense of needless repetition, "the darker part of her story" (III,533). The prelude to the rape, and the event itself, are thus described from both Lovelace's and Clarissa's point of view.

Because her gloomy father has abandoned her, Lovelace will, after the abduction, be her father. She cannot escape him. The verbal fate meted out to her in her father's curse is continuous with the literary fate Lovelace weaves for her in his multifaceted narrative. After he finds her in Hampstead, Lovelace thinks of himself as her omnipotent sovereign, "Robert the Great," her Jupiter, a godlike prince who can assume any role necessary to complete his design: "I can suit myself to any condition, that's my comfort" (III,33). First he recapitulates her exact movements, as if to become one with the very ambiance of her flight, then he dons his disguise: a great horseman's coat buttoned over the lower part of his face, a little powder over

his hat, stirrup stockings over his legs to give him "a good gouty appearance." He could not have chosen a disguise more calculated to terrify her
when he finally does reveal himself. She sees him coming up the stairs (and
he glimpses "a little piece of her") but takes no notice of him until, attempting to pay her a compliment, his accent slips: "She started, and looked at me
with terror" (III,41). There is a confrontation of pure panic. She gives "three
violent screams" and falls into a fit.

In scenes like these, Richardson forces his heroine's unconscious fears
into horrified consciousness. At home, Clarissa feared her gout-ridden father
stumping up to her room and killing her in his rage (I,212). Lovelace has now
administered another shock in the guise of a hobbling old man, whose
sudden appearance in his true colors also reenacts that earlier surprise in the
garden of her father's house when "he threw open a horseman's coat" and
confronted her (I,176).

Lovelace's great success in eventually getting Clarissa out of Goody
Moore's rooming house is owing largely to his gift for immersing and
insinuating himself into the women's world at Hampstead—a gift strength-
ened by his knowledge of grandmother wisdom—and his skill at directing
the women in the parts he wishes them to play. The paradigm for his success
is apparent in the way he is able to win over the anonymous landlady near
the Moores': he has his servant Will tell a story about how Clarissa, "mother-
spoilt," "skittish," and headstrong, "but the finest creature that ever the sun
shone upon, had three or four times played his master such tricks" (III,30);
and the good people obligingly consent to see Clarissa in the stereotyped
role of young mistress as a fine runaway horse. The whole Hampstead
passage is an indictment of the credulity of good people, particularly good
women, and this scene in particular develops a peculiarly feminine intensity,
an atmosphere to which Lovelace adapts with remarkable verve and self-
possession. In answer to the good woman's rather bold question, "was
madam ever a mamma?" (III,32), Lovelace, now in his own person, can
assert that "it is her own fault that she is not," keeping up the ruse of an
unconsummated marriage to his advantage throughout his dealings with
these women. In order for his plot to succeed, however, he must have only
women around him, as his effective banishment of Mr. Rawlins (who is
concerned about whether Clarissa is indeed Lovelace's wife) demonstrates:
Lovelace, like an indignant man-midwife, insists "That women only are
proper to be present on this occasion . . . and I think myself obliged to them
for their care and kind assistance." But Clarissa now cannot bear to be
touched by him. With her apron over her face and the women present, she
screams at Lovelace, "Begone, begone: touch me not!" Clarissa here is
extremely vulnerable, on the verge of complete mental collapse, and Lovelace, with a great show of concern and pity, manages to ally himself with the
ordinary good women witnessing the unhappy spectacle of a "mother-

spoiled" child having a grown-up temper tantrum. Lovelace plays upon "a
delicate string," the Tomlinson association with her relatives, to provoke
Clarissa's further rage in front of the women and elicit further concern for
himself.

After her father's curse, Clarissa had lamented that her "fate [was] depending, as it seems, upon the *lips of such a man*" as Lovelace (II,263) and
she implored Nancy's prayers that the first part of the curse be lifted. As that
first part nears fulfillment, she sees Lovelace as the physical instrument of
the fatal curse: his hands have been pulling, or restraining, or encircling, or
fondling her since the flight from her father's, and his lips have been just as
active, speaking or kissing. She cannot stop referring to his hands. Lovelace
says, "I would have pressed her hand, as I held it, with my lips":

> Unhand me, sir . . . I will not be touched by you. Leave me to my fate.
> What right, what title, have you to persecute me thus? . . . I will receive
> nothing from your hands . . . you have no *right* to invade me thus . . .
> once more leave me to my fate (III,45).

Until now, Lovelace has been her fate. She here senses that her fate is
something beyond them both. Belford will much later characterize this force
as the "womb of fate," but Clarissa does not now give voice to an image for
her sense of personal destiny. She cannot see what her fate holds or means.
Lost in a "moral wilderness," she can only rely on herself. In her quandary,
she holds to her present knowledge of Lovelace as the "*Vilest of men*—My
name is Lovelace, madam—*Therefore* it is that I call you the *vilest of men*"
(III,70). This is the only time that she allows herself to play on his name, and
she does it with something like the wit of Christ before the Pharisees. He has
proved himself "loveless" to her; his name is his character and his fate, for
she will be "loveless" to him also. Lovelace parries the wildness in her
manner to intensify her "*disorder*" before the attending women. After he
artfully evades the solemn Biblical thrust of her direct questions, as if they
were in a court of law ("art thou really and truly my wedded husband? Say!
answer without hesitation" [III,70]), she affirms to the women that she has
not given him her hand, that there was no marriage. Then she asks to be left
alone: "leave me to make the best of my hard lot. O my dear cruel father! . . .
thy heavy curse is completed upon thy devoted daughter! I am *punished* . . .
by the very wretch in whom I had placed my wicked confidence!" (III,71).
She has carried the curse within her, syllable for syllable, and endorses the
ironic truth of Lovelace's spoken name at the same time that she senses the
first part of the curse reaching fulfillment. Again, as so often in heroic
literature, name and fate coincide in a moment of bitter knowledge. Clarissa
is crushed by the sheer weight of words. She finally collapses in tears: "Good
Heaven . . . what is at last to be my destiny! Deliver me from this dangerous

man; and direct me!" (III,74). She feels that God will show her no "gleam of
the Divine grace or favour" (III,73) while she is in Lovelace's power, and this
belief seems borne out by the women's immediately prevailing upon her to
stay at Mrs. Moore's until Captain Tomlinson, Lovelace's chief instrument,
comes with new proposals. Tomlinson still has her confidence, and can
appeal to her love for her mother as he manages to persuade her to stay till
the false Lady Betty arrives to help complete the movement back to Sinclair's.

   That the "womb of fate," as partially embodied in Lovelace's whores, his
paid tools, and particularly now in the good women of Hampstead, seems to
be working against Clarissa's welfare is most dramatically apparent in the
Widow Bevis affair. Clarissa, armed in the knowledge of her innocence and
worthiness, is determined to go to church: "Her whole person was informed
by her sentiments. She seemed to be taller than before. How the God within
her exalted her, not only above me, but above herself!" (III,153). If Lovelace
is doing his best to play the role of a pagan god, a protean Jupiter-Apollo, he
recognizes in Clarissa a god of another kind, but he is not able to identify that
divinity. Clarissa gradually emerges for the reader, although not for Lovelace, as a female counterpart to suffering Job, whose God seems to be
actively seeking his destruction, and to Christ, who seems also to have been
abandoned by his heavenly father. In her own mind, Clarissa is now deserted by both her natural father and her heavenly one, and while she is at
church hoping to "receive benefit of the divine worship," Lovelace in-
tercepts Nancy's damaging letter by having the Widow Bevis impersonate
Clarissa. Lovelace had anticipated this letter as "the hinge on which the fate
of both [Clarissa and Nancy] must turn":

   what a hair's-breadth escape have I had! . . . What a perverse girl is this,
   to contend with her fate; yet has reason to think that her very stars fight
   against her! I am the luckiest of men! But my breath almost fails me,
   when I reflect upon what a slender thread my destiny hung (III,157).

   Lovelace is right to thank his lucky stars, but in large part he made the
circumstances of his luck by his mastery of male and female roles: the
hot-blooded widow, another "Devil's factor," will do whatever he asks, and
his skill in mimicking a woman's voice at a crucial point saves the deception.
Furthermore, he has been able to win the good women over to his side so
successfully that even the circumspect Miss Rawlins functions as his unwitting agent when she urges Clarissa to dispense with her supposed condition
of "separate beds" (III,67), and the stolid goody Moore becomes just another
London bawd for Lovelace when he gloats, "I had not made a bad exchange
of our professing mother, for the unprofessing Mrs. Moore" (III,87). He
continues: "though not permitted to lodge there myself"—as he had done at

Mrs. Sinclair's, he again manages to rent all the rest of the rooms—"I have engaged all the rooms she has to spare, to the very garrets . . . at her own price . . . my spouse's and all" (III,101), in order to isolate Clarissa further under his ever-watchful attention. In London, Lovelace knows his adopted family of bawds and whores "of figure" so intimately that he can transfer that knowledge to the world of respectable women of business, transforming them into another little "professing" community to further his ends without their knowledge. Even Brown's Mother Creswell always kept her "family as neat and sweet, poor girls, as any alderman's daughters in the City of London,"[59] and Lovelace speculates, "What a happy man shall I be, if these women can be brought to join to carry my marriage into consummation" (III,62). Lovelace's presence hovers over and within Mrs. Moore's establishment as ominously as Mrs. Sinclair's does over her own, and the Fates— Lovelace's "Fates," who are traditional bawds or matchmakers as well as spinners—are above them all: before Nancy's Miss Townshend can rescue Clarissa, "my dear Miss Harlow and I [so the Fates, I imagine, have ordained] shall be fast asleep in each other's arms in town" (III,172).

Richardson gives Clarissa the task of telling Nancy about the prelude to the rape long after it happens and in far more detail than does Lovelace. What happens to Clarissa from the moment she allows herself to be taken from Hampstead by Lovelace and his "aunt" and "cousin" up until her second escape from Mrs. Sinclair's house is of critical importance to her very capacity for telling about the actual rape and how she will do it. In effect, a different Clarissa recounts the rape from the one who suffered it, and we must have a sense of this Clarissa before we can comprehend what the rape, and the direction of her life after it, mean to her. Until she can write about herself again with some composure and independence, we must continue to rely on Lovelace's view of her.

On the night of the rape, Mrs. Sinclair, the fatal bawd with "her huge arms akembo . . . her masculine air, and fierce look," storms in, probably at Lovelace's direction, to terrify Clarissa just before the laudanum finally takes hold. Again Lovelace gives us the image of a wild horse in Clarissa's "turning her head hither and thither, in a wild kind of amaze":

> The old dragon straddled up to her, with her arms kemboed again, her eyebrows erect, like the bristles upon a hog's back, and, scowling over her shortened nose, more than half hid her ferret eyes. Her mouth was distorted. She pouted out her blubber-lips, as if to bellows up wind and sputter into her horse-nostrils; and her chin was curdled, and more than usually prominent with passion (III,195-96).

In a description which owes something to the Augustan satirists' account of the features of a Dissenting minister in the throes of inspiration, Lovelace's mind boils over with animal images, from land, sea, and mythology, to convey the inhuman force of his despicable Pythia. But he can only describe the phenomenon, he cannot penetrate its meaning. In Lovelace's account of the rape, just before the crime is actually committed, we see his eyes fastened not on Clarissa but on "the old beldam," depicted contemptuously in all the disorder and distortion of her bestial nature. We last see Lovelace trying to pacify her and reconcile Clarissa to "the true mother of his mind," the most influential person in his life.

"And now, Belford, I can go no farther. The affair is over, Clarissa lives. And I am Your humble servant, R. Lovelace." It is necessary for Richardson to affix Lovelace's name to the crime. This seals it. Lovelace, like Macbeth in Act V, can go no farther; he was in "too far to recede"[60] (III,132). The affair, or seduction progress, has ended and with it his real subject, but "Clarissa lives." The affair had been an extended operation or experiment on a human subject who was the vehicle for, and mirror of, his love of plotting, directing, subjugating, and somehow the patient survived. It is almost as if Lovelace had not expected her to.

After the rape, Clarissa is comatose; in Lovelace's words, "sunk into a state of absolute—insensibility" (III,200). Her descent is complete, but "Clarissa lives." She begins a new life in the shadow of death. Lovelace, the objective naturalist, has had a specimen of her future resentment in the "speechless agony" of her display of the marriage license "to Heaven," and fears that the large dose of laudanum administered by Mrs. Sinclair might have "damped her charming intellects." Lovelace's favorite adjective for Clarissa now is not merely repetitive but appalling.

Clarissa resumes life after her rape without speech but with a series of mad letters—torn, scratched through, scribbled all over up, down, and sideways, thrown under the table, "blistered with the tears even of the hardened transcriber," Dorcas—all expressions of her mutilated spirit, and her dismembered body.[61] The human voice speaking, even in rage, is still a form of communion. The divorce between Clarissa and Lovelace is now so complete that she cannot speak to him or to anyone, not even to herself, not even to God. What she is at this moment can only be written. It is more than painfully ironic that Lovelace's depersonalizing aesthetic vision, which sees Clarissa as a beautiful assemblage of separable parts, has in fact (and inevitably) now created a genuine psychic fragmentation. One theme runs through these fragments: "I am tired of myself . . . whatever they have done to me, I cannot tell; but I am no longer what I was in any one thing" (III,205). Lovelace cannot bear to transcribe them or even read them because the theme applies to him as well as to her, though he cannot see it. She has lost her self, and she has lost her name. As she suffered after receiving the letter containing her father's curse and the expulsion of her image from his house, so she suffers now, only more intensely, as she tries to expel her *own* image, her *own* sense of self, in an anguished fragment to her omnipresent father: "My name is—I don't know what my name is! I never dare to wish to come into your family again!" (III,206). Then too one of the instigators of the familial rape had been a woman, her sister Arabella, and that assault "broke her heart" as this one disrupts her sense of identity.

Her letter to Lovelace shares with the grieved utterances of Ophelia and Desdemona a certain fairy-tale or nursery-rhyme poignance ("What, Lovelace, have you done with Clarissa Harlowe? . . . Sent her beyond sea"), all the more affecting in their hopelessness, because fairy tales always end happily for this life, and we know this one will not.

These fragments of paper are part of Clarissa's lot, her psalms of lament. They testify, in Biblical and Shakespearean echoes, to her present broken and fragmented condition, a transitional state from a self-in-life to a self-in-death. She no longer knows her name, and she does not know her destiny— these will be given to her: "My head is gone . . . Alas! you have killed my head among you" (III,210-ll). The rape of the intellect is an integral part of the assault committed upon her by Sinclair with her "worse than mannish airs . . . she is a frightful woman! If she *be* a woman" (III,211), but Clarissa sees that the woman is only a "fearful mask" for Sinclair.[62] Under the mask is something else—neither man nor woman, not even human—which she has seen in both Lovelace and Sinclair.

We next see Clarissa's direct confrontation of Lovelace on her own initiative, one of the only such occurrences in the novel. She is a figure now of enormous dignity, with a "fixed sedateness" in her look, apparently "the effect of deep contemplation" (III,218-19). Somehow, through another remarkable act of courageous will, she is "collected," and she has found a way to speak again to her tormentors. Clarissa has fixed her resolution never to have Lovelace, but more important, she will keep her own soul inviolate. This resolution concentrates all her spiritual force into a presence of shimmering moral power. Clarissa might now almost be called a deity because the term transcends the masks of masculine, feminine, or human, a counterbalancing force to the demonic power of Sinclair and her implement, Lovelace. Clarissa asks Lovelace, in her own indelible rendering of Hamlet's "My fate cries out!", "Whether . . . you intend to hinder me from going whither my destiny shall lead me?" He cannot speak. She tells him that he shall never make her his wife: "all my prospects are shut in—I give myself up for a lost creature as to this world" (III,222). She is then forced to remain in the house with only Lovelace's love standing between her and the terror urged upon him by the women, who wish to have five days for "*breaking*" so "skittish a lady" (III,228) down to their level or below. This language suggests that the women—and Lovelace—are in the service of a demonic

impulse that goes beyond nature and beyond conventional Christian notions
of Satan and evil, although Clarissa invokes these notions. The sense of evil
here is beyond even Clarissa's power to understand and articulate, but she
knows that something else is calling her as she repeats her plea, with added
intensity: "Hinder me not from going whither my mysterious destiny shall
lead me" (III,232). Midway between the human and the divine, she dimly
senses that her mysterious destiny is a religious one, but she is not free from
periods of frenzy and the longing for immediate extinction (III,238).

Clarissa's triumph over Lovelace and the women, and her emergence as a
person of godlike influence, armed with the power of outraged innocence
and moral condemnation, occurs when she is called down to face charges
before the mock tribunal of Lovelace and his family in the "penknife scene."
(We noted, in Chapter 22, a similar moment in *Pamela*, when B. staged his
mock-trial and search for the heroine's letters after his final attempted rape.)
She enters "with a majesty in her person and manner . . . which then shone
out in all its glory!" This is Clarissa at the peak of her heroic passion in the
world of her own epic, the glorious power of her innocence now forcibly
exerted in the face of evil. Lovelace again can see only the outer shell of her
person, godlike though it may be, but while Clarissa may consider herself "a
lost creature as to this world" (III,222), she here defines herself as a free
person in the sense of possessing individual and unique being, an old
meaning often applied to royalty: "I am a person, though thus vilely betrayed, of rank and fortune. I never will be his" (III,288). In addition to this
apprehension of her inherent nobility, Richardson calls upon the power of
folk belief to make us envision a good witch with her own powers of
damnation ("I . . . will have no mercy upon you!"), facing down the combined
wicked witchcraft of bawds and whores, with their intoxicating potions, vile
deceptions, and malice. It had been Lovelace's intention to intimidate
Clarissa with all the women behind him, remove her to her room, and take
her by force, if necessary, in a second rape, this time to be performed with
the patient fully conscious. Instead, in the full possession of her "SENSES"
(III,289), she intimidates *them*, passes a kind of Last Judgment on them all
(as well as a withering critical review of the low farce which Lovelace has
given them to act), and retires to her room, "taking one of the lights."
Lovelace never sees her again.

Away from him, and in great perturbation of mind, she can again write
her letters to Nancy, and attempt to meditate in private on what has
happened to her: "Once more have I escaped—but alas! *I*, my *best self*, have
not escaped!"(III,321). We have in this passage a deeper representation of
Clarissa's sense of self than in the penknife scene. By her "best self" she
seems to mean the good person she once was, with all her excellent advan-
tages, attributes, and potential for virtuous action in this world, the self she
reveres Nancy for still possessing. Clarissa was never in full control of her

body, her physical self, after the first rape, the abduction from Harlowe Place. She was always vulnerable to Lovelace. Now she thinks of her violated body, her best self, her individual identity, as one lost thing, but she remains in control of her spirit, her will, her soul, the inviolate heart of the self which she believes every person to possess. The self Clarissa so urgently wants to be separated from is the raped self, "the lost creature as to this world," which she associates with her past, her "story," a heavy tale to disburden herself of. Later, at her arrest for debt, near complete collapse, she murmurs, "my name *was* Clarissa Harlowe: but it is now *Wretchedness*" (III,427), echoing the word *"wretch"* (for Lovelace) in her father's curse.

Although she could present herself before Lovelace and his women, and in the eyes of the world, as a "person . . . of rank and fortune," in private communion with her "best . . . dearest . . . *only* friend," the other who mirrors her "best self" now lost, she acknowledges that she no longer has a social identity, an "I." Only angels are more pure than her friend because they have "shaken off the encumbrance of body." She asks forgiveness for her rambling. "My peace is destroyed. My intellects are touched. . . . What a tale have I to unfold! But still upon *self*; this vile, this hated *self!* I will shake it off, if possible. . . . "(III,321). Her language, not her conscious mind, tells that she wishes to become an angel. She trusts that she is still a child of God, that through her will and God's grace her immortal soul will be her medium to a "mysterious destiny." But ashamed of her "rhapsody" (which of course expresses her true feelings about her predicament), she assumes the submissive, rational tone of objective description in her reply to Mrs. Howe's unexpected letter: "My story is a dismal story. It has circumstances in it that would engage pity, and possibly a judgment not altogether unfavourable" (III,323).

She will attempt to maintain this rational tone in her future correspondence, but the tale, in its progressive unwrapping of one layer after another of the apparent reality (the minutely detailed scenarios of deception) that Lovelace has woven around her, will not allow for a consistently impersonal narrative. Clarissa is now the laborious searcher, or researcher, of her lost self, as was Lovelace, in the more literal sense, when trying to locate her after her first escape. Just as he had resolved, if necessary, to advertise for her as "an eloped wife" in the *Gazette*,

> She had on a brown lustring night-gown, fresh, and looking like new, as everything she wears does, whether new or not, from an elegance natural to her. A beaver hat, a black ribbon about her neck, and blue knots on her breast. A quilted petticoat of carnation-coloured satin; a rose diamond ring, supposed on her finger; and in her whole person and appearance, as I shall express it, a dignity, as well as beauty, that commands the repeated attention of every one who sees her (II,525),

so she advertises for the villain Tomlinson to Mrs. Hodges, her Uncle
Harlowe's housekeeper:

> He is a thin tallish man, a little pock-fretten; of a sallowish complexion.
> Fifty years of age, or more. Of a good aspect when he looks up. He
> seems to be a serious man, and one who knows the world. He stoops a
> little in the shoulders. Is of Berkshire. His wife of Oxfordshire; and has
> several children. He removed lately into your parts from Northampton-
> shire (III,334).

These descriptions characterize their writers' personalities and differing
approaches toward historical inquiry. Lovelace's description of Clarissa is
almost entirely based on externals—the night-gown, the hat, the ring, the
"elegance," the "dignity"; Clarissa's portrait of Tomlinson is more inward
looking—there is nothing about his clothing, he "seems" to be serious. The
result of all of Lovelace's inquiries is that he finds out what he wants to hear
and exults in his knowledge. He is always the historian of the future, making
things happen, then shaping them to his advantage. His researches are
self-promoting. Clarissa too discovers what she expects to discover, and even
more than she expects. What she learns is a series of negatives. No, Hannah
Burton cannot attend her—the poor girl is too ill (III,326). No, Mrs. Norton
declares, the family was not at Uncle Harlowe's on his birthday (III,327).
No, Lady Betty Lawrance "wrote not" to her nephew on the 7th of June, and
concludes with the phrases "neither I nor my steward," "I wrote not," "Nor
have I," "Neither shall I" (III,333). No, Master Harlowe is "acquented with
no sitch man" (III,335) as Captain Tomlinson. And so it goes—negative
confirmation of Clarissa's worst suspicions. Negative history, every answer
tending to affirm that her whole life with Lovelace for these past few months
has been a worthless dream of his (and her own) devising. But the past has
not been empty—it has been filled with error, distortion, the "complicated
wickedness" of his fabrications. Now she will put the record together. The
past, like her lost self, will not go unremembered. The only reality will be in
the written record, and the letters, for Clarissa and for Richardson, are this
record.

The effect of Clarissa's researches into her own past is that of a biographer
recounting the recent demise of an illustrious person. If Clarissa Harlowe
has indeed "died," who then is the person inquiring, confirming, and recording all this? That person has no name, only a mysterious fate, and a highly
contingent existence. If God would not help her while she was in Lovelace's
power, perhaps he will now that she has escaped. But Clarissa is not aware
that the God within her, whom even Lovelace is aware of, has emerged to
help her prevail. Although the action takes place within a far more complex
and tragic texture, Clarissa, like Moll Flanders after Newgate, is a different

person from the nineteen year-old girl who lost her honor to Lovelace. She must have been a changeling to receive a fate such as this, or so she intimates to her old nurse, Mrs. Norton: "Surely you are mine own mother; and, by some unaccountable mistake, I must have been laid to a family that . . . cast me from their hearts" (III,337). She is looking for new mothers and finds them in this faithful correspondent and friend of her spirit, and in yet another widow, this time a good one, Mrs. Lovick: "There seems to be a comfortable providence in *this* at least" (III,339).

Her efforts are bent now on having the second part of her father's curse revoked (III,326,339,340), but Nancy's satirical letter, written in ignorance, stings her into gathering strength to tell her friend the story of the rape: "how my heart sinks under the thoughts of a recollection so painful" (III,353). She is grief-stricken at so painful a recollection of her lost self, but Clarissa must tell her friend all in a shattering account that takes a huge toll. Bearing this tale to her friend is an agonizing birth effort reminiscent of the anguish of separating from her mother and then from her honor at the hands of Lovelace and his whores. In Homer, and in Greek tragedy, the heroes have their fates bound, tied to them from birth, as R. B. Onians has shown in such convincing detail,[63] and something similar occurs in *Clarissa* to both the heroine and Lovelace. Clarissa draws a lot which is impressed upon her heart when she cuts herself off from her mother and her father, and it finally kills her. She does not will her physical dissolution, but she does not fight against it either. She dies of a broken heart, of a heart seizure inflicted by repeated blows or attacks of shock and grief, a not unlikely case history under the circumstances. After a heroic effort of historical reconstruction in her letters of inquiry to discover her lost self, she is in the curious position of telling her friend how she became that lost creature, how she "died."

Controlled by Belford's image of the "womb of fate" and by the metaphor of a difficult case in midwifery, Clarissa's return to Mrs. Sinclair's takes place with the two ladies and their counterparts at the house delivering Clarissa's "best self" over to Lovelace and the corrupted world to "run," in his words, "the fate of a thousand others of her sex—only that they did not set such a romantic value upon what they call their *honour*; that's all" (III,199). Clarissa is now a "niece" to the pretended ladies, like the "nieces" of Mrs. Sinclair, while "Lady Betty" acts as a "mediatrix" for Lovelace. The ladies go to work on her, but occasionally, like inexperienced practitioners who need to refer to their manual, they must resort to Lovelace's "instructions" as to how to proceed with her, a script hidden in their stays (reminiscent of Mrs. Jewkes). The women want something out of her—her consent to come away with them; Clarissa, the perfect patient, says "tender," "obliging," "respectful things": "The wretch himself then came forward. He threw himself at my feet. How was I beset! The women grasping one my right hand, the other my left" (III,355).

The passage is a more subtle recapitulation of Pamela's struggle between the "torturing midwife" Jewkes and B. dressed as a woman, and more important, perhaps, Clarissa is besought with an intensity as great as her own when she implored her mother for her consent not to have to marry Solmes. Clarissa is paralyzed into confusion by her deference to social convention and good manners, much as her own mother was rendered passive to the machinations of her son and daughter by similar considerations. "I was stupid to their hands," says Clarissa later, and the phrase could apply to both daughter and mother, for Clarissa, like Moll, is her mother's daughter, just as Lovelace is Mother Sinclair's true son. The task of recounting all this "grows too heavy"; "I was very ill, and obliged to lay down my pen. I thought I should have fainted" (III,357). This illness stems from seeing herself at such a distance: her historical subject, poor Clarissa Harlowe, is "the poor devoted" over whom the women triumph, "What a devoted victim must I be in their eyes!" (III,364). She sees herself being drawn down to her fate, as in a dream, and she can do nothing but watch and tell with horror.

The heroic narrator, thus distanced, is not free from her own lapses in judgment: "O my dear! What risks may poor giddy girls run, when they throw themselves out of the protection of their natural friends, and into the wide world?" (III,363). Clarissa was not a giddy girl and her friends did not protect her. Clarissa the devoted seems to be in a trance, and so does the narrator at times in reliving the ordeal. She is drawn back to Mother Sinclair's as inexorably as Moll is drawn back to Mother Newgate: "My feet complied against my speech and my mind"; she is "led to the coach"; she is "thoughtless" of danger as the coach winds its way down through the London labyrinth:

> But think, my dear, what a dreadful turn all had upon me, when, through several streets and ways I knew nothing of, the coach slackening its pace, came within sight of the dreadful house of the dreadfullest woman in the world, as she proved to me (III,364-65).

This colloquial use of "turn," meaning a momentary shock caused by sudden alarm or fright, with the added sense of an attack of faintness or nausea, is a woman's term. This is Lovelace's "turn" upon Clarissa. In the slow-moving, claustrophobic atmosphere of this passage through a London street we are close to Moll Flanders and her "turning" of the little dancing student, only now the student will suffer death. As when she recounts the first great trick Lovelace played on her, Clarissa refers to herself in the third person: "Lord be good unto me! cried the poor fool." At what level of the human spirit Clarissa's return to Mrs. Sinclair's is enacted I do not know, but it is a deep level, and the "womb of fate" looms large there. We noticed the sexual configuration of the two houses, the outer entry, the passageway, and the "elegant" inner house. Clarissa was drawn back into that house to experience her own mortality in a sexual act that will be her death, and as she reconstructs the action through her writing, she relives the pain of the event, surrounded by the female operators who will deliver up her honor to Lovelace. Perhaps in her grief after the rape and before her effort to record it, when the Bible was her only book, she was addressed by voices like this:

> And when thou art spoiled, what wilt thou do? Though thou clothest thyself with crimson, though thou deckest thee with ornaments of gold, though thou rentest thy face with painting, in vain shalt thou make thyself fair; thy lovers will despise thee, they will seek thy life. For I have heard a voice as of a woman in travail, and the anguish as of her that bringeth forth her first child, the voice of the daughter of Zion, that bewaileth herself, that spreadeth her hands, saying, Woe is me now! for my soul is wearied because of murderers (Jeremiah 4:30-31).

In Clarissa's narrative, "the poor fool" trembles and sighs as if her heart would burst. Lovelace too, and even the pretended Lady Betty, are gasping for breath: "You will faint, child—we must cut your laces" (III,365). Clarissa, an eighteenth-century woman whose freedom of movement is restricted by "stays" (the word suggests staying in one place, or one's place), had to have her laces cut with her mother also, but at this point the laces have been transformed into the bonds of life itself. At the crucial moment of her fate, the multiple meanings of the names within the name of her antagonist coalesce. In the oral form of the name he is *loveless*; and the literal written form, *lovelace*, means not simply the desire for fine adornment in his personal dress, but the love of possession ("lace" is derived from *laqueus*, a noose, snare, trap), love of the bonds and strings and cords of his web over her, the snare of fates (the persons and the situations) he has fashioned to hold her bound in his wide embrace: "He pulled the string [of the carriage]. What need to have come this way? . . . My dearest life, *why* this apprehension?" (III,365). The women of the house, nurses and midwives to rape, Mrs. Sinclair in the forefront, lead the "poor sacrifice" through the gathering crowd, then through the passage to "the fatal inner house," and assist Clarissa's weaning with their "London milk" laced with laudanum. Mrs. Sinclair at first is everything the accomplished midwife is told to be: "Never was anybody so gentle, so meek, so low voiced . . . drawling out, in a puling accent, all the obliging things she could say" (III,368). Clarissa, having shut herself up for a long wait in the chamber that had once been hers, kneeling, praying, moving about the room, feeling herself growing "heavier and heavier," finally meets Lovelace and his gaze, and sees the same malign leer she first saw in the women's eyes:

His sentences short, and pronounced as if his breath were touched. Never saw I his abominable eyes look as then they looked—triumph in them!—fierce and wild . . . such a leering, mischief-boding cast!" (III,370).

The world "abominable" is derived by folk etymology from *ab homine*, away from man, inhuman, as "wretch" has the root meaning of outcast. Lovelace's look is demonic, and fatal. And as in his own account of those moments, the last image for her, as for him, are of the women, especially Mrs. Sinclair and her "worse than masculine violence": "some visionary remembrances I have of female figures, flitting, as I may say, before my sight; the wretched woman's particularly" (III,372).

34. *"Wisdom* was her *birthright"*

Through most of this discussion we have noticed, in a variety of ways, the far-reaching influence of women upon Clarissa's fate. We have considered her mother's separation from her shortly before the unwilling flight from Harlowe Place; Clarissa's mortification under her father's curse as conveyed in her sister's terrible letter; Lovelace as the "natural philosopher of women" who skillfully manipulates women—whether his own theatrical family of bawds and whores or the respectable women of Hampstead—into moving Clarissa ever nearer to sexual conquest. At the same time, however, he lets himself fall further under the dominance of "the true mother of his mind," Mrs. Sinclair. The influence of all the women in the novel on Clarissa (including such lesser figures as Mrs. Howe, Aunt Hervey, Mrs. Norton, the widows Sorling and Bevis, among others) can be seen as varied expressions of Belford's suggestive metaphor, "the womb of fate," Richardson's final image for the hidden force that disposes and allots Clarissa's life and death, an image ultimately derived from the Greek Fates who were birth spirits, spinners, and midwives.

We noted the difficulty of interpreting Clarissa's credulity where Lovelace was concerned, their secret and fateful correspondence, and Clarissa's own sense of her "strange fatality." She prided herself on "avoiding everything, *precautiously* . . . that might make [her] happy or unhappy"; she had prudence, caution, and wisdom beyond her years ("it has always been my observation, that very few people in courtship see each other as they are" [I, 291]), but not where Lovelace was involved or his women, with their cynical grandmother wisdom so much like the libertine's own view of life: "My charmer is as cool and as distinguishing, though not quite so learned in her own sex, as I am" (III, 186). Not so learned about those of her own sex who see *each other* only as objects to be exploited or as creatures without souls. This degraded sense of self in such women is perhaps best illustrated in the memorable dialogue between Clarissa and the two whores, Sally and Polly, after Clarissa's arrest for debt. Sally defends Lovelace, the man who ruined her, and puts Clarissa's credulity in yet another light: "Don't speak against Mr. Lovelace, *Miss Harlowe*. He is a man I greatly esteem. . . . And, 'bating that he will take his advantage where he can, of *us* silly credulous women, he is a man of honour" (III, 440-41). Throughout the novel, the women who do Clarissa the most harm, beginning with her mother and sister and ending with Sally and Polly, are precisely those who have the lowest estimate of themselves as free and worthy persons, just as those who are Clarissa's most cherished friends, Nancy Howe and Mrs. Norton, have the greatest self-esteem. Although it is disturbing that Clarissa is reduced to the whores' level in her disgust with self, she will move beyond self into the mysterious region of spiritual transformation, while they remain mechanical, unfeeling, and rapacious.

Lovelace senses early that Clarissa is a good judge of people, that she is even wise, but he nevertheless continues to perceive her through the defining principles of his natural philosophy of women. Iago-like, he muses upon her as that most curious of all human creatures, the reasoning lady, and characterizes himself as an inventive spirit:

> She *may* doubt. She *may* fear. The wise in all important cases will doubt, and will fear, till they are sure. But her apparent willingness to think well of a spirit so inventive, and so machinating, is a happy prognostic for me. Oh, these reasoning ladies! How I love these reasoning ladies! 'Tis all over with them, when once love has crept into their hearts: for then will they employ all their reasoning powers to *excuse* rather than to *blame* the conduct of the *doubted* lover, let appearances against him be ever so strong (II,214).

But Lovelace deceives himself here: Clarissa does not love him and is only deceived into having a better opinion of him.

At times, however (for example, in the aftermath of her detecting his theft of one of her letters), and in a way curiously reminiscent of Mrs. Jewkes confronting the cunning Pamela—as if there was something here even so experienced and knowing a ladies' man as Lovelace could not begin to comprehend—the libertine Apollo wonders whether "this lady has something extraordinary in her head," either beyond ordinary mortal ken or gained by means of secret intelligence:

> It won't do. She is of baby age. She cannot be—a Solomon, I was going to say, in everything. Solomon, Jack, was the wisest man. But didst ever hear who was the wisest woman? I want a comparison for this lady. Cunning women and witches we read of without number. But I fancy *wisdom* never entered into the character of a woman. It is not a requisite of the sex (II,273).

Lovelace here further reveals both his knowledge of grandmother wisdom and his ignorance of another kind of wisdom. We have seen enough of "cunning women and witches" by this time to appreciate Lovelace's apparently vast acquaintance with the Mother Sinclairs and Dolly Welbys of the world, in person and in lore. Up to the very end, like a cunning man-midwife, he attributes Clarissa's strange "harping so continually on one string, dying, dying, dying" not only to his operations leading up to and including the rape, but to her possible pregnancy ("I hope all this melancholy jargon is owing to the way I would have her be in . . . . [she] fancies she is breeding death, when the event will turn out quite contrary" [IV,41]). But Lovelace cannot find the female equivalent for Solomon. Perhaps this is owing to his ironic patriarchal notion ("I am a very Jew in this") that women have no souls. He once acknowledges that as a child he refused to read the book of Proverbs because of his aversion to Lord M's incessant "old saws" (II,329); this ignorance deprives him, however, of the knowledge of another Hebrew tradition which tells of Wisdom being a woman, as in Proverbs 8. Richardson, never regarded as a great reader, is nonetheless on record as an admirer not only of heroic literature but also of the Wisdom books of the Bible. We know this from an amusing letter to his intimate and lively friend of the spirit, Lady Bradshaigh, whose name he enjoys making a "high-low" pun on, characteristically at his expense:

> I believe, Madam, that if such a low-classed scribbler as he is, who is now addressing himself to the Lady of Haigh, could but bend his mind to reading, he would better employ his time in collecting the wisdom of past times, than in obtruding upon the world his own crudities. He has, for a trial, classed under particular heads, alphabetically, the Proverbs of Solomon, Ecclesiastes, the Book of Wisdom, and Ecclesiaticus, and called it . . . *Simplicity the True Sublime.* Those books are a treasure of morality.[64]

The two chief attributes of the feminine spirit of wisdom in Proverbs and the Wisdom of Solomon are speaking the truth and radiance. The wisdom of Proverbs is first of all a voice:

> Hear; for I will speak of excellent things; and the opening of my lips shall be right things. For my mouth shall speak truth; and wickedness is an abomination to my lips. All the words of my mouth are in righteousness (8:6-8).

The seventeenth-century praisers of women stressed the innate superiority of woman's eloquence to man's, and pointed out that language begins with them; similarly "Wisdom," dwelling "in the beginning" with the Lord, brings her voice to the "sons of men":

> Women are . . . naturally more eloquent of *Speech,* than Men, and their Tongues more *apt* and *voluble* to cloath their thoughts in Language . . . . Did not every one of us first learn to speak from no other *Tutors* than our *Mothers* and *Nurses*?[65]

> For from *their voyce* men learne to frame *their owne,* to be understood of others. For in our infancy, we learne our language from them. Which men (therein not ingratefull) have justly termed our *Mother tongue.*[66]

In the Wisdom of Solomon, "Wisdom is glorious, and never fadeth away . . . and found of such as seek her. . . . To think therefore upon her is perfection of wisdom. . . . and the giving heed unto her laws is the assurance of incorruption":

> for in her is an understanding spirit, holy, one only, manifold, subtil, lively, clear, undefiled, plain, not subject to hurt, loving the thing that is good, quick, which cannot be letted, ready to do good, kind to man, stedfast, sure, free from care, having all power, overseeing all things, and going through all understanding, pure, and most subtil, spirits. For wisdom is more moving than any motion; she passeth and goeth through all things by reason of her pureness (*Wisdom of Solomon*, 7:22-24 [AV])[67]

Now the two chief attributes of Clarissa are her radiant beauty, physical and moral, and her eloquence, spoken and written. Richardson exalts her, in her dying state, as body gives way to spirit ("I never saw so much soul in a woman's eyes as in hers," says Belford) into a recognizably human approximation of that spiritual state of wisdom. As Wisdom was present at the birth of creation, so for Clarissa, "*wisdom* was her *birthright*" (IV,493).

The most poignant and complex association of Clarissa with Wisdom occurs early in the narrative and sets the tragic tone of the denouement. Under virtual house arrest and perplexed as to what her present course of action should be, Clarissa hears the evening song of the nightingale emanating from the wood house (the setting of her clandestine correspondence with Nancy) as she closes the shutters to her window, and she is reminded of the "charming Ode to Wisdom," "By a Lady," and strongly tinged with Milton's "Il Penseroso," the last three stanzas of which she has set to music "as not unsuitable to my unhappy situation" (I,274). A sympathetic reading of this austere hymn reveals that Clarissa is herself the nightingale of the first stanzas:

> The solitary Bird of Night
> Thro' the thick Shades now wings his Flight,
>   And quits the Time-shook Tow'r;
> Where shelter'd from the Blaze of Day,
> In philosophic Gloom he lay,
>   Beneath his Ivy Bow'r.

We saw that Clarissa too had her own creative ivy bower, now unused in her plight. Like the nightingale of "Il Penseroso," who in "sweetest, saddest plight . . . shunn'st the noise of folly, / Most musical, most melancholy," Clarissa finds "a calmer moment. Envy, ambition, high and selfish resentment, and all the violent passions are now . . . asleep all around me," and she enjoys this "gentler space" to sing her own plaintive ode and to meditate on Nancy's letters. It is "Friday Midnight": the speaker of the ode hears the "solemn Sound, / Which midnight Echoes waft around" (I,275) and her thoughts tend toward Wisdom, a feminine personification in the ode of both the philosophic Wisdom of the Greeks (as expressed in Pallas Athena [I,275] and the spirit of Plato [I,276]) and the Hebrew tradition. Wisdom

> loves the cool, the silent Eve,
> Where no false Shows of Life deceive
>   Beneath the Lunar Ray.
> Here Folly quit each vain Disguise,
> Nor sport her gaily-colour'd Dyes,
>   As in the Beam of Day.[68]

Night is more *real* than day for the Lady and for Clarissa. Reading this poem again after tracing the misery of Clarissa's persecution, rape at midnight, dismemberment, and recollection in letters to Nancy Howe of her lost self, reminds us that the nightingale's solemn song rehearses the peculiarly horrible rape and mutilation of Ovid's Philomela, whose tongue Tereus cut out and who preserved her story in a web of needlework for the perusal of her sister, Procne. Philomela is a notable precursor of Richardson's Clarissa, particularly in her lamentation after the rape, and Tereus, in his eloquence and single-minded passion, makes a convincing prototype of Lovelace. Ovid's deepest response to all this is the tragic question, "Ye gods, what blind night rules in the hearts of men!"[69]

Although Richardson's response to the tragedy of Clarissa is nowhere in the novel expressed so explicitly, it may also be represented in the more philosophical meaning of the image of night. This is the night of Melancholy in "Il Penseroso," calm, silent, pensive, suffused by a "dim religious light." Here in the ode night represents a level of experience transcending the transitory daylight world; it is the realm of "mental Sight," of the "Lunar Ray" of Truth, of Plato's "sacred spirit," "Of Perfect, Fair, and Good," of the imagination itself: "[Wisdom's] Breath inspires the Poet's Song." Then the frame of reference shifts from the classical world to the Biblical:

> No more to fabled Names confin'd;
> To Thee! Supreme all-perfect Mind,
>   My Thoughts direct their Flight.
> Wisdom's thy Gift, and all her Force
> From Thee deriv'd Eternal Source
>   Of intellectual *Light!*

Oh send her sure, her steady Ray,
To regulate my doubtful Way,
   Thro' Life's perplexing Road:
The Mists of Error to control,
And thro' its Gloom direct my Soul
   To Happiness and Good.

Beneath her clear discerning Eye
The visionary Shadows fly
   Of Folly's painted Show,
She sees thro' ev'ry fair Disguise,
That all, but VIRTUE's solid Joys,
   Is Vanity and Woe.

We are back with the Wisdom of Proverbs and Solomon, the penetrating, steady ray of intellectual light which drives away the deluding and false perceptions of Folly. This is a view of life the young, untried Clarissa aspires to; it is the view of life to which, after all her suffering, she attains in her dying state; and it is a view of life in this world ("Folly's painted Show") worth setting beside Lovelace's final satiric vision of society as "a great fair," and of Clarissa's place in it, expressed as a little allegorical mock romance, the fruit of a cynicism which has no place for Clarissa's Wisdom:

But here, in the present case, to carry on the volant metaphor (for I must either be merry, or mad), is a pretty little miss just come out of her hanging-sleeve coat, brought to buy a pretty little fairing; for the world, Jack, is but a great fair, thou knowest; and, to give thee serious reflection for serious, all its toys but tinselled hobby-horses, gilt gingerbread, squeaking trumpets, painted drums, and so forth.

Now behold this pretty little miss skimming from booth to booth, in a very pretty manner. One pretty little fellow called Wyerley perhaps, another jiggeting rascal called Biron, a third simpering varlet of the name of Symmes and a more hideous villain than any of the rest, with a long bag under his arm, and parchment settlements tagged to his heels, ycleped Solmes; pursue her from raree-show to raree-show, shouldering upon one another at every turning, stopping when she stops, and set a spinning again when she moves. And thus dangled after, but still in the eye of her watchful guardians, traverses the pretty little miss through the whole fair, equally delighted and delighting: till at last, taken with the invitation of the *laced-hat orator*, and seeing several pretty little bib-wearers stuck together in the flying coaches, cutting safely the yielding air, in the one go-up the other go-down picture-of-the-world vehicle, and all with as little fear as wit, is tempted to ride next.

In then suppose she slyly pops, when *none of her friends are near her*: and if, after two or three ups and downs, her pretty head turns giddy, and she throws herself out of the coach when at its elevation, and so dashes out her pretty little brains, who can help it? And would you hang the poor fellow whose *professed trade* it was to set the pretty little creatures a flying?

"Tis true, this pretty little miss, being a *very* pretty little miss, being a *very much-admired* little miss, being a very *good* little miss, who always minded her book, and had passed through her sampler doctrine with high applause; had even stitched out in gaudy propriety of colours, an Abraham offering up Isaac, a Samson and the Philistines, and flowers, and knots, and trees, and the sun and the moon, and the seven stars, all hung up in frames with glasses before them, for the admiration of her future grandchildren: who likewise was entitled to a very pretty little estate: who was descended from a pretty little family upwards of one hundred years' gentility; which lived in a very pretty little manner, respected a very little on their own accounts, a great deal on hers (III,316-317).

Lovelace is the *"laced-hat orator"* who leads the pretty miss into the "picture-of-the-world vehicle" (i.e., Mrs. Sinclair's bawdy house) and sends her flying. The satiric tradition, best exemplified in Pope, of women as spinning, turning, giddy, witless pretty dolls reaches a kind of culmination with Lovelace, who is here a Bunyan without faith; he knows that "the whole world is governed by appearance" (III,64) and this world—including Clarissa—is nothing but a whore tinselled over. With this satiric dismissal of his goddess, Lovelace dismisses his chief subject and the chief business of his life: no matter how earnestly he may anguish and recant later, Lovelace's occupation is gone, as he recognizes in the subdued lament not many pages later: "What heart, thinkest thou, can I have to write, when I have lost the only subject worth writing upon? . . . Having lost her my whole soul is a blank" (III,388).

35. Belford as Executor and Clarissa

In ways which we explored in Chapter 28, Clarissa and Lovelace have each been and ever will be the other's fate. But there is now a reversal of emphasis: as Lovelace was Clarissa's fate up until her shining moral victory over him and his women and her ingenious escape from the house, so now until his death, Clarissa is Lovelace's fate. Finally outside of his sphere of influence, she exerts the same strange influence upon him which he once exerted upon her. Half-mockingly, Lovelace at first sensed Clarissa as his fated wife: "Fate is weaving a whimsical web for thy friend, and I see not but I shall be inevitably manacled" (II,182). He *would* be manacled, but to Mrs. Sinclair and her whores.

Now, late in the novel, he uses the same word for Clarissa, and with the same perplexed intensity, that she used for him in trying to make sense of the "strange diligence" with which he pursued her: "Strange, confoundedly strange, and as perverse [that is to say as *womanly*] as strange, that she should refuse, and sooner choose to die [O the obscene word! and yet how free does thy pen make with it to me!] than be mine" (III,508). He returns to Hertfordshire to confront Nancy Howe (like Tereus: "With such crimes upon his soul he had the face to return to Procne's presence"[70]), but he is no longer joking when he asks, "I must know my fate. I will go abroad once more, if I find her absolutely irreconcilable." In a memorable instance of *fatum* as utterance, Clarissa had earlier sensed that her "fate was depending . . .upon the *lips*" of Lovelace. He now says, "I hope she will give me leave to attend upon her, to know my doom from her own mouth" (IV,25).

Clarissa's effect upon Lovelace now, whether she wills it or not, is to force him to reflect upon his crimes, but her influence upon Belford has the force of regeneration. She becomes for him the mortal personification of Wisdom, and whoever seeks and finds her will become immortal. Belford in turn exerts new influence over Lovelace, apparently derived through his association with Clarissa: if Clarissa is now Lovelace's fate, Belford is the instrument of that fate in Lovelace's eyes. We noted at the outset of this discussion that Clarissa makes Belford her legal executor; that term comes to have increased significance when we consider Belford as executor not only for Clarissa, but particularly for Lovelace and for Mother Sinclair.

Lovelace had wished to hear his doom pronounced from Clarissa's own lips, but Clarissa has her own agent to perform this task. Just after Clarissa's final escape from Sinclair's house, Belford's tone to Lovelace begins to take on the accents of doom: "now wilt thou be inevitably blown up: and in what an execrable light wilt thou appear to all the world! Poor Lovelace! Caught in thy own snares! Thy punishment is but beginning!" (III,307). And when he first hears of Sinclair's arrest of Clarissa, Lovelace raves, "A curse upon all my plots and contrivances! . . . .Thou toldest me that my punishments were but beginning. Canst thou, O fatal prognisticator! canst thou tell me where they will end?" (III,419). Lovelace comes to see Belford as a torturer who breaks off his letters at crucial points and leaves his anguished reader in suspense. When he finally does give Lovelace the news of Clarissa's death (according to their prearranged formula), Belford the oracle cannot forebear a note of contemptuous dismissal: "I have only to say at present: Thou wilt do well to take a tour to Paris; or wherever else thy destiny shall lead thee!!!" (IV,342). Lovelace is now a character in search of his fate, and Belford obligingly writes it for him.

From the outset, Lovelace has had a more traditional sense of fate—of the Fates as ancient spinners who weave a web to ensnare and fix men—than Clarissa, with her more emotional apprehension of fate as an active force, like a hand throwing her forward, or a shaping word, or an ineluctable lot. Her sense of fate begins with feelings of great physical agitation and ends with the knowledge of a mysterious destiny, that is, Providence. Lovelace senses, near his life's end, after the deaths of his chief accomplices, McDonald ("Tomlinson") and Sinclair, that "something has been working strangely retributive" (IV,438), and Belford chooses to repeat to him his very words. What makes these sentiments more than conventional moralizing about Providence is that Lovelace now sees Belford as the author of a tragic script in which Lovelace himself is the victim. It is as if the Fates have given Belford enormous power—control over the very threads of life—to conclude the tragedy of Clarissa and mete out the doom of everyone associated with her: as Mrs. Norton had said of the child Clarissa (echoing the Biblical tale of Joseph), "all our lives were bound up in your life":

> Fate, I believe, in my conscience, spins threads for tragedies, on purpose for thee to weave with. Thy Watford uncle, poor Belton, the fair inimitable [exalted creature! and is she to be found in such a list!], the accursed woman, and Tomlinson, seem to have been all doomed to give thee a theme for the dismal and the horrible! And by my soul, *thou dost work it going*, as Lord M. would phrase it (IV,450).

Lovelace pays homage to Belford's extraordinary "knack of painting everybody whom thou singlest out to exercise thy murdering pen upon," and humbly requests: "But wilt thou write often when I am gone? Wilt thou then piece the thread where thou brokest it off?" (IV,450-51). As Clarissa felt herself to be after receiving her father's curse, Lovelace now seems almost passively devoted in the face of the apparently inevitable executive literary power which Belford possesses in Clarissa's service. Belford comes to have nearly the same authoritative oracular influence over Lovelace as Clarissa's father once exerted over his daughter.

But transcending this effect, Lovelace and Belford seem to be two sides of Richardson the artist. There is much of Richardson's own mischievous wit and ingenuity in Lovelace's remarks on the status of women and his omniscient plotting; but with Lovelace in decline, Richardson, drawing upon the potent age-old metaphor of the spinning fates, invests the literary Belford with his own moral and artistic authority. He makes him Clarissa's executor and preserver of her story, a kind of ideal editor, the artistic role Richardson finds most congenial and meaningful for himself. Belford is also a kind of editor for Lovelace, since he has all of his letters, and acting on his own discretion, decides to supply Clarissa with Lovelace's accounts of critical parts of the story, such as the fire scene (IV,74-75). The materials of her own history which Clarissa pieces together, with Belford's help, come to constitute her true story and a justification of her conduct to her friends, and running through this "tragical story" is a series of imitations of and extracts from Holy Scripture, beginning with her Biblical lamentations in the deranged fragments she composed after the rape and evolving into a whole "book of *Meditations*" (IV,290).[71] These imitations are based almost entirely on the Wisdom literature of the Old Testament (particularly Job ["O that my words were now written! Oh that they were printed in a book!"—19:28]) and the Psalms, and they form Clarissa's personal scripture, or Wisdom book, written for her own use. Belford recounts to Lovelace how he has renewed his own interest in reading the Bible by collating Clarissa's meditations with the original text. For Belford and for us, this text *is* Clarissa.

In looking back over this novel of seduction, one should not be surprised by the accumulated references throughout to Clarissa's body, and to the particular parts of her body—her face, eyes, hair, neck, breasts, hands and feet, skin, veins, "The finest waist in the world" (II,141). But the emphasis at this late point has more to do with the state of Clarissa's physical health: "I have no appetite. Nothing you call nourishing will stay on my stomach. I do what I can. . . . I have engaged . . . to avoid all wilful neglects" (IV,13). Richardson's model, at least in part, for Clarissa's tragic demise seems to have been the tragedy of Job. One of the most remarkable features of that book is the detailed chronicling on almost every page, literally and metaphorically, of Job's physical afflictions and degeneration. But unlike Job, Clarissa's physical health is not restored. Her remarkable body, once hardy and beautiful, glowing with the health of her outdoor regimen, withers away under the pressure of her grief. As she passes her nineteenth birthday (July 24), we sense more and more urgently her personal presence manifested not in her body but in her writing, in her letters. There was of course a similar development in Pamela. In an almost comic yet poignant respect, she came to *be* the clothing of her letters, herself a concealed text.

Clarissa, in a much more protracted, arduous, and complicated process, undergoes a complete translation, or transformation, of body into language. It seems to be her destiny to keep on writing, even when she knows that the activity is inimical to her physical health ("the mind will run away with the body at any time," she says [IV,10]). She literally takes her fate into her own hands by writing herself out. The ruined and fragmented Clarissa reintegrates her spiritual self by writing her "tragical story," and story and spirit become one. She becomes her own spiritual text, her own scripture. These letters are thus charged with a peculiar kind of vitality: as her presence increases in the letters she writes, the influence of the Old Testament on her behavior seems all the more pronounced. Now that her father has taken off the weight of his "heavy malediction," she will solicit for a "last blessing" (IV,63). If we sense truly how the written record has become essential to Clarissa, or *essentially* Clarissa, we may understand why—on her knees— she implores her "ever-honoured mamma" for forgiveness and a blessing: "Let me, on a blessed scrap of paper, but see one sentence to this effect under your dear hand" (IV,84). Everything significant to Clarissa now has to be in writing (her story, her last will and testament, the withdrawal of the second part of her father's curse, her letters to her family to be sent after her death, even the note to be given to Lovelace to read if he gazes at her dead body [IV,417]), and it all relates to her Job-like sense of her own suffering. Finally, in her last phase, the power of the two most important men in her life, her father and Lovelace, must be met and overcome.

Toward the end of her confinement in her father's house she once overheard her father, behind the yew hedge, "utter these words: Son James, to you, and to Bella . . . do I wholly commit this matter. That I was meant, I cannot doubt" (I,411) ("And the Lord said unto Satan, Behold, all that he hath is in thy power" [Job 1:12]). In requesting Lovelace's letters from Belford, Clarissa believes that the "vile man" will condemn himself out of his own mouth (since his "base arts . . . will be best collected from those very letters" [IV,61]), so she can then "appeal with the same truth and fervour as he did, who says": "*O that one would hear me! and that mine adversary had written a book! Surely I would take it upon my shoulders, and bind it to me as a crown!*" (IV,61; cf. Job 31:35-36). We have noted at several points that Clarissa senses her "lot" in life as one imposed, inflicted, and bound upon her through the actions and words of Robert Lovelace; this passage is the culminating and most powerful expression of her sense of that lot. Lovelace has inflicted a terrible fate upon her body, her physical self, yet Clarissa will vanquish him and transcend that fate by taking the record of it, in Lovelace's own words, upon her own head and proudly bind it to her as a crown for all to see. This gesture is in direct contrast to Pamela's final putting of herself, of her story, literally into the hands of Mr. B., of letting him "wind up the Catastrophe of the pretty Novel." Clarissa's story will incorporate and prevail over Lovelace's, her fate will be the stronger.

This is not a conventionally Christian heroine and hers is not a conventionally Christian story. Clarissa emerges at the end less as a figure of Christian forgiveness than as an Old Testament goddess of suffering Wisdom who evolves in her brief lifespan from girl to woman to saint to angel, and finally into a genuine deity in Belford's eyes as opposed to the spurious goddess which Lovelace "makes" in his own perverse erotic imagination. By taking over in good faith the roles of father and brother to Clarissa which Lovelace had appropriated and then betrayed even more thoroughly than had her own mean-spirited father and brother, Belford becomes her executor (the one who "follows her up," pursues, and collects her story). Belford is Baruch to Clarissa's Jeremiah, and as a libertine converted to a better life under her influence, he becomes her counterpart to the apostle Paul (a convert "sent forth" to proclaim her sacred virtues). Anna Howe too contributes her hagiographical epistle to the Clarissa story; indeed, much of the last quarter of the novel could be called hagiography.

In the parcel sealed with "three black seals" which Belford breaks open after her death (IV,353), there are eleven letters to the members of her family and other interested parties. These seals and posthumous epistles, reminiscent of the apocalyptic letters and seals of the book of Revelation, record a kind of resurrection of Clarissa. She rises from the dead in these letters like an exterminating angel (like the *real* angels of the Bible) whose forgiveness is more shattering than outright condemnation. The reader recalls Lovelace's anguished complaint to Belford that Clarissa would forgive her family before she would forgive Lovelace ("Surely thou must see the inconsistence of her *forgiving* unforgivingness, as I may call it" [III,508]); one also thinks of her triumph, after her "death" in the rape, over Lovelace and his family of whores. Now she will exact a kind of revenge, or is it justice, upon her own family. The most curious thing about these letters is that, owing partly to an adroit and persistent repetition of the word "now," they preserve the illusion of having been written to the moment.

The dying Clarissa writes her letters on the assumption (for which she had "the strongest assurances" from the Almighty) that by the time they are read she will actually *be* the angel who speaks to her auditors in these mortal, yet immortal, accents, and so she appears before her father "with exulting confidence now" to congratulate him for having been "the means of adding one to the number of the blessed" (IV,360). This crushing compliment, which has the effect of giving him all the credit for her promotion, reduces the thunderous father's once awful presence to sackcloth and ashes and

materially hastens his own departure from the world (IV,534). A similar
effect, though muted, is dispensed in the other letters. It is not quite fair,
however, to leave Clarissa in her posthumous angelic manifestation. It is her
death—its image and her attitude toward it—which is of more concern to
Richardson, and perhaps to his reader. An account of Clarissa's death also
demands an account of the death of Mother Sinclair, her terrible female
antagonist whose demonic influence over Lovelace makes her the only other
force (besides Clarissa's father) powerful enough to wean Clarissa from the
world.

36. The Rape of Sinclair

Lovelace was deeply affected by Belford's painting of the demise of the people closest to him—Belford's account of the deaths of Mrs. Sinclair and Clarissa. It is natural for readers to compare the two deaths as examples of holy and unholy dying, and of course Richardson wants us to make the proper moral applications, but the more significant initial comparison is that between Clarissa's rape and Sinclair's death. The whole long scene of this death, a gross and startling underworld parallel of the error, mortification, and rape of Clarissa, might be called the Rape of Sinclair by Death. Belford, now acting as Richardson's London spy, is called as if by the devil (IV,380) to Mrs. Sinclair's house where the "old wretch" is dying of her own "mortification" (the word is used three times) incurred by restless impatience after breaking her leg in a drunken fall downstairs at night. He moves first through an obscene assemblage of whores "just . . . risen perhaps from their customers in the fore house, and their nocturnal orgies"[72] (IV,381) and midnight revels:

> But when I approached the *old wretch*, what a spectacle presented itself to my eyes!
> Her misfortune had not at all sunk, but rather, as I thought, increased her flesh; rage and violence perhaps swelling her muscular features. Behold her, then, spreading the whole tumbled bed with her huge quaggy carcass: her mill-post arms held up; her broad hands clenched with violence; her big eyes, goggling and flaming-red as we may suppose those of a salamander; her matted grizzly hair, made irreverent by her wickedness (her clouted headdress half off), spread about her fat ears and brawny neck; her livid lips parched, and working violently; her broad chin in convulsive motion; her wide mouth, by reason of the contraction of her forehead (which seemed to be half lost in its own frightful furrows), splitting her face, as it were, into two parts; and her huge tongue hideously rolling in it; heaving, puffing, as if for breath; her bellows-shaped and various-coloured breasts ascending by turns to her chin, and descending out of sight, with the violence of her gaspings (IV,382).

As in Tom Brown's description of his fat bawd ("a ton of female fat saluted us"), the first thing to salute Belford's incredulous sight is Mrs. Sinclair's increased flesh, and again we notice, as with Mother Jewkes in *Pamela*, the "goggling" eyes, only this time inflamed and red like those of the archetypal witch-bawd, Mother Shipton (see Chapter 4). She is no longer a woman but a magnified and distorted image of outraged animal Nature, "howling, more a wolf than a human creature," her noise "more like that of a bull than a woman!" (IV,380). Richardson's Mother Midnight (like Mother Jewkes) is always, it seems, something other than woman: she is more masculine than feminine, and in her death throes, she is identified again and again with animals (hog, ferret, dragon, whale, horse, spider). She had always been in metamorphosis; now she erupts. The passage has the impact of a natural disaster, an earthquake. It brings to mind Ovid's affecting account of Earth's agony in the chaos wrought by Phaeton's fall:

> . . . Earth, who, encircled as she was by sea, amid the waters of the deep, amid her fast-contracting streams which had crowded into her dark bowels and hidden there, though parched by heat, heaved up her smothered face. Raising her shielding hand to her brow and causing all things to shake with her mighty trembling, she sank back a little lower than her wonted place, and then in awful tones she spoke.[73]

Mrs. Sinclair's "naturally big voice" is hoarsened by her ravings, but unlike Ovid's Mother Earth, she can only call down curses—in a passage heavy with cursing—on "every careless devil" in her house for not taking better care of her.[74] Belford "more than once thought himself to be in one of the infernal mansions" and felt "half poisoned by the effluvia arising from so many contaminated carcasses" (IV,384-85).

The description of Mother Sinclair's agony is indeed worthy of epic comparisons—the literary Belford had already compared her daughters to "Virgil's obscene harpies, squirting their ordure upon the Trojan trenches" (IV,381)—and fitting for the large implicit role she plays in the novel as Lovelace's true mother. But Milton's *Paradise Lost* is the chief epic analogue to the death of Sinclair. If, as we have seen, Mother Jewkes and Colbrand have certain affinities with Milton's Sin and Death, the death of Sinclair has more and deeper connections. For Richardson as for Milton, the relevant scriptural text is James 1:15: "When lust hath conceived, it bringeth forth sin: and sin, when it is finished, bringeth forth death." In *Paradise Lost*, Death, the Son of Sin and Satan, rapes his mother and engenders a brood of yelping hell hounds who feed continually on their mother's entrails. In *Clarissa*, Mrs. Sinclair and her figurative son, Lovelace, stand to each other as new versions of Sin and Satan. The bawd Sinclair, surrounded by her dependent and infernal daughters, is Richardson's graphic re-invention of the ancient figure of Sin for a readership no longer interested in conventional religious symbols. We have noticed before in this study the emblem of the goddess fate standing on the globe of the world, and the image of the bawd symbolizing the world. Like Tom Brown's bawd, Sinclair is a "globe" of iniquities, pocked and seamed and furrowed like the earth, but her "huge quaggy carcass" is in violent commotion, gripped by a strong fever and con-

sumed, like Ovid's Earth, with unnatural heat. Fastened upon by death, her
heavings and puffings and rollings are an outrageous and prolonged parody
of the sexual couplings from which she has made her living. Her death, like
Clarissa's rape, apparently takes place in the inner house, and she too is
surrounded by prostitutes who "now and then flitted in" (Clarissa recalled
"female figures, flitting, as I may say, before my sight" [III,372]). In both
cases there are "operators" (IV,386), first the bawd and her crew assisting
Lovelace's "operations" upon Clarissa; now two French surgeons contemplating the amputation of Mrs. Sinclair's leg, not with any hope of saving
her but "for an experiment only." As Belford's description of Sinclair's
tortured body evoked a magnified image of the "quaggy" earth with "mill-
post arms" and breasts like literally rolling hills, so the doctors (in language
which recalls Arbuthnot, the master of Scriblerian medical satire) magnify
even more that deadly feature of her topography, Sinclair's swollen leg:

> They told me the fracture was high in her leg; that the knee was
> greatly bruised; that the mortification, in all probability, had spread
> half-way of the *femur*: and then . . . did they by turns fill my ears with an
> anatomical description of the leg and thigh, running over with terms of
> art; of the *tarsus*, the *metatarsus*, the *tibia*, the *fibula*, the *patella*, the *os
> tali*, the *os tibiae*, the *tibialis posticus* and *tibialis anticus*, up to the *os
> femoria*, to the *acetabulum* of the *os ischion*, the *great trochanter*,
> *glutaeus*, *triceps*, *lividus*, and *little rotators*; in short, of all the muscles,
> cartilages, and bones that consitute the leg and thigh from the great toe
> to the hip; as if they would show me that all their science had penetrated
> their heads no farther than their mouths; while Sally lifted up her hands
> with a Laud bless me! Are all surgeons so learned! But at last *both* the
> gentlemen declared that, if she and her friends would consent to
> amputation, they would *whip off her leg in a moment* (IV,385).[75]

Belford is thinking of the execution for high treason when he says that the
poor wretch is to be "lanced and quartered" to increase the surgeons' profit:
in a sense, this is Sinclair's crime against Clarissa, and the Sex. Belford
finally undertakes "to be the denouncer of her doom" and acts the part of a
clergyman attempting to console the condemned woman before her execution. In a darker sense, however (and one we have noted throughout the
discussion of Belford as Clarissa's agent of fate), it seems as if a large part of
Belford's role as Clarissa's executor (one who "follows up" but who also
"pursues") is to be the verbal executioner of her mortal enemies. Clarissa's
death precedes Mother Sinclair's: the old wretch howls her regret for having
"been the means of destroying an angel," and explicitly holds herself and her
girls responsible for Lovelace's "not doing her justice" (IV,383).

37. Death and Deliverance

> Beareth all things, believeth all things, hopeth all things, endureth all things.
>
> (I Corinthians 13:7)

> The better fortitude
> Of Patience and Heroic Martyrdom
> Unsung
>
> (*Paradise Lost.* IX.31-33)

The death of Sinclair is a grand exercise in epic satire meant to shock; the death of Clarissa is not so elaborate a set piece, and though it is in one sense a fitting end to the heroine of a Christian epic, it must arouse mixed responses in any thoughtful reader. From the very beginning, we are aware that Clarissa has expressed, if not a longing for death, at least a remarkable receptivity to it: "I have sometimes wished that it had pleased God to have taken me in my last fever, when I had everybody's love and good opinion" (I,4). At the end her spiritual mother, Mrs. Norton, reminds her of this "dangerous fever" (which afflicted Clarissa at the ages of nine and eleven), adding, with the wisdom of Silenus, "what a much more desirable event, both for you and for us, would it have been had we *then* lost you!" (IV,49). Reading this from her second mother, Clarissa could hardly feel the finality of her tenure in the world more acutely. It is all over.

Nancy Howe always sensed that Clarissa was somehow not meant for this world of men: "The result is this: that I am fitter for *this* world than you; you for the *next* than me—that's the difference" (I,43). Clarissa becomes an extreme embodiment of the notion that men and women are not at home with each other in this world. She is in harmony with nature, with her creative imagination, and with the night, but not with other people (not even with Nancy, finally) nor with the self she wishes to shake off (III,321). Her imagination can accommodate the night, the loss of the self, and death, and transform these into images closer to her desires. Early in the novel, her image of death is one of Gothic horror, the vault or house of the dead, but even this alternative is preferable to a life under the sway of Solmes:

> O my dear mamma, save me, save me if you can, from this heavy evil! I had rather be buried alive, indeed I had, than have that man! (I,87).

> I will undergo the cruellest death—I will even consent to enter into the awful vault of my ancestors, and to have that bricked up upon me, rather than consent to be miserable for life (I,380).

What almost redeems Clarissa's frequent hyperbole (including the occasionally wooden rhetoric of her later denunciations of Lovelace) is that we

Frau Welt, **early fifteenth-century illumination. (From Codex Latinus monacensis, Bayerische Staatsbibliotek MS 8201, fol. 95, Munich. Reproduced from Roland Mushat Frye's** *Milton's Imagery and the Visual Arts: Iconographic Tradition in the Epic Poems.* **Copyright © Princeton University Press, 1978.)**

Frau Welt, fifteenth-century woodcut. (British Library, London. From Frye, *Milton's Imagery and the Visual Arts*. See above.)

know she *means* it, and we sense the boundaries to which she has been pushed, and pushed beyond.

Clarissa's death brings up those most difficult questions attending her role as a Christian heroine, questions that center on her moral imagination, an amalgam of intense creative force, credulity, and hope:

> But if it shall come out that the person within the garden was his corrupted implement . . . do you think, my dear, that I shall not have reason to hate him and myself still more? I hope his heart cannot be so deep and so vile a one: I hope it cannot! (I,485).

Closely allied to this belief is her unquenchable hope "*before* the capital enormity" (III,374), that things would turn out for the best between herself and her family:

> I had thoughts indeed several times of writing to my cousin but by the time an answer could have come, I imagined all would have been over, as if it had never been: so from day to day, from week to week I hoped on . . . . He might not have been in haste to come, hoping the malady would cure itself . . . (I,423-24).

A good part of the genuine tragedy of Clarissa lies in this sense of hope. She is a precursor of the life-sustaining hope, a belief in one's own essential goodness and in that of others, that has impelled many to go passively and unwittingly to their doom believing that things have to get better. Her misguided hope is most poignantly evident when she is in the presence of Lovelace's false Lady Betty and Cousin Charlotte:

> Yet, thought I at the time, with what intermixtures does everything come to me that has the appearance of good. However . . . my lucid hopes made me see fewer faults in the behaviour of these pretended ladies, than recollections and abhorrence have helped me since to see . . . (III,363).

Up to this point, *Clarissa* may be, after *King Lear*, the greatest representation in English literature of the hopelessness of hope, the tragedy of hope. The heroine comes to see the futility of her good hopes after the rape, and characteristically places more blame or "hate" on herself than on Lovelace:

> yet, I hate thee not (base and low-souled as thou art!) half so much as I hate myself, that I saw thee not sooner in thy proper colours! That I hoped either morality, gratitude, or humanity, from a libertine . . . (III,221).

She comes to the conviction—not a speculation or a belief, and earned, she thinks by her sorrow and suffering—that the only hope worth having in the hard school of this life is in "the better hope" of the life to come, "an excellent school! my dear Mrs. Norton, in which we are taught to know ourselves, to be able to compassionate and bear with one another, and look up to a better hope" (IV,2). In effect, Clarissa exchanges her "best self" for the "better hope."

The doorway to the better hope is death, and her strong shaping imagination, as well as her suffering, gradually soften the image of death into a source of pleasure and renewal:

> what is the result of all? It is this: that I must abide by what I have already declared—and that is . . . that I have much more pleasure in thinking of death than of such a husband [as Lovelace] (III,519).

> And what, after all, is death? 'Tis but a cessation from mortal life: 'tis but the finishing of an appointed course: the refreshing inn after a fatiguing journey: the end of a life of cares and troubles; and, if happy, the beginning of a life of immortal happiness (III,521).

As she balances between life and death, Clarissa spells out, in a powerful vision of both the living and dying condition, her own explanation of the doctor's diagnosis of grief and her new affirmation of "the better hope":

> I am persuaded, as much as that I am now alive, that I shall not long live. The strong sense I have ever had of my fault, the loss of my reputation, my disappointments, the determined resentment of my friends, *aiding* the barbarous usage I have met with where I least deserved it, have seized upon my heart: seized upon it, before it was so well fortified by *religious considerations* as I hope it now is . . . . God will soon *dissolve my substance*: and *bring me to death, and to the house appointed for all living* (III,522-23).

Clarissa says she succumbed to death before her heart was fortified by religious considerations; presumably if these considerations had been strong enough, she would not have suffered this fatal seizure of the heart. She is emphatic about not willing her death:

> so I should think it . . . criminal, were I now *wilfully* to neglect myself; were I *purposely* to run into the arms of death (*as that man supposes I shall do*), when I might avoid it . . . . When appetite serves, I will eat and drink what is sufficient to support nature. A very little, you know, will do for that (III,522).

But her body, her ruined "self," will not let her live. She has no appetite but for writing herself out in letters. She seems to be in the grip of a powerful unconscious death wish. The period of her knowing she will die until her dissolution is now near its end; in her meditation "*On being hunted after by the enemy of my soul*," she lamented: "*He hath made me dwell in darkness, as those that have long been dead*" (IV,140), a reminder of the ominous warning of her grisly early nightmare of how Lovelace, in her words,

> carried me into a churchyard; and there, notwithstanding all my prayers and tears, and protestations of innocence, stabbed me to the heart, and then tumbled me into a deep grave ready dug, among two or three half-dissolved carcasses; throwing in the dirt and earth upon me with his hands, and trampling it down with his feet (I,433).

For Mrs. Sinclair, death came as a violent and prolonged rape; for Clarissa, rape was a violent and prolonged death attended by ruthless nurses. Now physical death comes to her as gentle and pleasure-giving: "but to me, who have had so gradual a weaning-time from the world, and so much reason not to love it, I must say I dwell on, I indulge (and, strictly speaking, I enjoy) the thoughts of death" (IV,258). Clarissa has been weaned or separated from the world in three senses: first, and literally, from her good nurse Norton; then at eighteen from her own weak mother; finally, from the terrible mother, Sinclair, the appalling embodiment of a corrupted earth. After all the links in the novel between women and houses, Clarissa finally dwells on death as "accommodations" on a journey into an untravelled country, as a "refreshing inn" at the end or her journey, as her allegorical "father's house," as "the house appointed for all living," as "her last house," her *"palace"* the coffin which she purchases, writes on as a desk, and adorns with appropriate symbols of her fate. The coffin, the epic heroine's shield of Achilles, is also an ironic gift for her father. He ordered the banishment of her image from his house; she returns to him in her *own* house, "when furnished" with her remains, leaving for him to decide whether it should be carried down to the ancestral vault.

We come round to her first image of death in the grave, but her last image, before she dies, is that of a good mother. Clarissa's last letter, written in her own hand, is addressed to her "dear Mamma Norton" ("O my blessed woman! My dear maternal friend! I am entering upon a better tour than to France or Italy either!" [IV,301]). Mrs. Norton, who cannot be with Clarissa at her death, is succeeded by the Widow Lovick, attending her to the very last, whose sheltering "motherly bosom" is the resting place for Clarissa's head in her final sleep (IV,332). Mother Death takes the place of Mother Midnight. Clarissa at the end is as death-absorbed as any Homeric hero going to his anticipated doom. Death becomes what remains of her daily life: "she can talk of death and prepare for it, as if it were an occurrence as familiar as dressing and undressing" (IV,215). Belford rhapsodizes over her heroic magnanimity, tranquility, courage, and presence of mind in preparing for death. Though she may not actively will her death, Clarissa calmly proceeds through an orderly ritual of preparation for "that great and awful moment" (IV,186) which is the fatal counterpart of the "critical" and "yielding" moments already discussed. The forethought that goes into this preparation is strangely reminiscent of Lovelace's "premeditated"—Clarissa uses the word many times—"violence" leading up to the rape. Thus Lovelace and Clarissa make elaborate, single-minded preparations for their respective "critical moments," but Clarissa's moment is an encounter with a spiritual lover in the maternal house of death.

Clarissa's individual death rite also affords Richardson a sweeping satirical reflection on the social death rite of marriage in his time; now that Clarissa is "dead," she is acceptable in marriage to everyone, not least to her tormentor: "Were her death to follow in a week after the knot is tied, by the Lord of Heaven, it *shall* be tied, and she shall die a Lovelace" (IV,69). Lovelace's "friends" now counterbalance Clarissa's "friends": before, she owed it to her family to marry Solmes; now, she owes it to the family of Lord M. to marry Lovelace. After her own family has thrown her off, after the family of Mother Sinclair is done with her, there is still this last family—respectable, influential, and enormously wealthy—which has its claims on her. All this is what Clarissa means by the world, although it must be acknowledged that how she will appear in the eyes of others (especially other young women) is one of the prime reasons she gives Nancy for not living in this world either as Lovelace's wife or in the single state (III,520-21).

In the extraordinary image of Clarissa sitting at her coffin-desk ("placed near the window, like a harpsichord") and "consuming from day to day" as she literally writes herself to death (addresses herself to death and in effect *becomes* her last letter, delivered to death), we see the accelerated unraveling of the self before it enters its "last house": like a person aging sixty years in a few months, Clarissa loses her senses one by one, sight, hearing, touch, and she even talks like an old woman, as if emulating her dear older friends, Mrs. Norton and the Widow Lovick, describing her "gradual and sensible death" as the manner in which "God dies away in . . . us all human satisfactions." Still she wonders that someone who has suffered as she has done "should be so long a dying." She has "charming forebodings of happiness" as she dresses herself in the habit of a bride, in "virgin white," to await her "outsetting."

The last scene is a carefully composed tableau: Colonel Morden kneeling beside the bed, holding Clarissa's hand; the women arranged around the room in appropriate postures of grief:

> My dearest cousin, said she, be comforted—what is dying but the
> common lot?—The mortal frame may *seem* to labour—but that is all!—It
> is not so hard to die as I believed it to be!—The preparation is the
> difficulty—I bless God I have had time for that—the rest is worse to
> beholders than to me!—I am all blessed hope—hope itself (IV,346).

Clarissa had anticipated that her actual dying would be painful: "I shall have
agonies, I doubt—life will not give up so blessedly easy, I fear" (IV,288), but
she experiences instead what seems to be a pleasurable "labour."

This final labor is attended by Morden on the right and Belford on the
left, two good men who take the place of the "pretended ladies" who drew
her back to Sinclair's house. The two men thus help deliver her soul in its
death labor. And she is "all blessed hope—hope itself." We have considered
the novel as a tragedy of hope, hopes that have come to tragic disillusion-
ment. A few pages earlier Belford had lamented: "Yet, alas! how frail is hope!
How frail is life!" (IV,308).[76] With her last words, Clarissa transcends her
history of hopeless hope. If Clarissa in her prolonged death rite has indeed
evolved into her own letters, text, "scripture," and language, her repetition
here of the divine "I am" in "I am all blessed hope—hope itself" is her final
self-definition, an immortal epitaph, spoken by her and written down by her
apostle. She *is* "all blessed hope—hope itself," she *is* "Happy indeed!" In the
end, her powerful moral imagination—allied to her Wisdom—affirms her
spirit and wills a beautiful and pleasurable entrance into her own heaven,
the final house of her spirit presided over by her "blessed Lord—Jesus," the
"bridegroom" who comes for her at midnight (Matthew 25.6), the divine
vanquisher of the false one who brought about her rape at midnight. The
death of Clarissa foreshadows Johnson's sober celebration of the virtues of
hope, love, patience, and faith at the very end of *The Vanity of Human
Wishes*: "With these celestial Wisdom calms the mind, And makes the
happiness she does not find." Clarissa as a figure of Wisdom affirms her hope
and her faith, an affirmation which makes both real for her in "that unavoid-
able moment which decides the destiny of man" (IV,354).[77]

PART FIVE:

TRISTRAM SHANDY AND "THE WOMB OF SPECULATION"

38. *Tristram* and Tristram

This requires a second translation:—it shews what little knowledge is got
by mere words—we must go up to the first springs (624).[1]

On 23 May, 1759, Laurence Sterne of York sent a package to the bookseller, Robert Dodsley, of London: "Sir With this You will rec^{ve} the Life &
Opinions of Tristram Shandy, wch I choose to offer to You first—and put into
your hands without any kind of Distrust both from your general good
Character, & the very handsome Recommendation of Mr Hinksman" (the
York bookseller).[2] Sterne had great confidence in Dodsley, and even greater
confidence in the anticipated popular appeal of his novel: "The Book will sell
. . . the World . . . will fix the Value for us both."[3] Sterne was offering his
little book up, via Dodsley, to the sometimes sordid ways of a world which
puts a price on everything. In the summer, Sterne, thinking of a friend who
had advised him "to get your Preferment first Lory," wrote feelingly to
another friend who had read the manuscript and thought "the vein of humor
too free and gay for the solemn colour of [Sterne's] coat":

> But suppose preferment is long acoming (& for aught I know I may not
> be preferr'd till the Resurrection of the Just) and am all that time in
> labour—how must I bear my Pains?—You both fright me with after-
> pains (like pious Divines) or rather like able Philosophers, knowing that
> One Passion is only to be combated by Another.[4]

These early readers must have had qualms about the sexual, even bawdy,
content of a book emanating from an Anglican divine, and Sterne jokes with
them about bearing the labor pains of literary generation till the end of time.
We note also the medical implication of driving one passion out with another. But the author himself had his own qualms: "after all, I fear Tristram
Shandy must go into the world with a hundred faults—if he is so happy as to
have some striking beauties, merciful & good Judges will spare it as God did
Sodom for the ten Righteous that are therein."[5]

Sterne did not receive from Dodsley the reply he had hoped for. Sometime in the fall of 1759 he wrote again to the bookseller offering this modest
suggestion:

> I propose . . . to print a lean edition, in two small volumes, of the size of
> Rasselas, and on the same paper and type, at my own expense, merely to
> feel the pulse of the world . . . . The book shall be printed here, and the
> impression sent up to you; for as I live at York, and shall correct every

proof myself, it shall go perfect into the world, and be printed in so
creditable a way as to paper, type, &c., as to do no dishonour to you,
who, I know, never chuse to print a book meanly.[6]

We know then that Sterne was conscientious about how *Tristram Shandy*
was to appear. He wanted a small book, portable, and neatly printed. The
admirable and indefatigable bibliographic efforts of Lewis Perry Curtis have
long since been accepted as establishing that the first two volumes of
Tristram Shandy were indeed published, under Sterne's supervision, in
York, in December, 1759.[7] Contemporary opinion, including the information of Dr. John Hill, asserted that York was the place of printing: "A parcel
of books were sent up out of the country; they were unknown, and scarce
advertised; but thus friendless they made their own way, and their author's."[8] Curtis went on to point out that the volumes were printed in the
shop of Ann Ward, the chief printer in York after the recent death of her
husband, Caesar, an old friend of Sterne's. From a survey of the typography,
water marks, press numbers, and signatures of copies of the first edition of
Tristram Shandy, Curtis noted that no press numbers appear in the first two
volumes of "the mysterious first edition of Sterne's novel" and argues convincingly that the widow Ann Ward, "in a small shop, which she could
readily supervise, . . . found no need to sully her neat pages with superfluous
figures," like press numbers, in the manner of a large London bookseller,
like Dodsley; in her Sterne found the very person to print *Tristram Shandy*
in a "credible way, as to paper, type, &c."[9]

Hence Mrs. Ward can be called the printing-house midwife to the book
Tristram Shandy, the real-life counterpart to the old woman and the brash
"scientifick operator," Dr. Slop, who between them manage to bring Tristram Shandy, the character, into the world.[10] But unlike Tristram, the
narrator and "small Hero" of the novel who, as everyone knows, has his nose
squashed by Dr. Slop's forceps, *Tristram Shandy* the book will "go perfect
into the world" from the matrix of the press and will not dishonor, like a
Scriblerian bastard, its bookseller or its author. Even before his appearance
in the world, Tristram Shandy is, and is not, his book. As a literary object,
Tristram Shandy will be perfect, permanent, elegant, simple—everything,
in other words, that Tristram Shandy is not. Even before the reader enters
the picture, Sterne plays with the notions of Tristram Shandy as book and as
protagonist, but both are artificial, made up things.

The actual first edition of *Tristram Shandy* is indeed a beautiful book.
One is struck first of all by how small the seven small octavo volumes really
are, with only seventeen or eighteen lines of print per page. The well spaced
words sit on the page in pristine lucidity. The Caslon roman pica type face
makes the words seem to hover on the page and almost smile at the reader.
There is much white space—between phrases, sentences, paragraphs— and

there are the familiar long dashes. The black page is now a dark gray, but the marbled page retains a remarkable freshness in its mixture of green, white, yellow, and red, as of something seen through a microscope. The reader seems to have entered a playful, philosophical dimension which encourages thought, speculation, humor, creation—an interchange or conversation between author and reader—yet the words on the page conserve and convey a mysterious sense of secret space, of possibility. For Sterne would seem to be as interested in the spaces for creation between the words, lines, and paragraphs as in the words themselves. The *entire* book is expressive, and the entire book, for Sterne and for his reader, includes the experience of the reader reading it.

39. *Tristram Shandy* as a Midwife Book

Sterne's book may be seen as many books and traditions congregating under the "anatomy," that form of literature, as defined by Northrop Frye, "characterized by a great variety of subject-matter and a strong interest in ideas," a form first mastered in English letters by Robert Burton, Sterne's master, in *The Anatomy of Melancholy* (1621).[11] It is appropriate, however, to notice for our purposes that the *OED* does not recognize "anatomy" as a distinct literary genre but more generally as the dissection or dividing of anything for the purpose of examining its parts—an analysis—and more specifically as the artificial separation of the different parts of the human body as in a model showing the parts discovered in dissection. It is this stress on the anatomy as *displaying* the human body (Sterne's metaphor for human nature) that I would like to apply to *Tristram Shandy*, with the qualification that Sterne's book is a tragicomic anatomy, focussing strongly on the theme of procreation, wherein the body and the mind are displayed by indirect and ironic means. *Tristram Shandy* might be called "the anatomy of mortality", "the anatomy of generation," or "the anatomy of human fate." What fascinated Sterne most, I believe, about Locke's theory of the association of ideas was the multitude of possibilities it afforded him as a literary anatomist for demonstrating how language and the body relate to each other. What follows is largely an analysis of Sterne's peculiar kind of narrative associationalism, an early form of free association which has its own carefully crafted artistic logic.[12]

Frye concedes that *Tristram Shandy* may well be a novel,[13] but Sterne's anatomy also comprises a history—owing to and extending beyond Locke—of "what passes in a man's own mind" (85) and the fictional history of a family; a musical structure and a version of literary pictorialism;[14] a courtesy book in which a new kind of courtier is fashioned in Uncle Toby; a satirical tragicomedy embodied in the first person author, Tristram; a philosophical meditation on human fate; and a midwife book, a unique, poignant, and hilarious culmination of a long tradition of English midwife books.

Tristram Shandy tells, in its peculiar way, a good deal about male and female generative functions; about the conception and gestation of the infant; about a difficult case in midwifery; about obstetrics and obstetrical instruments; about pediatrics. As a midwife book, it must, willy-nilly, embody attitudes towards its reader (or user), towards birth and death, towards midwives, parents, children, child rearing, and women in particular, towards the value and meaning of human life. Almost all the earlier midwife books afford an intermittent meditation on human mortality, and in their preoccupation with examining and describing the parts of generation and their functions, they are little anatomies in the strictest sense.[15]

198

The surviving English midwife books (and those translated into English) beginning with Richard Jonas's translation of Eucharius Rösslin's *Rosengarten (The byrth of Mankynde,* 1540) are absorbing human documents in themselves, the well thumbed and frail relics of many an itinerant midwife and many a curious reader. Many of these books are in so dilapidated a condition that copies in the British Library (and elsewhere) are held together by tied laces, like ancient items of apparel. Most of the books, dating from the sixteenth and seventeenth centuries, were cheaply printed and were meant to be carried around and passed from hand to hand. Though they abound with instructions to midwives for the safe delivery of mother and child in normal and difficult labors, the books are not simply about childbirth: since most of them are concerned, in one way or another, with how men and women propagate their kind, they are in part the sex manuals of their day.[16] Sterne, who had undoubtedly read and pondered over at least a few of these little emblems of mortality,[17] says on several occasions in *Tristram Shandy* that he writes for the patient, curious, and inquisitive reader, and that, in his words, "My way is ever to point out to the curious, different tracts of investigation, to come at the first springs of the events I tell" (66). A good writer, he reminds us, will dive deep into the "first causes" of human ignorance and confusion to come up with satisfactory accounts of things (85). The Fates themselves are present "from the first creation of matter and motion," and preside over the eventual conjunction of Toby and the Widow Wadman, the culminating action of the book (552). These first springs for Sterne have many figurative meanings, but the literal sense seems to be human generation and human origins, and that is what the midwife books are essentially about.

Although Sterne's book has many things in common with the midwife literature, as one would expect from an author who will follow no man's rules (8), his work also differs sharply from them in many respects. He will write a midwife book, but one unlike any that has gone before.[18] Both Sterne and the authors of the books of generation share an acute concern for their readers, but whereas the midwife authors almost all assert some sort of preliminary admonition ("I requyre all suche men in the name of God, which at any tyme shall chaunse to have this boke, that they use it godlye . . . utterly exchuynge all rebawde and unsemely communication of any thynges contayned in the same"),[19] Sterne's Tristram seems to welcome all readers, male and female, as long as they are attentive to and patient with his unusual way of telling a story.

Sterne's narrative method of proceeding digressively, not chronologically, forcing the reader to make his own sense of the proceedings, is also in sharp contrast to the midwife authors, who repeat at length in unfolding the secrets of generation that they have taken all manner of pains to be intelligible to the meanest understanding.[20] Tristram says, "I know there are

readers in the world, as well as many other good people in it, who are no
readers at all,——who find themselves ill at ease, unless they are let into the
whole secret from first to last, of every thing which concerns you" (7). And
the book embodies a secret (or secrets) about human nature, just as Moll
Flanders has her secret name and identity, and Pamela and Clarissa have
their inviolate private selves. At this early stage in the novel, Sterne himself
perhaps does not know what the secret is, but it has something to do with the
generation, constitution, and education of his hero. If the midwife authors
want the reader to be instructed about the secrets of generation, Sterne
wants his readers to be entertained and to divine the whole secret on their
own.

Sterne and the midwives also play upon the literary convention that their
books are identical with the subjects which they treat. The midwife book is
represented as a little midwife, or an exposed infant, or a young mother.
Wolveridge presents a small, pretty child-midwife whose country dress is an
extension of the "clothing" of the child in the womb:

> Go little Book, I envy not thy hap,
> Mayst thou be dandled in the Ladies lap;
> I hope the Ladies will not disdain,
> Th'art clean, though in a home-spun dress, and plain:
> Nor mayst thou to a gaudy Garb aspire,
> Thy native Idiom is thy best attire. . . . [21]

Jonas hopes his "lytell treatyse" will be as "frutefull" in instruction as is the
laboring woman in the fruit of her womb,[22] and Raynold, who declares that
he has revised his whole book from "top to too," equates the "labour and
paynes" in writing his book with those of the laboring woman, comparing the
book itself to the "anathomye of a ded woman." The book is pictured as a
woman whose secret parts are opened, as the reader becomes a midwife-
physician to the book. Or, in another image, the book itself becomes the
midwife: "I thought it shold be a very charitable and laudable dede . . . yf by
my payns this lytell treatyse were made to speake Englysshe," so that the
book might "supply the roome and place of a goud mydwyfe."[23]

Now Tristram Shandy is his book too, and his author's brain child, but in
more varied and intriguing ways. Sterne, an appreciative reader of the Old
Testament and of Swift, was familiar with the tradition of men and women as
creatures cut and sewn in layers out of the fabric of flesh by a God who is
both midwife and tailor. Man's body, like a book, is an emblem of mortality.
A book too is sewn together; it has a spine, a cover like a suit of clothes, and
pages which are the layers of its flesh to be turned over or peeled off, until
you come to the end—then nothing. Johnson was right in one sense when he
said, "Nothing odd will do long. Tristram Shandy did not last."[24] But

Tristram Shandy, the elegant little book, did last. The book seems to be immortal to the same degree that its author and main character were all too mortal. (Laurence Sterne's name is not on the title page of the first editions.) The fate of a book is its words (and the empty spaces around them), and what happens between the book and its reader. As we write a book, or read one, we are living it, or reliving it. *Tristram Shandy*, like the midwife books and *Rasselas* and almost all the self-help books ever devised, is originally a little pocket book, designed to be part of one's dress, to be carried about like a little homunculus or child in a pocket womb, to be *worn*, usually close to the heart or to the private parts of the body. In one respect, the book is as much the reader's child as it is the author's; in another, it is an intimate companion, a friend, a guide. It makes one think of the inspired motto uttered by Knowledge, "Everyman, I will go with thee and by thy guide, In thy most need to go by thy side." Books are self-conscious objects in the eighteenth century, some ostentatiously, others more modestly so. Like a man, or a woman, any book is an enigma; if "*the periwig maketh the man*" (499), it may also disguise him, and you can't tell a book by its cover. Tristram Shandy—character, creative act of writing, and book—was Sterne's close companion for the last nine years of his life.

The book is in a double sense identical with its subject: it embodies both Tristram's life and opinions and Sterne's act of writing, which was *his* life during a period of extreme ill health, with one tubercular crisis after another. Tristram's opinions stand midway between his "life" and the "life" of Sterne's writing. An opinion is indeterminate, unfixed, a belief based not on absolute certainty or positive knowledge but only on what seems true to one's own mind. It is an evaluation, an impression, and often it has a moral dimension. To discern Tristram's relationship to his book is exceedingly difficult, but it would appear that for Tristram, as for Clarissa (different as they may be in other respects), the act of writing is the act of living: I write therefore I am. Tristram's book is ultimately an attempt to discover himself by divining his origins and identity within the context and history of his immediate family. The writing of his story is also a way of authenticating his existence, and preserving his opinions, leading to a philosophic reverence for life, "being determined as long as I live or write (which in my case means the same thing) never to give . . . a worse word or a worse wish, than my uncle *Toby* gave the fly which buzz'd about his nose all *dinner time*,—'Go, —go poor devil,' quoth he, '—get thee gone, why should I hurt thee? This world is surely wide enough to hold both thee and me'" (162).

Both Sterne and the midwives are further preoccupied with the mechanics of human sexual intercourse leading to conception, with the condition of the child in the womb, and with the experience of birth. We shall look more fully at what the midwife books have to say about the act of human propagation in considering Walter Shandy, the patriarch of the family. It is well to

recall at this point, however, that most of the midwife books before the
mid-eighteenth century follow tradition in assigning the father the most
important role in conception. Furthermore, Louis Landa has convincingly
shown Sterne's apparent debt to contemporary speculation about
embryology.[25] There were two schools of thought concerning human conception, the ovists and the animalculists. The ovists (including Harvey,
Swammerdam, and de Graaf) believed in the dictum, *ex ovo omnium*; the
animalculists, led by Leeuwenhoek and inspired by his discovery of the
spermatazoa, believed that a miniature of the person-to-be, a homunculus,
was preformed not in the egg, but in the human spermatazoa. Landa quotes
Patrick Blair, a Fellow of the Royal Society, who notes that an animalcule of
masculine seed contains a whole man and the particles in the ovum contain
its food; the "new arriv'd Child . . . who after being fatigu'd by so long a
Journey, and through so many difficult and unaccessible Roads," has need of
refreshment to rouse his spirits and make him grow up into a lively boy.[26]
Tristram Shandy, character and book, partakes of both schools. Tristram
originates as an animalculan "Homunculus," a creature presented to us as a
tiny manikin,

> a BEING guarded and circumscribed with rights . . . created by the
> same hand,—engender'd in the same course of nature,—endowed with
> the same loco-motive powers and faculties with us;—That he consists, as
> we do, of skin, hair, fat, flesh, veins, arteries, ligaments, nerves, carti-
> lages, bones, marrow, brains, glands, genitals, humours, and articula-
> tions;—is a Being of as much activity,—and, in all senses of the word, as
> much and as truly our fellow-creature as my Lord Chancellor of En-
> gland. (5)

This lovely satirical anticlimax, reminiscent of the Scriblerians' description of
an "artificial man" who "will not only walk, and speak, and perform most of
the outward actions of the animal life, but (being wound up once a week) will
perhaps reason as well as most of your Country Parsons,"[27] has the effect of
casting little Tristram from the beginning as a man and not a man—an
individual person with inalienable rights, but also as a little alien endowed
with the same qualities "with us," a creature who is "as much and as truly"
human as . . . well, *who*? (As soon as an individual starts making the
comparison he or she is in trouble.) The definition raises the question: in
what does (or should) mankind's essential nature consist? This may be the
primary question which the novel raises and, in its circuitous, riddling, and
secretive way, attempts to answer.

   Tristram is his father's animalculan son and "my father" is also the creation
of Tristram. Father and son coexist in a mutual act of creation in the novel.
Tristram's *book*, on the other hand, which embodies its fictional author,

might be said to have an ovarian origin, since Tristram is glad that he has begun the history of himself from his conception, and that he is "able to go on tracing every thing in it, as *Horace* says, *ab Ovo*" (7). Now this process is not quite the same thing as *ex ovo omnium*, but it suggests a feminine matrix for the novel—the mind-womb of the actual author. As we have noted, Sterne often refers to his own mind under the proverbial aspect of the womb. In the "Sermon on Conscience," Yorick—with language that evokes the intuitive knowledge a mother has of her child—sees the mind in its conventional feminine (or Psychean) form: "But here the mind has all the evidence and facts within herself;—is conscious of the web she has wove;—knows its texture and fineness" (126). Toward the end of the book, Tristram, in looking back from the end of the last chapter and "surveying the texture of what has been wrote" (an account of Walter and Elizabeth discussing the Widow Wadman and Uncle Toby), implies that the difficult task of literary creation is kept going, and the book is augmented by those elusive feminine personifications, capricious "FANCY," "WIT," and "PLEASANTRY (good natured slut as she is)" (614). Finally Walter Shandy, in concluding his search for the "Seat of the Soul" in the cerebellum, that "delicate and fine-spun web," sees both the "soul" (Psyche, "Anima") and its domain in feminine terms (149) without seeming to realize it.

Walter's own mental processes are a carefully presented exemplification and demonstration of his son's theory of the hypothesis: Tristram says, "It is the nature of an hypothesis, when once a man has conceived it, that it assimilates every thing to itself as proper nourishment; and, from the first moment of your begetting it, it generally grows the stronger by every thing you see, hear, read, or understand" (151). Walter's hypotheses usually begin with the physical phenomenon and spin out into the intangible, Tristram's start with the metaphysical and come humorously back to the generative body. In his discourse to Toby on the nature and function of Woman, Walter is interrupted (not for the first time in the novel): "Now, if a man was to sit down coolly"—whenever Walter or any other male in the Shandy world "sits down coolly" to do something, whether to discourse rationally or to "plant cabbages," the reader can expect difficulty—

> Now, if a man was to sit down coolly, and consider within himself the make, the shape, the construction, com-at-ability, and convenience of all the parts which constitute the whole of that animal, call'd Woman, and compare them analogically.—I never understood rightly the meaning of that word,—quoth my uncle *Toby*.—ANALOGY, replied my father, is the certain relation and agreement, which different —Here a devil of a rap at the door snapp'd my father's definition (like his tobacco-pipe) in two,—and, at the same time, crushed the head of as notable and curious a dissertation as ever was engendered in the womb of speculation;—it

was some months before my father could get an opportunity to be safely
deliver'd of it:—And, at this hour, it is a thing full as problematical as the
subject of the dissertation itself. . . . (102-3)

For Tristram, clearly, Woman and the feminine is a far more complicated
and problematical subject than it is for his father. One gathers from *Tristram
Shandy* and Sterne's letters that by playing the dual role of Tristram and
Yorick in his life and in his writings, Sterne, like Richardson, indicated his
fascination and preoccupation with women, with images of women, and with
feminine beauty and sensibility.[28] Though there are no major female
characters in *Tristram Shandy* until the Widow Wadman's influence is felt in
books eight and nine, the novel (and the letters, too, for that matter) teem
with women and figurative extensions of the feminine, as a glance at the
following characters and personifications shows: Mrs. Shandy and Tristram's
friend, Jenny, who share a certain "greatness of soul" (44); Yorick's wife, the
old "motherly midwife", Aunt Dinah "backsliding" in her orbit, the Beguine
and her massage, Susannah and Bridget; and later the mad Maria, Tom's
widow, the statuesque Janatone who carries "the principles of change within
her frame" (490), the abbess and the novice of Andoüillets, and the "sun-
burnt daughter of Labour" with the dark chestnut hair who will invite frail
Tristram to a country dance in his travels through France (537-8).

In figurative terms, in contrast to the polar countries, there is the "warm-
er and more luxuriant island" of England, a loving mother who pours down
the passions "amongst us in such a flowing kind of decent and creditable
plenty" (197) that no one has cause to complain—the language is reminiscent
of that used by an earlier English divine, Robert Herrick, whose work is also
impregnated with images of women. There is Sterne's female reader,
"Madam," alluded to in a variety of tones; there is "a true Virgin-Dedication"
(15), part of which, Tristram assures us, is reserved for "the Moon, who . . .
of all PATRONS and MATRONS I can think of, has most power to set my
book a-going, and make the world run mad after it" (16-17). Joining the
feminine psychic powers of Wit, Pleasantry, and Fancy (614) are Curiosity
and Desire (543), and a host of other female personifications, the greatest of
which are the Muses (the "Powers" Tristram mentions earlier), the "ungracious Duchess," Fortune, the Fates, and of course, a fecund, many-sided,
maternal Nature. The midwife book was often called "the Woman's Book."
In a Shandyan world plagued with male obtuseness, arrogance, debility, and
impotence (as well as female obtuseness, moral and mental frailty, and
frustration), Sterne's midwife book, through the double vision of "Tristram"
and "Yorick," shows an exceptional *human* sensitivity to the feminine origins
of life and creation—physical, mental, and imaginative.

The "womb of speculation" (102-3) is as suggestive a term for Sterne as the
"womb of fate" is for Richardson. Let us return for a moment to the

Homunculus. When the as yet unnamed "little gentleman" arrives at his place of reception, the womb, the animal spirits which were to have escorted him there have been dispersed and "his muscular strength and virility [are] worn down to a thread" (6). His impaired virility at the start of life recalls that of his father in his late middle age. For the midwife authors, the thread of life begins as the growth of "very many and very small fibers or hairs," as we saw in Wolveridge's account.[29] In Sterne's midwife book, however, the thread is almost evanescent at the outset. Moreover, the little traveler, like his father after his sexual exertion, is "miserably spent," and in his "sad disorder'd state of nerves," lies down "a prey to sudden starts, or a series of melancholy dreams and fancies for nine long, long months together,"[30] a miniature counterpart to Walter's own subsequent nocturnal anxieties about the child-hood development of his second son. The prenatal experience of Tristram, like that of the foetus described in some midwife books, is far from the nirvana-like state proposed by modern theorists about life before birth. As he begins his nine-month sojourn in the womb of his mother, the Tristram homunculus exists also in a womb of anxious speculation.

The midwife books before 1720 do not have much to say about the journey of the masculine seed to its "cherishing" place in the womb, but they reiterate the notion of "the disease of the nine months," and they comment vividly on the actual birth of the child. It was widely held at this time that labor was initiated not by the contractions of the uterus but by the efforts of the healthy child, ripe for his freedom, to break out of the prison of the womb: Wolveridge describes the moment when the infant in the womb begins its movement toward birth, impelled with "great strugglings and force" to break the "ligaments, reins, and coats in which it is involved." The womb opens, the fluids flow down, and the infant now free of the womb itself begins to smell the air and "being desirous of his life" turns himself toward the "outlet of the matrix."[31] But as vigorous as the child is, he nonetheless "draws his death after him."[32] Sterne was probably aware of the new discov-ery, enunciated most accurately by Smellie, of the womb's active (and the child's passive) role in the mechanism of labor.[33] The birth of Tristram is presented not from the infant's point of view but almost entirely externally, as Sterne focuses our attention on the passive and vulnerable state of the child as victim by examining the bungling activities of Dr. Slop, whose figurative birth into the novel occurs shortly before Tristram's.

Besides its concern with the process of labor, another important feature which *Tristram Shandy* shares with earlier midwife literature is the con-ventional panegyric on the nature of man. This is Wolveridge's fairly typical version:

> It being no less virtue and prudence to preserve a child when begotten, than content and pleasure in begetting; in both which, both Sexes are,

and ought equally to be concerned . . . let us . . . contrive, how that
creature man may be preserved, from the beginning of his Conception,
to the hour of his birth, and that with safety too to her that bore
him.—And truly, it may be worth the while, if we consider the excellency of man, whom some call (as like unto God, so) the Interpreter of
the gods. *Pythagoras* calls him The Measure of all things; and *Plato* calls
him The Wonder of Wonders. *Theophrastus* styles him The Great
Pattern of the Universe. *Aristotle* terms him A Politick Animal, born for
society, whom God made with his face upright; whereas all other creatures look with their faces downwards. . . . *Synesius* terms man the
Horizon of all corporeal and incorporeals. *Tully* calls him a Divine
creature, full of Reason and counsel; whom *Pliny* also calls the Epitomy
of the World, and delight of Nature: And whom all with one consent,
call, a *Microcosme*, a little world in a bigger.[34]

But Sterne presents this motif unconventionally. We have just seen what
Sterne does with the microcosm idea in the story of the Tristram homunculus, and Sterne will several times play with the imagery of miniatures as
emblems of mortality. Wolveridge begins his panegyric with the notion of
the mutual influence of the sexes on their offspring, an influence to which
Tristram alludes wistfully in the opening sentence of his book ("I wish either
my father or my mother, or indeed both of them, as they were in duty both
equally bound to it, had minded what they were about when they begot me"
[4]). At the opening of Book V, which might be called Corporal Trim's book
with its focus on his masterly re-enactment of the entire phenomenon of
human corporeality in the fall of a hat, Tristram begins on a note of fatigue:

Shall we for ever make new books, as apothecaries make new mixtures,
by pouring only out of one vessel into another?
Are we for ever to be twisting, and untwisting the same rope? for
ever in the same track—for ever at the same pace? . . .
Who made MAN, with powers which dart him from earth to heaven
in a moment—that great, that most excellent, and most noble creature of
the world—the *miracle* of nature, as Zoroaster in his book
called him—the SHEKINAH of the divine presence, as Chrysostom—
the *image* of God, as Moses—the *ray* of divinity, as Plato—the *marvel* of
Marvels, as Aristotle—to go sneaking on at this pitiful—pimping—
pettifogging rate? (343)

Sterne has just played the trick (not unknown to Swift in his "Verses on his
own Death") of scorning plagiarists in a passage he himself has copied out of
that arch copyist Burton's *Anatomy of Melancholy*, and his panegyric on man

prefaces a chapter "Upon Whiskers" which take their proper place just under noses in the novel's typology of sex.[35] Making new books out of old ones would seem to be a trope for making new human beings out of old ones, and Sterne, in this passage, seems to be pleading for something out of the ordinary—something like a miracle—in the age-old process of creating new human beings. Tristram then goes on to wish for the presence of a "good farcical house" to hold all the literary imitators in "*Great Britain, France, and Ireland*" and "sublimate them, *shag-rag and bob-tail*, male and female, all together" (343). That is, he wants to purify them into something new and better.

There are early indications of this impulse to create a new human being. Despite several references to his "dear, dear *Jenny*," Tristram does not want his reader, especially his fair reader, to imagine that he is a married man, or that he keeps a mistress. He wants to keep the relationship between himself and Jenny a secret. Might not Jenny be a child, or even his "Friend!" "Surely, Madam, a friendship between the two sexes may subsist, and be supported without—Fy! Mr. *Shandy*:—Without any thing, Madam, but that tender and delicious sentiment, which ever mixes in friendship, where there is a difference of sex" (49).[36] Sterne goes out of his way to point out to Mrs. F. in a letter that even though his Nose . . . is an inch at least longer than most of my neighbours . . . I am a two footed animal without one Lineament of Hair of the beast upon me, totally spiritualized out of all form for conubial purposes. . . . I am moreover of a thin, dry, hectic, unperspirable habit of Body—so sublimated and rarified in all my parts That a Lady of yr . . . Wit would not give a brass farthing for a dozen such: next May when I am at my best, You shall try me—tho I tell You before hand I have not an ounce & a half of carnality about me."[37] Sterne's appearance at this time was ghastly, his carnality wasted by consumption, but his joking offers glimmers of what might be called a Shandean theory of the sublimation of the sexes into a new being who like Uncle Toby blends and embodies the virtues of courage and gentleness.[38]

Thus it might be said that Sterne's midwife book, like its predecessors, is also a kind of sex manual, but one which offers its instruction indirectly by means of a thoroughly individual and complex process of innuendo, humorous analogy, and often covert allusion, even while incorporating much of the "hearty good women's" uninhibited sense of sexual humor. What this means, of course, is that the book is capable of almost unlimited sexual inference. *Tristram Shandy* is a midwife book which documents the coming to birth of laughter and a new kind of person, sublimated beyond male and female in the hero, Tristram Shandy, as fathered and mothered by his beloved spiritual mentor, Uncle Toby, who teaches him what it means to be humane not through words but through his actions. The jog-trot, hobby-horsical, back-and-forth copulative rhythm of the novel generates, ultimately, the philosophy of "true *Shandeism*," expressed in quasi-medical language.

We may better understand this new philosophy by turning back again to George Cheyne's *The English Malady*. The human body, according to Cheyne, is a "Machin" of an infinite number and variety of pipes and channels, all filled with various fluids perpetually running forward, or returning backward "in a constant *Circle*" and sending out little branches to nourish and maintain the living body.[39] In Tristram's words,

> True *Shandeism*, think what you will against it, opens the heart and lungs, and like all those affections which partake of its nature, it forces the blood and other vital fluids of the body to run freely thro' its channels, and makes the wheel of life run long and chearfully round. (337-8)

The explicit birth mechanism of this new medical philosophy is described in an address to the gentle reader (301-02), a passage equal in importance for Sterne's midwife book as the bequest of Clarissa's writings to Belford is for Richardson's novel. In his characteristically roundabout and sexually joking way, Tristram says that despite the fanciful and careless attitude he has so far displayed toward the reader, he has "lusted earnestly and endeavoured carefully . . . that these little books, which I here put into thy hands, might stand instead of many bigger books" (301). This portable, unpretentious little book,

> If 'tis wrote against anything, 'tis wrote . . . against the spleen; in order, by a more frequent and a more convulsive elevation and depression of the diaphragm, and the succussations of the intercostal and abdominal muscles in laughter, to drive the *gall* and other *bitter juices* from the gall bladder, liver and sweet-bread of his majesty's subjects, with all the inimicitious passions which belong to them, down into their duodenums (301-02).

Cheyne says:

> The *Spleen* or *Vapours*, as the Word is used in *England*, is of so general and loose a Signification, that it is a common Subterfuge for meer Ignorance of the Nature of Distempers. All *Lowness of Spirits, Swelling of the Stomach, frequent Eructation, Noise in the Bowels or Ears, frequent Yawning, Inappetency, Restlessness, Inquietude, Fidgeting, Anxiety, Peevishness, Discontent, Melancholy, Grief, Vexation, Ill-*

Humour, Inconstancy, lethargick or *watchful Disorders*, in short, every Symptom, not already classed under some particular limited Distemper, is called by the general Name of *Spleen* and *Vapours*.[40]

One would be hard pressed to come up with a better list of splenetic grievances as dramatized in the novel, particularly in the behavior of Walter Shandy and Tristram.

Cheyne goes on to argue, as we noted before in the context of Pamela's "fits," that "any acrid, sharp, or corroding Juice," like the "*gall* and other *bitter juices*" referred to by Tristram, may occasion "*Convulsions, Spasms, Gripes* or Pains" which are communicated through the entire body, "continuing till the offending Matter is by such violent Action or Motion worked off, or removed."[41] Cheyne explicitly compares this process to the expulsion of the child in birth ("in the same Manner as the *Foetus*, by its Motion or Pressure, raises those *Throws* and *Convulsions* in the Mother, that bring it into the World") and concludes:

> Thus *Choler, Wind, sharp* and *porracious* Juices, occasion those *Fits* and *Convulsions* in the Bowels . . . being the Struggle of Nature to throw them out, which are commonly call'd *Hysterick Fits*; and thus any *irritating, acrid,* or *sharp* Humour or Steam, according to the Place wherein they are lodged, or the Sensibility of the Part affected, occasions all the various and different Degrees or Kinds of *Convulsions* that are common in *Nervous* Disorders.[42]

Hence Tristram's account of the mechanism of the birth of laughter is a parody of conventional medical accounts of the gestation of nervous disorders, with a characteristically positive stress on the therapeutic function of laughter. Sterne through Tristram is for turning hysteria into hilarity. Tristram uses much the same Latinate medical diction as Cheyne to describe a healthy kind of "working off" or expulsion downwards of gall through the convulsive and purgative effect of laughter.[43] But there is more to his description. Every reader of *Tristram Shandy* knows that all through the novel (as in Swift's *Tale of a Tub* and other great satires of the body), there is an implied equivalence between the "upper" and "lower" organs and functions; the diaphragm had long been recognized as the muscular partition separating the spiritual organ, the lungs, from the guts, and the *OED* further informs us that "to move the diaphragm" meant to excite laughter: "It still moues my Diaphragme, what once moued the Spleene of Cyrus," says John Gaule in 1629. Sterne's stress on the effect of his little book on the reader as exciting "a more frequent and a more convulsive elevation and depression of the diaphragm" may be a covert recollection of certain descriptions in the literature of midwifery of the supposed up and down motion of the womb during coition.[44] Sterne seems to suggest an affinity between the convulsive pleasures of laughter and coition, as he does in other parts of *Tristram Shandy*, notably the passage on Tickletoby's mare.

The philosophy of true Shandeism then incorporates Sterne's idea of "sublimation," and the portable pocket "midwife book," *Tristram Shandy*— at once a feminine construct and a masculine "life" story—works in two ways. It is first of all a comic emblem of the activity of the members of generation. Second (and related to this activity), in a novel full of references to machines and mechanism, the book itself functions as a comic instrument, like a "*petite Canulle*" (58) or a "good farcical house" in miniature, for creating a new person in the reader, male or female, effecting a conversion from depression and nervous disorder (the "Spleen") to emotional health through the shaking up, purgative, liberating, and refining process of Shandean laughter.

40. The Midwife and Dame Nature

—Nature is nature, said *Jonathan* (365)

Besides Tristram and the immediate members of his family circle, we are introduced early to some of the other central figures in this odd book of generation. The first is the world itself, "this scurvy and disasterous world of ours," a "vile, dirty planet . . . made up of the shreds and clippings of the rest," "one of the vilest worlds that ever was made" (10). It is an artificial, patched-up world, a sloppy job. Tristram's bemused stress on the vileness (or baseness or cheapness) of his world (and he clearly speaks only of his own experience) prepares us for "what the world calls fortune," an "ungracious Duchess" who singles out the small hero, Tristram, for her "continual sport" in a set of "pitiful misadventures and cross accidents" (10). Fortune is characterized as a powerful woman with a special interest in Tristram; she is joined as a force in the book by her sister power, Fate (or the Fates, or the "destinies") who appear at critical moments in the action, particularly in the last third of the novel as spinners and patchers up of the fabric of human life. A vile world made up of the shreds of better ones, and an ungracious fortune, are of a piece with the uncourtly Dr. Slop who will have such great influence on Tristram's getting into the world and his constitutional preparation for living in it and dealing with it.

But like so many other of the active participants in the novel (Tristram's father and mother, Toby and the Widow, Trim and Bridget, the reader—"Sir" and "Madam"), the midwife also comes in two sexes:

> In the same village where my father and my mother dwelt, dwelt also a thin, upright, motherly, notable, good old body of a midwife, who, with the help of a little plain good sense, and some years full employment in her business, in which she had all along trusted little to her own efforts, and a great deal to those of dame nature,—had acquired, in her way, no small degree of reputation in the world;—by which word *world*, need I in this place inform your worship, that I would be understood to mean no more of it, than a small circle described upon the circle of the great world, of four *English* miles diameter, or thereabouts, of which the cottage where the good old woman lived, is supposed to be the centre.— She had been left, it seems, a widow in great distress, with three or four small children, in her forty-seventh year . . . she was at that time a person of decent carriage,—grave deportment,—a woman moreover of few words. . . . (11-12)

good
parora

We do not need to rehearse at this point the various descriptions of the good midwife already presented in this book. It will be sufficient to recall that as far back as 1540 Richard Jonas was speaking of "honeste and motherlye mydwyfes" in his *The Byrth of Mankynde*. What may here be noted is the affectionate tone of Sterne's traditional picture of the country midwife, a tone sharply contrasted by his presentation of the modern "scientifick operator," Dr. Slop. Part of the satire of Sterne's unique midwife book is the presentation, in the rivalry between the innovative "modern," Slop, and the grave, notable "old" village midwife, of the acrid controversy in England in the 1750s between the new man-midwives armed with their instruments, particularly the forceps designed by Dr. William Smellie, and the old-fashioned female midwives who relied almost solely on their experience and what they liked to consider their innate and uniquely feminine mastery of "touching." Jean Donnison gives an illuminating account of the controversy,[45] drawing particular attention to the work of Mrs. Elizabeth Nihell, the most outspoken of the female midwives, and the one most gifted for doing satirical battle with men. All through the seventeenth and early eighteenth centuries male-midwives, as we have seen, often accused their female counterparts (and often with good reason) of being rash, giddy, officious, drunken, ignorant, and arrogant. Mrs. Nihell in her *Treatise* adroitly turns these charges back on contemporary male practitioners, particularly the long-suffering Smellie, adding a few touches of her own. As if thinking of Pamela's sad outfit, she suggests an appropriate costume for the new man-midwife: "I would advise, for the younger ones, a round-ear cap, with pink and silver bridles. . . . As to the older ones, a double-clout pinned under their chin could not but give them the air of very venerable old women."[46] Mrs. Nihell's book came out the same year as *Tristram Shandy* and her account of the new man-midwife shares some features with Sterne's portrait of Slop. Mrs. Nihell asserts that nature has bestowed on the female sex a peculiar assiduity and competence in aiding women in labor; certain men may occasionally display this ability, but then it seems more forced than natural to them. "Women . . . have more bowels for women." For all the boasted erudition of men, she cannot help noting "a certain clumsy untowardly management" that plainly shows this skill to be merely an "acquisition of art, or rather the rickety production of interest begot upon art."[47]

Mrs. Nihell's appeal to nature serves to recall that behind the description of the good midwife lies, in the literature relating to birth, a traditional interpretation of Nature as a wise but limited artisan, usually represented as a woman, who reveals herself in her Book for those who know how to read it. This notion goes back to the "father of English midwifery," William Harvey. Before Harvey, many things were "*concealed in the darkness of Impervestigible Nature*," but he refused "to be tutored by other men's commentaries, without making tryal of the things themselves: especially, since *Natures Book* is so *open*, and *legible*." For Harvey and his optimistic disciples, "Nature, truly, is Her self the most faithful Interpreter of Her own Secrets . . . to us, the whole Theatre of the World is now open," as compared with the "narrow limits of *Greece*."[48]

The secrets of Nature, then, are a woman's secrets; Nature's book—the whole phenomenal world—is a woman's book; and those secrets are, after Harvey, now largely open to those adepts who trust and will be guided by Her. William Sermon, whose description of the midwife was central to the discussion of Moll Flanders' Governess and Pamela's adversary, Mrs. Jewkes, summed up for his midwife audience the seventeenth-century French-Galenist sense of Dame Nature as a midwife, ordained by God, "the best Midwife." For Sermon, midwives ought to know, above everything else, that "Nature, the handmaid of the great God," has given to everything in the world its beginning, growth, appropriate condition, perfection, and decline, phases which are manifested most impressively in the mother's bringing forth of a child in birth: "for Nature surpasseth all, and in that she doth, 's wiser than either Art, or the Artist, what ever she be, or the best and most cunning Workman that may be found."[49] Nature has her own wisdom greater than that of any other female artisan or male workman. Finally, the great seventeenth-century man-midwife and friend to Harvey, Sir Percival Willughby, knew that women in former ages always had a "better, invisible midwife to assist them, Dame Nature . . . Eve's midwife."[50]

But even for Harvey, though Nature is an artisan of good sense and proportion, she is subject to certain limitations. He stresses "Aristotle's . . . one foundation, namely, *Natures Perfection*; which in all her workmanship, hath nothing *short*, nor nothing *superfluous*, but always disposeth matters for the best. . . . which is to be understood of Her, as often as she acts freely, and by choice. But sometimes she acts otherwise, being as it were under constraint, and put beside her purpose." The reasons for her acting otherwise are vague, attributable to "defect" or "superfluity of matter," "default" in Nature's instruments, or "outward impediments."[51]

By Sterne's time, certain investigators of Nature, though still applauding her wisdom and sense of harmony, were more inquisitive about the curiosities which resulted from a kind of boredom or inadvertency on the part of Dame Nature:

> Whatever degree of accuracy and wisdom nature employs in the composition and frame of the human body, we have oftener than once seen her swerve from these, and, as it were, forget herself. . . . It should seem . . . that this common parent, tired out and spent with producing every day the same things, over and over, in the same order, did now and then quit that uniformity . . . [producing a variety of] *lusus naturae*."[52]

With the notion of Nature as a bored or capricious parent, tired of the
same dull round of imitation, we enter the natural world of the Shandy
family, particularly Tristram's world. This is not a world of *lusus naturae* as
such, but one of vagaries and eccentricities on the part of Nature and her
human offspring. Although the old midwife inhabits the same local space as
Tristram, her world is one of regularity and uniformity; appropriately
enough for one who presides over the apportionment of navel strings, she
dwells in the exact center of that precisely defined circle of four English
miles—a circle carefully set off from "the great world"—for Tristram the
vilest world that ever was made. The old midwife is a widow, past childbearing, of grave deportment, and taciturn. Unlike our previous Mother Midnights, however, she seems an entirely good creature, though ultimately
limited and circumscribed. The midwife's Dame Nature is identical with the
one who presides over the homogeneous Danish nation, "neither very
lavish, nor . . . very stingy in her gifts of genius and capacity to its
inhabitants;—but, like a discreet parent, was moderately kind to them all,"
whereas "in this unsettled island," in general, and specifically for the Shandys, "we are all ups and downs in this matter . . . nature, in her gifts and
dispositions of this kind, is most whimsical and capricious; fortune herself
not being more so in the bequest of her goods and chattels than she" (25).
The root of the words "nature" and "genius" is the same; Nature produces
genius, and the true English nature is here virtually equated with fortune.
    "Nature had been prodigal in her gifts to my father beyond measure, and
had sown the seeds of verbal criticism as deep within him, as she had done
the seeds of all other knowledge" (230). It is nature as this goddess of
extremes ("you are a great genius;—or tis fifty to one, Sir, you are a great
dunce and a blockhead . . . the two extremes are more common" in England
[25]) that has produced Walter, the compulsive theorist who proceeds to
alter the text of Erasmus's discourse on the uses and applications of long
noses to suit his own meaning. Erasmus' Dame Folly is not far from the
prodigal Dame Nature of this passage, and her gift of profound verbal
criticism puts us in mind once again of Fate (fatum) and her predilection for
the word. The sense of Nature as a visual artist of figurative language or poet
of appearances is conveyed in "the sweet look of goodness which sat upon my
uncle *Toby*'s [brow] . . . and Nature had moreover wrote GENTLEMAN
with so fair a hand in every line of his countenance, that even his tarnish'd
gold-laced hat and huge cockade of flimsy taffeta became him" (601). Nature
for Sterne as well as the Shandys has a mysterious and varied personality;
she is a rich complex of moods and extremes, with a sense of humor and a gift
for irony.[53] Even Dr. Slop, when he confronts his green medical bag "tied
and cross-tied . . . with . . . a multiplicity of round-abouts and intricate cross
turns," recognizes, at least fleetingly, the intricate and forbidding model of a
womb which Obadiah has fashioned for him.[54] Tristram reflects,

I think in my conscience, that had NATURE been in one of her nimble moods, and in humour for such a contest—and she and Dr. *Slop* both fairly started together—there is no man living who had seen the bag with all that *Obadiah* had done to it,—and known likewise, the great speed the goddess can make when she thinks proper, who would have had the least doubt . . . which of the two would have carried off the prize. My mother, madam, had been delivered sooner than the green bag infallibly (166).

The old midwife had her carefully circumscribed four-mile circle in nature's domain (11). Trying to impose their order on Nature's multiple phenomena, the literati of Strasbourg believed that "nature, though she sported—she sported within a certain circle;—and they could not agree about the diameter of it" (259); but for Tristram, Nature, though a "dear Goddess," makes us behave in inexplicable ways, and is herself like the traditional seventeenth-century images of woman as a many-roomed house or secret cabinet, as a piece of fine cloth with many folds and wrinkles, or as an elaborate network or labyrinth—a mysterious figure full of dark sides and impenetrable crannies. In *Tristram Shandy*, generative Nature is represented as an all enveloping, shaping, maternal birth spirit closely associated with fate, and the Fates.[55] Tristram, just after inadvertently throwing his fair sheet of writing into the fire instead of the foul one, tosses his wig up to the ceiling and, as if instructing his female auditor—who is always addressed on delicate female subjects—in a difficult case in midwifery, points out that the "dear Goddess" Nature,

by an instantaneous impulse, in all *provoking cases*, determines us to a sally of this or that member—or else she thrusts us into this or that place, or posture of body, we know not why—But mark, madam, we live amongst riddles and mysteries—the most obvious things, which come in our way, have dark sides, which the quickest sight cannot penetrate into; and even the clearest and most exalted understandings amongst us find ourselves puzzled and at a loss in almost every cranny of nature's works; so that this, like a thousand other things, falls out for us in a way, which tho' we cannot reason upon it,—yet we find the good of it, may it please your reverences and your worships—and that's enough for us (293).[56]

The dear Goddess has a form, for all her mystery; she is a woman, and in this passage she is Willughby's "invisible midwife," enveloping us, thrusting us into this or that gesture "we know not why . . . yet we find the good of it." As Tristram said in reference to whether his father should have taken off his wig with his right hand or his left, "need I tell you, Sir, that the circumstances with which every thing in this world is begirt, give every thing in this world its size and shape;—and by tightening it, or relaxing it, this way or that, make the thing to be, what it is—great—little—good—bad—indifferent" (158). These begirding circumstances too are Nature, a Nature who, though seemingly inexplicable and even allied to error, ultimately works to originate, sustain, and enhance human life.

41. Yorick, the Black Page, and Marriage Articles

The first thirty pages of *Tristram Shandy* provide a kind of prelude to the story of Tristram and his birth in the account of the life and death of Parson Yorick, his forerunner. After 900 years, all of Yorick's Danish blood, and the "cold phlegm and exact regularity of sense and humours," which are evident in the old midwife and the Danish nation in general, seem to have run out. Yorick, like Tristram and Sterne himself, is an odd creature, "mercurial," "sublimated," "heteroclite," a gay satirist "with an invincible dislike and opposition in his nature" to the affectation of gravity: "the very essence of gravity was design, and consequently deceit" (25-26). This opposition is reenacted in Sterne's satiric depiction of the designing, heavy-handed man-midwife, Dr. Slop. Yorick, like Tristram, has a difficult time with a nasty and dirty world, but whereas he falls victim to the world and dies of a broken heart, Tristram prevails. This chapter explores the elegiac significance of Yorick for Tristram, and two unexpected manifestations of the midwife and fate.

We have noted in several ways in which *Tristram Shandy* calls our attention to itself as a tactile, visual object, as do the midwife books which precede it. One of the most striking examples of Sterne's nonverbal summons to his reader's sensibility, and to the "first springs" of the narrative, is the famous black page.[57] Yorick, whom the reader has come to know as a friendly man associated with new birth, generosity, play, freedom, mirth, candor, and genial satire, is on his deathbed, "within a few hours of giving his enemies the slip for ever" (30). He beseeches Eugenius to take a view of his head, "bruised and mis-shapen'd by the blows of his enemies" in the travail of his life. We recall that "there is a fatality attends the actions of some men. Order them as they will, they pass thro' a certain medium which so twists and refracts them from their true directions that, with all the titles to praise which a rectitude of heart can give, the doers of them are nevertheless forced to live and die without it" (23). We turn page thirty-one of *Tristram Shandy* in simultaneous motion with Yorick's eyes as they follow Eugenius to the door (a last journey in a book which abounds with mortal journeys) and our eyes are pulled into another doorway, the black vertical rectangle on page thirty-three. A book in the act of being read is itself a series of openings, each page a door leading to the next. In the act of perception which reading entails, the black page keeps pulling our eyes away from the epitaph for Yorick on the facing page. It distorts and blurs the language, as if pulling it over into the void; it casts an inescapable pall.

Sterne performs here, in his own extraordinary way, the exacting role of the elegiac satirist. Other great ones in English literature before him—Donne, Milton, Swift, Gray—all had a preternatural interest in the links between birth and death, and all had to invent, perhaps for obscure reasons of poetic survival, a simulacrum of themselves which dies on their pages before they themselves will die: Donne in his own funeral sermon, Milton in "Lycidas," Swift in the "Verses on his own Death," Gray in his "Elegy." Yorick performs that same function for Sterne. The parson seems to be there as a counterweight to his fraternal twin, Tristram (Sterne's other self) who will *not* die of a broken heart. There is "a footway crossing the churchyard close by the side of [Yorick's] grave" and passengers repeat his epitaph [*Alas, poor Yorick!*] in "a variety of plaintive tones." Aside from purposes of identification, there seems to be a deep need in human nature to affix the name of the individual person after the experience of death, as well as after the experience of birth.

We all receive an individual name at birth, like a birthmark; we receive that name again in death, often with an embellishment, marked on a stone. Yorick is kept alive in a sense by the plaintive repetition of his epitaph, and his ghost is laid to rest by Sterne himself when he tells the story of the "Ill-fated sermon" on Conscience (142-43). After the epitaph, we ponder the blank doorway again, and when we feel ready to pass beyond and through it, we turn the page where it appears again, like the repetition of Yorick's epitaph—an echo, a second shock. Sterne's book is an immortal elegy for mortality, life goes on, and waiting for us on the other side of the doorway is that good old "motherly" body, the midwife: "It is so long since the reader of this rhapsodical work has been parted from the midwife, that it is high time to mention her again to him, merely to put him in mind that there is such a body still in the world" (35). The reader is reminded that it has been a long time since he has been parted from his own midwife. After the black pages Sterne begins all over again with his midwife, and with the reader. The black page somehow does not cast quite the pall it did before (perhaps because it is now on the left, behind us), and we learn more about "this good woman": she seems to stand waiting between Sterne and his reader: "But as fresh matter may be started, and much unexpected business fall out betwixt the reader and myself, which may require immediate dispatch . . . we can no way do without her" (35). The midwife seems to have a figurative function here for Sterne and his reader: her presence is felt before and just after the black pages, and she seems to be there before life and after death. She is a medium between birth and life as she is between Sterne and his reader, in order to help remind us that we must exercise some of her careful, life-promoting function in bringing Tristram to life in our own imaginative experience as we progress through the book.

Shortly after reintroducing the figure of the midwife, Tristram tells us he is writing a history book. Of the many writers of fictional histories in the eighteenth century, Sterne (like Arbuthnot or Fielding) would probably have been aware of the common root for "history" and "story," learning by inquiry. Tristram represents himself as a research historian or research biographer, with

> Accounts to reconcile:
> Anecdotes to pick up:
> Inscriptions to make out:
> Stories to weave in:
> Traditions to sift:
> Personages to call upon: . . . there are archives at every stage to be look'd into, and rolls, records, and documents; and endless genealogies, which justice ever and anon calls him back to stay the reading of (37).

Out of a diverse matrix of historical materials, from Uncle Toby's word of mouth anecdotes to written records, one document, shrouded in tautological legal jargon, stands out from the others: "my mother's marriage settlement" (36).

In order to find out the secrets of his life history ("the history of myself") from the very moment of his conception forward, he must in a sense search his own mother, uncover her own private wishes and deliberations. This search is another way of tracing everything in his life story "*ab Ovo.*" The language of the document makes an elaborate pretence of allowing for and anticipating all possible contingencies relating to Elizabeth Mollineux's "bearing and bringing forth children" (38). But because Walter Shandy insists on an additional clause ("which indeed had never been thought of at all, but for my uncle *Toby Shandy*" [40, 43]) enforcing a subsequent lying-in at home instead of London in the case of a false alarm, "the whole weight of the article" falls entirely upon Tristram, just as the sash-window is to fall upon him later, again owing indirectly to Toby. "So that I was doom'd, by marriage articles, to have my nose squeez'd as flat to my face, as if the destinies had actually spun me without one" (41). Tristram is fated by his mother's, father's, and uncle's *words* (spoken and written) to his misfortune ("I was begot and born to misfortunes" [41]) as effectually as if the fates who spin men's lives—the original ancient midwives with their scissors and thread measuring out and sewing up the umbilical cords of life, or Nature herself, bored with the uniformity of her generative task—had whimsically decided to leave something out.

Sterne's version of "in the beginning was the word" stresses the ordinariness of the old spinners of fate. The whims of the Shandys coincide with—are in fact, identical to—the whims of those imposing personifications Nature, Fortune, and Fate, and he keeps reminding us that those abstractions are originally only the extensions of humdrum human frailty and imperfection. But in the spaces between those ordinary whims and acts (like the gap between Toby's well meaning suggestion and the working of Dr. Slop's forceps) occurs the inexplicable mystery which in everyday usage we persist in calling fate or the nature of things. In a passage where Walter is said to fall with his nose flat to the quilt, thus reenacting Tristram's fall into life, Sterne approaches the mystery again with a pronouncement to his feminine reader, "Attitudes are nothing, madam,—'tis the transition from one attitude to another—like the preparation and resolution of the discord into harmony, which is all in all (276-7)." *Tristram Shandy* is the transition; the novel itself is a "womb of speculation."

42. Walter Shandy and "the Books of Generation"

Woe unto him that saith unto his father, what begettest thou? or to the
woman, What hast thou brought forth?

(Isaiah 45:10)

Tristram Shandy begins and ends with the image of human copulation,
and for Walter Shandy it is not a happy image: Tristram starts the story of his
life with a wistful account of his parents' *coitus interruptus* in the act of his
begetting; Walter is last seen lamenting to his wife the bestial nature of
coition ("a passion, my dear . . . which . . . makes us come out of caverns and
hiding-places more like satyrs and four-footed beasts than men" [645]).
Sterne also provides his reader with hints and reflections on a great deal of
lore relating to human sexual intercourse, much of it connected in some way
or other with Walter Shandy, the systematic philosopher *manqué*, the patriarch and father of the Shandy family, the bearer and expediter of the
Homunculus who will become Tristram Shandy and who, it is hoped, will
perpetuate the house and line of the Shandys. Walter's role as a father,
particularly as a propagator, is of great concern to him and to Uncle Toby
("Brother *Shandy* . . . you do increase my pleasure very much, in begetting
children for the *Shandy* family at your time of life.—But, by that, Sir, quoth
Dr. *Slop*, Mr. *Shandy* increases his own.—Not a jot, quoth my father. . . .
My brother does it, quoth my uncle *Toby*, out of *principle*" [115-16]).
   Many of the authors of midwife manuals, male and female, deemed it
necessary to comment on the issue of pleasure in intercourse, "It being no
less virtue and prudence to preserve a child when begotten, than content
and pleasure in begetting; in both which, both sexes are, and ought equally
to be concerned."[58] "Now that these different Sexes should be obliged to
come to the Touch, which we call Copulation," the parts are "endow'd by
Nature with a delightful and mutual Itch."[59] Without "Delight in Copulation
. . . the fair Sex neither desire martial Embraces [sic], nor have Pleasure in
them, nor conceive by them."[60] Mrs. Sharp exclaimed that "were not the
pleasure transcendentally ravishing to us, a man or woman would hardly
ever die for love."[61] As we have seen in the Introduction, the womb,
according to Plato, was thought to be an animal with an almost independent
sensory existence inside the body. The French midwife Dionis explains that

> In *Hysterick* Cases . . . it moves sometimes upwards and sometimes
> downwards, with so much force and violence, as shews that [the] Liga-
> ments have little power over it. . . . The Womb has Nerves . . . [which]
> make it very susceptible of Pleasure or Pain, and of Sympathy with all

221

the others Parts of the Body; when 'tis ill or well, all the Body is sensible
of it; wherefore it is called the Clock, which shews the bad or good state
of Health in Women.[62]

Correspondingly, Mrs. Sharp stresses, in another tradition going back to the
locus in Plato, the fury, power, and "abundance of pleasure" in the male
member in intercourse, and notes that "the Yard is placed betwixt the
thighs, that it may stand the stronger to perform its work with all the force a
man is able."[63] Dionis elaborates on how the nerves fill with blood and
become so stiff "that the Yard grows furious and seeks to be satisfy'd: the
Animal has no more command of itself, and Man very often forgets and loses
the Exercise of his Reason."[64]

It was distressing to Walter Shandy and to earlier English thinkers like Sir
Thomas Browne that "so exalted and godlike a being as Man" should be
dominated by "a passion which bends down the faculties" and "couples and
equals wise men with fools"[65] (645), but his attitude toward intercourse is
more complex than this: if Toby takes pleasure in Walter's capacity for
propagation, Walter at one point, carried away with an imperial fancy,
compliments his brother with,

> tis piteous the world is not peopled by creatures which resemble thee;
> and was I an *Asiatick* monarch . . . I would oblige thee, provided it
> would not impair thy strength—or dry up thy radical moisture too
> fast—or weaken thy memory or fancy . . . which these gymnicks in-
> ordinately taken, are apt to do—else, dear *Toby*, I would procure thee
> the most beautiful women in my empire, and I would oblige thee,
> *nolens, volens,* to beget for me one subject every *month* (586).

Walter is careful to qualify his enthusiasm because it was a commonplace
notion that inordinate indulgence in sexual intercourse was debilitating: "no
wonder that those that use immoderate Copulation, are very weak in their
Bodies; seeing their whole Body is thereby deprived of their best and purest
Blood, and of the vital Spirits."[66]

Tristram defines his father early in the novel as "an excellent natural
philosopher" (6); we have examined Lovelace as the natural philosopher of
women. Not surprisingly, Walter, like Lovelace, fancies himself an authority
on women. He too has his maxims. He says to Toby in his letter about
women, "Always carry it in thy mind, and act upon it, as a sure maxim,
Toby—that women are timid . . . and thou knowest, dear *Toby,* that there is
no passion so serious, as lust" (591-2). But when he invokes the delicacy of
Diogenes and Plato to recalcitrate against sexual passion, and asks "wherefore, when we go about to plant a man, do we put out the candle," he seems
to forget or ignore another tradition, recalled by Dionis: "when the Philoso-

pher was ask'd, what he was doing? he answer'd boldly, That he was planting a Man. And pray, what more harm is there in planting a Man, than a Cabbage?"[68]
Tristram picks up this anecdote in his chapter on story lines. He gives the "precise line" of the development of his fifth volume showing five little c's in the middle of it. These c's may be a mischievous allusion to five others in Burton's diagram of the female reproductive organs in his *Essay*,[69] especially since Tristram's c's stand "for. . .nothing but parentheses, and the common *ins* and *outs* incident to the lives of the greatest ministers of state" (474) and since Tristram continues with a mock encomium of straight lines, to the "excellency" of which he aspires: "This *right line*,—the path-way for Christians to walk in! say divines—The emblem of moral rectitude! says *Cicero*— The *best line*! say cabbage-planters" (474-75). All this is comically refuted of course in the opening chapter of Volume VIII, the beginning of the account of Toby's Amour, when Tristram defies, alliteratively,

the best cabbage planter that ever existed, whether he plants backwards or forwards, it makes little difference in the account . . . I defy him to go on cooly, critically, and canonically, planting his cabbages one by one, in straight lines, and stoical distances, especially if slits in petticoats are unsew'd up—without ever and anon straddling out, or sidling into some bastardly digression" (539).

Passages such as this one help to define further what Sterne means by the "backward and forward" movement of a novel which dramatizes, on many levels, the act of creation.

In general, it may be said that almost all descriptions of intercourse in the literature of generation up to the mid-eighteenth century characterize the act as an itching, furious, violent engagement combining ecstatic pleasure, loss of self-control, and debilitation. With such an emphasis on the fury and animality of the sexual organs in coition, one would expect the midwife authors, in language which Sterne parodies, to give advice on how to behave in preparing for a successful act of propagation: "since the Act is the Foundation of Generation . . . some Care ought to be taken and consequently some Advice given, how to perform it well. . . . let every thing that looks like Care and Business be banished from their thoughts."[70] Walter Shandy maintained that one of the three chief causes necessary to produce a mentally superior and successful child into the world (besides the preservation of the cerebellum in the birth labor and his being given a good Christian name) was "the due care to be taken in the act of propagation of each individual, which required all the thought in the world, as it laid the foundation of this incomprehensible contexture in which wit, memory, fancy, eloquence, and what is usually meant by the name of good natural parts, do consist" (149).

Walter knew further that in order to produce healthy, active children, "the Act of Coition should be perform'd with the greatest Ardour and Intenseness of Desire imaginable, or else they may as well let it alone."[71] A little further on in *Aristotle's Master Piece* (a book which Sterne almost certainly knew in one of its many editions), women are advised "to lay aside all Passions of the Mind, shunning Study and Care as Things that are Enemies to Conception." For if a woman were to conceive under such adverse circumstances, however wise and prudent the parents might be, the children would be at best mere fools because the understanding and judgment of the parents (from which the children derive their own rational faculties) are confused through a "multitude of Carès and Cogitations." This is demonstrated by many examples of learned men, "who after great Study and Care having performed their conjugal Rites with their Wives, have often begot Children, which have indeed been the *Fruits* of their Bodies, but not the *Issue* of their Brains."[72]

The midwife book which perhaps comes closest to summing up the received doctrines of what is necessary for generation, and which anticipates Walter Shandy's melancholy sense of the poignant mortality of the act, is that of the Scottish physician, James McMath. McMath prescribes first of all a male possessed of a "most *Vivace Constitution*" since he gives the principal impression and force to the offspring; secondly, a female possessed of a fecund womb to safely conserve and cherish both of the prolific seeds; then "their *Genial Embrace* . . . or a truly *Venereous Congress*: To which they haste . . . chiefly, from that signal *Delite*, and enchanting *Pleasure* found therein." For if it were not for this solace from general human misery, even though the joy is short-lived, "*Sadness* and *Drooping* coming instantly after, yea even during the *Pleasure* of this *Dance*," hardly anyone would indulge in sexual intercourse, and "Mankind would soon wear out."[73] We may set this account beside that of the self-important Maubray, who must be heard in his own voice to be appreciated, a worthy predecessor of John Burton:

> *As* to the *unsuccessful Act* of *Coition* . . . the *Parties* ought not to encounter with full *Stomachs, Bellies,* or *Bladders*; much less when *Both,* or *Either,* are *weary, fatigu'd, depriv'd of Sleep, angry, troubled in Mind,* or in any other real respect *out of Order.* For in these Cases, it is very detrimental to the *Health* of such imprudent Parents; and (if *Conception* follows) it infallibly *intails* some respective *Evil* upon the *Innocent Production*: Because all of the *Affections* or *Disturbances* of their *Minds,* virtually devolve upon the Embryo. . . . *Wherefore,* in fine, as this *Affair* is to be undertaken with a serene and contented *Mind,* a chearful and undisturbed *Heart,* so it ought to be perform'd with *Moderation* and *Decency*: Not in any *brutal Manner* or *Posture*; but according to the rational Law and proper *Instinct* of *Nature.*"[74]

We may now consider in detail Walter's "Lamentation" (296-97) to Uncle Toby, who sits precariously under both the chimney piece and "Ernulphus's curse" which was "laid upon the corner" of it. The conversation takes place in the military disorder of the tea parlor as Walter takes one of the chairs which had formed the corporal's breach. It is a fit setting for the disorder of a mind which feels itself the victim of heaven's "heaviest artillery," the whole force of which is directed against the prosperity of his unfortunate child. "Unhappy *Tristram!* child of wrath! child of decrepitude! interruption! mistake! and discontent! What one misfortune or disaster in the book of embryotic evils, that could unmechanize thy frame, or entangle thy filaments! which has not fallen upon thy head, or ever thou camest into the world!"

This last sentence focuses Walter's dilemma. Tristram's hapless father seems to be victim as well as satirical personification of a change in perspective, from the seventeenth to the eighteenth century, on how to represent the act of human propagation. The older midwife books stress not only that due care be taken in the act, but also the doctrine that the more "merry," "vivacious," carefree, forceful, and "brisk" the act of coition, the more active, healthy, intelligent, and robust the child. The later midwife books, like Maubray's, play down the intensity of animal vigor and loss of self-control ("Ecstasy") perceived by the earlier writers, and play up the notion of decent, moderate, restrained sexual relations. This change of perspective and emphasis corresponds to a similar movement from a richly organic account of generation to a more "scientifick" and mechanical one. In reflecting on his son's catastrophic conception, Walter's divided and discouraged mind combines both an old organic metaphor for generation ("entangle thy filaments") and a newer mechanical one ("unmechanize thy frame") in one phrase. He seems to have read (or understood) the literature of generation too late, or more probably, after having gathered together all the old and new ideas about propagation available to him, Walter Shandy for once does not seem to know what to believe except that Tristram was

> produced into being, in the decline of thy father's days—when the
> powers of his imagination and of his body were waxing feeble—when
> radical heat and radical moisture . . . were drying up; and nothing left to
> found thy stamina in, but negations. . . . But how were we defeated! You
> know the event, brother *Toby*,—'tis too melancholy a one to be repeated
> now. (296)

Walter Shandy here sounds like an old soldier recalling a disastrous campaign, and the subtle transfer of Uncle Toby's idiom to Walter's situation implicates Toby in his brother's failure. It was Toby himself who inadvertently helped Tristram pinpoint the night of his conception by relating the anecdote of how Mrs. Shandy's untimely question about the clock interrupted Tristram's father not just in the act of coition but in the critical moment, apparently, of his ejaculation, "when the few animal spirits [he] was worth in the world, and with which memory, fancy, and quick parts should have been convey'd—-were all dispersed, confused, confounded, scattered, and sent to the devil."[75]

Walter then blames himself for not trying an experiment in mental relaxation which has the subtle effect of shifting to poor Mrs. Shandy the burden of all Tristram's misfortunes:

> Here then was the time to have put a stop to this persecution against him;—and tried an experiment at least—whether calmness and serenity of mind in your sister, with a due attention, brother Toby, to her evacuations and repletions—and the rest of her non-naturals, might not, in a course of nine months gestation, have set all things to rights. . . . What a teazing life did she lead herself, and consequently her foetus too, with that nonsensical anxiety of hers about lying in in town? I thought my sister submitted with the greatest patience, replied my uncle *Toby*— I never heard her utter one fretful word about it—she fumed inwardly, cried my father; and that, let me tell you, brother, was ten times worse for the child. (297)

Walter's predicament may be summed up as follows: on the one hand, he has tried on his part to exercise that "due care to be taken in the act of propagation of each individual, which required all the thought in the world"; on the other hand, whether subscribing to the earlier theory that the act of propagation must be accompanied by all the ferocious animal attributes, as well as the abundant animal spirits, delineated in the midwife literature, or subscribing to the later notions of decency and moderation, he and his wife have failed disastrously on both counts. Built into his predicament is the difficult question, which none of the seventeenth-century theorists bother to consider, of how calmness and serenity of mind can coexist with the violent genital congress they consider necessary for conception. In other words, from the standpoint both of reproductive theory and Shandean reflection, it is a wonder that anyone ever gets conceived, much less born.

It may be said that Walter was if anything too methodical. "My father, you must know . . . was, I believe, one of the most regular of men in every thing he did, whether 'twas matter of business, or matter of amusement, that ever lived" (8). It was a precisely logical and regular transition for him to move from the ritual of winding up the clock "with his own hands" on "the first Sunday night of every month" to "the other little family concernments" with Mrs. Shandy. Was not the womb "called the Clock, which shews the bad or good state of Health in Women" (Dionis), and did not Dr. John Burton himself regard the womb "to be as extraordinary a Piece of Mechanism, as any in the whole Body"?[76] Hence it was as logical in its own way, via the theories of the association of ideas and the sympathy of the womb, for Mrs. Shandy to interrupt her husband with *"Pray, my dear . . . have you not forgot to wind up the clock?,"* as it was for Walter Shandy to proceed from the "large house-clock" to the winding up of other concernments. For in his attitude toward woman as an animal mechanism, Walter would seem to be a kind of theoretical or philosophical "midwife" in the intellectual tradition of Maubray, Giffard, Chapman, and Burton, and his representation of women becomes as much a target of Sterne's satire as will the similar attitudes of the official "scientifick operators."

Walter laments the obstinacy of his wife "in trusting the life of [his] child . . . her own life, and with it the lives of all the children [he] might, peradventure, have begot out of her hereafter," to the ignorance of an old woman (100), and he goes on to chide his poor brother about his ignorance of women, particularly his not knowing "so much as the right end of a woman from the wrong" (101). Woman, considered theoretically, is hardly more than a convenient vehicle for Walter, although in reality a recalcitrant and obstinate one at times. But at the end of his "Lamentation," Walter reveals a more sinister dimension to his view of women, that is, the idea of an all-encompassing inimical fate: "Cripple, Dwarf, Driviller, Goosecap—- (shape him as you will) the door of Fortune stands open—O *Licetus! Licetus!* had I been blest with a foetus five inches long and a half, like thee—fate might have done her worst."

43. Slop, Burton, and Bawdry

Dr. Slop is first introduced not by his name but by his role: he is "a scientifick operator . . . who . . . had expressly wrote a five shillings book upon the subject of midwifery, in which he had exposed, not only the blunders of the sisterhood itself,—-but had likewise superadded many curious improvements for the quicker extraction of the foetus in cross births, and some other cases of danger which belay us in getting into the world" (44). Slop is the practical counterpart of the theoretical operator (the "good natural philosopher" [101]), Walter Shandy, and the activities of both animate Sterne's unique revision of Swift's great satirical theme of the "mechanical operation of the Spirit."

Dr. Slop is in some respects a caricature of the Yorkshire man-midwife, Dr. John Burton, educated, like Swift's Moderns, at the University of Leyden. As early as his *Treatise on the Non-Naturals* (York, 1738), Burton was proud to enlist himself with "the Moderns [who] with a great deal of Reason, have quite exploded [the old] fantastical Way of philosophizing; and with much Industry and Success, have endeavour'd to account for every thing that relates to the Animal Oeconomy upon Mechanical Principles." Burton argues as if Reason were a quantifiable entity, enough of which would annihilate any outmoded mental notion. For him, as for George Cheyne, the "human body [is] to be consider'd as a Machine," but Burton goes his own characteristic way when he charges that this machine is to be used "no better, than any other Part of the material World; because herein, we can't come to any knowledge of its Mechanism, without taking it in Pieces like any other Machine, and considering all the Parts as so many Springs, Wheels, and the like Mechanical Powers. . . . they are throughout the Whole, to be consider'd as so many Mechanical Instruments."[77] Burton, who is quite conscious that his own *"Diction and Style"* in the *Treatise* are but *"dry* and *lean,"*[78] seems to have stepped right out of the satirical universe of self-condemned Swiftian victims. As much as it was necessary for the modern science of obstetrics to develop a consistent and uniform language for the mechanism of parturition—and certainly Burton, with his explanation of the muscular nature of the uterus, provided a significant emphasis—it is clear that Burton's overriding reduction of all human functions to purely mechanical ones made him almost a ready-made satiric target for Sterne's novel. But Sterne invented the name.

One is affronted by the conjunction of Doctor and Slop—a professor of rubbish, a sloppy practitioner. He is linked from the start with mud and excrement. Burton wrote at length on "Retention and Excretion" in his *Treatise*, but Slop is not simply Burton. He is a comic representation, in the guise of a "scientifick" man-midwife, of the figure of the torturing midwife-bawd. Though his first appearance is anything but intimidating, there is a stress upon his "sesquipedality of belly, which might have done honour to a serjeant in the horse-guards," echoing the description of the fat bawd's girth. He is "a little, squat, uncourtly figure" (105) almost as wide as he is broad (like Brown's "ton of female fat"), "coming slowly along . . . waddling thro' the dirt" on his poor diminutive pony—recalling other waddlers like Mother Bentley and Mrs. Jewkes.

When Obadiah and his huge coach horse hit him, Dr. Slop is born into the novel in the "dirtiest part of a dirty lane," in terror and hydrophobia, with an "explosion of mud" (106) and water. As Burton claims to have exploded older notions of physic, Sterne has exploded Burton into Slop. Of the several arrested images in windows and doorways we have noticed in these novels, Dr. Slop's "full minute and a half, at the parlour door"—*"unwiped, unappointed, unanealed"*—takes a unique place (107). Sterne's Tristram keeps asking the reader to imagine and visualize Slop. We have noticed in the various portraits of the bawd an emblem of the world, and Slop too is such an emblem. He is a rotund figure transubstantiated into the first elements of the earth, mud and water, in a collision which underlines his affinity with this "vile, dirty planet," made up of "the shreds and clippings of the rest." Slop is not only an emblem of lumpish mortality, he is a type of the Shandy world. That Tristram comes to exist in the world at all is owing solely to the intervention of Slop and his forceps, clumsy as they are. The old midwife is *not* able to deliver the child.[79] Tristram's birth is artificial, making him in a sense an artificial man. Thus Slop is the perfect agent for introducing Tristram into the Shandy world, and his performance in the birth reinforces the notion of life as a *manufactured*, highly contingent affair. In Defoe there is a constant reiteration of the joy in technical mastery, the celebration of the manufactory impulse, offset by sinister associations with the hand of Mother Midnight. In *Tristram Shandy* the stress on a manufactory impulse calls attention to history, narration, and life itself as an uncertain fiction, a series of artifices, subject to negligence, botchery, and muddle.

As for the "many curious improvements" Slop introduced, Burton makes the following announcement in his Preface to *An Essay Towards a Complete New System of Midwifery* (1751), giving us his notion—unlike Harvey's "open" and "legible" Nature—of an opaque Nature whose secrets must almost be forced out of her by rational analysis:

> there are, in this *Essay*, a great many *Remarks* and *Methods* of *Practice* entirely new, that are founded upon Reason and Experience, . . . the surest Foundation in the Practice of all Branches of *Physic*. For, as

Nature discloses herself in an obscure Manner, we must strictly observe
her Operations, by which we shall see the Facts; and then a thorough
Knowledge of *Philosophy* and *Anatomy* will enable us, by such Guides,
to penetrate into her secret Principles.[80]

One can detect in this blunt theoretical pronouncement the germ of the
blunt practical behavior of Dr. Slop when called upon to minister to poor
Mrs. Shandy in her crisis.

Burton, sounding like an historical prototype of Dickens' Gradgrind, was
to rehearse this "factual" credo right up to the end of his last treatise on
midwifery, the mean spirited, unprovoked, and interminably sarcastic *Letter to William Smellie* (1753). This tone seems to be the logical outcome of
his attempt to substitute mechanical for human nature: "And as the Art of
delivering a Woman of her Child and Secundines is entirely a mechanical
Operation, whether it be done by turning the child in the Womb, to extract
it by the Feet, or by Assistance of Instruments, so the mechanical Laws or
Rules are to be our general Guide."[81]

Slop as a mechanical operator appears in a variety of memorable stances
and gestures in the novel, but running through them all is a consistent and
defensive insensitivity to the feelings of others. Like the old midwife-bawd,
Slop is also indecent, but in a way different from Tristram. Slop loves to
inject his puns and double-entendres at inopportune times, often for insulting effect. Wit for him is not genial or humorous in a good-natured, Shandean way, but works as a form of separation from others, a kind of self-applause, and an insulation from or defense against others. In this, he has an
affinity with the cruel wit of Walter Shandy. Slop's wit fences himself off,
Tristram's wit bridges the gap between himself and others.

Nonetheless, despite his insulation from others, Slop serves to call attention to certain recurring motifs and linguistic connections in the novel. One
of these motifs is a series of allusions to the head, often with a sexual or
obstetric significance. Walter Shandy rebukes Toby over his obsession with
the jargon of military fortification, "I would not have my head so full of
curtins and hornworks.——That I dare say, you would not, quoth Dr. *Slop*,
interrupting him, and laughing most immoderately at his pun" (110-11). Slop
is the first to make the connection between Toby's language of fortification
and the female anatomy, one of the major linguistic parallels in the novel.

Sterne enjoys calling attention to the interconnections and verbal equivalences among the rhetorics of the arts of love, obstetrics and military
fortification as they occur in this "cyclopaedia of arts and sciences" (122).
These parallels help tie together the three main transactions of the book, the
generation and birth of Tristram, the interplay among the members of the
Shandy world, and the transformation of Uncle Toby's hobby-horse into the
affair with the Widow Wadman. As Walter unwittingly invoked the ancient

cuckold joke on his own head, Toby unwittingly evokes the ancient parallel between fortifications and a woman's virtue. "Besiegers seldom offer to carry on their attacks directly against the curtin, for this reason, because they are so well *flanked*. ('Tis the case of other curtins, quoth Dr. *Slop*, laughing)" (111). But because of the infinite and autonomous punning possibilities of language itself, when one rich verbal context is set beside another, the joke goes beyond the "noble science of defense" to include the noble art of midwifery. Sterne seems to suggest that language itself is a character in *Tristram Shandy*, maybe the chief one, another capricious female like Fortune or Nature or Fate.

Toby's reference to the "curtin" and "half-moon" recall the old midwives' birth stool, described by Wolveridge as "strong," "cut with a hole, in the shape of the moon," "with a skirt of cloth . . . around it, to keep away the air," a kind of formidable instrument of defense to preserve the laboring mother against what were thought to be the fatal effects of cold air entering the womb.[82] At Toby's mention of "the double tenaille," Walter explodes with "By the mother who bore us!" just as poor Mrs. Shandy is crying out in the pains of labor; "nothing will serve you but to carry off the man-midwife.— *Accoucheur*,—if you please, quoth Dr. *Slop*" (112-13) reminding Walter that midwifery, as well as the science of defense, has its fine French appellations.[83] It would appear that Toby, with his interminable lecture on outworks covering "such places as we suspect to be weaker than the rest" (112) is in unconscious alliance with Nature to prevent Dr. Slop from getting anywhere near Mrs. Shandy's "covered-way." "Truce!—truce, good Dr. *Slop!*—stay thy obsteric hand;—return it safe into thy bosom to keep it warm" (109). The hidden causes which retard its operation are not just the secret articles which Mr. and Mrs. Shandy agreed to about midwives, but the hidden resources of a labyrinthine and self-inventive flow of words from Toby's mouth which Walter can halt only by wishing "the whole science of fortification, with all its inventors, at the devil,—it has been the death of thousands,—and it will be mine, in the end" (113). Toby is patient of this injury, and it is here that Sterne chooses to tell us of his uncle's truly defensive nature, one that shelters, nurtures, and protects—"I know no man under whose arm I would sooner have taken shelter" than the maternal Toby. There is something beyond Dr. Slop's self-important pride as an accoucheur, some hand greater than his "obstetric hand." Toby "was of a peaceful, placid nature,—no jarring element in it" (113); his "good nature," his unforced flow of words, are in harmony with that greater power. But beyond even Nature, in the novel, is an ironic power called the Fates, to be considered in more detail in appraising Toby's Amour with the Widow Wadman.

Sterne's presentation of Dr. Slop—his insensitivity and his links with Burton and bawdry—takes on more complex and affecting overtones in Book

V of the novel. There is the Doctor's response to Trim's medical lecture on
the siege of Limerick, in which he and Toby nearly lost their lives to
dysentery ("the flux") as they lay "in the middle of a devilish wet, swampy
country" (401). Trim concludes that "the radical moisture is nothing in the
world but ditch-water" and Slop, with characteristic sarcasm and pedantry,
roundly confutes him: since "The radical heat and moisture . . . is the basis
and foundation of our being," Trim must "have had the misfortune to have
heard some superficial emperic discourse upon this nice point" (402). In the
muted replies by Walter, Toby, and Yorick to this observation, we hear a
poignancy which Slop has completely missed: Trim and Toby suffered their
emperic discourse in the flesh. The full sense of Slop's immunity to this is
conveyed without words in the transitional space between the chapters.

Burton too has his telling transitions. There is a story in his *Essay* which
may be set beside this passage. In the middle of a series of female anatomical
definitions, he tells of the case of one Mary English who having come to him
apparently pregnant, was found to have a large tumour; after a suppression
of urine was extracted, she was sent home, "where she continued about two
Months longer, with the same Symptoms, but never had a Child since; and I
am informed, she died soon after. But to return—6. The Figure of the
Womb is like a flatten'd Pear, or rather a Triangle with the Corners rounded
off."[84] This leap is not unlike Swift's "Tale Teller": "But to return to Madness. . . . "

The dialogue between Dr. Slop and Susannah, the housemaid, short as it
is, concentrates much of what Sterne has to say about his man-midwife, the
all too mortal agent of Tristram's introduction into mortality. The exchange is
not only a caricature of the dialogues in midwife manuals of the man-midwife
and his unlearned female assistant, but also a parody of Burton's obstetrical
rhetoric.[85] The cataplasm or poultice is ready to be tied to Tristram's injured
penis after the accident with the sash-window. (It must be observed that
poultices were also used in the treatment of venereal disease.) Susannah
(whose name evokes the image of the beautiful young woman spied on while
bathing by two lecherous elders in the apocryphal book of Susannah), out of
real or feigned modesty, is reluctant to hold the candle close enough for Slop
to see what he is doing. He pretends to have found her out: "I think I know
you, madam . . . Dr. *Slop* clapped his finger and his thumb instantly upon
his nostrils" in a gesture which arouses the young woman's indignation as it
signals a joke at the expense of the surname Smellie ("Adrianus Smelvgot").
"*Susannah*'s spleen was ready to burst at it. . . . Come, come, Mrs. Modesty,
said *Slop*, not a little elated with the success of his last thrust" (412). The
specific emphasis on Slop's finger, thumb, and thrust in this context (compare "the subordination of fingers and thumbs to ****" [184]),[86] recalls
Burton's quarrel with other midwives (including Smellie) over the flexibility
of the "*Os Coccygis*" in childbirth ("what, prima facie, [the reader] may think

a very trifling Affair," Burton says, anticipating Sterne's style without the irony);[87] the passage also recalls Burton's sense of the vulnerability of the genital organs in podalic version: "Therefore, as soon as the Operator perceives, by the Softness and Fleshiness of the Parts, what Part presents, he must immediately thrust up against the Buttocks with all his Strength, but without committing Violence to the Child's *Os Coccygis*, or its Parts of Generation."[88] It had been traditionally argued (as Smellie was to do in his *Treatise*) that the midwife could assist a woman in a retarded childbirth by introducing a finger into her anus or vagina. Burton in his *Letter* deferred sarcastically to Smellie's "great Modesty":[89] here his customary pedantic gravity in attempting to demolish the efficacy of this maneuvre is a vivid premonition of Dr. Slop who mangles and dislocates the object of his obstetrical care. Burton proceeds:

> Nay, I'll venture to affirm, that by introducing a Finger or Thumb, either into the *Anus* or *Vagina*, it will take up more Space betwixt the *Coccyx* and *Os Pubis*, than any Person can make the *Os Coccygis* give way, without breaking or dislocating it: And how much those Parts must be bruised, with such a Force as would be here required, any Person may easily judge, and may imagine what bad consequences may thence arise.[90]

The exchange between Slop and Susannah now takes an explicitly bawdy turn, and the dialogue almost seems to degenerate into a discussion between a bawd (or pimp) and a whore. To Susannah's implication of "popish shifts," Slop returns, with a nod, "better . . . than no shift at all, young woman," and when she accidentally sets fire to his wig, Slop bursts forth twice with "You impudent whore! . . . (for what is passion, but a wild beast)," the expletive as worthy of Sinclair as is the epithet for her. "I never was the destruction of any body's nose," Susannah howls in reply, putting Slop (and herself) in the umbrage of prostitution, since the accoucheur and the French disease destroy noses with equal effect if not dispatch (412-13). No wonder Walter Shandy refers to Slop as "a son of a w——" for exalting himself, and debasing Tristram to death, by making ten thousand times more of Susannah's accident with the window sash than there were grounds for (433); Tristram himself, in his flight across France from "DEATH," says "this *son of a whore* has found out my lodgings"; Death then interrupts him in the telling of a funny story (480). Thus Slop and Death are both characterized as rude, obstreperous sons of whores who, at the beginning and end of his life of interruptions, find Tristram out. And both are torturing midwives who catch Tristram by the nose or by the throat, one his deadly instrumentality into this vile world, the other his hostile nemesis out of it.

44. Two Images of Mortality

Viewed in the light of the literature of midwifery and bawdry, Slop is not simply a caricature of John Burton. He is also a complex representative of a science which, in the wrong hands, could be deadly, a figure who just manages to bring Tristram into this mortal world alive, but who makes the child and his mother undergo needlesss torture. We have seen several remarkable and varied activities of the torturing midwife-bawd, from the quiet but sinister "I-know-what-you're-thinking" games of Moll Flanders' witchlike Governess to the melodramatic physical and emotional violence wrought by Mrs. Jewkes in *Pamela* and especially by Mrs. Sinclair in *Clarissa.* Sterne's Dr. Slop is the tragicomic culmination of this conventional figure in eighteenth-century fiction, but he is a *man*-midwife. Sterne using the masculine figure of Slop carries the satire of the ignorant midwife the next logical step beyond the obvious targets of deadly older women torturing young and vital ones: Burton, Chapman, Giffard and company, for all their considerable technical ingenuity and expertise, betray in their language a certain blindness to the suffering *human* nature of their patients, mother and child. While Mrs. Shandy in her lying-in upstairs undergoes a catastrophic series of reverses, Slop down in the parlor insists on the midwife's coming down to report to him ("I like subordination, quoth my uncle Toby"), parodies Toby's mlitary jargon, tears the skin off the poor man's hand with a demonstration of his forceps (cf. "From what has been said, it is evident my Forceps are better than any yet contrived"),[91] intimates the danger to the child's genitals if the midwife is mistaken in her diagnosis of the presentation, and finally trips, "pretty nimbly, for a man of his size, across the room to the door" and Mrs. Shandy's apartment. One is reminded again of Burton's experiments with narrative method: "Having now brought the Child into its proper Posture for Birth, I shall return to the Mother, whom we left labouring under several Complaints, and very unweildy with her Burden."[92] Mrs. Shandy's burden too is now under great pressure. Walter Shandy has learned in Adrianus Smelvgot's treatise

That the lax and pliable state of the child's head in parturition, the bones of the cranium having no sutures at that time, was such, that by force of the woman's efforts, which, in strong labour-pains, was equal, upon an average, to a weight of 470 pounds averdupoise acting perpendicularly upon it;—it so happened that, in 49 instances out of 50, the said head was compressed and moulded into the shape of an oblong conical piece of dough, such as a pastry-cook generally rolls up, in order to make a pye

234

of.—Good God! cried my father, what havock and destruction must this make in the infinitely fine and tender texture of the cerebellum!" (150).

Smellie, with a choice of images that rivalled Burton's for tactile vividness, focused on the vagaries of the forehead in the mechanism of birth. He noted that every pain would force it farther down and,

> when delivered, it will rise in form of an obtuse cone or sugar-loaf, and in that case the crown of the head will be altogether flat. But if instead of the *Vertix* [crown] or forehead, the *Fontanelle* should first appear, the space from the forehead to the crown will then rise in form of a sow's back. . . . And in all laborious cases, the *Vertix* comes down and is lengthened in form of a sugar loaf, nine and forty times in fifty instances.[93]

Arthur Cash has incisively discussed Walter Shandy's theory for preserving the cerebellum in delivery and what it owes to John Burton's remarks (on the cerebrum and podalic version) in the *Essay* and *Letter*.[94] I would like to stress that Walter in these passages is perhaps the first philosopher of the birth trauma and should be listened to, but not perhaps for reasons he would particularly approve of. Walter, like Freud, Otto Rank, and the Primal therapists long after him, takes seriously the fact that in its passage toward delivery the head of the infant undergoes great physical pressure (though not 470 pounds!), a shock that may well have an effect on the subsequent psychological development of the individual. Sterne exaggerates and makes fun of Walter's concern as he does his theories of noses and proper names, but as absurd as Walter's theories always appear on the surface, they have a deep reference to man's sexual identity (the Nose theory), and to man's fate seen as a function of character and language (the Name theory).

Walter's observations on the birth trauma reveal two of Sterne's favorite fragile images—seen in terms of birth—for the human condition; man as a piece of malleable matter, whether dough or clay; and man as a piece of cloth or fine texture. The "delicate and fine-spun web" of the mind, which after birth is "no better than a puzzled skein of silk—all perplexity,—all confusion within side (149, 151) may here be compared with the "large uneven thread" (463) in Tristram's brain which was bequeathed him by his father, despite all his fruitless efforts to preserve the web from injury. The image of the "oblong conical piece of dough, such as a pastry-cook generally rolls up in order to make a pye of," added to the fact that the crown of the head is molded in birth by the female genitals and then expertly guided out by the midwife with his tong-like forceps, somewhat like a cook maneuvering bread out of the oven, recall another of Burton's jokes at Smellie's expense. In discussing the many cases and examples culled from his extensive obstetric practice, Smellie had said in his Preface

> Nor will the reader, I hope, imagine, that such a fund will be insufficient for the purpose; or that this treatise is cooked up in a hurry, when I inform him, that above six years ago I began to commit my lectures to paper, for publication: and from that period, have from time to time altered, amended, and digested what I had written, according to the new lights I received from study and experience.[95]

This passage gave Burton the opportunity for chastising Smellie to "so far forget yourself, that what you flatly deny in one Part, you either doubt of, or acknowledge in another, which is the more amazing, as you tell us, *you was six Years in cooking up this Treatise.*"[96]

Tristram has earlier informed us that "attitudes are nothing . . . 'tis the transition from one attitude to another . . . which is all in all" (276-77). The same might be said of the transitions between words which reveal the first springs of our being. Again, as important as words are for him, it is what happens in the spaces between them that is everything for Sterne, an idea and effect reinforced by Sterne's ubiquitous dash. These strategically placed long dashes have aural and visual significance: they indicate brief pauses in the voice speaking to us, pauses which suggest the actual working of a rapid, sensitive, and reflective mind; they also indicate spaces for the reader to make his or her own reflections. The dashes enhance the mutual, reflective give and take between Sterne and his reader. As mere empty spaces, they also remind us of the essential discontinuity of the narrative—and of mortal life. Trim conveys the finality of the death of young Bobby Shandy by dropping his hat on the floor and saying, "'Are we not here now,—-and gone in a moment?'—There was nothing in the sentence—'twas one of your self-evident truths we have the advantage of hearing every day" (362). "There was nothing in the sentence": Tristram, transcendant child of negations (322), is acutely aware of the emptiness of the all too apparent, the significance of the mysterious life around it. In Tristram's account of Trim's performance, Sterne—recalling Smellie's "crown" and "sugar loaf" head— exemplifies his thesis about transition by bringing attitude and word together in the interim between Trim's stance and the soft thud of his hat on the floor:

> —"Are we not here now;"—continued the corporal, "and are we not"— (dropping his hat plumb upon the ground—and pausing, before he pronounced the word)—"gone! in a moment?" The descent of the hat was as if a heavy lump of clay had been kneaded into the crown of it—Nothing could have expressed the sentiment of mortality, of which

it was the type and fore-runner, like it—his hand seemed to vanish from under it,—it fell dead,—the corporal's eye fix'd upon it, as upon a corps,—and *Susannah* burst into a flood of tears.

An "*old cock'd hat,*" (549), as we know from a later frenzied excursion through "niches," "furr'd caps," and "pyes," is a cant term for the female sex organs. Trim's infinitely striking demonstration of man's mortality is the work of an expert midwife in reverse. The hat drops as if clay had been kneaded into the crown of it. In this reenactment of human transience, Trim emerges as another kind of practitioner, a sleight-of-hand artist, a magician, in whose hat and gesture the moments of birth, sex, and death are fused.

Tristram implores his readers, who are rushing toward their own oblivion "like turkeys to market" (362) with something like the force of gravity, to meditate on Trim's hat, and toward the end of the book, as a prelude to the last stage of Toby's Amour, provides this mock-solemn (and bawdy) resolution of the baking metaphor:

> We live in a world beset on all sides with mysteries and riddles—and so 'tis no matter—else it seems strange, that Nature, who makes every thing so well to answer its destination, and seldom or never errs, unless for pastime, in giving such forms and aptitudes to whatever passes through her hands, that whether she designs for the plough, the caravan, the cart— . . . you are sure to have the thing you wanted; and yet at the same time should so eternally bungle it as she does, in making so simple a thing as a married man.
>
> Whether it is in the choice of the clay—or that it is frequently spoiled in the baking; by an excess of which a husband may turn out too crusty (you know) on one hand—or not enough so, through defect of heat, on the other— . . . I know not. . . . (625)

Toward the end of this odd and puzzling book of generation, the mystery and irony previously associated with nature seems subtly to shift, as we shall see, to the Fates. The goodness of Nature is still very much evident, but now her limitations are sadly apparent. She does not simply err occasionally in making married men, she bungles the job every time, and not simply "for pastime." The suggestion now, as we approach the climax of the novel and recall Tristram's earlier spirited denial of being married, is that there is something unnatural in the very notion of the conventionally married man, or in the conventional way the two sexes have of coming together, procreating, and getting along with each other.

45. Toby, Namur, and "the sweet fountain of science"

> Man is but a Lump of Clay Kneaded together with Tears, and would be
> the most dull and Phlegmatick thing imaginable, had not Nature . . .
> furnisht him with variety of passions. (*Sad and Deplorable News from
> Fleet-Street, or, A Warning for Lovers*, 1674)

Dr. Slop is almost the precise opposite of Uncle Toby, but each is
presented to us as a man of clay. We recall Slop in the Shandy doorway in all
the "majesty of mud" (107) after his collision with Obadiah near "an acute
angle of the garden wall" (105). Toby is, and always will be, intimately
associated with "the rood and a half of ground" lying at the bottom of his
kitchen garden:

> When FATE was looking forwards one afternoon, into the great transac-
> tions of future times,—and recollected for what purposes, this little
> plot, by a decree fast bound down in iron, had been destined,—she
> gave a nod to Nature—'twas enough—NATURE threw half a spade full
> of her kindliest compost upon it, with just so *much* clay in it, as to retain
> the forms of angles and indentings,—(443)

Like two influential old women who communicate merely by nods and
winks, a kindly disposed gardener, Nature, takes her orders from a silent
and inflexible Fate as Toby and Trim go about "taking the profile" (444) of a
female plot of earth with their packthread and piquets: "the nature of the
soil,—the nature of the work itself,—and above all, the good nature of my
uncle *Toby*" all conspire to transcend the labor and toil and trouble of life in
the joy of serious creative play. Slop is a bungler, Toby a creator; the squat
Slop is like a "serjeant in the horse-guards," the round-faced Toby is a
captain in H.M.'s army; Slop is "uncourtly," Toby is a "Gentleman" (601);
Slop looks dirty and talks bawdy, Toby radiates kindly innocence and looks
askance at talking bawdy (603); whereas Slop mangles Tristram's nose and
nearly crushes Toby's knuckles with his forceps, Toby shelters and nurtures
the young Tristram; and yet . . . Slop is a deadly obstetrical agent of fate,
who still manages somehow to bring Tristram to birth, while Toby is a
wounded soldier who conducts harmless military operations which somehow
result in Tristram's near castration. The contrast between Slop and Toby
begins in clearcut fashion and ends in a puzzle of mixed threads, like
eveything else in the Shandy world.
  Nature "formed [Toby] of the best and kindliest clay—had temper'd it
with her own milk, and breathed into it the sweetest spirit—she had made
him all gentle, generous, and humane—she had fill'd his heart with trust and

confidence" (626). Toby is Nature's Adam, a man of her finest clay. He is Sterne's gentle successor to Fielding's robust Parson Adams. Toby is all original innocence and pure-spirited generosity, a figure of primal man in his goodliest aspect, as Slop is primal in his ill-fashioned deformity. Yet in another sense, both Toby and Slop are the offspring of chance collision and accident—Slop in his encounter with Obadiah and the coach horse, Toby in his accident at Namur.

Now in the eighth and ninth books, the story toward which everything has been pointing—the affair of Toby and the Widow Wadman—can be seen as a sequence of metamorphoses from the time that Toby, "the foremost of created beings" (452) and the quintessence of good-natured mortality, was refashioned by his accident and by his response to it. Toby the child of nature became something else—part child, part man, part woman, part hobby-horse—because of the severe physical injury sustained in his encounter with the stone that crushed his *os pubis* and *os ilium* while he stood exposed "upon the point of the advanced counterscarp, before the gate of *St. Nicolas*, which enclosed the great sluice,*" just before "the English made themselves masters of the covered way" before the gate in the siege of Namur in 1695 (81). Again we have a major character framed for our reflection at a critical moment in his life on the threshold of a new beginning.

As we can see, most of the terms used by Sterne that are derived from the science and art of fortification are given sexual connotations in *Tristram Shandy*, and we have already met with several of them in considering Dr. Slop. What Toby has suffered at Namur is akin to the birth shock of Tristram; Toby, however, has undergone an agonizing and protracted parody of both a difficult act of birth and the shock of being born during a difficult birth. The female pelvis was a battleground for eighteenth-century man-midwives who sought to give a precise description of the bones surrounding the uterus. The bones referred to above are the ones constantly alluded to by Smellie and other man-midwives after 1740 in their preliminary accounts of the female pelvic anatomy.[97] Fielding Ould remarked that even in the most "favourable Labours, poor Women endure as much Pain as Mortals are well able to endure."[98] The stone that hit Toby was large and irregular, but it was the gravity (79) of it, and not its projectile force, that inflicted the injury. Toby's wounding was an impossible nightmare birth in which the stone, like a head too large to pass through the pelvic cavity, crushed his bones and groin while he stood exposed within a feminine configuration of ditches and masonry, a pelvic basin of fortified military ground. After the injury he was confined to his room for four years suffering "unspeakable miseries" (79).

Tristram takes pains to point out to Madam reader that Uncle Toby's "most extream and unparallel'd modesty of nature . . . almost to equal . . . the modesty of a woman" (66), was neither congenital nor owing to the good influence of the conversation of women, but to the blow he suffered at

Namur (67). It becomes clear that his modesty is an obsession indissolubly fused with his military hobby-horse. Toby is still as innocent as the "child unborn," as modest as "a sweet young girl" partly because the whole story of his hobby-horse leading up to his encounter with the Widow is presented as a process of displaced sexual energy and gestation, curiously similar to Pamela's "Correspondence" with Parson Williams.

Tristram draws his uncle's character from his hobby-horse, "as tender a part as [a man] has about him" (115), and in the following theoretical comment on the phenomenon, plays upon the indecent association of hobby-horses and loose women going back to Shakespeare[99] to show that the hobby-horse is a kind of sexual partner:

> doubtless there is a communication between [a man and his Hobby-Horse] of some kind . . . by means of the heated parts of the rider, which come immediately into contact with the back of the HOBBY-HORSE.—By long journies and much friction, it so happens that the body of the rider is at length fill'd as full of HOBBY-HORSICAL matter as it can hold (77).

Toby's hobby-horse, a child's game (played with adult resources) of building model fortifications to parallel the campaigns of Marlborough, began with a map of Namur to help him out of the difficulty of forever having to explain how and where he got his wound, and progressed, "before he was two full months gone" (88), into the study of military architecture, a pursuit which was also a form of self-therapy (after the teachings of Dr. James Mackenzie [83]), since by mastering his subject he hoped to be able to discuss it without becoming emotionally upset (87). But Toby's emotions were aroused in a different way. He took "intense . . . delight" in poring over his map and drinking deep at "the sweet fountain of science" (88).

In the third year of his home study course he progressed to the subject of ballistics where, in a process parallel to Tristram's search for his own origins, Toby attempted to locate the precise Parabola or Hyperbola of the cannon-ball that was the original cause of his blow (90). He navigated through phrases like "the parameter, or *latus rectum*, of the conic section" and "the angle of incidence, form'd by the breech upon the horizontal plane" (which recalls the "acute angle of the garden wall" where Dr. Slop suffered his "transubstantiation"), military language that mocks anatomical obstetric references, and brings to mind the new mathematical procedures, practiced by Smellie and Levret, of discussing the mechanism of labor in terms of the exact shape and situation of the pelvis, the precise dimensions of the child's head, and particularly the rules governing the movement of bodies in different directions—that is, the science of ballistics.[100] Glaister notes that before Smellie accurately described the mechanism of labor, the prevailing view was that the infant "was propelled by the uterine force, *a tergo*, in a straight path into the world, just as a bullet is shot out of a cannon."[101] The story of the origin and development of Toby's hobby-horse clearly parallels and parodies the contentious evolution of modern obstetrics in the mid-eighteenth century.

Long before the hobby-horse takes on the tangible form, as recommended by Trim, of rebuilding the siege towns on the bowling green, Tristram describes Toby's obsession by employing the feminine images of an intricate labyrinth, a "bewitching phantom, KNOWLEDGE," a tempting serpent, all of which he urges Toby to flee as for his life (90). Tristram's "stop! my dear uncle *Toby*—stop!—go not one foot further" recalls his injunction to Slop to stay his obstetric hand, but the story proceeds as inevitably as birth or death, as if in spite of its author. It would seem that Fate and Nature have provided the script which Tristram merely elaborates. After all this, instead of calming Toby's passions, Trim's project only serves to enflame them: "the more [Toby] consider'd it, the more bewitching the scene appeared to him" (98). "Painted . . . upon the retina of my uncle *Toby*'s fancy" was the scene of the bowling green, cut off from the garden by the "tall yew hedge," and enclosed on the other three sides by "rough holly and thickset flowering shrubs" (98), a clear secluded space for private pleasures which heightens Toby's "blush of joy" (97). One is reminded of the medieval *hortus conclusus*. "Never did lover post down to a belov'd mistress with more heat and expectation than my uncle *Toby* did, to enjoy this self-same thing in private" (98).[102] The theme of witchcraft, so potent in the workings of Moll's sense of her Governess and Pamela's awareness of Mrs. Jewkes, as well as in the activities of Lovelace and Mother Sinclair, takes, in this novel, the subtle form of Toby's "bewitching Phantom" and the aura that surrounds the Widow Wadman.

So the project grows in intricacy and scope during the fourteen years that the Widow Wadman, in love with Toby, bides her time, and the reader recognizes the possibility that this whole process is a way for Toby to undo and rise above the horror of that new birth shock at Namur. The fortifications on the bowling green are his one love, but during the demolition of Dunkirk—the interval that led to the Peace of Utrecht—Toby's story undergoes one more metamorphosis: the labyrinth of his beloved fortifications are exchanged for "this mystick labyrinth" of love (469) embodied in the fair Widow Wadman, the physical culmination of every comparison ever made in the annals of love between a woman and a fortified town. Sterne the anatomical humorist, in his recreation of three of the central life acts in human existence, birth, death, and the coming together of the sexes, seems to have left the story of romantic love for last so he can play off all the associations with obstetrics and defense he has carefully fashioned up to this point.

46. The Widow Wadman and Toby: Birth, Sex, and the Fates

The Widow Wadman is a beautifully enigmatic figure of a woman partly because much of her actualization in the novel depends upon the reader's imaginative powers. In what serves as a satire on his male readers' fantasies about women, Sterne explicitly invites his reader ("Sir" not "Madam" this time) to sketch the Widow's picture on the blank page, to recreate her after his own desires. The widow always exists for the reader, male or female, in a state of semi-realization somewhere between the naked page and the imagination. She becomes for a moment the book itself, a reminder of the tradition of the woman as book, at once open, fresh, as sweet and exquisite as anything in Nature (472), yet like Donne's mistress in Elegy XIX, a "mystic book" as well. The blank white page stands in precise contrast to the framed black one, but over each hovers the image and suggestion of new feminine possibility.

There may indeed be one page in Tristram's "thrice happy book . . . which MALICE will not blacken, and which IGNORANCE cannot misrepresent" (472), but it gradually becomes apparent, if only just apparent, that Sterne, with infinitely delicate jest, links the Widow Wadman with the extensive literature of those other widows who kept houses of questionable repute. The Widow is first mentioned in connection with the "shock"—his final blow—which Toby received after the demolition of Dunkirk (101,208). The role played by Fate in the affair of Toby and the Widow is adumbrated early: "there was a strange and unaccountable concurrence of circumstances which insensibly drew him in, to lay siege to that fair and strong citadel" (208). It is not until well into the sixth volume, when the "Fatal interval of inactivity!" (464) occasioned by Dunkirk gives the Widow Wadman, assisted by Fate and Nature, the opening to reverse the metaphor and lay siege to Toby's fair citadel of modesty. She learns to speak his language. She also learns how to wait, and how to move slowly but deliberately at the right time, aided too by the "delusive, delicious" consultations of Toby and Trim on the demolition: "the magic left the mind the weaker—STILLNESS, with SILENCE at her back, entered the solitary parlour, and drew their gauzy mantle over my uncle *Toby*'s head;—and LISTLESSNESS, with her lax fibre and undirected eye, sat quietly down beside him in his arm chair" (465). The Widow is in a conspiracy with the whole mystery of space, intervals, "vacancy" (549), darkness, "Silence . . . weav[ing] dreams of midnight secrecy" (592), stillness, relaxation, and a host of feminine personifications (including Fate and Nature) in her complex siege upon Uncle Toby who, in his "unmistrusting ignorance of the plies and foldings of the heart of woman" (455), is hardly a match for her.

When Toby and Trim first hastened down from London in 1701 "to take possession of the spot of ground" on Toby's small estate in Yorkshire, they were put up for the night in Widow Wadman's house. The only character Sterne will give of the widow is that she was "A daughter of *Eve . . . That she was a perfect woman*" (546). A woman who makes "a man the object of her attention, when the house and all the furniture is her own," mixes him up with something of her own interior or muted light (as opposed to "broad daylight") and her own "goods and chattels," the things around her which are invested with her presence. Thus it was, through a reiterated process of thought, that Toby got "foisted into her inventory—And then good night" (546). The beautiful and highly "concupiscible" Mrs. Wadman in her seven years' widowhood, with her own house and furniture, is indeed a figure of power and mystery. We have seen a series of widows in Defoe and Richardson associated with all manner of female frailty and wickedness—Moll's Governess, the Widow Bevis, Mother Sinclair. Cynical Father Poussin noted that "there is hardly a village within twenty Miles round *London*, but affords a kind Residence to one or more *Widows*, who have had *Husbands*, to whom they had the Misfortune to be never *Married*, and who by being tied down to certain yearly Stipends, (the Wages of their *youthful Labours*,) are oblig'd to pass the latter Part of their Days in a retired Manner."[103]

It would certainly be wrong to see the Widow Wadman in such dark colors—after all she has a marriage settlement which she reads with devotion. But all the business about her "house and furniture," "her inventory," her role as a "daughter of Eve" is "matter copulative and introductory" (547) to the story of the Widow, Bridget (her waiting-maid generously given to Corporal Trim), and the corking pin. In this extraordinary "ordinance of the bed-chamber," the pin seems to stand to the Widow's long Queen Anne nightshift as she wishes Toby to stand to her (547-48); "she ruminated till midnight upon both sides of the question" and finally kicked the etiquette of the corking pin into shivering atoms. The Widow is far from being a Mother Sinclair, but she is Toby's Mother Midnight, a voluptuous Eve to his pristine and modest Adam.

The Fates, who certainly all foreknew of these amours of widow *Wadman* and my uncle *Toby*, had, from the first creation of matter and motion (and with more courtesy than they usually do things of this kind) established such a chain of causes and effects hanging so fast to one another, that it was scarce possible for my uncle *Toby* to have dwelt in any other house in the world, or to have occupied any other garden in *Christendom*, but the very house and garden which join'd and laid parallel to Mrs. *Wadman's*; this, with the advantage of a thickset arbour in Mrs. *Wadman's* garden, but planted in the hedge-row of my uncle *Toby's*, put all the occasions into her hands which Love-militancy wanted; she could observe my uncle *Toby's* motions, and was mistress

> likewise of his councils of war; and as his unsuspecting heart had given
> leave to the corporal, through the mediation of *Bridget*, to make her a
> wicker gate of communication to enlarge her walks, it enabled her to
> carry on her approaches to the very door of the sentry-box; and some-
> times out of gratitude, to make the attack, and endeavour to blow my
> uncle Toby up in the very sentry-box itself. (552)

Sterne reserves his richest commentary on Fate for the story of Toby and the
Widow. At the end of Book 7, Tristram seems to be more deeply in touch
with this own mortality (and fatality) than ever before when in the midst of
his "delicious riot" of speculation on the last days of the Christian faith and
the ushering in of a new age of heathen gods at sexual play—"what jovial
times!"—he is pierced with the thought that he "must be cut short in the
midst of [his] days" (495). The female Fates are the first gods; they not only
preside over events, they cause them.[104] Immediately preceding the Fate
passage, the Widow, in all the trappings of Toby's new hobby-horse, stands
"ready harnessed and caparisoned at all points to watch accidents" (552)
which makes her a mortal counterpart to the Fates who stand behind the
accidents and errors to which even kindly Dame Nature is subject. The
Widow, like Milton's Eve, has her own garden with a "thick-set arbour" to
spy upon unsuspecting Toby and we may imagine the holly, yew, and dense
shrubs surrounding Toby's bowling green as merely extensions of the
Widow's garden, of her own organic encircling potency. The wicker gate
made for her by Trim enables her "to carry on her approaches to the very
door of the sentry-box" of his citadel.

In this box, an extraordinary transaction occurs: the Widow is pre-
determined to light Toby's candle at both ends (554). That Toby is capable of
being so ignited is not to be doubted, and what follows in Chapter XVI of
book 8 is the apotheosis of the theme of matter and motion (or Sterne's sense
of transition being all in all in this life), and the culmination of the arts of
love, birth, and death in one concentrated comic episode.

I have tried to show that Toby's childlike nature, his sexual modesty (a
persistence in "total ignorance of the Sex"), and his devotion to the history
and reduplication of military fortifications combine to hold him in a kind of
arrest or suspension from ordinary reality. His is a self-contained world that
has its own all consuming pleasures. In a sense, he is married already, the
masculine and feminine sides of his good nature coexisting in self-sufficient,
if arrested and precarious, harmony. Perhaps this is the real meaning of his
modesty. Toby has now been gestating in this womb of his own making, this
elaborately constructed and defended reversal of the blow of Namur, for ten
full years, the duration of Marlborough's active career in the War of the
Spanish Succession (1702-1712), and a span of time that recalls the nine or
ten months of pregnancy as established in the midwife books. The Widow

seems to understand all this about Toby and intuit that he may be ready, or may be made ready, for a new kind of pleasure. She wishes to deliver him from the illusory but protective matrix of his fortifications into the ordinary world of male and female sexuality by undoing, with all the skill and experience and dexterity of which she is consummate mistress, the elaborate citadel of modesty which Toby inhabits, and by moving ever closer to the secret of his genital ability or disability, redirect the masculine passion he has expended on his hobby-horse toward its proper object—namely, herself.

The language for the Widow's critical encounter with Toby in his sentry-box is an elaborate parody of the rhetoric of siege warfare. Even more compellingly, however, it is also a parody of obstetrical language, and Sterne is minutely careful in his rendering of every gesture of the encounter, just as Smellie, or even Burton, tried to be in articulating their life-and-death directions for proper delivery. As the Widow moves into the sentrybox and ever closer toward Toby's "main body," she extends "her right hand; and edging in her left foot at the same movement" (554) takes hold of his map, the very map which once extricated him from the pain and sorrow of fruitless explication. Next she must deliver him of his tobacco-pipe, which of course has "no arterial or vital heat" in the end of it (555), like the *funis umbilicus*. Then Toby "would lay his hand flat upon" the map (which implies that there were more than one of these skirmishes) and "by a manoeuvre as quick as thought," having placed her own hand by his on the map and "opened a communication, large enough for any sentiment to pass or repass, which a person skill'd in the elementary and practical part of love-making, has occasion for—," she brings her forefinger and thumb into action which "naturally brought in the whole hand."[105] Toby's hand, before it is removed, receives "the gentlest pushings, protrusions, and equivocal compressions" imaginable, and his calf under the table receives similar ministrations from her leg (556). The Widow is mistress of the touch, in all the sexual, obstetric, artistic, and other senses which we have noted since *Moll Flanders*, "so that my uncle *Toby* being thus attacked and sore push'd on both his wings—was it a wonder, if now and then, it put his centre into a disorder?" The mention of wings (like touch a term redolent of meaning in several contexts), recalls the military signification of "divisions. . .on each side of the main body or *centre* of an army" (*OED*, 7), and also serves as a final ironic contrast with Dr. Burton's forceps, the "Wings" of which clasped the child's head like a portable vise.[106]

The Widow puts Toby's "centre into disorder," but she has not yet penetrated his secret, and not to be outdone by Trim's fair Beguine and her rubbing maneuver, she forms a new attack in a moment by means of "a mote—or sand—or something" (576) in her left eye.[107] At this point, Sterne invokes a comparison, by way of the earlier Burton, between the eye of the Widow and that of the celebrated Greek courtesan, Rhodopis of Thrace. The

links between the widow and her famous sisterhood of antiquity and modern
times are made delicately but firmly as the affair moves toward its conclusion. The Widow's "venereal" (578) eye is not rolling, romping, wanton,
sparkling, petulant, or imperious (578), not at all like the eyes of Sally and
Polly in Widow Sinclair's entourage; it is rather a "speaking" eye, "whispering soft—like the last low accents of an expiring saint." Not that Mrs.
Wadman is anything other than a beautiful and concupiscible widow, but
Sterne's language makes comparisons with the inverted religious order of
eighteenth-century prostitution inevitable, and the widow's eye "did my
uncle *Toby's* business" (578).

"My uncle *Toby* knew little of the world" (580), and almost nothing about
women. The Widow Wadman is a perfect woman, and a worldly one, much
more refined and sophisticated than all the other widows and "housekeep-
ers" that have preceded her in these pages. As with Moll Flanders, "the
Devil, who never lies dead in a ditch, had put into her head" (581) further
misgivings about "the monstrous wound" upon Toby's groin, and these
misgivings lead to Toby's final shock and the undoing of all the Widow's well
laid plans. Sterne has now arrived at the "choicest morsel" in his story of
Uncle Toby and the Widow. Toby, refurbished in his laced cloaths, white
ramillie-wig, and red plush breeches, and Trim, a rejuvenated corporal, now
mount their own campaign upon the Widow and Bridget, but Toby has
misgivings: "I declare, corporal I had rather march up to the very edge of a
trench—A woman is quite a different thing . . . I suppose so. . . . " (583).

Toby standing, in all his finery, "looking gravely at Mrs. Wadman's
house," musing about the loss of his sweet liberty and the fate of Trim's
brother Tom who married the Jew's widow at Lisbon, is one of the most
pensive moments in the novel. Sterne dwells on and elaborates the moment
with the bawdy yet touching story of Tom and the widow's sausage-making.
The outcome of the story parallels that of Toby and his Widow's encounter in
the sentrybox, and it is yet another of Sterne's capsule metaphors of mortality, a comic anatomy of sausage-midwives as fates ("cutting the strings into
proper lengths") who will soon be swept away by the deadlier fate of the
Inquisition. The fleeting mortality of the characters under his pen seems to
prompt in Sterne a brief meditation on the mortality of the creator who gives
them their nature and fate. Or does he only seem to create them? At this
point, the relation between Sterne the creator and Fate the creator seems
blurred beyond discrimination:

> . . . Time wastes too fast: every letter I trace tells me with what rapidity
> Life follows my pen; the days and hours of it, more precious, my dear
> *Jenny!* than the rubies about thy neck, are flying over our heads like
> light clouds of a windy day, never to return more—every thing presses

on—whilst thou art twisting that lock,—see! it grows grey; and every
time I kiss thy hand to bid adieu, and every absence which follows it, are
preludes to that eternal separation which we are shortly to make.—
—Heaven have mercy upon us both (610-11).

As the story of Tom and the Jew's widow spins on and on, Walter Shandy,
who stands with his wife at "the fatal angle of the old garden wall, where
Doctor *Slop* was overthrown by *Obadiah* on the coach-horse," frets at the
nonsensical doings of Toby's and Trim's "two noddles" while the issue of the
event with the Widow is "hanging in the scales of fate" (611-12). Bridget
awaits in the house "with her finger and her thumb upon the latch benumb'd
with expectation" while Mrs. Wadman, "with an eye ready to be deflowered
again" (619), perhaps darning up the slit, fatelike, in her apron (633), "sat
breathless behind the window-curtain of her bed-chamber," a curtain which
has taken the place of Toby's military curtins. "Let us go into the house"
(620)—and two more blank pages follow, reminding us of the page left blank
for the male reader to paint the Widow as she exists in his own mind after the
lineaments of his mistress. A London brothel in the eighteenth century
offered a similar prospect: the visitor could choose, from among the many
charming portraits adorning the walls, the woman who most coincided with
his heart's desire. [108] After these blank pages (for Chapters XVIII and XIX)
there occurs the curious digression on the poor maid Maria, whose banns
were forbidden by the curate of the parish and who subsequently went mad.
She is placed here, perhaps, as a poignant counterbalance to the web of
associations clinging to the Widow Wadman. She is a reminder, especially to
Sterne's male readers, "of what a *Beast* man is" (631) in relation to women, as
a predator or as the goat Tristram compares himself to, in the eighteenth
century or after, a beast who may yet be capable of the innocence and
generosity of an uncle Toby or the compassion of a Tristram.
"The Eighteenth Chapter" (633) is finally presented in Chapter XXV,
spelled out in scriptural black letters. Toby is introduced so quickly into the
parlor that Mrs. Wadman barely has time to "lay a Bible upon the table, and
advance a step or two towards the door to receive him" (633). We are familiar
with this gesture, from Mother Creswell to the more refined hypocrisies of
Mother Sinclair instructed by Lovelace, but the Widow's stratagem is far
more delicate than the schemes of these other Mother Midnights. When
"My uncle *Toby* laid down his pipe as gently upon the fender, as if it had
been spun from the unravellings of a spider's web" (643), realizing for the
first time that the Widow's thousand virtues, especially "the compassionate
turn and singular humanity of her character" (642) have all been in the
service of an overriding curiosity (however natural and understandable)—
"the weak part of the whole sex" (368)—Toby receives in this final stage of his

siege upon this fair citadel a second shock no less painful, in its quiet intensity, than the terrible one at Namur. It would seem, finally, that what Toby and the Widow represent are two vital but incompatible powers in a fictional universe which is the frustrated comic counterpart of Richardson's in *Clarissa*.

EPILOGUE

Lifelines:
The Language of Fate and
the Transcribed Self

The reader who chooses to review the Introduction cannot help but notice the many references to cutting, tying, sewing, spinning, weaving, dressing, stitching—to men and women as figurative creatures of clothing. A traditional image, running all through the Introduction, is the thread of life and its relationship to fate. It is this thread which is the crucial metaphoric link between the figure of Mother Midnight and the gradually unfolding lives of the protagonists of these four novels. The thread of life mirrors the fundamental duality of fate: it is both continuous and discontinuous. Fate is body and spirit, good and evil, feminine and masculine—personal yet impersonal, potent yet finite, generative yet terminal, or as Kierkegaard puts it in his most deliberately ambiguous fashion, "Fate may mean two things exactly opposite, since it is a unity of necessity and chance." The paradox of continuity in discontinuity is reflected in the image of the midwife who must sever the umbilicus, the lifeline to the mother, that we may be born into life. Mother Midnight for a time presides over the thread of the main character's fate, but we must remember that the character is always weaving this thread through her or his writing (in all the senses we have suggested for this term), a thread which issues into a unique destiny outside and away from Mother Midnight's influence. Perhaps the chief consequence of our search for and examination of Mother Midnight is this figure's role as a catalyst to further speculation about the meaning of a character's unique fate and language, and the meaning of fictional creation itself.

In the light of the historical context and mind set I have attempted to delineate in the Introduction—based primarily on the Psalms, Job, the scriptural motif of God's "book of life," and contemporary seventeenth and eighteenth-century writings—every person is a text who unites the metaphor of clothing (the language of the body and appearance) with the metaphor of the book (the language of words). A book is sewn, and the child is sewn in the womb; his progenitors and namers are his parents. As we observed at the end of Chapter 2, the child's parents, like authors, give the child a title, a name, and the name is an emblem or talisman for the child's fate. The person is thus a book of clothes, an enigma there to be read by any prospective reader. With our name, we have been given a compressed script for our life, but with our appearance, gestures, and verbal language we must, throughout the course of our life, write the book of our own unique fate upon the consciousness of the world we move in. In this sense, the person *is* the thread of his or her own life.

Defoe, Richardson, and Sterne were well advanced in years when they wrote their fictions. They were men who had seen much of the world, lived actively in it, and who had experienced, in uniquely different ways, a profound immersion in the written word: Defoe through his long, diverse, almost manic career as a popular writer, Richardson as a man of business, a prolific and distinguished printer, Sterne as a gregarious parson who wrote contemplative sermons and was, moreover, a wide-ranging, idiosyncratic reader and mischievous scholar. Each author had a keen interest in the experience of women—particularly, as I have tried to show explicitly and by implication, in the secrets of women's wisdom relating to human procreation. I have argued that in certain respects the Socrates of Plato is an ancient prototype of these writers. In establishing himself as a philosophical midwife to men's minds, Socrates became a self-styled expert on the midwives' lore of his time. He was a kind of medium between the sexes, as is Defoe when he virtually fuses himself with his creation, Moll, in retailing the secrets of a "Woman debauch'd from her Youth"; as is Richardson in reviving his childhood role of impersonating lovers, writing and editing their letters for them; as is Sterne in recreating himself through the androgynous Tristram, an all-licensed, self-deprecating, philosophic fool, full of opinions about the act of creation, who tells bawdy stories about his family culminating in the affair of Uncle Toby and the Widow Wadman. As mediums between the sexes, Defoe, Richardson, and Sterne are literary fates to their fictional creatures.

In reflecting on the chief characters of the novels—Moll, Pamela, Clarissa, Lovelace, Tristram—much of our attention has centered on how they view their own lives, particularly on how they present their lives *in their writings*. What distinguishes these protagonists from others in major eighteenth-century British fiction is the extraordinary relationship of each to her or his own *story* or narrative, and in the case of Pamela, Clarissa, Lovelace, and Tristram, to the *act* of writing itself. Defoe, Richardson, and Sterne seem to take great pleasure in the act of verbal revelation, and their main characters—their fictional offspring and alter egos—are all great storytellers or writers. Each of these highly verbal, highly expressive protagonists is at once a character in a fiction, a name, and a literal text to be read by an outside reader, and in the case of Pamela and Clarissa, by readers within the novel itself. The titles of the four novels (as well as Fielding's and Smollett's novels) all include the *given* name, the new name chosen by the author/ parent. Each novel is thus a person and a book, a carefully contrived objective version of the person-as-book. And as the author fuses with his created character, so the character fuses with her or his book.

We saw in Psalm 139 and in the case of Pamela that the sewer gives way to the writer, the *textus* or fabric sewn with the needle is superseded by the text composed with the pen. The author of the Psalms and Richardson the novelist posit an important link between the metaphors of sewing and writing. The hand twisting and turning in the spinning motion of the fate, or the sewing motion of the midwife tying off the navel cord, is at one with the hand moving a pen in the act of writing, and the line of writing, like Pamela's trembling "Lines," is another thread of life, or as Lovelace puts it to Belford, "Fate . . . spins threads for tragedies, on purpose for thee to weave with." The narrative of each of the great writing characters in the four novels then *is* the thread of her or his own fate—the line of writing is the line of life—and each character writes out that fate. But each must undergo the encounter with Mother Midnight.

Let us recall that from the beginning, the midwife is an enigmatic figure of mystery and power, at once strange and familiar, an uncanny creature. A figure of enormous antiquity, her function, as defined from Plato through Galen on into the eighteenth century, has remained quite stable. The very definition of the three roles of the cunning woman (to decide whether a particular man and a particular woman are capable of begetting children, and then to make the match; to be able to tell the signs of pregnancy; to assist at the mother's delivery) linked her with the preternatural power of the witch and the unsavory activities of the bawd. Moreover, all the characteristics of the traditional midwife (her age—an older woman, past childbearing; her wisdom of the world; her skill in predicting human consequences; her use of scissors and thread in her work) allied her with the sinister mythical figures of the Three Fates of the Greeks (originally birth spirits), the daughters of Night, who presided over the thread of life, spinning it into being, apportioning it to each individual, and cutting it off when the life was done. The midwife-fate was always a figure of *worldly* wisdom, and often androgynous, with the female element predominating. At the critical moment of birth, the midwife-fate of folklore determined the child's destiny in a milieu saturated with chants, charms, ritualistic utterances, and women's talk. We noted further how in seventeenth-century midwife lore the cunning woman was thought to have power to determine the child's sexual and verbal capacity by how long or short she cut the navel cord. Hence the midwife could make a girl modest and keep women in their place from birth by giving them a short cord. The midwife's overall function was an extension of that primary metaphor, drawn from the Old Testament, of man as a creature whose body God sews in the womb and whose members God records in his own book of life.

The torturing midwife of the seventeenth and eighteenth centuries was associated with the powers of the black witch and, even more important to our study of these novels, with the bawd. The emphasis on imparting the arts of stitching and dressing made the bawd a figurative worldly mother to her opulently dressed adopted daughter, the whore. Always linked to her

house, her own sovereign and ominous domain, the traditional London
bawd (fat, taciturn, nocturnal, witchlike, a former whore) transformed, by a
kind of manufactory process, naive young women from the country, her raw
material, into rich salable commodities (the whore as an eighteenth-century
fashion model and vendor of sweet kisses, pretty smiles, charming looks, and
all the arts of pleasing), and ultimately into complete artists—through verbal
and sexual attraction—of ensnarement to men. The creatures and creations
of libertines and the authors of books about prostitution, the whores make
victims of their male creators. But the whore was also a person "dead to law,"
full of self-contempt, and intent on reducing other young women to her
level—a self-punishing victim caught in a destructive cycle even if she did
escape early death and become another "Mother to the maids." Standing
behind Mother Midnight, as we have seen, is the variety and enormous
power of the mother figure in literature (often folk literature), a literal or
figurative mother and rearer of children, or a stepmother, grandmother,
godmother, witch, widow, aunt, nurse, governess, duenna, housekeeper.
But the chief characteristic of Mother Midnight, for our purposes, is her
connection with fate.

The word "fate" has appeared in a variety of senses and contexts in this
work. The most important of these have to do with fate as a process and fate
as a powerful human figure who acts as an agent within that process. Fate is
three old women who spin the thread of life, fate is what is given to one at
one's birth, and fate is also the life spun. Fate as the totality of one's life is
what Moll glimpses in her encounter with the Governess, and it is the
outcome of a life in Arabella's contemptuous forecast of her sister's inevitable
"fate" as a "common creature." Within that lifespan fate may be perceived as
a binding phase or condition, as when Moll says it was her "Fate" to be poor
and friendless, or when Pamela says of her inability to go or stay, "What a
Fate is this!," a prelude to the "Fate that awaits her" from Mr. B. And at the
end of *Tristram Shandy* the binding nature of fate is imaged conventionally,
within a highly innovative framework, as the chain of causes and effects. The
power of fate is represented in the novels in two principal ways, as an outside
force, like a hand impelling or compelling the protagonist (Moll's sense of
fate "pushing" her on and the stress on manual action in the narrative,
Pamela's fear of the hand of Jewkes, Clarissa's vulnerability at the hands of
Lovelace and her sense of being thrown and bound by fate, Tristram in Dr.
Slop's bungling hands or Toby in the expert ones of the Widow Wadman),
and as has been equally apparent, this power resides in words. The dual
nature of the thread of fate has its counterpart in the dual nature of the word,
spoken or written (silent or unwritten). To choose just one example, Clarissa
and Lovelace are each other's fates in their mutual shaping through intensely
sexual *verbal* conflict. Fate is a word, a name, a prophecy, a curse, a decree,
a language. There is a rhetoric of fate operating in each of the four novels,

and this rhetoric is the most significant and binding of languages. There are then several agents of fate at work in these fictions, but the most influential of these is Mother Midnight.

Emerson said that "Fate is unpenetrated causes." It is not surprising that a figure with the unpropitious lineage we have just reviewed should, in her various manifestations in our four novels, constitute not an unpenetrated but an apparently impenetrable source of anxiety, in one form or another, for the title character. In *The Courage to Be* (1952), Paul Tillich, speaking of the human condition in every age, called "fate . . . the rule of contingency, and the anxiety about fate is based on the finite being's awareness of being contingent in every respect. . . . Fate is usually identified with necessity in the sense of an inescapable causal determination. Yet it is not causal necessity that makes fate a matter of anxiety but the lack of ultimate necessity, the irrationality, the impenetrable darkness of fate." Tillich notes further that "the anxiety of death is the permanent horizon within which the anxiety of fate is at work," and that "fate would not produce inescapable anxiety without death behind it." Ultimately, Mother Midnight is an image of anxiety about the fate that waits for all of us, normally just below the threshold of consciousness, in death. Tied most closely to fate through a quality of malign mystery, Mother Midnight poses a threat to the protagonist's innermost sense of being. If we look back at the life stories of these four characters, we shall see that some of the deepest, most intensely mortal moments of their being are lived in the presence of their Mother Midnight and her figurative offspring or counterparts. We have a sense, in the suffering of the female protagonists especially, of the anxiety of fate.

In the Introduction and in the discussion of Pamela, our examination of the representation of the womb and women in the medical and quasi-medical lore of the era revealed that woman, in large part subject to the vagaries of her womb—that highly sensitive and suggestible source of melancholy, frenzy, disease, extravagancy of mind, and error—was thought to be a creature tender, delicate, soft, weak, timid, and vulnerable, susceptible to and capable of more intense sensations of pleasure and pain because the passions of grief, joy, anger, and fear make greater impressions on her. The early English (and French) novel is intimately bound up with feminine experience, with women as authors and as subjects of fiction. Perhaps women, in the eyes of these novelists, made better subjects because more happens *to* and *within* them—they are better fictional exemplars, in this sense, of the human condition than men—and certainly Defoe, and especially Richardson, were well aware of writing for a predominantly female audience. In any event, each of the three great female protagonists we have discussed is, in her own way, an exceptionally impressionable, sensitive, and above all, apprehensive creature, and Tristram and Toby demonstrate their own peculiar versions of melancholy, consternation, and dismay. At the same time, each of these major characters is presented, and sees herself or himself as, an extraordinary and unique person in the world who tries to maintain precarious control over the telling or writing of a life story which represents what they consider to be of most value in their lives. We shall conclude by briefly reviewing each character in turn in the light of how they deal with their anxiety and try to preserve their uncommon story in response to their experience of Mother Midnight.

One of Moll Flanders most crucial moments (discussed in Chapter 13) is her interview with the Governess shortly after her lying-in when the "impenetrable" old beldam prevails upon her to divulge the secrets of her married life and, touching Moll "to the Quick," terrifies her with her apparent knowledge of the circumstances of Moll's coming into the world and her going out of it by the steps and string. This moment is mirrored in Moll's ordeal in Newgate (Chapter 15), the prison which functions as the ancient counterpart and mother to Mother Midnight and Moll's own mother, where the inmates have given the heroine the fatal name of Moll Flanders and who seek, like the whores who wish to humble Clarissa, to reduce Moll to their level.

Like the other three title characters, Moll, as Defoe puts it in the Preface, is represented as "suppos'd to be writing her own History," only "the original of this Story is put into new Words" to make the style more modest. In a deep and primitive way, Moll attempts to preserve her true story within her true Name by not revealing the secret of that name to Mother Midnight or anyone else, even the writer of the Preface, presumably. This unknown name is the title of her unwritten history. But after opening her soul to the minister in Newgate, escaping execution, and establishing her new foundation in the new world, the more secure and autonomous older Moll, perhaps a more exceptional person now than ever because of her survival in the prosperity of a kind of comic afterlife, takes control of her story. She feels confident and presumably eager enough, so the fiction goes, to "write her own History," in all its fullness and variety, through the agency of a trustworthy and sympathetic reporter/editor, "the Pen employ'd in finishing her Story." Having evolved into her own Governess, Moll can now tell the story she could not tell to Mother Midnight, though she still protects her true name. Moll Flanders, the notorious name given to her by Mother Newgate, evolves into the name Moll *chooses* for her story, in effect becomes the "true Name" she will now go by in the world and for all posterity. In other words, Moll becomes strong enough to take Moll Flanders as her true name. This is the final sense in which Moll is her own midwife: she becomes namer, mother, author of herself.

The adolescent Pamela, like the young Moll Flanders, is a highly equivocal creature and, through her lively talk and genius for self-display through the right costume, an even more expressive actress. Pamela too is more expressive than Moll in the variety of her apprehensions, a medley of feelings building in intensity from uncertainty, misgiving, foreboding and suspicion to a threshold of genuine fear: superstitious fear of a witch, fear of being searched, fear of rape alternating with paralyzing depression, then reaching a climactic level of terror, panic, agony and hysterical convulsions followed by a return to anxious uncertainty. Her fears are always directly related to Mr. B. and to his primary instrument, Mrs. Jewkes, but it is not too much to say that the horizon of her anxiety before marriage is, literally, death. Pamela's rhetoric of fate and her relationship to the impenetrable Jewkes ("Why, *Jezebel!* . . . would you ruin me by Force?") might suggest that the heroine is in more danger from her Mother Midnight than from Mr. B. (141, 116). As the childlike Moll feared her Governess' virtual appropriation of her true Name and destiny, so the child/woman Pamela fears Mrs. Jewkes's physical plundering of her person and her writings, and finally her assistance in—or managing—the rape which will mean her death as much as it will for her successor, Clarissa.

As long as Pamela maintains control of her writings, whether hiding them under a rosebush or sewing them to her petticoats, she is a figure of extraordinary independence, vitality, and autonomy. Even the little history of her sixteen years of righteous innocence which she recounts for Jewkes before the final attempted rape acts to clothe and shield her vulnerable nakedness from B.'s hostile intentions. This little history is a more explicit counterpart to Moll's recital to her Governess of her marital history. Pamela's exfoliating autobiography, written around her body, is the Fable, or Romance, or Novel which includes all the important characters in her life story. These writings, suffused and literally one with Pamela's experience, personality, and presence, preserve the story of how she kept her virtue—in a deep sense they *are* her virtue, her best self, a significance Richardson preserves in his carefully chosen title for the novel. When she allows B. to possess this text, Pamela, dressed in her own words, becomes the living simulacrum of her own fate—the book of her fate.

Though she heroically overcomes her fears, vanquishes her Mother Midnight, and eventually establishes a groundwork of trust with B., Pamela does so at a great cost. Finally getting what she hardly dared to wish for, she virtually lets B. make her over into his idea of a wife, surrendering to him both her self and her story. This is how Pamela's Virtue is rewarded. As a fiction of loss, *Pamela* is an incipient tragedy, a natural, brilliant, but rather awkward precursor of the epic tragedy of *Clarissa*. Put another way, Pamela sometimes acts as if B. were her only reader, and that helps to account for the wildly mixed reception the novel has met with from its own time to the present. Pamela's ultimate fate, as is the case with any book, is her unknown reader, and that reader, male or female, may be left with something of the same anxiety about Pamela's successful defence of her virtue in becoming Mrs. B. as the heroine felt when that virtue was under attack.

Perhaps the most difficult thing to acknowledge about Clarissa is that her strongest feelings of affection are for women, and the most difficult thing to accept about Lovelace is that he carries out the rape of Clarissa largely under the influence of his own female tools, Mrs. Sinclair, her whores, and other women, an influence I have discussed particularly in Chapters 30 and 31. Lovelace and Clarissa both care a very great deal about how they will appear in the eyes of their respective worlds, for Lovelace the interrelated worlds of libertinism and prostitution, for Clarissa the respectable world of women. The country lady Clarissa (as Richardson defines her in the Postscript of the novel) is the victim of both of these worlds, and in a profound sense the victim of women. This in no way diminishes Lovelace's individual responsibility for his treatment of her. The "strange Fate that attends our Sex" (Chapter 9), the betrayal of women by women, becomes personified most richly and vividly (of all four novels) in that strange creature, Mother Sinclair, and all her progeny: Lovelace, her "son," and all the women in her house who contribute to Clarissa's suffering and agony. It is true, as I have tried to demonstrate, that the members of Clarissa's immediate family also do her incalculable harm, especially her father through the curse conveyed by Arabella, but they too are at least partially manipulated by Lovelace. Before the rape, Lovelace says to Belford, "leave this sweet excellence and me to our fate: that will determine *for* us, as it shall please itself: for, as Cowley says:

> An unseen hand makes all our moves:
> And some are great, and some are small;
> Some climb to good, some from good fortune fall:
> Some wise men, and some fools we call:
> Figures, alas! of speech!—For destiny plays us all." (II,397)

It is clear that at the height of his powers and success, Lovelace identifies himself with the unseen hand, but he will also come to recognize for himself that he has been manipulated by Mother Sinclair and the women below, and perhaps ultimately by destiny itself.

Clarissa's evolving sense of fate differs significantly from Lovelace's. Early in her relationship she sees herself as one who is "singled out to be a very unhappy creature," one whose young wisdom, by a "strange fatality," a "perverse fate," seems to be turned to foolishness. When Lovelace first gets

her to London she sees fate as a violent compelling force, and Lovelace
becomes in her mind virtually the personification of her ineluctable lot, her
fate "too visibly in his power" as she becomes his possession, whether
married or unmarried. Later, as Lovelace falls more and more under the
influence of the women below, Clarissa comes to see him as the physical
instrument of her father's curse ("my guilt . . . stares me every day more and
more in the face; and still the more, as my fate seems to be drawing to a
crisis, according to the malediction of my offended father!" [III,110]), but
she senses her fate as something still peculiarly *her own* ("leave me to my
fate"), outside of the combined power of Lovelace and Sinclair, and beyond
any of them in its significance. After the rape, the old self, name, and image
lost, she still has sufficient courage and resourcefulness to help preserve her
soul by facing down and vanquishing her tormentors, physically freeing
herself from the demonic union of Lovelace/Sinclair, and going whither her
"mysterious destiny" shall lead her. She comes to know the full circumstances of the deceptions Lovelace has practiced on her, and this knowledge
augments the saintlike power she attains in her isolation from him and her
intensifying collaboration with Belford (her executor and avenger), with
whom she reestablishes a semblance of the trust she had lost with all men.
Moll Flanders chronicles nearly the entire life of a sexually active woman
through menopause into a prosperous old age. Clarissa, her curious counterpart, encapsulates the entire life cycle of a chaste woman in her nineteen
years, and both characters end by entrusting the "publication" of their life
story to a man.

Richardson says in his Postscript that he intended to "investigate the great
doctrines of Christianity under the fashionable guise of an amusement." As
Pamela with her Petticoat papers became the book of her own fate, so
Clarissa, in a more profoundly religious sense, transforms herself into her
own "book of Meditations," a transcribed self which binds Lovelace's story to
hers and transcends it in the uniquely personal scripture of her letters. This
book is then vouchsafed to the care of Belford, her literary executor, at once
a kind of ideal reader and representative of the author. Clarissa becomes a
goddess of suffering Wisdom who, after a long wished-for and pleasant
transition in death (and we recall that death became for her as familiar as
dressing and undressing), and with a final divine self-definition of her fate as
"I am all blessed hope," is translated for her family and friends into a
triumphant epistolary angel meting out to all the characters in her story a
peculiarly devastating sort of forgiveness.

Tristram Shandy, like his female predecessors, sees himself as an exceptional person, and he is the most fully developed of the four as a writing
character. We are to believe that Moll's story is re-written for her; Pamela
writes nearly all of her own story and then hands it over to her most
influential reader; Clarissa, with extraordinary devotion and courage, and as

long as she can move a pen, writes out the entire version of her story (alongside the versions of Anna Howe, Lovelace, and Belford), which turns out to be an all-inclusive narrative, subsuming the fates of all the other major and minor characters within her fate. Tristram, who of the four title characters is most fully fused with his own author, is imagined to be fashioning the history of the Shandy family, and he works away at his job over a much longer period of time than any of the other writing characters, weaving a narrative exceedingly rich in a variety of metaphors of the thread of life, memorable images of mankind's tenuous and disjunctive mortality.

Mother Midnight in the other three novels presides over a painful period of regeneration for the heroine. In this novel the hero is afflicted with anxiety even before he is born, and Sterne, the anatomist of fate, divides the traditionally androgynous and ambivalent Mother Midnight figure into her female and male components, giving to the female the un-Shandean motherliness, regularity, and affinity with Nature of the good midwife, and to the male the indecency and insensitivity of the bawd, and the presumption, impatience, and incompetence of the rash, torturing midwife whose procedures have mortifying lifelong consequences for the hero in a Shandean world where things almost always fall apart. As the fumbling, forceps-wielding improvisor of a new male technology, Slop is the technological father of Tristram. Yet Slop seems to function for Tristram as the living personification of the threat of disruption or annihilation, and Burton/Slop united constitute a satiric end-product of a natural philosophy, or science which, if it does not exactly banish the female from nature, treats her with insensitivity, suspicion, and contempt.

Sterne invents Tristram, and Tristram attempts an historical inquiry into his past and reinvents his biological father and his spiritual parent and mentor, Uncle Toby, the protagonist of his concluding romance. As Toby attempts, unconsciously, to reverse the trauma of his wound at Namur by painstakingly re-creating his fortifications on the bowling green out of the same materials and milieu which brought about his grievous injury, so Tristram, out of the material of words whose heavy weight has inflicted injury even before his conception (in his parents' marriage articles), compensates for the accidents of his birth and near castration by writing out his melancholy life in a "second translation" (or his own "obstetrical romance," as Lodwick Hartley call it), creating a book which functions as an inexhaustibly comic member of generation for true Shandeism. It was the word which doomed Tristram; it is the word which redeems him for immortality. Yet ultimately Uncle Toby is Tristram's most representative emblem of the human condition, for despite the blended masculine/feminine gentleness of his influence on Tristram Shandy, Gentleman, at the end Toby and his Mother Midnight, who with all her arts is no more able to deliver him into the world of marriage than Tristram's original midwife was able to deliver him into life, are as much the victims of their own fate as anyone else in the Shandy world. As Lovelace wondered whether destiny was "playing" him at the end, Sterne leaves us with two questions: is Tristram writing the fiction or is Fate writing him; and what is the nature of that fate? The most Shandean of nineteenth-century philosophers, Søren Kierkegaard, wrote a discourse on the concept of dread, by which he meant approximately the same thing Tillich did by anxiety, and what Sterne meant by melancholy. If we were to ask, says Kierkegaard, "what is the object of dread, the answer as usual must be that it is nothing . . . But what then is signified more particularly by the nothing of dread? It is fate." For Kierkegaard, who also said that "He who has to explain fate must be just as ambiguous as fate is," fate is "nothing" and it is also the "secret friend" of genius. In the other three novels we have examined, the title character, after the ordeal of the experience with Mother Midnight, is still able to establish trust with someone just outside the narrative ("Defoe" as ghost writer) or another character within the fiction (Mr. B., Belford) and so preserve her story. For Tristram, this trust can only be established with the reader, female or male, an unknown quantity, a fate. Sterne is happy to create a space, a form, and even a sex for his reader, if only that reader will reinvent him in mortal sympathy and friendship.

NOTES

PART ONE: INTRODUCTION: "THE BIRTH OF FATE"

1. *The Ladies Companion, or The English Midwife* . . . by William Sermon, Doctor in Physick . . . (London . . . printed . . . at the *Adam* and *Eve* in *Little-Britain,* 1671) 3-5; cf. James Guillimeau, *Child-Birth, or The Happy Deliverie of Women* (London, 1612) 82-83, originally published in Paris in 1609 under the title *De l'heureux accouchement des femmes* (see Heinrich Fasbender, *Geschichte der Geburtshülfe* [Jena: Fischer, 1906] 130). My title for this part is taken from "The Rape of the Lock," canto II, 1.142; of the many links between birth and fate in seventeenth-and eighteenth-century poetry, stanza 3 of Cowley's "The Muse" (1656; where the Muse appears as a wise figure of fate), ll.845-860 and 1173-76 of Dryden's *Annus Mirabilis*, and many passages in his translation of the *Aeneid*, and in Pope's Homer, are noteworthy.

2. Plato, *Theaetetus*, trans. John McDowell (Oxford: Clarendon Press, 1973) 11-15.

3. *Ladies Companion* 3.

4. *Theaetetus* 12.

5. *Ibid.* 13.

6. *Ladies Companion* 5. Cf. also the "jury" of midwives who might be called upon to determine if a woman was a witch.

7. Cf. Erich Neumann, *The Great Mother: An Analysis of the Archetype*, trans. Ralph Manheim, Bollingen Series, 47 (Princeton: Princeton UP, 1955) 321; Richard Brixton Onians, *The Origins of European Thought About the Body, the Mind, the Soul, the World, Time and Fate* . . . (Cambridge: Cambridge UP, 1951), chap. 4, "The Weaving of Fate," and pp. 352-53, 392-94; and Eliot's "Sweeney Agonistes."

8. Pierre Danet, *A Complete Dictionary of the Greek and Roman Antiquities* . . . (London, 1700), under "Parcae," n.p.

9. P. Galtruchius [Gautruche], *The Poetical Histories. Being a Compleat Collection of all the Stories Necessary for a Perfect Understanding of the Greek and Latine Poets, And other Ancient Authors*, 3rd ed. (London, 1674) 75.

10. Danet, under 'Terra,' n.p.

11. Hesiod, *The Homeric Hymns and Homerica*, trans. H. G. Evelyn-White (Loeb Classical Library, London, 1914), *Theogony* 95.

12. Gautruche 71.

13. Danet, under "Parcae."

14. William King, *An Historical Account of Heathen Gods and Heroes. Necessary for the Understanding of Ancient Poets*, 2nd ed. (London, n.d. [1711?], ("of the *Parcae*") 158.

15. Danet, under "Fatum," n.p.

16. *Ibid.*

17. Gautruche 71.

18. Under "Parcae."

19. King 158.

20. Robert Burton, *The Anatomy of Melancholy*, ed. Holbrook Jackson (Everyman's Library, 1932), I, 206.

21. *Clarissa's Ciphers: Meaning and Disruption in Richardson's "Clarissa"* (Ithaca: Cornell UP, 1982) 79. I find this the most stimulating recent discussion of *Clarissa*.

22. Hesiod 95.
23. *A Handbook of Greek Mythology* (New York: Dutton, 1959) 24.
24. Pp. 231-32.
25. Madeleine Riley, in her account of childbirth in the English novel, notes that in the eighteenth century childbirth seems to have been regarded "as a natural, frequent event involving all the community in which the mother lived. They recognised that it was an event which was likely to include death, which would require humour, endurance, and good luck. In the childbirth scenes in these [eighteenth-century] novels there are many characters, some giving advice and assisting at the birth, some coming in to chat, eat and drink: the atmosphere is convivial, busy and easy going. The women in labour are, for the most part, brave and practical," *Brought to Bed* (London: J. M. Dent, 1968) 130.
26. Sermon 107.
27. See especially the extended accounts in Jane Sharp, *The Midwives Book: Or The Whole Art of Midwifery Discovered* . . . . (London, 1671) 22-23, 212-16, and *Aristotle's Compleat Master Piece: In Three Parts: Displaying the Secrets of Nature in the Generation of Man* . . . , 27th ed. (London, 1750) 73-74.
28. See Henry à Daventer [Hendrik van de Venter], *The Art of Midwifery Improv'd* . . . , 3rd ed., corrected (London, 1728), for an account of the midwife's tools, excluding "Instruments," 110-19, 321; cf. James Wolveridge, *Speculum Matricis; or The Expert Midwives Handmaid* . . . (London, 1671) 24-25.
29. Sermon 107.
30. Pp. 23, 214. Not all writers on generation shared these beliefs. The great de Graaf (1641-73) considered "the saying of midwives, that the penis will be larger if the umbilical cord in a new-born baby is not tied next to the navel but cut away, is a silly one." In a comment which would be relevant to *Tristram Shandy*, he added "what the physiognomists say is not part of eternal truth either, to wit that the size of the penis corresponds with the shape of the nose," Regnier de Graaf, *On the Human Reproductive Organs*, trans. H. D. Jocelyn and B. P. Setchel, *Journal of Reproduction and Fertility*, Supplement no. 17 (Oxford: Blackwell Scientifc Publications, 1972) 46.
31. Sharp 215-16.
32. Sharp 212-13.
33. Pp. 230, 223.
34. Sir Walter Ralegh, "What is our life? a play of passion," 1612.
35. "The Preface," n.p.
36. Wolveridge 2. Cf. the wording of the *Compleat Midwife's Practice* (London, 1656) 65, and *The English Midwife Enlarged* (London, 1682) 1. See Herbert R. Spencer, *The History of British Midwifery from 1650 to 1800* (London: J. Bale, 1927), appendix I.
37. Wolveridge, "The Preface." Other midwife authors are more circumspect about prying into God's creation. James McMath will only narrate the conventional account of the formation of "this *Noble Fabrick*" because "this be matter of most hard *Explication*, so that our great *Creator* seems to have reserved this *Mystery* to himself alone, and would not, proud man should dive into the most small beginnings of his work," *The Expert Midwife: A Treatise of the Diseases of Women with Child, and in Child-Bed.* . . . (Edinburgh, 1694) 20. McMath may have in mind Ecclesiastes 11:5: "As thou knowest not what is the way of the spirit, nor how the bones do grow in the womb of her that is with child: even so thou knowest not the works of God who maketh all."

38. Jacob Rueff asks, "What will frame and instruct our mindes better, than to have considered the end of so excellent and wonderfull a building and worke-manship? What is more pleasant and beautiful, than to have understood the artificiall framing and forming of our proper Nature and body, which we inhabit and continually abide in?", *The Expert Midwife or An Excellent and most necessary Treatise of the generation and birth of Man* (London, 1637) 55. Cf. Austin, below, and McMath 27ff.

39. For God's control of the birth process and delivery, cf. also Isaiah 46:34 and 66:9.

40. *Aristotle's Compleat Master Piece* 9, 13.

41. William Harvey, *Anatomical Exercitations, Concerning the Generation of Living Creatures: To which are added Particular Discourses, of Births, and of Conceptions, &c* . . . (London, 1653) 501-02.

42. Gautruche 13. Penelope Shuttle and Peter Redgrove note that "Hera" and "Astarte" both mean womb, and that "Pallas Athena" means literally "vulva-vulva," *The Wise Wound: Menstruation and Everywoman* (London: Gollancz, 1978) 178.

43. The best historical discussion of representations of and attitudes towards the womb and its supposed influence on female behavior is found in Ilza Veith, *Hysteria: The History of a Disease* (Chicago: U of Chicago P, 1965), passim.

44. *The Female Physician. Containing all the Diseases incident to that Sex . . . To which is added, The Whole Art of New Improv'd Midwifery . . .* By John Maubray, M.D. (London, 1724) 393.

45. Harvey, *Anatomical Exercitations* 502. Cf. Robert Burton, *The Anatomy of Melancholy*, I, 234-35.

46. Cf. *Timaeus* (91bcd): "in men the organ of generation becoming rebellious and masterful, like an animal disobedient to reason, and maddened with the sting of lust, seeks to gain absolute sway, and the same is the case with the so-called womb or matrix of women. The animal within them is desirous of procreating children, and when remaining unfruitful long beyond its proper time, gets discontented and angry, and wandering in every direction through the body, closes up the passages of the breath, and by obstructing respiration, drives them to extremity, causing all varieties of disease, until at length the desire and love of the man and the woman, bringing them together and as it were plucking the fruit from the tree, sow in the womb, as in a field, animals unseen by reason of their smallness and without form . . . " (Jowett trans.). Cf. Montaigne's reference to this passage in "On some verses of Virgil" (*Essays*, III, 5), arguably the single most comprehensive and influential commentary on women's sexuality, women's role, and marriage in the Renaissance.

47. Quoted in Veith 23; cf. 7-8.

48. This and the following images for the womb come, respectively, from William Austin, *Haec Homo: Wherein The Excellency of the Creation of Woman is described. By way of an Essay . . .* (London, 1637) 93; Thomas Raynold's translation of Eucharius Rösslin's *Rosengarten* (1512), entitled *The byrth of mankynde, otherwyse named the woman's booke . . .* (London, 1545) 10; Rueff 51; Sharp 35; McMath 37, 10, 7; and Sharp 39.

49. Sharp 134-38. Thomas Forbes notes that the "caul," or that portion of the amnion which occasionally envelops the head of the child at birth and is thought superstitiously to portend greatness (among other things) goes by several references to clothing in various languages, such as "shirt," "helmet," "cap," "hood," "veil," "little cloth," "mask," "little birth shirt," "Virgin's shift," and so on (*The Midwife and the*

Witch [New Haven: Yale UP, 1966] 97-98). He notes further that "witches were reputed to prize cauls highly as potent aids in evil-doing" (101).

50. Sharp 372.

51. Jean Donnison, *Midwives and Medical Men: A History of Inter-Professional Rivalries and Women's Rights* (London: Heinemann, 1977) 33. Cf. also the valuable pioneering commentary on the profession of midwifery by Alice Clark, *Working Life of Women in the Seventeenth Century* (1919; rpt. New York: A. M. Kelley, 1968) 265-85.

52. Percival Willughby, Gent., *Observations in Midwifery. As Also the Country Midwife's Opusculum or Vade Mecum* [1642], ed. Henry Blenkinsop (Warwick, 1863) 32. Willughby is generally considered the greatest English authority before the eighteenth century on the practice of midwives; he was a friend of William Harvey's.

53. Donnison, quoting Willughby 11.

54. *Ibid.* 11.

55. *The Midwife and the Witch* 113.

56. Kittredge, *Witchcraft in Old and New England* (Cambridge, Mass.: Harvard UP, 1929) 4. Perhaps the best representation of such a witch in English literature is Ford, Rowley, and Dekker's *Witch of Edmonton* (1621), Mother Elizabeth Sawyer: "Reverence once / Had wont to wait on age; now an old woman / Ill-favored grown with years, if she be poor, / Must be called bawd or witch" (IV.i.149-52).

57. *Ibid.* 5

58. For background on the "cunning woman" see Wallace Notestein, *A History of Witchcraft in England from 1558 to 1718* (Washington, D.C.: American Historical Association, 1911) 20-22; and also Thomas Cooper, *The Mystery of Witch-craft* (London, 1617): "Good Witches, Blessers, Wise, and Cunning-women," 203; Ned Ward, *The London Spy compleat, in Eighteen Parts . . .* " reprinted from the edition of 1700" (London, 1924), part xv: "Of *Astrologers* and *Wise-Women*," 361-62; Sermon, *The Ladies Companion* 3-5; Maubray, *The Female Physician*: "the Cunning Expert *Midwife*," 219; Kittredge's discussion of John Bale's "Idolatry," 34-35; Forbes, *The Midwife and the Witch*, chap. 8; and particularly, Keith Thomas, *Religion and the Decline of Magic* (New York: Scribner's, 1971), chap. 8. Cf. *sage femme* and Daumier's representations.

59. McMath, *The Expert Mid-Wife*, "Preface," n.p.

60. See Forbes, *The Midwife and the Witch* 118-27.

61. [Richard Head?], *The Life and Death of Mother Shipton, Being not only a true Account of her Strange Birth, and most Important Passages of her Life, but also of her Prophecies* (London, 1684) 9-10, 1.

62. Ned Ward, *The Whole Pleasures of Matrimony: Interwoven with Sundry Delightful and Comical Stories . . . To which is added, The Destructive Miseries of Whoring and Debauchery* (London, n.d. [1700?] 56-59); the midwife's talkativeness, particularly about sex, was proverbial: "at a Gossipping-Feast, the Works of Generation are so large and so pleasing a Theme, that there is no fear of wanting fresh matter to discourse on," 115. One of Ward's "comical stories," in verse, concerns Betty the Chambermaid: "Now *Betty* by the wise and prudent Care / Of Mother Midnight, straightways does prepare / Herself for Men's reception out of hand, / For she'll not now be under the command / Of anyone, since she's a Woman grown, / But will set up a calling of her own" (157-58). Jacob Rueff dilates on "the wicked Arts and policies of Old Witches and Harlots" relating to midwifery, abortion, and child-murder in *The Expert Midwife* 58-61.

63. Donnison 34.

64. *The Character of a Towne-Misse*, (London, 1675) 4.

65. *The Whores Rhetorick* (London, 1683; rpt. Edinburgh, 1836) 25-26. Mother Creswell is presented here as a true *sage femme*, learned in philosophy, astronomy, and metaphysics—"then I advanced to the Books of Generation," 20. For a scholarly discussion of "Prostitutional" literature see Roger Thompson's *Unfit for Modest Ears: A study of Pornographic, Obscene, and Bawdy Works Written or Published in England in the Second Half of the Seventeenth Century* (London: Macmillan, 1979) 57-95.

66. *The Night-Walker: or, Evening Rambles in search after Lewd Women, with the Conferences held with Them, & c.* . . . (London, 1696) 23.

67. Joseph Gay [i.e., J. D. Breval], *The Lure of Venus: or, a Harlot's Progess. An Heroi-Comical Poem. In Six Cantos . . . Founded upon Mr. Hogarth's Six Paintings . . .* (London, 1733) 7-8. The bawd in this plate is conventionally identified as Mother Needham (see *Hogarth's Graphic Works*, comp. Ronald Paulson [New Haven: Yale UP], I, 144-45).Some notable bawds and whores in seventeenth-century drama would include Madonna Fingerlock and Madame Horseleech in both parts of Dekker's *The Honest Whore*, 1604-5; Franceschina, the courtesan, and Mary Faugh, the bawd, in Marston's *The Dutch Courtesan*, 1603-5; old Cataplasma, the periwig maker/bawd of Tourneur's *The Atheist's Tragedy*, ca. 1609; Webster's *The White Devil*, ca. 1611, Vittoria Corombona, a Venetian courtesan; Madam Decoy, a procuress in Shirley's *The Lady of Pleasure*, 1635; the courtesans Angelica Bianca and La Nuche, and the bawd, Petronella Elenora, in both parts of Aphra Behn's *The Rover*, 1677-81; Mrs. Clacket, a "City Baud and Puritan" in Behn's *The City Heiress*, 1682, and the bawd, Driver, in her *The Town Fop*, 1676; Lady Du Lake and her two whores in Dryden's *The Wild Gallant*, 1662; Mrs. Joyner and Mrs. Crossbite, the two "Bawds" in Wycherley's *Love in a Wood*, 1672; Coupler, the old bawd in Vanbrugh's *The Relapse*; and the variety of bawds, whores, and bullies who appear throughout the comedies of Shadwell, especially in *The Humourists*, 1671, *Epsom Wells*, 1673, *A True Widow*, 1679, and *The Woman Captain*, 1680.

68. [Robert Gould], *Love given o're: Or, a Satyr against the Pride, Lust, and Inconstancy, & c. of Woman . . .* (London, 1683) 4-5.

69. *The Whores Rhetorick* 10-12.

70. *The London Bawd: with her Character and Life. Discovering the Various and Subtle Intrigues of Lewd Women . . .* 4th ed. (London, 1711) 4-8. Cf. another of Ned Ward's energetic bawds: "How now, Old Beldam; Whither are you Trotting in such wonderful haste this morning? . . . She's so Naturally Prone to Corrupt others, that her highest Felicity consists in Seducing her own Sex to what, she knows by Experience, ends . . . in most Sorrowful Reflections. . . . She's an Absolute *Politician* in the business of Intrigue. . . . She's a rare Assistant to a *Midwife*, and a Merry Old Matron at a Gossiping, or a Christning; has as many Smutty Stories at her Tongue's end, as an Old Parish Clerk. . . . Her Face is as full of Wrinkles as a Vintner's Bar-board is of Chalks. . . . she is the very Emblem of the Serpent that betray'd *Eve*," *The London Terraefilius: or, the Satyrical Reformer . . .* (London, 1707) 7. An influential prototype of the ancient bawd is Ovid's Dipsas (*Amores* I, viii): "She's the local witch— / can reverse the flow of water, / whirl the magic wheel, cull herbs, / brew aphrodisiacs, / guarantee the weather, / cloud or sunshine, / blood red stars . . . or a blood moon—I've seen both. / She's a night-bird . . . Well, this creature tried to corrupt my innocent girl / and she's very persuasive— poisonously so" (*Ovid's Amores*, trans. Guy Lee [New York: Viking, 1968] 27. Cf. also the "duenna" figures in *The Roman de la Rose* and *Don Quixote*, part II.

71. William Austin, *Haec Homo* 55-58, 63, 92-93.

72. *A Discourse of Women . . . Translated out of the French into English . . . .* (London, 1662) 41.

73. *The Compleat Midwifes Practice. In the most weighty and high Concernments of the Birth of Man. . . .* (London, 1656) 121-22. The "Dying Midwife" is reputed, on the title-page, to be the great Louise Bourgeois, "Midwife to the Queen of France," and author of *Observations diversés* (1609). The "Dying Midwife" further cautions her daughter "Never [to] keep the cawl called *Amnios*, which covers the head and shoulders of the childe, for Sorcerers to make use of," 120.

74. *Pretty Doings in a Protestant Nation. Being a View of the Present State of Fornication, Whorecraft, and Adultry, in Great Britain. . . .* Written Originally in *French* by Father Poussin . . . . (London, 1734), pp. 38-39.

75. *The London Bawd* 113.

76. *The Whores Rhetorick* 63, 73-75.

77. *The Works of Mr. Thomas Brown. In Prose and Verse; Serious, Moral, and Comical. . . .* (London, 1707), I, 167-68. "Thus then it is plain, a whores work is no more than to be well skilld in legerdemains, to know how to raise a Fog, and artificially to throw it before the Fops Eyes: then all her Cheats, Slights and Juggles pass for Honesty, Sincerity and Plain-dealing" (*The Whores Rhetorick*, 114).

78. *The Covent-Garden Magazine. . . .* (London, Jan. 1773), II, 66.

79. Ned Ward, *The Insinuating Bawd: and the Repenting Harlot. . . .* (London, n.d. [1699]), n.p.

80. William Alexander, *The History of Women, From the Earliest Antiquity to the Present Time. . . .* (London, 1779), II, 34, 85.

81. *Pretty Doings in a Protestant Nation* 13-14.

82. Mandeville, *A Modest Defence of Publick Stews* 42.

83. *Pretty Doings* 6-7.

84. In considering the conditions necessary for human procreation, the French surgeon and midwife Pierre Dionis posits "a Woman of a sound Constitution, without any natural Defect, full fourteen Years of Age, in the Arms of her Husband, whom she's perfectly fond of, and allows to do whatever he pleases, in obedience to Nature," *A General Treatise of Midwifery . . .* (London, 1719) 75.

85. *Pretty Doings* 6-7; cf. "She being thus equipt for *Venus* sport, / She takes a Lodging in *Salisbury-Court*, / And sets up, being charming, young, and fair, / The good old trade of Basket-making there," Ned Ward, *The Whole Pleasures of Matrimony*, p. 155. "Basket-making" could also refer to conveying a bastard away in a "Hand-basket" (*ibid.* 157) or to whore-mongering in general. Cf. also the last couplet of Gray's "The Candidate": "Damn you both for a couple of Puritan bitches! / He's Christian enough, that repents, and that stitches."

86. *The Crafty Whore: Or, The misery and iniquity of Bawdy Houses Laid open, In a dialogue between two Subtle Bawds. . . .* (London, 1658) 7.

87. *The Night-Walker*, Sept. 1696, p. 25. The strait-laced Hannah Woolley emphasizes, in *The Gentlewoman's Companion; or, a Guide to the Female Sex* (1675), that "Chambermaids" are to "Dress well," and "work Needle-work well," 207, 209-10.

88. *Pretty Doings in a Protestant Nation* 4.

89. W. De Archenholtz, *A Picture of England* (London, 1797) 302-03, 307-09, 316. See also L. Fernando Henriques, *Prostitution and Society*, vol. II: *Prostitution in Europe*

and the New World (London: MacGibbon and Kee, 1963) 144-45, for further quotations from pp. 118-99 of the 1789 edition of *A Picture of England*. Henriques' chapter on prostitution in "London in the Eighteenth Century" is a detailed and useful survey. Cf. also "the gay Dress and jaunty Airs of some of these Strumpets might have led [a foreigner] into a Mistake concerning their Condition," *Some Considerations Upon Street-Walkers* (London, n.d. [1725]) 14.

90. *The Whores Rhetorick* 110.

91. *Ibid.* 38.

92. *The History of Women* I, 7-8.

93. Henricus Cornelius Agrippa, *The Glory of Women: Or a Looking- Glasse for Ladies* . . . trans. H.[ugh] C.[rompton] Gent. (London, 1652) 2, 15-16.

94. Henricus Cornelius Agrippa, *Female Pre-eminence: or the Dignity and Excellency of that Sex, above the Male* . . . trans. H.[enry] C.[are] . . . (London, 1670) 16.

95. *Haec Homo* 133.

96. *The History of Women*, I, 314-15, 326-27, 336; cf. Tom Brown: "the chief Vertue in the Ladies Catechism is to please; and Beauty pleases Man more effectually than Wisdom," *Amusements Serious and Comical*, 1700, 63.

97. *The Whores Rhetorick* 36, 43, 39-40.

98. *Ibid.* 42, 215.

99. William King 158.

100. The whore must maintain a close professional relationship with some "Venereal Doctor. These are as necessary in the war of *Venus*, as in that of *Mars*; because the casualties are as different as that may befall a Female Combatant, as any the most adventurous and daring Souldier. The Lady is on duty every day, and being sometimes forced in her single person to face whole Armies of fighting Men, and Volleys of Shot, it is odds but some of them hit, and disable her from further service . . . " (*The Whores Rhetorick* 124-25).

101. *Ibid.* 215-16, 41-43. In this connection it may also be noted that women were often compared to books: the perfections of nature "are collected . . . in [woman], whom we may call, a *Draught* of the whole Creation in *Miniature*, or a *Copy* of that vast Volume done in exquisite *short-hand*" (*Female Pre-eminence* 17); in his famous "Elegy XIX" Donne refers to women as "mystic books" and asks his mistress to show herself to him "As liberally as to a midwife"; Ned Ward refers to gentlemen "Who admire Books as they do Women, for the Newness of their Faces" (*The Secret History of Clubs*, "The Preface," n.p.); a "stale Virgin" is referred to as "an old Almanack out of Date" in *Aristotle's Compleat Master Piece* 30-31. The motif of "woman as book" is particularly evident in connection with prostitution and "prostitutional" literature: in the "brothel" scene of *Othello*, the Moor asks rhetorically (alluding to Desdemona), "Was this fair paper, this most goodly book, / Made to write 'whore' upon" (IV. ii. 70-71). Marston's *Dutch Courtesan*, Franceschina, is described as "adulterate as some translated manuscript." In his dedication John Taylor equates his book with its title: *A Common Whore* (London, 1622), and the "Epistle to the Reader" of *The Whores Rhetorick* contains an extended metaphor of the woman as book; the accomplished whore later switches the metaphor to men: "Reading men is the great Work of her Life," p. 135. Cf. also "*Ju*[lietta] is not overworn, therfore not past turning, and a good *two leav'd book* left to look in still" (Gusman in *The Wandring Whore* [London, 1660], part 5, p. 3).

102. *The Whores Rhetorick* 144, 116-17.

103. *Ibid.* 144, 152.
104. *A Modest Defence of Publick Stews* 9 (my emphasis), 42.
105. *The Whores Rhetorick*, p. 221. Maximillian E. Novak notices the resemblance between Moll Flanders' dialogue with her "Mother Midnight" and Mother Creswell's with Dorothea in "Defoe's 'Indifferent Monitor': The Complexity of *Moll Flanders*," *ECS* 3 (1970) 351-65; rpt. Kelly, p. 416. Cf. Swift on the Struldbruggs: "As soon as they have compleated the Term of Eighty Years, they are looked on as dead in Law."
106. *The Crafty Whore* 23.
107. *Tell-tale Cupids Lately discover'd* (London, 1735) 49.
108. *Nocturnal Revels: or, the History of King's Place, and Other Modern Nunneries* . . . 2nd ed. (London, 1779), I, 187-88.
109. *Pretty Doings in a Protestant Nation* 29-30.
110. Samuel Richardson, *Pamela*, ed. T. C. Duncan Eaves and Ben D. Kimpel (Boston: Houghton Mifflin, 1971) 410.
111. *The London Bawd*, pp. 5, 7. Cf. also: "Whores are all knowing in that maxim of changing Names and Qualities, from one part of the Town to another; when they become crackt in their reputation" (*The Whores Rhetorick* 113). Victor Turner's discussion of "liminal *personae*" is relevant to the representation of Mother Midnight and the figures in her power: "Liminal entities are neither here nor there; they are betwixt and between the positions assigned . . . by law, custom, convention, and ceremonial. As such, their ambiguous and indeterminate attributes are expressed by a rich variety of symbols in the many societies that ritualize . . . cultural transitions. Thus, liminality is frequently likened to death, to being in the womb, to invisibility, to darkness, to bisexuality, to the wilderness, and to an eclipse of the sun or moon," *The Ritual Process: Structure and Anti-Structure* (1969; rpt. Ithaca: Cornell UP, 1977) 95. Cf. also his commentary on the "*Isoma*" (a ritual of procreation) with respect to the ensuing discussion of Clarissa, Lovelace, and Sinclair (*ibid.* 11-20).
112. See Henriques quoting Archenholtz (II, 89-90), *Picture of England*, p. 144.

NOTES TO PART TWO: "MOLL'S FATE"

1. Ned Ward, *The London Spy* 243.
2. Daniel Defoe, *The Fortunes and Misfortunes of the Famous Moll Flanders.* . . . , ed. G. A. Starr (London: Oxford Univ. Press, 1971) 128. Hereafter all quotations from this edition (including the "Introduction") are cited by page number in the text and in the notes.
3. Although a sequel to the novel did appear in 1730 giving an account of Moll's governess under the name of "Jane Hackabout," the work has not been attributed to Defoe (see *Moll Flanders*, ed. Edward Kelly [New York: W. W. Norton, 1973] 6n). The title of this sequel is *Fortune's Fickle Distribution: In Three Parts. Containing, First, The Life and Death of Moll Flanders. Part II. The Life of Jane Hackabout, her Governess; who was an Attorney's Daughter, a Lady's Woman, a Whore, a Bawd, a Pawnbroker, a Breeder up of Thieves, a Receiver of Stolen Goods, and at last died a Penitent. Part III. The Life of* James Mac-Faul, Moll Flanders's *Lancashire Husband.* . . . In the "Preface," the reader is cautioned about how careful a young woman must be concerning her chastity, "for when once the Modesty of a Woman is gone, she is capable of any Mischief the Devil can put her upon; there being no Creature in the World so voracious as a wicked

Woman" (n.p.). The story of "Jenny Hackabout" is a conventional one, but it has particular passages relevant to *Moll Flanders* which will be cited in the following notes.

4. *The London Spy* offers these synonyms for "Mother Midnight": "*Matron in Iniquity*," "Reverend Doctress of *Debauchery*," "old *Mother* of the *Maids*," "*Mother Belzebub*," "Mother *Grope*." There is also a "Father Midnight," the watch (Ned Ward, *The London Spy* 9, 29, 32, 33, 57, 35. Cf. Starr's note, *Moll Flanders* 391); cf. also Ward's *The Secret History of Clubs* (pp. 303-04) for a lively and detailed account of the bawd's "Business of Intrigue."

5. The best historical discussion of the origin of the character and name of "Moll Flanders" is Gerald Howson's "Who Was Moll Flanders?" *TLS* (18 Jan. 1968) 63-64; rpt. in Kelly 312-19; cf. Howson's *Thief-taker General: The Rise and Fall of Jonathan Wild* (New York: St. Martin's, 1970) 156-70. Cf. also David Blewett's relevant discussion in *Defoe's Art of Fiction* (Toronto: U of Toronto P, 1979) 55-92.

6. *To the Palace of Wisdom: Studies in Order and Energy from Dryden to Blake* (Garden City, New York: Doubleday, 1964), rpt. in Kelly 381-82.

7. Cf. G. A. Starr on Moll's "recurring attachments" to older women, each of whom she "learn'd to call Mother" ("Introduction" to *Moll Flanders*, p. x). It is noteworthy that the epithet "Mother" was often used for particular midwives, bawds, or witches.

8. The name "Cleave" may have historical significance (see Starr's note, p. 376) but it is also a sexual pun: "Therefore . . . a man . . . shall cleave unto his wife: and they shall be one flesh" (Genesis 2: 24). "My Lady *Cleave*" (117) is slang for a wanton woman (cf. *Moll Flanders*, ed. Kelly 93n).

9. Cf. Juliet McMaster, "The Equation of Love and Money in *Moll Flanders*," *Studies in the Novel*, 2 (1970) 136-37. For what follows, cf. Robert Burton on gold as "the great goddess we adore and worship . . . If we lose it, we are dull, heavy, dejected, discontent, miserable, desperate, and mad. Our estate and *bene esse* ebbs and flows with our commodity . . . 'Tis the general humour of the world" (*The Anatomy of Melancholy*, III, 20).

10. "Jenny Hackabout," after leaving off the trade of bawd because of the expense of "keeping off Indictments, bribing the Informers, and other Accidents," became so successful a midwife "that there was scarce a Whore about Town but was her Customer"; Jane was also expert at disposing of children to "Gypsies" as soon as they were born for "forty shillings" (*Fortune's Fickle Distribution* 109-10).

11. *London Spy* 9. This pimp is also an expert pickpocket.

12. *Ladies Companion* 92.

13. Daventer, *The Art of Midwifery Improv'd* (1728) 12.

14. Cf. Ned Ward's "Bawdy Governess"—"an *Amphibeous* Necessary, between *Bawd* and *Midwife*," "an old experienc'd Lady, whose wrinkl'd *Brows*, and hypocritical Eloquence, seem'd to shew she had run thro' all the changeable Conditions incident to the complying Nature of the *Female Sex*," who after delivering a young unwed country girl, "cherish'd me up," in the victim's words, "with Caudle and boil'd *Chickens* till I was almost surfeited; so that I was grown so lusty in a Fortnights time that the Old *Beldam* would have merrily insinuated I had gather'd Strength enough for Humane Consolation," *The Rise and Fall of Madam Coming-Sir: or, An unfortunate Slip from the Tavern-Bar, Into the Surgeon's Powdering-Tub* (Suffolk, n.d.—ca. 1700) 25-27. See Starr's note, p. 381. Moll's Governess (who had also "run thro', it seems in a few Years all the eminent

degrees" of a disgraced "Gentlewoman" [5], "Nurs'd . . . up" her charge as well (though before the delivery) with "a Chicken roasted and hot" (166-67).

15. In John Lyly's *Mother Bombie*, "the wise woman of Rochester is visited by Vicina, a young woman who wishes to have her fortune told: "Thou has touch'd me to the quick, mother. I understand thy meaning and thou well knowest my practice," *Mother Bombie*, ed. A. Harriette Andreadis (Salzburg Studies in English Literature . . . no. 35, 1975) 200.

16. Daniel Defoe, *The History of the Devil*, part II, chap. 9.

17. Cf. Terence Martin's provocative "The Unity of *Moll Flanders*," *MLQ* 22 (1961), rpt. in Kelly 363-64. I disagree, however, that the Governess, "on analysis, is found to exist in quantitative terms" (371). Cf. also Miriam Lerenbaum's compelling suggestion that Moll begins her career as a thief while "undergoing her climacterium" in "Moll Flanders: 'A Woman on her own Account,'" in Arlyn Diamond and Lee R. Edwards, eds., *The Authority of Experience: Essays in Feminist Criticism* (Amherst: U of Massachusetts P, 1977) 114-15.

18. *Amusements Serious and Comical And Other Works*, ed. Arthur L. Hayward (New York: Dodd, 1927) 23.

19. Moll's stooping to tie the lace of the child's "Clog" and the deliberateness of "I turn'd the Child about" may be compared with "the greatest Article of all in the Art of Midwifery . . . that of Turning the Child. . . . Whatever the Posture be, (except when . . . the Child comes right) you should search for the Feet . . . When you have found one, secure it by tying it with a Ribbon . . . draw them down . . . so low, that you may make use of your other Hand . . . in turning the Child," *The Midwife rightly instructed: or, the Way, which all women desirous to learn, should take, to acquire the true knowledge and be successful in the practice of, the art of midwifery. By T. Dawkes,* Surgeon (London, 1736) 16. Cf. the description and illustration of "clogs" (overshoes tied with ribbons) in C. Willet and Phillis Cunnington, *Handbook of English Costume in the Eighteenth Century*, 2nd ed. (London: Faber, 1964) 171, 173.

20. See Starr's note, 388.

21. Dawkes's *The Midwife Rightly Instructed* is cast in the form of a dialogue between a man-midwife and his "Deputy," a young woman named "Lucina." Cf. Maubray, *The Female Physician* (1724) 176.

22. *Ladies Companion* 6.

23. *Ibid.* 6.

24. Maubray, *The Female Physician* 181.

25. Cf. Everett Zimmerman, *Defoe and the Novel* (Berkeley: U of California P, 1975) 101.

26. Moll's sense of being taken "infallibly" is conveyed in rhetoric similar to that of official accounts of criminal acts in the Old Bailey "sessions papers"; cf. *"Ann Festrop*, of St. *Brides*, was indicted for privately stealing a Guinea and a half . . . from the Person of *Robert Spicer*, on the 18th of *February* last. The Prosecutor deposed that as he was going along *Fleet-street* about one a Clock the night aforesaid, the Prisoner took hold of him, and his Cloak slipt off; that while his Hands were employ'd in putting it on again, she pickt his Money out of his Fob; that he felt her Hand under his Waistcoat, and seiz'd her at the instant; but did not search her. The Constable deposed that he heard the Prosecutor call out Watch, and that he and the Watchman brought the Prisoner to the Watch-house. *James Boddington* deposed, that he hearing the Prosecutor call, Watch, turn'd back and saw him have hold on the Prisoner, saying, she had pickt his Pocket.

Two Watchmen corroborated the former Evidence, and farther deposed that the Prisoner was a common Night-walker. The jury found her Guilty. Death.", *The Proceedings on the King's Commission of the Peace*, . . . *and Goal-Delivery of Newgate, held for the City of London, and County of Middlesex, at Justice-Hall in the Old Bayly* (1/4 March 1721) 1-2.

27. Moll's skillful deliverance of herself from the "Crowd" may be compared with Ned Ward's less successful experience of the Lord Mayor's Day "Mob" (at "the End of *Blow-Bladder-Street*") as a kind of violent womb of humanity: "Whilst my Friend and I were . . . staring at the Spectators . . . such a Tide of *Mob* over-flow'd the Place we stood in that the Women cry'd out for Room, the Children for Breath, and every Man . . . strove very hard for his Freedom. For my own part, I thought my Intrails would have come out of my Mouth, and I should have gone shotten Home, I was so closely Imprisoned between the Bums and Bellies of the Multitude, that I was almost squeez'd as flat [as] a Napkin in a Press, that I heartily would have joyn'd with the *Rabble* to have cry'd *Liberty, Liberty*" (*London Spy* 298-99; cf. also 251-52). Cf. one of the earliest descriptions of labor in the midwife manuals: "Also it shalbe very good for a tyme to retayne and kepe in her brethe for because that thorow that meanes the guttes and intrailles be thrust together and depressed downeward," *The byrth of Mankynde newly translated out of Laten into Englysshe*. . . . , trans. Richard Jonas (London, 1540) 20.

28. Dawkes, *The Midwife Rightly Instructed*, pp. xi, 7-8.

29. *The Female Physician*, 169.

30. John Maubray, *Midwifery Brought to Perfection. By Manual Operation; Illustrated in a Lecture* . . . (London, 1725), p. ii.

31. See Miriam Lerenbaum's "'A Woman on her own Account'" (cited above) and Nancy K. Miller, *The Heroine's Text: Readings in the French and English Novel, 1722-1782* (New York: Columbia UP, 1980) 15, 19-20, for a similar emphasis on Moll as (in Miller's phrase) an "eponymous heroine."

32. *The Early Masters of English Fiction* (Lawrence: U of Kansas P, 1956), rpt. in Kelly 347.

33. Before her actual Newgate ordeal, the scene of Moll's worst suffering was Virginia, a colony "half-Peopled" with the human refuse of Newgate: "there are more thieves and Rogues made by that one Prison of *Newgate*, than by all the Clubs and Societies of Villains in the Nation" (87), in the words of Moll's mother. After Virginia Moll becomes a criminal. After Newgate she becomes a new and prosperous woman. "Virginia" and "Newgate" represent the two poles of Moll's experience, and both names imply a fresh beginning.

34. G. A. Starr notes, in a suggestive phrase, that Moll has "a stronger sense of her unfulfilled destiny than of her actual identity" (xvii). I believe that by this point in her story Moll's "destiny" (or fate) and "identity" (her true self) have come together.

35. Michael Shinagel, "The Maternal Paradox in *Moll Flanders*: Craft and Character," *Cornell Library Journal*, 7 (1969), rpt. in Kelly 410.

36. Moll even shows signs of attaining to Mother Midnight's traditional alternate role of match-maker, in this case to her own son: responding to his mother's inquiry as to why he is still unmarried, Humphrey replies "that *Virginia* did not yield any great plenty of Wives, and since I talk'd of going back to *England*, I should send him a Wife from *London*" (337).

Notes to Part Three: "Pamela's Book of Fate"

1. Richardson to the Rev. Johannes Stinstra, 2 June 1753, in *Selected Letters of Samuel Richardson*, ed. John Carroll (Oxford: Clarendon, 1964) 231-32.
2. *Ibid.*, 1741, 41.
3. *Ibid.* 232.
4. *Ibid.* 41. Cf. T. C. Duncan Eaves and Ben Kimpel, "The Publisher of *Pamela* and Its First Audience," *Bulletin of the New York Public Library* 64 (1960) 143-46, and Eaves and Kimpel, *Samuel Richardson: A Biography* (Oxford: Clarendon, 1971) 88-89. Cf. also Parson Tickletext's first letter to Parson Oliver in *Shamela* on "a little book which this winter hath produced."
5. *Selected Letters* 321.
6. *Ibid.* 41.
7. Samuel Richardson, *Pamela: or, Virtue Rewarded*, ed. T. C. Duncan Eaves and Ben D. Kimpel (Boston: Houghton Mifflin, 1971) 94. Hereafter all page citations to this editon are in the text.
8. *Selected Letters*, to Lady Bradshaigh, 1751, 184.
9. Presumably this involved going into the master's bedroom. See Judith Laurence-Anderson's allusion to the sexual case history of William Byrd discussed in Lawrence Stone's *The Family, Sex and Marriage in England 1500-1800* (London: Weidenfeld and Nicolson, 1977) 565, in "Changing Affective Life in 18th-century England and Samuel Richardson's *Pamela*," *Studies in Eighteenth-Century Culture* 10 (1981) 449; note also her use of J. Jean Hecht, *The Domestic Servant Class in the 18th Century* (London: Routledge & Kegan Paul, 1956) and her reminder of the consistent exploitation by their masters of female domestic servants in the era and on into the nineteenth century.
10. Cf. the story of a "young Gentlewoman" debauched by a handsome youth with the help of "his *Mothers' Housekeeper*, who was a Crafty, Sly, Old Crack" (*The Night-Walker* [1696] 23).
11. It may be argued that Mrs. Jewkes and the Swiss manservant, Colbrand, are Richardson's domesticated but no less repugnant versions of Milton's Sin and Death, the former with her keys and laboring gait, the latter with his extraordinary size, hideous grin, threatening black aspect, sword, horrid strides, and inclination toward rape as Pamela sees him in her dream (147-48). The chief features of Milton's Death and Colbrand are of course reminiscent of gigantic villains in medieval English romance.
12. "Parsley-Bed" was, like the stork, a childish epithet for where babies come from. Cf. Ned Ward: "I was never so scar'd since I pop'd out of the Parsley-Bed" (*The London-Spy* 36; cf. also 154).
13. Pamela delivers the equivalent of a secret hand-written newsletter to her parents by this means. Even the man in the local post-house, who "owes all his Bread to the Squire . . . has his Instructions" (118).
14. Roland Barthes, *Critical Essays*, trans. Richard Howard (Evanston, Ill., 1970) 107-09. For an instructive exercise on "Closet-work" in *Pamela*, see Robert Folkenflik, "A Room of Pamela's Own," *ELH* 39 (1972) 585-96.
15. In Charles Johnson's tragedy *Caelia* (London, 1733), cited by Ira Konigsberg, *Samuel Richardson and the Dramatic Novel* (Lexington: U of Kentucky P, 1968) 40 ff., in connection with the plot of *Clarissa*, the pregnant heroine is put by her faithless lover

into the power of a "Midwife" (7), one Mrs. Lupine, a London bawd. Mother Lupine, "in the main hearty and honest" (8) but "a very strange Woman" to Caelia (9), bears considerable resemblance to the jolly Mrs. Jewkes: "Why, my pretty one, thou won't breed thy little one a Saint, or an Idiot, if thou feed'st him with nothing but Sighs and Tears" (9); "Ods my Life! you are a fine Creature; this is Beauty-fair. . . . Hum! She has Spirit, I find . . . quite right!—She is a delicious Morsel, faith" (31).

16. For further examples of the midwife-bawd connection, see Chapter 3 above.

17. Willughby, *Observations in Midwifery* (1642) 32. Cf. Dawkes, *The Midwife Rightly Instructed*, who cautions the midwife to hand a dangerous case over to a physician rather "than by a vain Ambition to enhance her own Reputation, to torture the poor Sufferer one Hour after another" (15).

18. Maubray, *The Female Physician* (1724) 172-73. Cf. also Dawkes xi.

19. Criticism concerning Mrs. Jewkes stresses her kinship with the "ogress or cruel step-mother" of fairy-tale (D. C. Muecke, "Beauty and Mr. B.," *SEL* 7 [1967] 473) and her transformation, in Pamela's eyes, into "a docile and useful servant" over the course of the novel (John A. Dussinger, "What Pamela Knew: an Interpretation," *JEGP* 69 [1970] 384). Jacob Leed points to a possible influence from Sidney's *Arcadia* in Richardson's grotesque portrait of Jewkes in "Richardson's Pamela and Sidney's," *AUMLA* no. 40 (1973) 242. Stuart Wilson notices the bestial imagery associated with Mrs. Jewkes in a sensitive psychological reading of the heroine's "prolonged, intense, and disruptive emotional experience" in the first half of the novel ("Richardson's *Pamela:*" An Interpretation," *PMLA* 88 (1973) 84-85.

20. Cf. the London bawd "who could *pray*, and roll her goggle eyes, / With *brandy*, *bawdy*, *piety* surprize" in "The Bawd. . . . By a distinguish'd Worshipper in the Temple of Venus" (London, n.d., 1780?).

21. See Chapter 6 above.

22. Dawkes xi.

23. *Ibid.* xi-xii. Dawkes reiterates to his midwife-charge, "Lucina": "I must tell you, it is too common a Complaint of the modest Part of Womankind, against the Women-Midwives, that they are bold, and indulge their Tongues in immodest and lascivious Speeches, to the Shame of their Sex in general, and to the Disquiet of the more sober and modest Part of them" (6).

24. Throughout the midwife literature, the function of the womb (often meaning the female genitals) is described under the dual metaphor of "sewing," as we have seen, and "sowing": "The Yard is as it were the Plow wherewith the ground is tilled and made fit for production of Fruit" (18); "Man in the act of procreation is the agent and tiller and sower of the Ground, Woman is the Patient or Ground to be tilled, who brings Seed also as well as the Man to sow the ground with . . . we women have no more cause to be angry, or be ashamed of what Nature hath given us than men have, we cannot be without ours no more than they can want theirs" (Sharp, *The Midwives Book* 18, 33). The womb is often described as "the Field of Generation" (*Aristotle's Master Piece* 18) or "the Field of Nature" (Guillimeau, *Child-Birth* 3-4). The image goes back to the *Timaeus* (91d).

25. Cf. the inebriated Mother Lupine: "Madam—I suppose—I suppose now you are satisfy'd. . . . I say, whe', I say, it is a mighty good thing to be sa—satisfied, as it were, in one's Man, for then, you know, one is—satisfied" (*Caelia* 23). The name "Jewkes" was probably pronounced something like "jokes," and may be an anti-Semitic pun.

26. In this connection, and to anticipate the later treatment of Pamela by B. and Jewkes, cf. this account, in "a Letter from a Reader" to Dunton's *Night-Walker* of the rape of a 14-year old girl: "After [the Bully] had been *Four hours in Bed with the Bawd*, he came out and *attempted the Girl*; but she refusing, and struggling with him, the Vile Woman got out of the Bed, *helpt him to tie the Girl's Hands behind her back, stopt her Mouth with her Handkerchief, and held one of her Legs till the Villain ravish'd her*" (Nov. 1696, 3); cf. also "The BAWD has private rooms and private doors, / Against their will to make the VIRGINS WHORES; / Some *Irish bullies*, who obey command, / And all the wretched bus'ness understand, / Whom no fond cries, or virgin tears can move, / '*Who gainst their wills, will give them what they love*;' / . . . In vain they strive—unequal is the strife;— / So bleeds the lamb beneath the butcher's knife: / Held down by numbers, soon the contest's o'er, / And all her boasted honour is no more . . . " (*The Bawd* 20-21). Cf. *Nocturnal Revels*, II, 16-19. Cf. also the reference in Donne's Elegy VII to "Natures lay Ideot": "Must I alas . . . breake a colts force / And leave him then, beeing made a ready horse?"

27. In a similarly light-hearted vein, Mrs. Jane Sharp reports that "by reason of the pain [initial entry] puts maids to a squeek or two, but it is soon over . . . some pain there will be for all this but not much" (*The Midwives Book* 50). Mrs. Jewkes has this practical answer to Pamela's query, "what would you do . . . if you was he [i.e., Mr. B.]. . . . Not stand shill-I, shall-I, as he does; but put you both out of your Pain" (116).

28. Maubray 173.

29. "The creator of Heaven and Earth . . . Commits the Life of every Child of his to your charg . . . and at your hands will He have an Accompt of it another day. . . . a Midwife ought to be as quick-sighted as *Argus* . . . . To conclude: Grave Matrons, be diligent in your Office," *A Directory for Midwives: or, A Guide for Women. In their Conception, Bearing, and Suckling their Children* . . . By Nich.[olas] Culpeper, Gent. Student in Physick and Astrologie . . . (London, 1651), The "Epistle Dedicatorie," n.p.

30. Cf. Maubray on the "evil eye" of the witch: "Witches, by their intent Desire to *hurt*, have been thought to bewitch Persons most perniciously by their steady malicious Looks only, directed and inforc'd by *Imagination*," 60.

31. Maubray 173.

32. Maubray 176; "She ought to be a true *Fearer* of God. Since Matters of the greatest *Moment* are commited to her *Care*," 173. For an example of the "Midwife's Oath" administered in the eighteenth century, see J. H. Aveling, *English Midwives, their History and Prospects* (London, 1872) 91-92. The traits of the good and bad midwife are worth comparing with the account of the good and bad bishop in Titus 1:7-11 and I Tim. 3:2-7.

33. Maubray 174. Cf. Sermon, "As concerning their minds: [midwives] must be wise, and discreet; able to flatter and speak many fair words, to no other end, but only to deceive the apprehensive women, which is a commendable deceipt, and allowed, when it is done for the good of the person in distress" (*Ladies Companion* 6).

34. Besides being synonymous with "a bold and abandoned woman," the name "Jezebel" (i.e. "unmarried") aptly fits Mrs. Jewkes, for her setting of the "two Fellows" on Williams recalls her Old Testament predecessor's plot (*I Kings* 21: 8-14) to set "two base fellows" on innocent Naboth as false witnesses in order to secure his vineyard. Mrs. Jewkes's "watchments" may also be related to the *topos* of Jezebel at the window (II Kings 9:30): "sometimes like *Jezebel*, she looks out at the Window" (*The*

Character of a Town-Misse, 1675, 5). Cf. the "Bawd" as an "Old Diabolical *Jezabel*" in chap. xxvi ("Of the Bawds Initiating Club") in Ned Ward's *The Secret History of Clubs* (1709) 304; cf. also "Jezebel's sad fate" in *A Discourse of Artificial Beauty, In point of Conscience between Two Ladies* (London, 1662) 8, and Robert Burton, *The Anatomy of Melancholy*, III, 94. In this same passage, Pamela's chagrined "I have often heard women blam'd for their Tongues: I wish mine had been shorter," and Mrs. Jewkes's "you must think it is no Pleasure to me to tie you to my Petticoat" (117), recall the old midwives' notion (discussed in Chapter 3) that tying the navel-string longer or shorter at birth affected the size of the "Tongue and privy Members" in both sexes.

35. That Pamela may have exaggerated Mrs. Jewkes's prowess as a "cunning woman" during the period of confinement is suggested by the housekeeper's response to the "Gypsey-like Body" (194) who accosts the two women to tell their fortunes in a provocative passage shortly after Mr. B.'s final attempt on Pamela's virtue. Ned Ward and the Elizabethan sources cited by Notestein always link "wise" or "cunning" women with gypsies. One would expect Mrs. Jewkes to have been especially wary of such a person, and though her suspicions of the woman increase, her unwonted neglect allows Pamela to receive the gypsy's "Billet" warning of Mr. B.'s proposed sham-marriage.

36. *The Ladies Companion* 95. Cf. Dawkes to his midwife: "To perform the *Manual Operation* is your Work: To do it well will be your Crown and Honour," 88. A woodcut from the works of Samuel Janson, a Dutch physician of the seventeenth century (reprinted in Donnison, *Midwives and Medical Men*, plate 2), shows a male-midwife blindly delivering a woman whose large skirt is pinned around his neck, giving him the anonymous appearance of the female midwives in attendance. Perhaps the idea for Mr. B.'s costume owes something to this practice.

37. Veith, *Hysteria* 170, 168.

38. Mandeville, *A Treatise of the Hypochondriack and Hysterick Passions* (London, 1711) 173-75. On the reasons for women's "weaker" constitution than men, see the physician John Freind's treatise on the menses, *Emmenologia*, 1729, "The Preface," and pp. 17-19.

39. Cheyne, *The English Malady: or, A Treatise of Nervous Diseases of all Kinds, As Spleen, Vapours, lowness of Spirits, Hypochondriacal and Hysterical Distempers, &c . . . .* (London, 1733) 262. Cf. Ian Watt, *The Rise of the Novel* 184, 202. In an assertion which has interesting implications for the psychology of love and superstition as represented in the novels of Defoe and Richardson, Cheyne notes in his "Preface": "I hope I have explain'd the Nature and Causes of Nervous Distempers (which have hitherto been reckon'd *Witchcraft, Enchantment, Sorcery, and Possession* . . .) from Principles easy, natural and intelligible" (x).

40. *A Treatise* 175-76.

41. *The English Malady* 218-20. Pamela's fits, thus defined, might be considered a defensive hysterical parody of orgasm. Cf. Mandeville in note 54 (Chapter 31) below.

42. It may be argued that Pamela, in response to B. and his treatment of her, undergoes a "phantom pregnancy" and "hysterical childbirth" in this scene. Cf. Ernest Jones's account of how Breuer was summoned to find his patient, Anna O. (whom he had considered an "asexual being"), "in the throes of an hysterical childbirth . . . the logical termination of a phantom pregnancy that had been invisibly developing in response to Breuer's ministrations. Though profoundly shocked, he

managed to calm her down . . . and then fled the house in a cold sweat" (quoted by
Janet Malcolm in an essay on the neo-Freudians, *New Yorker* 24 Sept. 1980:61); rpt. in
Psychoanalysis: The Impossible Profession [New York: Knopf, 1981] 12-13). Cf. Pierre
Janet, *The Major Symptoms of Hysteria* (1929; rpt. New York: Hafner, 1965), particularly
his discussion of "hysterogenic points" and the symptoms of hysteria (98-103): "In
amorous emotions . . . there are genital sensations. . . . What difficulty is there in
understanding that in all these emotions of regret, of love, of remorse, this image of a
physical sensation intervenes and plays the part of a starting-point?" (99-100).
43. The story of Griselda and the constancy of her will in the face of inhuman
persecution might well be considered the paradigm for Richardson's fiction in his first
two novels, and for much subsequent fiction (e.g. *The Portrait of a Lady*). Cf. Sarah
Fielding's allusion to "Patient Grizzle" in *The Correspondence of Samuel Richardson*, ed.
Anna Laetitia Barbauld (London, 1804), II, 70.

NOTES TO PART FOUR: CLARISSA AND "THE WOMB OF FATE"

1. Samuel Richardson, *Clarissa or, the History of a Young Lady* (Everyman's Library
edition, London, 1932; rpt. 1967). All citations are in the text. Richardson partially
quotes this passage, including "the womb of fate," in his "Author's Preface" to the novel,
p. xv.
2. On the tragic elements in the novel, see John A. Dussinger, "Richardson's Tragic
Muse," *PQ* 46 (1967) 18-33; William J. Farrell, "The Style and Action in *Clarissa*," in
Samuel Richardson: A Collection of Critical Essays, ed. John Carroll (Englewood Cliffs,
N. J.: Prentice-Hall, 1969) 92-101; John Carroll, "Lovelace as Tragic Hero," *UTQ* 42
(1972) 14-25; Margaret Doody's discussion of Richardson's use of Restoration heroic
drama in the depiction of Lovelace as tyrant-hero and Clarissa as tragic heroine ("the
hero's 'Nemesis'") in *A Natural Passion* 107-27; and William Park, "*Clarissa* as
Tragedy," *SEL* 16 (1976) 461-71.
3. Alexander, *The History of Women*, "Of Delicacy and Chastity," II, 1-5.
4. Cf. Richardson's own view (expressed in a letter to Aaron Hill) of intending to
have Clarissa's love of Lovelace "imputed to her—she herself not acknowledging it"
(*Selected Letters*, 29 Oct. 1746, 72-73), but cf. also his comment in the "Postscript" to the
novel: "It was not intended that she should be in love, but in liking only" (IV,558).
5. Cf. "the Product of Fate's Womb" in *The Harlot's Progress. Being the Life of the
noted Moll Hackabout, in Six Hudibrastick Canto's . . .* , 6th ed. (London, 1740) 51.
Richardson's use of this image may have been influenced by his friend Edward Young's
Night-Thoughts (1742-44), a rambling, at times incoherent but popular meditation on
human life covering nine "Nights" (or chapters) and saturated with images of birth, fate,
and death: e.g. "In this shape, or in that, has fate entail'd / The mother's throes on all of
woman born, / Not more the children, than sure heirs, of pain"; we "spin out eternal
schemes, / As we the fatal sisters could out-spin, / And, big with life's futurities, expire";
"'all men are about to live,' / Forever on the brink of being born"; "Death is the crown of
life"; "Man makes a death, which nature never made," *The Works of Edward Young*
(Boston: Houghton Mifflin, n.d.) 11, 16, 17, 61, 62. Cf. also another Latin word for the
womb, "volva" (a wrapper, covering) derived from the same root as "volvo" (to roll, turn
around, open, ponder, undergo), often linked in Latin poetry to the activity of the fates
(e.g., *Aeneid* I, 262; III, 375-376).

6. The best discussion of the design of the novel is Frederick W. Hilles's "The Plan of *Clarissa*," *PQ* 45 (1966) 236-48; rpt. in *Samuel Richardson: A Collection of Critical Essays*, 80-91. Hilles notes the seasonal structure of the novel (82), points out that the serpent emblem on the coffin is the emblem of both eternity and "fate": "In my end is my beginning" (82), reminds us that "Clarissa is a country girl" who possesses "attributes that connote fresh air, healthy domesticity" (86), and that "although Lovelace is nominally a Christian, he constantly swears by pagan gods" (90).

7. Cf. Richardson's comment on the curse and on the relationship between the sexes in a happy marriage in the next chapter.

8. *Selected Letters*, to Frances Grainger, 22 Jan. 1749/50, 145-46.

9. *Selected Letters* 200.

10. Cf. Janet Todd, *Women's Friendship in Literature* (New York: Columbia UP, 1980) 35. The chapter on Richardson includes perceptive discussions of Clarissa and her mother, and of Clarissa's friendship with Anna Howe.

11. It is quite possible that Richardson had read Mandeville's *Modest Defence of Publick Stews*, 1724, where the description of a libertine has several points of contact with Lovelace: e.g. "A Man of Pleasure may indeed make this *Copulative Science* his whole Study; and by Idleness and Luxury prompt Nature that way," 22; cf. also "The experienc'd Man . . . has try'd several Women. . . . Women have establish'd a Maxim, that Rakes make the best Husbands," 37. Cf. *Pretty Doings* 49-50. Lovelace refers to his "worthy friend" Mandeville at III, 145. My emphasis in this chapter on Lovelace as the "natural philosopher" of women is reinforced by Brian Easlea's pertinent discussion (which came to my attention too late to incorporate into the argument here and elsewhere) of the masculinist cosmology developed and promulgated by sixteenth- and seventeenth-century natural philosophers in Chap. 3 of *Science and Sexual Oppression: Patriarchy's Confrontation with Woman and Nature* (London: Weidenfeld and Nicolson, 1981), especially pp. 83-86 on the possession of female nature, and p. xi.

12. Dryden's translation of "Ovid's Art of Love, Book I," in *The Works of John Dryden*, vol. IV: Poems of 1693-1696, ed. A. B. Chambers, William Frost, and Vinton B. Dearing (Berkeley: U of California P, 1974) 505. Subsequent page references to this edition are placed in the text. Cf. also Lovelace's affinity with the male lover depicted in Ovid's *Amores*.

13. Again Mandeville is relevant: those women who are "naturally more Chaste . . . [and] have very strict Notions of Honour . . . must be reduced by long and regular Sieges, such as few Men have the Patience or Resolution to go thro' with" (*A Modest Defence* 42-43).

14. "The Art of Love, Book II" in *The Art of Love, and Other Poems*, trans. J. H. Mozley (London: the Loeb Classical Library, 1929) 83.

15. In his first letter Lovelace concedes, seemingly for rhetorical effect, that Clarissa is the only one of the Harlowe's to have a soul (I, 144).

16. "Talk of blooming Charms and Graces, / All is Notion, all is Name; /Nothing differs but their Faces, / Every Woman is the same" in "A Dissertation on the Dignity, Benefit, and Beauty of *Ugliness*," in Christopher Smart's *The Midwife, or Old Woman's Magazine* . . . (London, 1751) 244. Smart recognized the multifarious roles of the old "midwife" as physician, wise woman, gossip, fortuneteller, bawd, whore, Gypsy, authority on sex, and put them all together into an effective Scriblerian persona for his "Magazine."

17. For a more specifically "psychological" reading of the similarity in "world view" between Richardson and Lovelace, see William J. Palmer, "Two Dramatists: Lovelace and Richardson in *Clarissa*," *Studies in the Novel*, 5 (1973) 13-21.

18. *Selected Letters*, 26 Jan. 1746/7, p. 82.

19. *Correspondence*, ed. Barbauld, 26 Dec. 1751, VI, 129.

20. *Ibid.* 130.

21. *Ibid.* 130-31.

22. *Ibid.* 133-34.

23. *Ibid.*, 24 June 1752, 190-91.

24. *Selected Letters*, 2 March 1752, 202-03.

25. *Ibid.*, 14 Feb. 1754, 292.

26. *Correspondence*, 7 Jan. 1744-5, I, 97-98.

27. Agrippa, *The Glory of Women* 6. See also Chapter 8 above.

28. Agrippa, *Female Pre-eminence* 16.

29. Austin, *Haec Homo* 105.

30. Cf. Richardson's image of Arachne for women in *Correspondence*, II, 220.

31. Cf. Dussinger, "Richardson's Tragic Muse," 33.

32. *Metamorphoses*, trans. Frank Justus Miller (London: Loeb Classical Library, 1916), I, 37-38.

33. Cf. the brief discussion of anxiety and "fate" in William Beatty Warner, *Reading Clarissa: The Struggles of Interpretation* (New Haven: Yale UP, 1979) 108, and Lovelace's allusion to his "adorable *Nemesis*" (II, 494). Though Warner's "reading" of *Clarissa*, particularly his account of her "book building," coincides with mine at several points, we arrive at different conclusions about her role and significance in the narrative. In many respects, *Reading Clarissa* is an indispensable study.

34. Austin, *Haec Homo* 141-53. The square brackets and emphasis are Austin's.

35. Dryden's translation of Ovid's *Metamorphoses*, Book I, in *The Works of John Dryden*, IV, 396.

36. Cf. Palmer, "Two Dramatists: Lovelace and Richardson in *Clarissa*," 8-10, and Lovelace's allusion to the Harlowes: "I myself, the director of their principle motions" (I, 494).

37. "Niece" was common slang for a prostitute: "The Old Woman coming in, I bid her sit down, and ask't her how long she had follow'd that Trade? *what Trade, Sir*, says she? I answer'd, of keeping Nieces. . . . O Sir . . . I have follow'd that Trade of being an Aunt . . . ever since I was not able to be any longer a Niece" (*The Night-Walker* 14). Cf. the "sham Nieces" of Lady Beldam in Aphra Behn's novella, *The Unfortunate Happy Lady: A True History* (ca. 1684), a remarkable precursor of Lovelace's deluding of Clarissa into a London brothel.

38. *The London Spy* 27-29.

39. *Amusements Serious and Comical*, ed. Hayward 97. Cf. the discussion of the bawd in Chapters 5 and 6 above. "Collared pig" is pork boiled, cut into small pieces, and pressed into the shape of a roll (*OED*).

40. *Ibid.* 99.

41. *Look e're you Leap: or, a History of the Lives and Intrigues of Lewd Women: with the Arraignment of their several Vices. . .* , l0th ed. (London, 1710?) 89, 93.

42. *Amusements*, ed. Hayward 99.

43. *The London Spy* 210.

44. *Ibid.* 28.

45. *Amusements*, ed. Hayward, 444. Cf. "You must not be unprovided of the *Whole Duty of Man, Practice of Piety*, and such like helps to Devotion; as having been from the beginning a great Pretender to Religion" (*The Whores Rhetorick* 63).

46. *Ibid.* 100.

47. Cf. Miss Fawkland's establishment on St. James's Street with its three adjoining houses, or "Temples," employing "nuns" of progressively graduated expertise; the third house was reserved for special customers and had no contact with the other two (described in Henriques, II, 149-150). (Cf. also the discussion of the bawdy house in Chapter 6 above). Archenholtz notes that the London bawds' "houses are neatly and sometimes magnificently furnished, they have waiting maids, house maids, livery servants, and some of them even keep a carriage" (*A Picture of England* 303). It may be argued that for Lovelace Clarissa is the ultimate "whore," set up in the best room of the mother bawd's house. Clarissa may then be seen as the "virtuous whore" who is made to go a London progress through all the conventional stages of a fallen woman yet who retains her integrity of soul. Margaret Doody notes, with regard to the description of Sinclair's house, that the "very phrases 'innermost house,' 'large handsome passage,' 'garden' and 'figures' have overtones of sexual metaphors" (*A Natural Passion* 196).

48. *Amusements*, ed. Hayward, 98.

49. *The London Spy* 30. Cf. the harlots' "eyes" with *Ecclesiasticus* 26: 9-11.

50. For a similar emphasis, see Judith Wilt, "He Could Go No Farther: A Modest Proposal about Lovelace and Clarissa," *PMLA* 92 (1977) 27.

51. Cf. Ned Ward's account of the "Bawds Initiating Club" where "the Lady-Abbess of the *Brothel-Monastery*" teaches her charges "how to swear like a Bully; Domineer like a Tyrant; be as Coy as a Maid; as Forward as a Widow; as Demure as a Holy-Sister upon a *Sunday* Morning" (*History of Clubs* 302-03). Lovelace, in his description, puns on "limberham," a lackey, usually in a sexual sense (*OED*).

52. Cf. "Old Mother Damnable, the Bawd," in *The London Bawd*, 1711, 15, 39. Antonia Fraser notes that "Mother Damnable was the nickname of a notoriously foul-mouthed character who dispensed ale" in the Restoration (*The Weaker Vessel* [New York: Random House, 1985], 456). Brown's "Mother Cresswell" describes her "deer park" in accents which recall Moll's Mother Midnight ("you look fat and fair Child"): "Thirty pair of haunches, both bucks and does, have been wagging their scuts at one another within the compass of one evening; and many noblemen, notwithstanding they had deer of their own, used to come to my park for a bit of choice venison, for I never wanted what was fat and good" (*Amusements*, ed. Hayward 443).

53. Cf. this discussion with Wilt, "He Could Go No Farther," 21-22, 27-28, and cf. *The Whores Rhetorick* on the worldly wisdom of the bawd and her knowledge of men as "books": "Mr. *Hobbs*, Child, says well, that Wisdom is nothing but experience; so by consequence the Bawd must surpass all Mankind in point of Wisdom, in as much as her experimental knowledge does exceed all others. She has read more Men than any mortal has Books, she has spent more oyl and more pains in quest of knowledge, than the most laborious of the ancient Philosophers," 85.

54. Cf. Lovelace's earlier comment: "I . . . watch her every step to find one sliding one; her every moment, to find the moment critical" (II, 42). Cf. Mrs. Fainall: "O Sir *Wilfull*; you are come at the Critical Instant. . . . pursue your Point, now or never" (*The Way of the World*, IV,i). Mandeville, in a digression on "the Violence of Female Desire"

and the female orgasm, provides yet another sense of the "critical moment": "The whole *Vagina*, [is] one continu'd *Sphincter*, contracting and embracing the *Penis*, while the *Nymphae* and adjacent Islands have their particular Emissions at that critical Minute" (*A Modest Defence* 40-41).

55. In an outburst which calls up visions of the bawd and her bully, Belford implores Lovelace not to give Clarissa, "no, not for one hour . . . into the power of that villainous woman [Sinclair], who has, if possible, less remorse than thyself" (II, 489). Also with respect to Mrs. Sinclair, Richardson appears to recall the legend of a particularly horrible version of the "torturing" midwife-bawd, the "Popish midwife" (perhaps Mrs. Elizabeth Cellier), who was reputed to have cut her husband into pieces and put his "quarters in ye Privy," as illustrated on playing cards from the reign of James II (see J. R. S. Whiting, *A Handful of History* [Dursley, Gloucs.: Alan Sutton, 1978]); five of the cards are illustrated with a note in *TLS*, 14 July 1978:791); in Belford's account of Clarissa's second escape, disguised as the servant, Mabel, Sinclair, "foaming at the mouth," directs this tirade at the poor wench: "I'll punish her for a warning to all betrayers of their trust. Put on the great gridiron this moment (an oath or a curse at every word); make up a roaring fire. The cleaver bring me this instant—I'll cut her into quarters with my own hands; and carbonade and broil the traitress for a feast to all the dogs and cats in the neighbourhood; and eat the first slice of the toad myself, without salt and pepper" (III, 313). Mrs. Cellier was accused of participating in the treasonous "Meal-Tub Plot" of 1680, and was to be created "Procuress and Midwife-General" under the new dispensation, according to *The Popes Letter, to Maddam Cellier In Relation to her great Sufferings for the Catholick Cause* . . . (London, 1680) 2.

56. "Allow me to try if I cannot awaken the woman in her? To try if she, with all that glowing symmetry of parts . . . be really inflexible as to the grand article?" (II, 42). Besides recalling the traditional poetic catalogue or "blazon" of the lady's beauties (cf. Shakespeare, Sonnet 106), Lovelace's description of Clarissa's "beauties" is the rake's version of one of the conventional philosophical definitions of beauty; cf. Robert Burton: "Others will have beauty to be the perfection of the whole composition, 'caused out of the congruous symmetry, measure, order and manner of parts; and that comeliness which proceeds from this beauty is called grace . . . '" (*The Anatomy of Melancholy*, III, 12). Also worth noting in this connection is Burton's inspired English-Latin collocation on the beauty of women's breasts (III, 80-81). Burton's descriptions stand behind Sterne's depiction of the Widow Wadman.

57. Tom Brown "peep'd into a *Fine Church*" on his way to Fleet Street "where you might see in one *Pew*, a Covey of Handsome, Bucksome *Bona Roba*'s, with High-Heads, and all the *Mundus Muliebris* of Ornament and Dress about them" (*Amusements Serious and Comical*, ed. of 1700, 124).

58. All along, Lovelace has indicated his preference for process over outcome: "*Preparation*, and *expectation* are in a manner everything . . . but the *fruition*, what is there in that?" (I, 172-73); "I have ever had more pleasure in my contrivances than in the end of them" (II, 147); "More truly delightful to me the seduction progress than the crowning act: for that's a vapour, a bubble!" (II, 337).

59. *Amusements*, ed. Hayward, 442.

60. Long before he concedes "I am in blood / stepped in so far . . . Returning were as tedious as go o'er" (III. iv. 137-39) Macbeth reflects, "we will proceed no further in this Business" (I. vii. 31). Macbeth, like Lovelace, was goaded to commit his crime by

a woman, and he too killed his conscience. Also, the crowd's exclamation at Cupid's captivity of Conscience and Modesty in *Amores* (Loeb ed.) I.ii. 34 seems to be alluded to in Lovelace's "*Io Triumphe!*" upon locating Clarissa in Hampstead (III, 20).

61. John Preston says that after the rape "Clarissa's state of mind is represented as the disintegration of a book" and he provides an arresting commentary on how her letters "embody some vital quality of the writer," *The Created Self: the Reader's Role in Eighteenth-Century Fiction* (New York: Barnes & Noble, 1970) 49, 54. Cf. also Terry Castle's discussion of "reading" as a model for the interpretation of experience and her comments on Clarissa's "mad papers" in *Clarissa's Ciphers* 50-54, 119-21.

62. Clarissa's plight may be compared with that of an unhappy young woman writing from Newgate to the bawd who helped ruin her: "I write like what I was, tho' I feel with Bitterness what I am. . . . I know not how you and he [her seducer] had concerted matters before-hand; but when he brought me to your House, he represented it to me as a new Lodging which he had taken for me. . . . You . . . cruel Woman, turn'd me out of Doors, poorer than you received me. I had Cloaths when I came to you splendid enough to adorn Beauty; when I left you, scarce Rags to cover it," *Some Considerations upon Street-Walkers* (London, n.d. 1725?) 17-18). One of the best discussions of the London bawd at mid-eighteenth century is John Campbell's *A Particular but Melancholy Account of . . . The Common Women of the Town*, London, 1752. Campbell inveighs against "the Extravagancy and Savage Dispositions of these human Brutes the Bawds, who are a thousand Degrees superior in Wickedness to those unfortunate Creatures who fall into their hands," 12, and his description of the bawd's power over unruly whores recalls Clarissa's arrest by Sinclair for debt: "but God help those unfortunate Creatures, they are Slaves to those Imps of the Devil the Bawds, whose Orders if they presume in the least to gainsay, nothing less than their Downfal ensues, they are immediately stript of their Cloathing, a Bailiff is sent for, who arrests them, and sends them to a Gaol for a round Sum," 14. Cf. *The Humours of Fleet-Street*, 1749, 42, for a similar account.

63. *The Origins of European Thought*, Chap. 4, "The Weaving of Fate," and 353, 392-93.

64. *Selected Letters*, 1752, 222 (quoted in Eaves-Kimpel, *Samuel Richardson* 571).

65. Agrippa, *Female Pre-eminence*, 1670, 28. This edition has the epigraph "*Women are strongest*" (I Esdras 3:12).

66. Austin, *Haec Homo* 133.

67. Cf. "Wisdom is rare, Lorenzo! wit abounds; / . . . . / But wisdom, awful wisdom! which inspects, / Discerns, compares, weighs, separates, infers, / Seizes the right, and holds it to the last; / How rare! In senates, synods, sought in vain, / Or if there found, 'tis sacred to the few; / While a lewd prostitute to multitudes, / Frequent, as fatal, wit . . . ," Young, *Night Thoughts*, Night VIII, 254. Cf. also the discussion of Sophia and wisdom in Martin C. Battestin, "Fielding's Definition of Wisdom: Some Functions of Ambiguity and Emblem in *Tom Jones*," *ELH* 35 (1968) 188-217; rpt. in *Tom Jones*, ed. Sheridan Baker (New York: Norton, 1973) 817-43.

68. For a discussion of how this "Ode," by Elizabeth Carter, came to appear in the novel, see Eaves-Kimpel, *Samuel Richardson* 214-16. Cf. Young: "A theme so like thee, a quite lunar theme, / Soft, modest, melancholy, female, fair! / A theme that rose all pale, and told my soul, 'Twas night" (*Night Thoughts*, Night III, 45). Young's "Narcissa" seems to be a forerunner of Clarissa.

69. *Metamorphoses* (Loeb ed.), I, 320-21.

70. *Metamorphoses* (Loeb ed.), I, 327.

71. In "Conscience and the Pattern of Christian Perfection in *Clarissa*" (*PMLA* 81 [1966]), an essay rooted in seventeenth- and eighteenth-century reflection, John A. Dussinger discusses the *Meditations* as they appear in the volume Richardson privately printed for friends (240-41). Walter J. Ong's discussion of writing, print, and death is particularly relevant to the present discussion of Belford (and Richardson) as Clarissa's editors: "Like writing, print is related to death, although the relationship is not exactly the same. It is even more definitive. Print comes in after death—that is, writing—has been accomplished. It works on the 'body' of the written text which it treats with respect and reverence, as a dead body should be treated. The writer has produced a 'body' because he has 'executed' his work . . . .Printers, like editors, feel deeply that they must deal with an unalterable, fixed text, and not with the spoken word. The text is sealed off from life and change. What was the author's final intention, his closing choice, the end product? 'Final,' 'closing,' 'end': these are editor's preoccupations," *Interfaces of the Word: Studies in the Evolution of Consciousness and Culture* (Ithaca: Cornell UP, 1977) 239.

72. Ned Ward describes the whores' "Brothel Sanctuaries, where they lay aside that Effeminacy that should be part of their Nature, and without Disguise let loose the very Devil that, to their Shame, possesses them, till wrinkl'd Age, a painful Decay, the slights of the World, and all the other miserable Consequences of a Wicked Life, either hurry them to Despair, or bring them to Repentance" (*History of Clubs* 307).

73. *Metamorphoses* (Loeb ed.) I, 79. Cf. Sinclair's death with the Sybil's prophetic rage in the sixth book of Dryden's *Aeneid*.

74. Cf. the harlot's curse on the bawd: "Curse on the female Tongue, that drew me in; / And for base Lucre, Taught me first to Sin: / May her Nose fall, her *Reines* and *Shinbones* Rot . . . May her Vile Womb Incessant Fury have; / And her Limbs drop by piece-meal to the Grave" (Ned Ward, *The Insinuating Bawd: and the Repenting Harlot* [London, 1699] 12. Also relevant to Mrs. Sinclair is the tradition of "the whore of Babylon" based on Revelation 17.5: "THE MOTHER OF HARLOTS AND ABOMINA-TIONS OF THE EARTH."

75. The iconographic figure of Sin, the World, or Frau Welt would seem to stand behind Richardson's portrait of the death of Sinclair. In *Milton's Imagery and the Visual Arts: Iconographic Tradition in the Epic Poems* (Princeton: Princeton UP, 1978), Roland Mushat Frye calls attention to two fifteenth-century illustrations of this figure: "The overall significance of the two images is the same . . . .In each instance a female body is balanced on a crane's leg, indicating instability. In the woodcut, there is only one leg, which is bitten by a cadaverous figure of Mors, to indicate the end of Sin in Death. In the manuscript illumination, Frau Welt has two lower limbs, one of them a serpent, also labeled Mors, which bites the crane's leg, labeled Vita, to show the end of all creaturely pretensions. In the woodcut, the right hand holds a cup signifying unchastity" (122; figures 97, 98; see above, opp. 186). The woodcut has further interesting links with the Fatum figure described by Danet in Chapter 2 above: both stand on a globe of the earth, and both hold urns. Danet also notes that Plutarch calls the Parcae "the three parts of the World." Finally, we have noticed certain similarities between Milton's Satan and Love-lace. And as the figurative son of Sinclair, Lovelace has a peculiar relationship to death: he invents Death as a real-life character for Hickman, he is the effective agent of Clarissa's demise, and he sees his own death as expiation for his crime.

76. Cf. Young on the tragedy of hope without immortality: "[Man's] immortality alone can solve / The darkest of enigmas, human hope; / Of all the darkest, if at death we die. / Hope, eager hope, th'assassin of our joy, / All present blessings treading under foot, / Is scarce a milder tyrant than despair / With no past toils content, still planting new, / Hope turns us o'er to death alone for ease" (*Night Thoughts*, Night VII, 163). Cf. also Young's final appeal to hope at the end of Night VII, 210-11.

77. Richardson in his "Postscript" argued that *Clarissa* conformed to the nature and design of "Tragedy" as described in Rapin's commentary on Aristotle's *Poetics*. The work might be called instead a tragic-epic, worthy of comparison to the scope and "fame of Virgil," in Aaron Hill's view, and modeled perhaps to some degree on the *Aeneid*. It observes these conventions: there is the traditional *in medias res* opening ("I am extremely concerned, my dearest friend, for the disturbances that have happened in your family"); the Christian heroine, or protagonist, undergoes a literal journey in two progressively contracting circles; the first from her father's house in Hertfordshire to St. Albans to Mrs. Sinclair's house in London to Mrs. Moore's in Hampstead and back to Sinclair's; the second from Sinclair's to the Smiths to the Rowlands' debtors prison and back to the Smiths. The body of Clarissa is finally returned to her father's house. These circles mirror the serpent emblem of eternity on Clarissa's coffin which, with its devices, functions as her heroic shield, or as her boat to the kingdom of the dead. (After noting the importance of the coffin to Clarissa, Belford asks Lovelace, "Dost thou think that, when the time shall come that thou shalt be obliged to launch out into the boundless ocean of eternity, thou wilt be able . . . to act thy part with such true heroism, as this sweet and tender blossom of a woman has manifested" [IV, 258].)

Before her first journey the heroine is fated to do battle with various members of her family who would inflict upon her, for life, the reptilian Solmes; James, and particularly Arabella, continue to assault Clarissa like avenging Furies after her flight from home. The battle with her family gives way to a prolonged struggle with her Protean antagonist and personified sexual fate, Lovelace, and his "family" of whores, led by the "old dragon," Mother Sinclair, the emblem of a corrupted world. (Edward Young says in *Night Thoughts*, "The world's a tutor more severe" than the Trojan war, "its lessons hard.") The heroine descends into a labyrinthine underworld of London prostitution (embodied in the "women below") and escapes twice from it, the second time after having lost her "honour" in a physical rape (the equivalent of the hero's mortal wound in battle), but having triumphed over her antagonist and with her "will" inviolate. As Young says, "The mother of true wisdom is the will."

With her will and purpose in life renewed, the heroine chooses to pursue her special fate by excluding Lovelace altogether from her life and making intricate formal preparations for her own death. This is followed by an elaborate public funeral. The overall action conforms to the fable of all great epics: the heroine is translated from one state (or condition) of being to another, and undergoes a physical homecoming to her earthly father's house and a spiritual one to her heavenly Father's mansion. Richardson intended *Clarissa* to be the great prose epic of the individual Christian soul. Her values are national values, and the heroine is the representative of a people (English womankind) and of Woman in Richardson's portrayal of how the sexes have defined (and refined) their roles so as to be at unending warfare with each other in this world.

There are, as well, some specific allusions to and echoes of the *Aeneid* (Dryden's translation). Lovelace says of Clarissa at a late point in the narrative:

. . . what comparison will *her* fate hold to Queen Dido's? And have I half the obligation to her, that Aeneas had to the Queen of Carthage? The latter placing a confidence, the former none, in her man. Then, whom *else* have I robbed? Whom *else* have I injured? Her brother's worthless life I gave him, instead of taking any man's; while the Trojan vagabond destroyed his thousands. Why then should it not be the *pious* Lovelace, as well as the *pious* Aeneas? For, dost thou think, had a conflagration happened, and had it been in my power, that I would not have saved my old Anchises (as he did his from the Ilion bonfire), even at the expense of my Creusa, had I had a wife of that name? . . . Let me tell thee, upon the whole, that neither the Queen of Carthage, nor the Queen of Scots, would have thought they had any reason to complain of cruelty, had they been used no worse than I have used the queen of my heart; and then do I not aspire with my whole soul to repair by marriage? Would the *pious* Aeneas, thinkest thou, have done such a piece of justice by Dido, had she lived? (IV, 31).

"Beauteous" Dido is similar to Clarissa (*Aeneid* I, 697), and her sister/confidante is also named Anna, the "filial," but Clarissa may perhaps more aptly than Lovelace be compared to "pious" Aeneas. The womb of fate may be said to exert as much influence on Aeneas as it does on Clarissa. Juno, linked to avenging fate from the start, hates Aeneas because the judgment of Paris went against her in favor of Aeneas's mother, Venus. Clarissa's siblings hate her in part because she was favored in her grandfather's will. In both works, a judgment favorable to the hero/heroine and outside of their control arouses envy and hatred of the protagonist. The radiant Clarissa, a superior woman, and the "serenely bright" Aeneas (I.825), a brave and just man, suffer unjust persecution and are each singled out by fate for a special destiny. Mrs. Sinclair's house is Lovelace's Trojan horse (Aeneid II) and Tomlinson his Sinon. (Cf. Ian Watt's discussion of Richardson's response to classical epic in *The Rise of the Novel*, 243–48.)

Notes to Part Five: *Tristram Shandy* and "the Womb of Speculation"

1. Laurence Sterne, *The Life and Opinions of Tristram Shandy, Gentleman*, ed. James Aiken Work (New York: Odyssey, 1940) 624. All citations are in the text.

2. *The Letters of Laurence Sterne*, ed. Lewis Perry Curtis (Oxford: Clarendon, 1935) 74.

3. *Letters* 74.

4. *Letters* 76. At other critical moments in his literary career, Sterne jokingly employs similar birth metaphors: "I miscarried of my tenth volume [of *Tristram Shandy*] by the violence of a fever, I have just got thro'—I have however gone on to my reckoning with the ninth, of which I am all this week in Labour pains; and if to Day's Advertiser is to be depended upon shall be safely deliver'd by tuesday," *Letters*, to William Combe, 7-9 Jan. 1767?, 294. Each volume of *Tristram Shandy* is for Sterne a child of his brain, produced with pain and subject to miscarriage during its gestation. He asks one correspondent, "how do you go on in this silly world? have you seen my 7 & 8 graceless Children—but I am doing penance for them, in begetting a couple more ecclesiastick ones [i.e, the Sermons of Yorick]," *Letters*, to Thomas Hesilrige, 5 July 1765, 251. And near completion of *A Sentimental Journey*, he informs Sir George Macartney: "I am going to ly-in; being at Christmas at my full reckoning—and unless what I shall bring forth is not *press'd* to death by these devils of printers, I shall have the honour of presenting to you a *couple* of as clean brats as ever chaste brain conceived" (*Letters*, 3 Dec. 1767, 405). It should be noted that Sterne may have chosen the name "Tristram" for his protagonist with Malory's

Sir Tristrams de Lyonesse in mind. Sir Tristrams' birth causes the death of his mother whose last words are "let calle hym Trystrams, that is as muche to say as a sorowfull byrth," *The Works of Sir Thomas Malory*, ed. Eugène Vinaver (London: Oxford UP, 1954), 277.

5. *Letters* 79-80. Cf. Defoe's references, in his "Preface," to the "Beauties" and "Beautiful Parts" of *Moll Flanders*.

6. *Letters* 80-81.

7. Curtis gave the advertisement from the *York Courant* of Tuesday, 12 Feb. 1760, no. 1790 [p. 3]. (He could not discover a copy of the newspaper for the year 1759.)

This Day is published,
Printed on a superfine Writing Paper and a new Letter,
In Two VOLUMES,
Price FIVE SHILLINGS neatly bound,
THE
LIFE AND OPINIONS
of
TRISTRAM SHANDY, Gent.

Curtis suggested the "new Letter" signifies that the font used in Sterne's book, Caslon's pica roman face, was apparently newly cast ("The First Printer of *Tristram Shandy*," *PMLA* 47 (1932) 783-84). The paper was foolscap, a not uncommon fine printing paper bearing a watermark picturing Britannia. The term "foolscap" derives from the fool's head and cap formerly used as a watermark, a fact peculiarly appropriate for Sterne, whose Tristram occasionally refers of course to his "cap and bells." For further commentary on the publication of *Tristram Shandy*, see Arthur H. Cash, *Laurence Sterne: The Early & Middle Years* (London: Methuen, 1975) 294.

8. Quoted in Curtis, "The First Printer," 779.

9. Curtis, "The First Printer," 787, 789.

10. For more on the literary convention of the printer as midwife, see Elizabeth Sacks, *Shakespeare's Images of Pregnancy* (New York: St. Martin's, 1981), 7-8. Cf. Mandeville's allusion to "the *Midwife* of a Printer" in *A Modest Defence of Publick Stews*, "The Preface," n.p.

11. *The Anatomy of Criticism: Four Essays* (Princeton, 1957; rpt. New York: Atheneum, 1966) 365.

12. Helene Moglen provides an informed discussion of how Locke's theory of association "opened to [Sterne] a new area of characterization and suggested a radical technique which allowed freedom while affording an underlying rational structure," *The Philosophical Irony of Laurence Sterne* (Gainesville: U of Florida P, 1975) 16; cf. also 1-18, 49-56. Eric Rothstein traces several sexual "associative" transitions in *Tristram Shandy* in *Systems of Order and Inquiry in Later Eighteenth-Century Fiction* (Berkeley: U of California P, 1975) 88-91.

13. "The digressing narrative, the catalogues, the stylizing of character along 'humor' lines, the marvelous journey of the great nose, the symposium discussions, and the constant ridicule of philosophers and pedantic critics are all features that belong to the anatomy," *Anatomy of Criticism* 312.

14. See especially William Freedman, *Laurence Sterne and the Origins of the Musical Novel* (Athens, Georgia: U of Georgia P, 1978) and William V. Holtz, *Image and Immortality: A Study of Tristram Shandy* (Providence: Brown UP, 1970). For a good

review of the "struggle to find some satisfactory definition or *genre* for *Tristram Shandy*," see Lodwick Hartley, *Laurence Sterne in the Twentieth Century: An Essay and a Bibliography of Sternean Studies 1900-1965* (Chapel Hill: U of N. Carolina P, 1966) 21-33. Hartley notes further that Sterne "probably knew the midwifery of the time at least as well as he knew Lockean psychology" (69).

15. Several of the midwife books use scriptural starting points (e.g. Psalms 22, 71, 139, and Job 10) for their meditations. A good example is James Wolveridge's *Speculum Matricis* (1671), "The Author to the Reader," n.p. See Robert A. Erickson, "The Books of Generation: Some Observations on the Style of the British Midwife Books, 1671-1764," in *Sexuality in Eighteenth-Century Britain*, ed. P. G. Boucé (Manchester: Manchester UP, 1982) 74-94.

16. Lawrence Stone, in his comprehensive survey of *The Family, Sex and Marriage In England 1500-1800* (London: Weidenfeld and Nicolson, 1977), 493, does not appear to have recognized this implication. Although it is true that the midwife books do not offer the kind of specific and technical information regarding foreplay, positions in intercourse, and prolongation of pleasure provided in the Chinese manuals, they give plenty of consideration to such matters as the appearance, constitution, and function of the genital organs, the "just" length of the phallus, the sensual delights of intercourse, the method for propagating a male child, the signs of conception and whether a male or a female has been conceived.

17. In the discussion of "the right end of a woman" (101-02) Sterne alludes to *Aristotle's Master Piece* (discussed in Chapter 3 above) and then quotes from *Aristotle's Problems* (see Work's note). Cf. also *Aristotle's Compleat and Experienc'd Midwife: In Two Parts* . . . (London, 1700). It may also be noted, with caution, that *A Facsimile Reproduction of the Unique Catalogue of Laurence Sterne's Library* (London, 1930), lists Sydenham's whole works (1717), Astruc on the *Veneral Disease* (1754), Maubray's *The Female Physician* (1724) and Cheyne's *The English Malady* (1733); the latter two works will be referred to later in this discussion. The catalogue lists books from Sterne's and other private libraries (cf. Cash, *Laurence Sterne* 203). With respect to the "right end of a woman," cf. "the right true end of love" as "the Centrique part" in Donne's Elegy XVIII.

18. There is a similar logic behind a *Sentimental Journey*: "I am well aware, at the same time, as both my travels and observations will be altogether of a different cast from any of my forerunners; that I might have insisted upon a whole nitch entirely to myself," *A Sentimental Journey through France and Italy by Mr. Yorick*, ed. Gardner D. Stout, Jr. (Berkeley: U of California P, 1967) 82.

19. *The byrth of Mankynde newly translated* (1540), n.p.

20. See particularly *The Compleat Midwife's Practice Enlarged. . . . A Work so plain, that the weakest capacity may easily attain the knowledge of the whole Art. . . . The Second Edition corrected* . . . (London, 1659); William Sermon, a physician who possesses "excellent Secrets" concerning childbirth and who has composed his book "in the most plain method" he could, nonetheless notes tentatively that "there will be found [in his book] those undeflowered secrets, which may be thought more fit for the Closets of discreet Ladies, then to be . . . exposed to publick view" (*The Ladies Companion*, 1671, the "Preface" and the "Dedication").

21. *Speculum Matricis*, "The Author to his Book," n.p. The "Go little book" convention may be taken from *The Anatomy of Melancholy*, introductory verses.

22. *The byrth of Mankynde* (1540), fol. viii.

23. *The byrth of mankynde* (1545), "The Prologue," n.p.
24. Boswell's *Life of Johnson* (Oxford Standard Authors's ed., London, 1904; rpt. 1965) 696.
25. "The Shandean Homunculus: The Background of Sterne's 'Little Gentleman,'" in *Restoration and Eighteenth-century Literature: Essays in Honour of Alan Dugald McKillop*, ed. C. Carroll Camden (Chicago: U of Chicago P, 1963) 49-68. Cf. Brian Easlea's discussion of *emboîtement* in *Science and Sexual Oppression* 74-76.
26. Landa 59.
27. *The Memoirs of Martinus Scriblerus*, ed. Charles Kerby-Miller (New Haven, 1950; rpt. New York: Russell and Russell, 1966) 141. Cf. Robert A. Erickson, "Situations of Identity in the *Memoirs of Martinus Scriblerus*," *MLQ* 26 (September, 1965) 393-94.
28. For the letters, see particularly Sterne's comparison of the vanity of an author "of [his] Stamp" to that of "a pretty Girl in the Hey day of her Roses & Lillies" (March 1760, 99), his defense of the novel against unchastity (30 Jan. 1760, 90), his sexual teasing of Mrs. Vesey (June 1761, 137-38), his characterization of Mrs. Montagu as a "Prophetesse" and "Goddess" (June 1764?, 215), his claim that he "must ever have some dulcinea in [his] head—it harmonises the soul" (August, 17651/4, 256), his advice to Mrs. Daniel Draper ("Eliza"): "you want nothing but firmness, and a better opinion of yourself, to be the best female character I know" (March 1767, 309), his repeated references to "poring upon" the picture of Eliza and carrying her image in his head (323, 333, 356, 365, 376, 377, 384) and to "Fate," usually as a kind of benevolent match-maker to his hoped-for marriage with Eliza (352, 363, 367, 381, 384), his assertion of her "Magicl authority over him" (i.e. "Yorick," 377), and finally his virtual self-identification with Eliza ("You are blessd with such a certain turn of Mind & reflection—that if Self love does not blind me—I resemble no Being in the world so nearly as I do You" (June, 1767, 355). A fruitful study might be made of Sterne's use of the term "Magick" and its contexts in *Tristram Shandy* and the *Letters*.
29. Quoted in Chapter 3.
30. "The Greatest disease that can afflict women, is that of the Nine moneths, the Cure of which wholly consists in their safe delivery" (Sermon, *The Ladies Companion* 2).
31. *Speculum matricis* 23-24.
32. *Child-Birth or, The Happy Delivery of Women. . . . by James Guillimeau. . . .* 1612, "The Author's Epistle Introductory to the Reader," n.p.
33. William Smellie, *A Treatise on the Theory and Practice of Midwifery . . .* 1752, I, 87-88. Cf. R. W. Johnstone, *William Smellie: The Master of British Midwifery* (Edinburgh and London: E. and S. Livingstone, 1952) 45.
34. *Speculum Matricis*, "The Preface," n.p. Cf. the panegyric in *The Anatomy of Melancholy* (Everyman ed.), I, 130.
35. In the curious chapter on "Whiskers" Sterne is more than ever preoccupied with the mystery of sex, and with the mysterious relationship between language and sex. Sex, or the power of generation, may stimulate a whole rhetoric of love, but the ladies of the court of Navarre, with their observations upon the Sieur De Croix, demonstrate how sex may also modify, distort, and even nullify language ("the word [whiskers] in course became indecent, and (after a few efforts) absolutely unfit for use" [347]). Cf. the bawdy-talking ladies of the court of Navarre in *Love's Labor's Lost* and Maria in *Twelfth Night*: "They that dally nicely with words may quickly make them

wanton [III. i. 14-15])." Frank Brady notes the equivalence of "whiskers" and testicles—and points out several other sexual puns—in "*Tristram Shandy*: Sexuality, Morality, and Sensibility," *ECS*, 4 (Fall, 1970) 44, 41-42, 45.

36. One is reminded of Richardson's comment on the similarity of the sexes, and Rilke's supposition that "perhaps the sexes are more related than we think, and the great renewal of the world will perhaps consist in this, that man and maid, freed from all false feeling and aversion, will seek each other not as opposites, but as brother and sister, as *neighbours*, and will come together as *human beings*," *Letters to a Young Poet*, trans. M. D. Herter Norton (New York: Norton, 1934; rev. ed. 1954) 38. This "great renewal" is Rilke's private version of the scriptural new heaven and new earth, where in Christ there is no male and female and where the sexes are not given in marriage, in effect a new version of "marriage" between the sexes. Sterne, in his own inimitable style, is suggesting something similar in *Tristram Shandy* and elsewhere to what Rilke and St. Paul are suggesting.

37. *Letters*, April 1765, 240-41.

38. Sterne in the *Letters* comments further on his "Leaness," "Spirituality," and "sublimated" condition at 215 and 332 ("I shall be sublimated to an etherial Substance by the time my Eliza sees me . . . but I was always transparent & a Being easy to be seen thro'"). As Sterne's health deteriorated, the joke attenuates into the recurring image of a "Shadow" (324, 326, 408).

39. Cheyne 4.

40. *Ibid*. 194. Cf. "I am glad that you are in love—'twill cure you (at least) of the spleen, which has a bad effect on both man and woman," Sterne to John Wodehouse?, 23 Aug. 1766?, *Letters*, 256.

41. *Ibid*. 219-20.

42. *Ibid*. 220.

43. For another account of birth as expulsion see Maubray, *The Female Physician*, 228-29. Here the birth process is compared explicitly to vomition, evacuation of feces and urine, extrusion of fuliginous matter by the heart and lungs, and effusion of genital seed by the testicles.

44. The normally circumspect Smellie allows himself the following remarkable anatomical digression on the mechanics of the sexual act: "In the woman, the friction of the *Penis* in the contracted *Vagina*, the repeated pressure and shocks against the external parts, the alternate motion upwards and downwards of the *Uterus*, with its appendages the *Ovaria*, Fallopian tubes, and round ligaments, produce a general titillation and turgency" (*A Treatise on . . . Midwifery*, I, 114). A few pages earlier, Smellie had noted that "In Coition, the Uterus yields three or four Inches to the Pressure of the Penis, having a free Motion upwards and downwards; so that the reciprocal Oscillation, which is permitted by this Contrivance, increases the mutual Titillation and Pleasure" (*Treatise*, I, 102). Smellie was echoing, almost certainly without intention, the information of one of the older midwives, Jane Sharp: "in the act of Copulation [the womb] is moved up and downe; somtimes it moves upward, that some women doe affirm that it ascends as high as their stomach" (*The Midwives Book* 33). Smellie's malicious obstetrical nemesis, John Burton, chided him for repeating "ridiculous old wives Notions" (*A Letter to William Smellie, M.D.*, 1753, 213) and the above indiscretion incited the following one from Burton: "I will not here enter into any Debate with you upon the Matter of Fact or Propriety of your Expression, but shall only observe, that to move the Uterus four Inches higher than its

usual *Situation*, will require a Man of *extensive Abilities*; but it requires no great Capacity to know that it is the Friction on the Clitoris, that increases the Pleasure in the Female, to which this *Oscillation* of the Uterus can no way contribute, therefore their *mutual Pleasure* cannot thereby be promoted" (*A Letter to William Smellie, M.D.* 68). Cf. Robert Burton on the "diaphragma" as "the instrument of laughing" (*Anatomy*, I, 152) and his discussion of the "tickling" and "titillation" of the midriff, which is "transverse and full of nerves" (I, 424).

45. *Midwives and Medical Men* 21-60. Cf. Brian Easlea on the "ousting of women from medicine" and the "possession of female nature" in the seventeenth and eighteenth centuries (*Science and Sexual Oppression* 83-8).

46. *A Treatise on the Art of Midwifery. Setting forth Various Abuses therein . . .* By Mrs. Elizabeth Nihell, Professed Midwife . . . (1760) 111n.

47. Nihell 89-90, 97.

48. *Anatomical Exercitations, Concerning the Generation of Living Creatures: To which are added Particular Discourses, of* Births, *and of* Conceptions, &c . . . (1653), from Sir George Ent's "Epistle Dedicatory," n.p.

49. Sermon, *The Ladies Companion* 6-7.

50. Willughby, *Observations in Midwifery* 42. Cf. "the best midwife, Nature," in Donne's *Metempsychosis: The Progresse of the Soule*, 1.402 (1601).

51. *Anatomical Exercitations* 325-26.

52. George Arnaud, *A Dissertation on Hermaphrodites* (London, 1750) 9-10. Cf. Shakespeare's sonnet 20: "Till Nature as she wrought thee fell a-doting, / And by addition me of thee defeated, / By adding one thing to my purpose nothing." But here the speaker is talking of an ideal youth, not a *lusus naturae*.

53. Sterne alludes to the life-preserving quality of "Nature" in a letter to John Hall-Stevenson, but again with a stress on her love of the remarkable joke: "I . . . recommended my affairs entirely to Dame Nature—She (dear goddess) has saved me in fifty different pinching bouts, and I begin to have a kind of enthusiasm now in her favour, and in my own, That one or two more escapes will make me believe I shall leave you all at last by translation, and not by fair death" (*Letters*, Oct. 1762, 186).

54. Obadiah's knots may be compared with George Counsell's intricate and highly detailed instructions for tying the navel string in *The Art of Midwifery: or, the Midwife's Sure Guide* . . . (1752) 22-27. The knots on the green bag also recall the old midwives' notion, rejected by Jane Sharp, that the knots on the umbilical cord "in number signifie so many Children, the reddish boys, the whitish Girls, and the long distance between knot and knot, long time between child and child" (*The Midwives Book* 216). Obadiah's knots may prefigure Tristram's hard life.

55. Again Rilke's great letter of 16 July 1903 is worth comparing in this context; if there is any explanation of the "whole secret" (7) of *Tristram Shandy* (and there is no explicit answer in the novel), what Rilke says here about "bowing to necessities that are greater than pleasure and pain and more powerful than will and withstanding," about the "secret" of being "reverent toward [one's] fruitfulness, which is but one, whether it seems mental or physical," about "the new human being" rising up and the "great motherhood" over all, all this may be considered as at least an approximate explanation (*Letters to a Young Poet* 36-38).

56. Yorick's sermon on "Self-Knowledge" exhorts us—in language similar to this evocation of labyrinthine feminine Nature—to retire into ourselves and search into

the "dark corners and recesses of the heart." In so doing, man will discover "many secret turns and windings" which will open and disclose themselves, and "in these labyrinths," he will trace out illaudable "hidden springs and motives for many of his most applauded actions," *The Sermons of Mr. Yorick* (Oxford: Shakespeare Head, 1927), I, 47. This variation on the ancient image of feminine "Error" stresses the darker, illusory, and unconscious substratum of the mind. It is Yorick's way of urging his listeners to find the good even of their own errors.

57. In this connection, see William V. Holtz's discussion of "Typography, *Tristram Shandy*, the Aposiopesis, etc." in *The Winged Skull: Papers from the Laurence Sterne Bicentenary Conference*, ed. Arthur H. Cash and John M. Stedmond (Kent State UP, 1971), 247-57, and also *Image and Immortality*, 80-89. Cf. also Douglas Brooks's relevant commentary on the black page and on the sexual significance of the number symbolism in *Tristram Shandy* in *Number and Pattern in the Eighteenth-century Novel: Defoe, Fielding, Smollett, and Sterne* (London: Routledge & Kegan Paul, 1983) 162-65.

58. Wolveridge, 'The Preface,' n.p. The title of this chapter is adapted from a phrase in *The Whores of Rhetoric* (1683) 25-26. See Introduction, note 65, above. Cf. Brian Easlea, "the fragile penis and sexual intercourse" (*Science and Sexual Oppression* 79-82).

59. *Aristotle's Compleat and Experienc'd Midwife* . . . (1700) 24.

60. *Aristotle's Compleat Master Piece* . . . (1750) 15-16.

61. *The Midwives Book* 45.

62. *A General Treatise of Midwifery* . . . (1719) 34-35.

63. *The Midwives Book* 31.

64. *A General Treatise* 74. Cf. the quotation from the *Timaeus* in Chapter 3, note 46. Robert Burton notes "the fury of this headstrong passion of raging lust" and its "unspeakable delight . . . which neither reason, counsel, poverty, pain, misery, drudgery, *partus dolor* . . . can deter [men] from" (*Anatomy*, III, 198).

65. One of the most vivid expressions of this notion is found in de Graaf: "So that the species might be propagated, Nature decided that the connubial act should be linked with an enormously pleasurable sensation. If She had not implanted this sensation in men and women, the human species would surely have perished. As André du Laurens elegantly puts it . . . , 'Who would have solicited and embraced such a filthy thing as sexual intercourse? With what countenance would man, that divine animal full of reason and wisdom, have handled the obscene parts of women, befouled with such great quantities of muck and accordingly relegated to the lowest part of the body, the body's bilge as it were? What woman would have rushed into a man's embrace unless her genital parts had been endowed with an itch for pleasure past belief? The nine months of gestation are laborious; the delivery of the fetus is beset with dreadfully excruciating pains and often fatal; the rearing of the delivered fetus is full of anxiety,'" *On the Human Reproductive Organs* 49 (Sterne alludes to de Graaf's writings on "the parts of generation" in his note to 636).

66. *Aristotle's* . . . *Midwife* 132.

67. It could be argued that Sterne, like Richardson, enjoyed playing the role of a quasi-libertine in his letters. Sterne sounds like a Shandyan Lovelace in describing himself as an Old Testament patriarch to Robert Foley in 1763 (193). Cf. also 213-14, and 393.

68. *A General Treatise* 73-74. Cf. Robert Alter's comment on cabbage planting in "*Tristram Shandy* and the Game of Love," *The American Scholar* 37 (1968) 319-20.

69. John Burton, *An Essay Towards a Complete New System of Midwifery* . . . (1751), between 36 and 37.

70. *Aristotle's* . . . *Master Piece* 37. Cf. Robert Burton, *Anatomy*, I, 215.

71. *Aristotle's* . . . *Master Piece* 50-51.

72. P. 57. Cf. Robert Burton, *Anatomy*, I, 213.

73. James McMath, *The Expert Mid-wife* . . . (Edinburgh, 1694) 21.

74. John Maubray, *The Female Physician* . . . (1724) 54-55. Cf. Mrs. Sharp: "**Much** might be said in Divinity against discontent, sullenness, and murmuring, which many women, especially, are too much guilty of; for it troubles the imagination, which should be pure in the act of conception" (*The Midwives Book* 179). It was thought of course that the power of a woman's imagination could impress itself upon the womb and hence upon the unborn child (cf. Maubray 62). There is little discussion of "Posture" in intercourse in the midwife books; Dionis "Won't enter into Particulars upon this Head" and only allows himself to observe "that the most convenient Posture for Generation, is that in which the Seed can be thrown directly into the Womb" (*General Treatise* 73). Again, cf. Brian Easlea, *Science and Sexual Oppression* 80.

75. Cf. Tom Brown's "Description of a Country Life": "in the critical minute of joy, when they ought to be all rapture and contemplation . . . they'll ask you a thousand foolish questions . . . as if one should interrupt a Popish priest at the elevation, and ask him what a clock it is." The parallel is pointed out and cited by W. A. Eddy in "Tom Brown and *Tristram Shandy* in *MLN* 44 (1929) 379. There is no question that Brown, whose works have been noted often in these pages, was an inspiration to Sterne as well as to the Scriblerians. Cf. Mandeville on "the critical minute" as the moment of orgasm, in Chapter 31, note 54.

76. *Essay* 11.

77. Pp. 1-2, 15-16.

78. Pp. viii-ix.

79. See Arthur H. Cash, "The Birth of Tristram Shandy: Sterne and Dr. Burton," in *Studies in the Eighteenth Century*, ed. R. Brissenden (Canberra, 1968) 152-53. This informative and amusing essay is reprinted in *Sexuality in Eighteenth-Century Britain*.

80. *Essay*, p. xiii.

81. *Letter* 117.

82. *Speculum Matricis* 28-31.

83. Cf. John Burton: "I can with the same Truth affirm, that [the obliquity of the womb] is the unanimous Opinion of all the best Accoucheurs of Character in these Kingdoms. For as I had frequent Opportunities of conferring and corresponding with several of the greatest Men in that Profession; so for my own private Satisfaction I have had this matter cleared up to me long since" (*Letter* 36-37).

84. *Essay* 13-14.

85. See particularly Dawkes's *The Midwife Rightly Instructed* . . . (1736), xxvi-xxviii. Dawkes goes so far as to announce to his apprentice, "Lucina," that "*Anatomical Knowledge* [is] a Privilege denied by Providence to your Sex" (17-18). In an early dialogue, Dawkes asks Lucina: "you can apply to Us *Surgeons* for Information, can't you? Yes, Sir; that's true: But alack! —Alack! what? Dear Sir!—methinks that's so strange! What's strange? Why Sir, to talk with you about such things; it looks so—Oh, what you're pleading upon the score of Modesty then!"

86. Brady notes at least fifteen allusions to fingers and thumbs in the novel (*"Tristram Shandy*: Sexuality, Morality, and Sensibility," 42).
87. In the light of what follows, it should be noted that the *os coccygis* could easily be confused with the *os coxendis* (hip bone, ischium, ilium) which had a bawdy significance: the bawd's initiate knew how "to elevate her Coxendis according to the School of *Venus*" (Ward, *History of Clubs*, 302).
88. *Essay* 193.
89. *Letter* 7.
90. *Essay* 6.
91. *Ibid.* 389.
92. *Ibid.* 101.
93. *A Treatise on . . . Midwifery*, I, 90. Cf. Swift's *Longheads*, which at first began a Custom among Midwives and Nurses of molding and squeezing, and bracing up the Heads of Infants; by which means, Nature shot out at one Passage, was forc'd to seek another, and finding room above, shot upwards, in the Form of a Sugar-Loaf" (in *The Mechanical Operation of the Spirit*), and Mirabell to Millamant in Congreve's *The Way of the World* (1700), IV, v: "I denounce against all strait lacing, squeezing for a shape, till you mold my boy's head like a sugar loaf."
94. "The Birth of Tristram Shandy," 139-42.
95. *A Treatise on . . . Midwifery*, I, iv-v. Cf. Tristram on his father's opinions: "No mortal claim'd them: they had cost him moreover as much labour in cooking and digesting as in the case above" (223). Tristram's "large uneven thread" may be compared with Robert Burton's image for the "affected style . . . like a prominent thread in an uneven woven cloth" (*Anatomy*, I, 111).
96. *Letter* 63. Smellie's unfortunate choice of the culinary image and his pastry-cook diction (the forehead "will rise in form of an obtuse cone or sugar-loaf") also left him open to other indecent associations. Bawds advertised in the daily papers as follows: "WANTED. A young woman, under twenty . . . it is proposed putting her under a Man-Cook of skill and eminence. She must get up small things, and even large ones occasionally . . . and know something of pastry, at least to make a standing crust" (*Nocturnal Revels*, II, 20). Cf. Ned Ward, *The Whole Pleasures of Matrimony*, 155, and Tom Brown, *Amusements*, ed. Hayward 443. Cf. also "the case of butter'd buns" and "the bakers [who] had all forgot to lay their leaven" in the story of the Strasburgers (255n).
97. See *A Treatise on . . . Midwifery*, I, 78ff, and the drawings of the bones of the female pelvis in Smellie's *A Sett of Anatomical Tables . . .* (1754). The language of obstetrics at times parodies the language of fortifications. Cf. James Drake's *Anthropologia Nova; Or, a New System of Anatomy* ("Drake's *Anatomy*," mentioned in *Tristram Shandy* 636): "The Uterus . . . is surrounded and defended by mighty Bones, before by the *Ossa Pubis*, behind by the *Os Sacrum*, on each side by the *Os Ilium*, and *Ischium*" (I, 292); "The Bones of the Pelvis . . . stand as a *Rampart*, fencing [the womb] against all external *Injuries*; That is to say, the *OS PUBIS* protects it *before*; the *SACRUM behind*; and the *ILIUM* on *each side*" (Maubray 186; "the uterus is surrounded as though by very secure walls," de Graaf 110.
98. *A Treatise of Midwifery. In Three Parts . . .* (Dublin, 1742) 49.
99. *Othello*, IV. i. 155. Cf. Brady, "*Tristram Shandy*," 41.
100. Cf. Smellie, *A Treatise*, I, 78ff, and André Levret, *L'Art des Accouchements demontré par des principes de physique et de mécanique* (Paris, 1753); cf. Cash, "The Birth of Tristram Shandy," 140n.

101. John Glaister, *Dr William Smellie and His Contemporaries. A Contribution to the History of Midwifery in the Eighteenth Century*(Glasgow, 1894) 174, 183.
102. Cf. A. R. Towers' discussion of the "displacement of Uncle Toby's sexual drives from their normal object (women) to a substitute object (fortifications)" in "Sterne's Cock and Bull Story," *ELH* 24 (1957) 20-24.
103. *Pretty Doings in a Protestant Nation* 15. Cf. G. S. Rousseau's relevant comments on the Widow Wadman and other widows in "Threshold and Explanation: the Social Anthropologist and the Critic of Eighteenth-Century Literature," *The Eighteenth Century: Theory and Interpretation*, 22 (1981) 133-37.
104. It would appear that the female gods and goddesses are the ones which most stimulate Sterne's imagination in *Tristram Shandy* and *The Letters*.
105. In describing "How to assist in Lingering Labor" of women "turned of thirty," Smellie notes that "The mouth of the womb and *Os Externum* . . . opens with greater difficulty in the first than in the succeeding labors . . . In these cases the *Os externum* must be gradually dilated in every pain, by introducing the fingers in form of a cone, and turning them round, so as to stretch the parts by gentle degrees; and the whole hand being admitted . . . it will be sometimes found necessary to insinuate the fingers with the flat of the hand between the head and the *Os internum*" (*A Treatise on . . . Midwifery*, I, 223).
106. See Plate III depicting Burton's forceps in Cash, "The Birth of Tristram Shandy," and cf. Burton's reference to the large screw "which serves to fix the Wings" of his instrument (*Essay* 386).
107. Contrast the chaste eye of Mrs. Shandy—"a thin, blue, chill, pellucid chrystal with all its humours so at rest the least mote or speck of desire might have been seen at the bottom of it, had it existed—it did not" (599-600). In the light of the midwives' and libertines' doctrine of "critical moments" (600), it is clear from this passage and others that Mrs. Shandy does not have the "yielding" sort. For what follows, cf. Robert Burton on "a wanton, a rolling, lascivious eye: a wandering eye," "those speaking eyes, courting eyes, enchanting eyes" (*Anatomy*, I, 89, 103), and his sources in II Peter 2:14 and Isaiah 3:16. Tristram's reference on this page to "the manual effervescencies of devotional tracts" may allude to the quasi-erotic rhetoric of certain devotional self-help manuals; cf.: "And to compleat all that *acme* of delight which the devout Seraphic Soul enjoys, when dead to the World, she devotes her self entirely to the contemplation and fruition of her Beloved . . . she moves in a direct and vigorous motion towards her true and only Good, whom now she embraces and acquiesces in, with such an unspeakable pleasure, as is only intelligible to them who have tried it," *A Serious Proposal to the Ladies, For the Advancement of their true/and greatest Interest. By a Lover of Her Sex* . . . (London, 1694) 70-71.
108. See John Dunton, *The Night-Walker* (1696): a procuress leads the Night-walker "into a Room which joyned to her Parlour, I found it hung round with Pictures representing all the Amours of Ovid's Heathen Gods, and amongst them were Intermixt the Pictures of her Ladies of Pleasure," 24; cf. also *The London Bawd* (1711) 155, and Tom Brown's Mother Creswell: "I kept a painter in my house perpetually employed upon fresh faces, and had as good a collection of pictures to the life as ever were to be seen in Lely's showing-room" (*Amusements*, ed. Hayward, 444).

SELECT BIBLIOGRAPHY
OF PRIMARY SOURCES

The following list includes books and pamphlets, mostly from the seventeenth and eighteenth centuries, which I have used in preparing this study. The list is not meant as a comprehensive guide to the midwife literature or to the literature pertaining to witchcraft or prostitution. Unless otherwise stated, all works cited were published in London.

Agrippa, Henricus Cornelius. *The Glory of Women: or a Looking-Glasse for Ladies: Wherein they may behold their own Excellency and Preheminence, proved to be greater than mans, by Scripture, Law, Reason and Authority, divine and human.* Trans. H.[ugh] C.[rompton]. 1652.

———. *Female Pre-eminence: or the Dignity and Excellency of that Sex, above the Male. An Ingenious Discourse.* Trans. H.[enry] C.[are]. 1670.

Alexander, William. *The History of Women, From the Earliest Antiquity, to the Present Time; Giving Some Account of almost every interesting Particular concerning that Sex, among all Nations, ancient and modern.* 2 vols. 1779. (Rpt. N.Y.: AMS Press, 1976.)

Ames, Richard. *The Rake: or, the Libertine's Religion.* A poem. 1693.

The Ape-Gentle-woman, or the Character of an Exchange Wench. 1675.

Archenholtz, W. de. *A Picture of England, containing a Description of the Laws, Customs, and Manners of England.* 1797.

Aristotle's Book of Problems. . . . Wherein is contained divers Questions and Answers Touching the State of Man's Body . . . the Twenty-Sixth Edition, n.d. [ca. 1750].

Aristotle's Compleat and Experienc'd Midwife: in Two Parts. 1700.

Aristotle's Compleat Master Piece: In Three Parts: Displaying the Secrets of Nature in the Generation of Man . . . to which is added, A Treasure of Health; or, the Family Physician . . . the Twenty-Seventh Edition. 1750.

Arnaud, George. *A Dissertation on Hermaphrodites.* 1750.

[Astell, Mary]. *An Essay in Defence of the Female Sex . . .* Written by a Lady. 1696.

Austin, William. *Haec Homo, Wherein The Excellency of the Creation of Woman is described.* 1637.

Barrett, Robert. *A companion for Midwives, Child-Bearing Women, and Nurses, Directing them how to perform their Respective Offices. Together with an Essay, endeavouring to shew the Influence of Moral Abuses upon the Health of Children.* 1699.

The Bawd: A Poem. . . . By a distinguish'd Worshipper in the Temple of Venus, n.d. [ca. 1780].

Beauty's Triumph: or, the Superiority of the Fair Sex invincibly prov'd . . . in three Parts, n.d. [1744?].

Behn, Aphra. *The Town-Fop; or, Sir Timothy Tawdrey.* 1676.

———. *The Rover; or, the Banished Cavaliers,* parts I and II. 1677-81.

———. *The City-Heiress; or, Sir Timothy Treat-all.* 1682.

———. *The Unfortunate Happy Lady: a True History,* n.d. ca. 1684 .

Bienville, J. D. T. de. *Nymphomania, or, a Dissertation concerning the Furor Uterinus.* Trans. E. S. Wilmot. 1775.

Bland, James. *An Essay in Praise of Women: or, A Looking-glass for Ladies.* 1733.

Blondel, J. A. *The Power of the Mother's Imagination over the Foetus examin'd.* 1729.

Bourgeois, Louise. *Observations diuersés sur la sterilité . . . foecondité, accouchements, et maladies des femmes et enfants nouueaux naiz.* Paris, 1617.

Breval, J. D. *The Art of Dress. A poem.* 1717.

Brinley, John. *A Discourse Proving By Scripture and Reason . . . That there are Witches.* 1686.

Brown, Thomas. *Amusements Serious and Comical, Calculated for the Meridian of London.* 1700.

———. *The Works of Mr. Thomas Brown, in Prose and Verse; Serious, Moral, and Comical.* 3 vols. 1707.

———. *Amusements Serious and Comical, And Other Works.* Ed. Arthur L. Hayward. New York: Dodd, 1927.

[Bunworth, Richard]. *The Doctresse: a plain and easie method, of curing those diseases which are peculiar to Women.* 1656.

Burton, John. *A Treatise on the Non-Naturals.* York, 1738.

———. *An Essay Towards a Complete New System of Midwifery, Theoretical and Practical. . . . Interspersed with Several New Improvements. . . . Part of which has been laid before the Royal Society at London, and the Medical Society at Edinburgh; after having been perused by Many of the most Eminent of their Profession, both in Great Britain and Ireland; by whom they were greatly approved of. All Drawn up and Illustrated with Several Curious Observations, and Eighteen Copper-plates.* 1751.

———. *A Letter to William Smellie, M.D.* 1753.

Burton, Robert. *The Anatomy of Melancholy. What it is, With all the kindes, causes, symptomes, prognostickes, and severall cures of it. . . . Philosophically, Medicinally, Historically open'd and cut-up. By Democritus Junior. With a Satyricall Preface conducing to the following Discourse.* The third Edition. 1628.

———. *The Anatomy of Melancholy.* Everyman's Library. 3 vols. New York: Dutton, 1932; rpt. 1964

The byrth of Mankynde newly translated out of Laten into Englysshe. . . Trans. Richard Jonas. 1540.

The byrth of mankynde, otherwyse named the womans booke. . . . Trans. Thomas Raynold. 1545.

[Campbell, John]. *A Particular but Melancholy Account of the Great Hardships, Difficulties, and Miseries, that those Unhappy and Much-to-be-pitied Creatures, The Common Women of the Town, Are plung'd into at this Juncture.* 1752.

Chamberlen, Peter. *A Voice in Rhama: or, the Crie of Women and Children.* 1647.

Chapman, Edmund. *Treatise on the Improvement of Midwifery, chiefly with regard to the Operation, second edition*. 1735.

The Character of a Town-Gallant; exposing the Extravagent Fopperies of some vain Self-conceited Pretenders to Gentility and good Breeding. 1675.

The Character of a Towne-Misse. 1675.

Cheyne, George. *The English Malady: or, A Treatise of Nervous Diseases of all Kinds, as Spleen, Vapours, Lowness of Spirits, Hypochondrical and Hysterical Distempers, &c*. 1733.

The Compleat Midwifes Practice. . . . from the experience not only of our English, but also of the most accomplisht and absolute Practicers among the French, Spanish, Italian, and other Nations. . . . with Instructions of the Midwife to the Queen of France . . . touching the practice of the said Art. 1656.

The Compleat Midwife's Practice Enlarg'd. In the most weighty and high Concernments of the Birth of Man. Containing Perfect Rules for Midwives and Nurses, as also for Women in their Conception, Bearing, and Nursing of Children. . . . a Work so plain, that the weakest capacity may easily attain the knowledge of the whole Art . . . The Second Edition corrected. 1659.

Congreve, William. *Love for Love*. 1695.

——. *The Way of the World*. 1700.

Cooper, Thomas. *The Mystery of Witch-craft. Discovering the Truth, Nature, Occasions, Growth and Power therof*. 1617.

Cotta, John. *The Triall of Witchcraft, shewing the true and right Methode of the Discovery*. 1616.

Counsell, George. *The Art of Midwifery: or, the Midwife's Sure Guide*. 1752.

The Covent-Garden Magazine; or, Amorous Repository. Calculated solely for the Entertainment of the Polite World, And the Finishing of a Young Gentleman's Education, vol. II, 1773.

The Crafty Whore: or, The misery and iniquity of Bawdy Houses Laid open, In a dialogue between two Subtle Bawds, wherein, as in a mirrour, our

City-Curtesans may see their soul-destroying Art and Crafty devices, where-
by they Insnare and beguile Youth, pourtraied to the life, By the Pensell of
one of their late, (but now penitent) Captives, for the benefit of all, but
especially the younger sort. 1658.

Culpeper, Nicholas. A Directory for Midwives: or, A Guide for Women, In
their Conception, Bearing, And Suckling their Children. 1651.

Danet, Pierre. A Complete Dictionary of the Greek and Roman Antiquities.
1700.

Daventer, Henry à [Hendrik van de Venter]. The Art of Midwifery Improv'd. 1728.

Dawkes, T. The Midwife Rightly Instructed: or, the Way, which all Women
desirous to learn, should take, to acquire the true Knowledge and be
successful in the Practice of, the Art of Midwifery. With a Prefatory Address to the Married Part of the British Ladies, concerning the Choice of
proper Women to be employed as Midwives; and Directions for distinguishing the Good from the Bad. Written principally for the Use of
Women. 1736.

Defoe, Daniel. Religious Courtship: being Historical Discourses, on the
Necessity of Marrying Religious Husbands and Wives only. 1722.

____. The Fortunes and Misfortunes of the Famous Moll Flanders. Ed. G. A.
Starr. Oxford UP, 1971

____. Moll Flanders. Ed. Edward Kelly. New York: Norton, 1973.

____?. Some Considerations upon Street-walkers. With a Proposal for lessen-
ing the present number of them, n.d. [1726].

____. The Political History of the Devil, as well Ancient as Modern. 1726.

____. Conjugal Lewdness: or Matrimonial Whoredom. 1727.

Dekker, Thomas. The Honest Whore, parts I and II. 1604-05.

A Dialogue between two young Ladies lately married concerning Management of husbands. 1696.

Dionis, Pierre. A General Treatise of Midwifery. 1719.

A Discourse of Artificial Beauty, In Point of Conscience, Between Two Ladies. 1662.

A Discourse of Women, Shewing Their Imperfections Alphabetically. 1662.

Douglas, John. *A Short Account of the State of Midwifery in London and Westminster.* 1736.

Drake, James. *Anthropologia Nova; or, A New System of Anatomy. Describing the Animal Oeconomy.* 2 vols. 1707.

Dryden, John. *The Wild Gallant.* 1662.

———. *Poems of 1693-1696.* Vol. 4 of *The Works of John Dryden.* Ed. A. B. Chambers, William Frost, and Vinton B. Dearing. Berkeley: U of California P, 1974.

[Dunton, John]. *The Night-Walker: or, Evening Rambles in search after Lewd Women, with the Conferences held with them, &c. To be publish'd Monthly, 'till a Discovery be made of all the chief Prostitutes in England, from the Pensionary Miss, down to the Common Strumpet. . . . Dedicated to the Whore-Masters of London and Westminster.* 1696.

Eliza's babes: or The Virgins-Offering. Being Divine Poems, and Meditations. Written by a lady, who onely desires to advance the glory of God, and not her own. 1652.

The English Midwife Enlarged, Containing Directions to Midwives. 1682.

Farquhar, George. *Love and a Bottle.* 1698.

The Female Advocate, or, an Answer to A Late Satyr Against The Pride, Lust and Inconstancy, &c. of Woman. Written by a Lady in Vindication of her Sex. 1686.

Fenton, Edward. *Certaine Secrete Wonders of Nature.* 1569.

Ferrand, James. *Erotomania. Or A Treatise Discoursing of the Essence, Causes, Symptomes, Prognosticks, and Cure of Love or Erotique Melancholy.* Oxford, 1640.

The Fifteen comforts of Matrimony. Or, a Looking-glass for all Those who have Enter'd in that Holy and Comfortable State. Wherein are sum'd up all those Blessings that attend a Married Life. Dedicated to Batchelors and Widdowers. 1706.

The Fifteen comforts of Whoring, Or, The Pleasures of a Town-Life. Dedicated to the Youth of the present Age. 1706.

The Fifteen Plagues of a Maiden-Head. Written by Madam B-le. 1707.

Fontanus, Nicolaus. *The Woman's Doctour: or, an exact and distinct Explanation of all such Diseases as are peculiar to that Sex.* 1652.

Foote, Samuel. *The Minor, a comedy.* 1760.

Ford, John, William Rowley, Thomas Dekker. *The Witch of Edmonton.* 1621.

Fortune's Fickle Distribution . . . Containing . . . The Life and Death of Moll Flanders . . . the Life of Jane Hackabout, her Governess; who was an Attorney's Daughter, a Lady's Woman, a Whore, a Bawd, a Pawn-broker, a Breeder up of Thieves, a Receiver of Stolen Goods, and at last died a Penitent. 1730.

Freind, John. *Emmenologia.* 1729.

Galtruchius, P. [Gautruche]. *The Poetical Histories. Being a compleat Collection of all the Stories necessary for a perfect Understanding of the Greek and Latine poets, and other ancient Authors*, third edition. 1674.

Gay, Joseph [J. D. Breval]. *The Lure of Venus: or, A Harlot's Progress. An Heroi-comical Poem. In Six Cantos . . . Founded upon Mr. Hogarth's Six Paintings.* 1733.

Giffard, William. *Cases in Midwifery.* 1734.

[Gould, Robert]. *Love given o'er: Or, a Satyr against the Pride, Lust, and Inconstancy, &c. of Woman.* 1683.

Graaf, Regnier de. *On the Human Reproductive Organs* [1672]. Trans. H. D. Jocelyn and B. P. Setchel. *Journal of Reproduction and Fertility*, Supplement nó. 17. Oxford: Blackwell, 1972.

Guillimeau, James. *Child-birth Or, The Happy Deliverie of Women. Wherein is set downe the Government of Women. In the time of their breeding*

Childe: Of their Travaile, both Naturall, and contrary to Nature: And of their lying in. 1612.

The Harlot's Progress. Being the Life of the noted Moll Hackabout, in Six Hudibrastick Canto's. 1740.

Harvey, William. *Anatomical Exercitations, Concerning the Generation of Living Creatures: To which are added Particular Discourses, of Births, and of Conceptions.* 1653.

[Head, Richard]. *The Life and Death of Mother Shipton. Being not only a true Account of her Strange Birth, and most Important Passages of her Life, but also of her Prophecies.* 1684.

———. *The English Rogue, or Witty Extravagant.* 1689.

Hesiod. *The Homeric Hymns and Homerica.* Trans. H. G. Evelyn-White. Loeb Classical Library. Heinemann, 1914.

Heywood, Thomas, and Richard Brome. *The Late Lancashire witches.* [1634].

Hippocrates. *The Presages of Divine Hippocrates.* 1634.

The History of Intriguing. 1735.

Hogarth, William. *Hogarth's Graphic Works.* Comp. Ronald Paulson. 2 vols. New Haven: Yale UP, 1965.

A Hue and Cry after a Man-Midwife, who has lately deliver'd the Land-Bank of their Money. 1699.

The Humours of Fleet-Street: and the Strand; Being the Lives and Adventures of the most noted Ladies of Pleasure; whether in the Rank of Kept-Mistresses, Or the more humble Station of Ladies of the Town. By an Old Sportsman, n.d. [1749].

Johnson, Charles. *Caelia: or, the Perjur'd Lover.* A play. 1733.

King, William. *An Historical Account of Heathen Gods and Heroes, Necessary for the Understanding of the Ancient Poets,* second edition. [1711?].

Levret, André. *L'art des accouchements demontré par des principes de physique et de mécanique.* Paris, 1753.

The Life of Mother Gin. 1736.

The London Bawd: with Her Character and Life. Discovering the Various and Subtile Intrigues of Lewd Women, fourth edition. 1711.

Look e'er you Leap: or, a History of the Lives and Intrigues of Lewd Women: with the Arraignment of their several Vices. 1710.

Lucian. *The Works of Lucian, translated from the Greek, by several Eminent Hands* ["The Dialogues of the Courtisans" trans. Thomas Brown]. 4 vols. 1711.

Lyly, John. *Endymion.* 1588.

———. *Mother Bombie,* ca. 1590.

McMath, James. *The Expert Mid-wife: A Treatise Of The Diseases of Women with Child, And in Child-Bed: As Also, Of the best Ways and Means of Help in Natural and Unnatural Labours.* 1694.

Malleus Maleficarum [ca. 1485]. Trans. Montague Summers. Pushkin, 1928.

[Mandeville, Bernard]. *The Virgin Unmask'd: or, Female Dialogues Betwixt an Elderly Maiden Lady and her Niece. . . . on Love, Marriage, Memoirs, and Morals,* &c. of the Times. 1709.

———. *A Treatise of the Hypochondriack and Hysterick Passions, Vulgarly call'd the Hypo in Men and Vapours in Women. In which the Symptoms, Causes, and Cure of those Diseases are set forth after a Method intirely new.* 1711.

———. *A Modest Defence of Publick Stews: or, an Essay upon Whoring, As it is now practis'd in these Kingdoms. . . . Written by a Layman.* 1724.

Marston, John. *The Dutch Courtesan.* 1603-05.

———. *The Malcontent.* 1604.

Massinger, Philip. *The City Madam,* a comedie. 1658.

Maubray, John. *The Female Physician. Containing all the Diseases incident to that Sex. . . . To which is added, the Whole Art of New Improv'd Midwifery*, 1724.

———. *Midwifery Brought to Perfection, By Manual Operation; Illustrated in a Lecture*. 1725.

Mauriceau, Francis. *The Accomplisht Midwife, Treating of the Diseases of Women with Child, and in Child-bed* . . . trans. Hugh Chamberlen. 1673.

The Midwife's Ghost, [a ballad]. 1680.

Mother Midnight's Miscellany . . . . By Mary Midnight, Midwife to all the Inhabitants of this Cosmos, and to the Choice Spirits in the Elysian Shades. 1751.

The New Popish Sham-Plot discovered, bs. n.d. [1680].

Nihell, Elizabeth. *A Treatise on the Art of Midwifery. Setting forth Various Abuses therein, Especially as to the Practice with Instruments.* 1760.

Nocturnal Revels: or, the History of King's-Place and Other Modern Nunneries. Containing their Mysteries, Devotions, and Sacrifices. Comprising also, the Ancient and Present State of Promiscuous Gallantry: with the Portraits of the most Celebrated Demireps and Courtezans of this period. . . . By a Monk of the Order of St. Francis, second edition. 1779.

Oliver, John. *A Present To be given to Teeming Women, By their Husbands or Friends. Containing Scripture-Directions for Women with Child, how to prepare for the hour of Travel.* 1688.

Ould, Fielding. *A Treatise of Midwifery.* 1742.

Ovid. *The Art of Love, and Other Poems.* Trans. J. H. Mozley. The Loeb Classical Library. Heinemann, 1929.

———. *Metamorphoses.* Trans. Frank Justus Miller. The Loeb Classical Library. Heinemann, 1916.

Paré, Ambroise. *The Workes of that famous Chirurgion Ambrose Parey, trans. Thomas Johnson.* 1634.

Pechey, John. *The Compleat Midwife's Practice Enlarg'd*, fifth edition. 1698.

Peele, George. *The Arraignment of Paris*, [ca. 1582].

Plato. *Theaetetus*. Trans. John McDowell. Oxford: Clarendon, 1973.

——. *Timaeus*. Trans. Benjamin Jowett. *The Collected Dialogues of Plato* . . . . Ed. Edith Hamilton and Huntington Cairns. Bollingen Series 71. New York: Pantheon. 1961.

A Pleasant Treatise of Witches . . . By a Pen neer the Covent of Eluthery. 1673.

The Popes Letter, to Maddam Cellier in relation to her great Sufferings for the Catholick Cause. 1680.

Portal, Paul. *The Compleat Practice of Men and Women Midwives, Or the true Manner of Assisting a Woman in Child-bearing: Illustrated with a considerable Number of Observations.* 1705.

Pretty Doings in a Protestant Nation. Being A View of the Present State of Fornication, Whorecraft, and Adultery, in Great-Britain . . . *Inscrib'd to the Bona-Roba's in the several Hundreds, Chaces, Parks, and Warrens, North, East, West, and South of Covent Garden; and to the Band of Petticoat Pensioners.* 1734.

Pugh, Benjamin. *A Treatise of Midwifery, Chiefly with Regard to the Operation. With Several Improvements in that Art.* 1754.

Quillet, Claude. *Callipaediae; or, an Art how to have handsome Children* . . . *To which is added Paedotrophiae; or, the Art of Nursing and Breeding up Children.* 1710.

A Rich Closet of Physical Secrets Collected by the Elaborate Pains of four several Students in Physick. 1653.

Richardson, Samuel. *Pamela or, Virtue Rewarded*. Ed. T. C. Duncan Eaves and Ben D. Kimpel. Boston: Houghton Mifflin, 1971.

——. *Clarissa or, the History of a Young Lady*. Everyman's Library. 4 vols. Dent, 1932; rpt. 1967.

——. *The Correspondence of Samuel Richardson*. Ed. Anna Laetitia Barbauld. 6 vols. 1804.

_____. *Selected Letters of Samuel Richardson*. Ed. John Carroll. Oxford: Clarendon, 1964.

Rösslin, Eucharius. *Der swangern frawen und hebammen Rosegarten*. Strasburg, 1512.

[Rueff, Jacob]. *The Expert Midwife or An Excellent and most necessary Treatise of the generation and birth of Man*. 1637.

Sad and Deplorable News from Fleet-Street, or, A Warning for Lovers. 1674.

Sadler, John. *The Sicke Womans Private Looking-glasse*. 1636.

Scot, Reginald. *The Discoverie of Witchcraft*. 1584.

A Serious Proposal to the Ladies, For the Advancement of their true and greatest Interest. By a Lover of Her Sex. 1694.

Sermon, William. *The Ladies Companion, or The English Midwife. Wherein is demonstrated, The manner and order how Women ought to govern themselves, during the whole time of their breeding Children; and of their difficult Labour, hard Travail, and Lying-in, &c*. 1671.

Shadwell, Thomas. *The Humourists*. 1671.

_____. *The Miser*. 1672.

_____. *The Virtuoso*. 1676.

_____. *A True Widow*. 1679.

_____. *The Woman Captain*. 1680.

_____. *The Lancashire Witches*. 1682.

Sharp, Jane. *The Midwives Book. Or the whole Art of Midwifry Discovered. Directing Childbearing Women how to behave themselves in their Conception, Breeding, Bearing, and Nursing of children*. 1671.

Shirley, James. *The Lady of Pleasure*. 1635.

Smart, Christopher. *The Midwife, or the Old Woman's Magazine. Containing all the Wit and all the Humour, and all the Learning, and all the Judgment, that has ever been, or ever will be inserted in all other Magazines . . . so that those who buy this Book will need no other,* n.d. [1751].

Smellie, William. *A Treatise on the Theory and Practice of Midwifery.* 3 vols. 1752-64.

——. *A Sett of Anatomical Tables, with Explanations, and an Abridgement of the practice of Midwifery.* 1754.

Sophia, or Woman not inferior to Man. 1739.

Sterne, Laurence. *The Life and Opinions of Tristram Shandy, Gentleman.* Ed. James Aiken Work. New York: Odyssey, 1940.

——. *A Sentimental Journey through France and Italy by Mr. Yorick.* Ed. Gardner D. Stout, Jr. Berkeley: U of California P, 1967.

——. *The Letters of Laurence Sterne,* Ed. Lewis Perry Curtis. Oxford: Clarendon, 1935.

Stone, Sarah. *A Complete Practice of Midwifery.* 1737.

[Swetnam, Joseph]. *The Arraignment of Lewd, Idle, Froward, and Unconstant Women: or, the Vanities of Them; (chuse you whether) With a Commendation of the Wise, Vertuous, and Honest Women,* n.d. [1690?].

Taylor, John. *A Common Whore With all these Graces Grac'd: Shee's very honest, beautifull and chaste.* 1622.

——. *A Bawd.* 1635.

Tell-tale Cupids Lately discover'd in the Eyes of a certain Court Lady, Now Displac'd. . . . To which are Added . . . The Secret History of Conie-Borough-Street . . . [and] The Banish'd Countess, 1735.

[Thicknesse, Philip]. *Man-midwifery Analyzed: and the Tendency of that Practice Detected and Exposed.* 1764.

Tourneur, Cyril. *The Atheist's Tragedy,* [ca. 1609].

Trusler, John. *Hogarth Moralized.* 1768.

Turner, Daniel. *The Force of the Mother's Imagination upon her Foetus in Utero, still farther considered: in the Way of a Reply to Dr. Blondel's last Book.* 1730.

Vanbrugh, John. *The Relapse.* 1696.

The Wandring Whore. A Dialogue Between Magdalena a Crafty Bawd, Julietta an Exquisite Whore, Francion a Lascivious Gallant, and Gusman a Pimping Hector. 1660.

[Ward, Edward]. *The Insinuating Bawd: and the Repenting Harlot. Written by a Whore at Tunbridge, and Dedicated to a Bawd at the Bath,* n.d. [1699].

_____. *The London-spy Compleat,* in Eighteen Parts, second edition. 1704.

_____. *The London Terraefilius: or, The Satyrical Reformer. Being Drolling Reflections on the Vices and Vanities of Both Sexes.* 1707.

_____. *The Secret History of Clubs. . . . with their Original: and the Characters of the Most Noted Members thereof.* 1709.

_____. *The Whole Pleasures of Matrimony: Interwoven with sundry Delightful and Comical Stories. . . . To which is added, the Distructive Miseries of Whoring and Debauchery. Of All Its Dreadful Concomitants,* n.d. [1710?].

_____. *Female Policy Detected: Or, the Arts of a Designing Woman Laid Open.* 1716.

_____. *The Rise and Fall of Madam Coming-Sir: or, An Unfortunate Slip from the Tavern-Bar, Into the Surgeon's Powdering-Tub.* Suffolk, n.d. [1720?].

Webster, John. *The White Devil,* [ca. 1611].

The Whore: a Poem. Written by a Whore of Quality, n.d. [ca. 1780].

The Whore's Rhetorick, Calculated to the Meridian of London; and conformed to the Rules of Art. In two Dialogues [1683], rpt. Edinburgh, 1836.

Wilkes, John. *An Essay on Woman.* 1763.

Willis, Thomas. *Dr Willis's Practice of Physick, Being the whole Works of that Renowned and Famous Physician.* 1684.

Willughby, Percival. *Observations in Midwifery. As Also The Country Midwifes Opusculum or Vade Mecum* [ca. 1680], *ed. from the original MS. by Henry Blenkinsop.* Warwick, 1863.

Wolveridge, James. *Speculum Matricis; or, The Expert Midwives Handmaid. Catechistically Composed.* 1671.

Woolley, Hannah. *The Gentlewoman's Companion; or, Guide to the Female Sex . . . With Letters and Discourses upon all Occasions. Whereunto is added, a Guide for Cook-maids, Dairy-maids, Chamber-maids, and all others that go to Service. The whole being an exact Rule for the Female Sex in General.* 1675.

Wycherley, William. *Love in a Wood.* 1672.

———. *The Gentleman Dancing-Master.* 1673.

Young, Edward. *The Complaint: or, Night-Thoughts on Life, Death and Immortality.* 1742.

SELECT BIBLIOGRAPHY
OF SECONDARY SOURCES

Aveling, J. H. *English Midwives, their History and Prospects*. London, 1872. Rpt. New York: AMS Press, 1977.

———. *The Chamberlens and Midwifery Forceps*. London, 1892. Rpt. New York: AMS Press, 1977.

Baird, Theodore. "The Time-Scheme of *Tristram Shandy* and A Source." *PMLA* 51 (1936): 803–20.

Barthes, Roland. *Critical Essays*. Trans. Richard Howard. Evanston, Ill.: Northwestern UP, 1972.

Blewett, David. *Defoe's Art of Fiction*. Toronto: U of Toronto P, 1979.

Bloch, Ivan [Iwan]. *Sexual Life in England, Past and Present*. Trans. William H. Forstern. London: Alder, 1938.

Boucé, Paul-Gabriel, ed. *Sexuality in Eighteenth-Century Britain*. Manchester: Manchester UP, 1982.

Brady, Frank. "*Tristram Shandy*: Sexuality, Morality, and Sensibility." *ECS* 4 (1970): 41–56.

Brooks, Douglas. *Number and Pattern in the Eighteenth-Century Novel: Defoe, Fielding, Smollett, and Sterne*. London: Routledge and Kegan Paul, 1983.

Carroll, John, ed. *Samuel Richardson: A Collection of Critical Essays*. Englewood Cliffs, N.J.: Prentice Hall, 1969.

———. "Lovelace as Tragic Hero." *UTQ* 42 (1972): 14–25.

Cash, Arthur H. "The Birth of Tristram Shandy: Sterne and Dr. Burton." *Studies in the Eighteenth Century: Papers Presented at the David Nicholl Smith Seminar 1966* (Canberra: Australian National UP, 1968), 133–54. Rpt. Boucé, *Sexuality in Eighteenth-Century Britain*, 198–224.

———. *Laurence Sterne: The Early and Middle Years*. London: Methuen, 1975.

Castle, Terry. *Clarissa's Ciphers: Meaning and Disruption in Richardson's Clarissa.* Ithaca: Cornell UP, 1982.

Chaber, Lois A. "Matriarchal Mirror: Women and Capital in *Moll Flanders.*" *PMLA* 97 (1982): 212–26.

Clark, Alice. *Working Life of Women in the Seventeenth Century.* 1919. Rpt. New York: Kelley, 1968.

Cunnington, C. Willet and Phillis. *Handbook of English Costume in the Eighteenth Century.* 2nd ed. London: Faber and Faber. 1964.

Curtis, Lewis Perry. "The First Printer of *Tristram Shandy.*" *PMLA* 47 (1932): 777–89.

Davis, Lennard. *Factual Fictions: The Origins of the English Novel.* New York: Columbia UP, 1983.

Donnison, Jean. *Midwives and Medical Men: A History of Inter-Professional Rivalries and Women's Rights.* London: Heinemann, 1977.

Doody, Margaret Anne. *A Natural Passion: A Study of the Novels of Samuel Richardson.* Oxford: Clarendon, 1974.

Doran, A. "Burton ('Dr Slop'): His Forceps and His Foes." *Journal of Obstetrics and Gynaecology of the British Empire* 23 (1913): 3–24, 65–86.

Dufour, Pierre [Paul Lacroix]. *Histoire de la Prostitution chex tous les peuples.* 6 vols. Brussels, 1851–54.

Dussinger, John A. "Conscience and the Pattern of Christian Perfection in *Clarissa.*" *PMLA* 81 (1966): 236–45.

——. "Richardson's Tragic Muse." *PQ* 46 (1967): 18–33.

——. "What Pamela Knew: an Interpretation." *JEGP* 69 (1970): 377–93.

Eagleton, Terry. *The Rape of Clarissa: Writing, Sexuality, and Class Struggle in Samuel Richardson.* Oxford: Blackwell, 1982.

Easlea, Brian. *Science and Sexual Oppression: Patriarchy's Confrontation with Woman and Nature.* London: Weidenfeld and Nicolson, 1981.

Eaves, T. C. Duncan, and Ben Kimpel. "The Publisher of *Pamela* and Its First Audience." *Bulletin of the New York Public Library* 64 (1960): 143–46.

——. *Samuel Richardson: A Biography*. Oxford: Clarendon, 1971.

Eddy, W. A. "Tom Brown and *Tristram Shandy*." *MLN* 44 (1929): 379–81.

Erickson, Robert A. "Starting Over with *Robinson Crusoe*." *Studies in the Literary Imagination*. Ed. Malinda Snow. 15 (1982): 51–73.

——. "Situations of Identity in *The Memoirs of Martinus Scriblerus*. *MLQ* 26 (1965): 388–400.

——. " 'The Books of Generation': Some Observations on the Style of the British Midwife Books, 1671–1764." Boucé, *Sexuality in Eighteenth-Century Britain*, 74–94.

Fasbender, Heinrich. *Geschichte der Geburtshülfe*. Jena: Fischer, 1906.

Flack, I. H. [Harvey Graham]. *Eternal Eve*. London: Heinemann, 1950.

Folkenflik, Robert. "A Room of Pamela's Own." *ELH* 39 (1972): 585–96.

Forbes, Thomas. *The Midwife and the Witch*. New Haven: Yale UP, 1966.

Foxon, David. *Libertine Literature in England, 1660–1745*. New Hyde Park, N.Y.: University Books, 1966.

Fraser, Antonia. *The Weaker Vessel*. New York: Random House, 1985.

Freedman, William. *Laurence Sterne and the Origins of the Musical Novel*. Athens, Georgia: U of Georgia P, 1978.

Frye, Northrop. *The Anatomy of Criticism: Four Essays*. 1957. Rpt. New York: Atheneum, 1966.

Frye, Roland Mushat. *Milton's Imagery and the Visual Arts: Iconographic Tradition in the Epic Poems*. Princeton: Princeton UP. 1978.

George, M. Dorothy. *London Life in the Eighteenth Century*. London: Kegan Paul, 1925.

Glaister, John. *Dr. William Smellie and His Contemporaries. A Contribution to the History of Midwifery in the Eighteenth Century*. Glasgow, 1894.

Green, William Chase. *Moira: Fate, Good, and Evil in Greek Thought*. Cambridge, Mass.: Harvard UP, 1944.

Harris, Anthony. *Night's Black Agents: Witchcraft and Magic in Seventeenth-Century English Drama*. Manchester: Manchester UP, 1980.

Hartley, Lodwick. *Laurence Sterne in the Twentieth Century: An Essay and a Bibliography of Sternean Studies 1900–1965*. Chapel Hill: U of N. Carolina P, 1966.

Hecht, J. Jean. *The Domestic Servant Class in the 18th Century*. London: Routledge and Kegan Paul, 1956.

Henriques, L. Fernando. *Prostitution and Society,* vol. 2 of *Prostitution in Europe and the New World*. 3 vols. London: MacGibbon and Kee, 1963.

Hilles, Frederick W. "The Plan of *Clarissa*." *PQ* 45 (1966): 236–48. Rpt. Carroll, *Samuel Richardson: A Collection of Critical Essays*, 80–91.

Holtz, William V. *Image and Immortality: A Study of* Tristram Shandy. Providence: Brown UP, 1970.

———. "Typography, *Tristram Shandy,* the Aposiopesis, etc." *The Winged Skull: Papers from the Laurence Sterne Bicentenary Conference*. Ed. Arthur H. Cash and John M. Stedmond. Kent State UP, 1971. 247–57.

Howson, Gerald. "Who Was Moll Flanders?" *TLS* (18 Jan. 1968), 63–64. Rpt. *Moll Flanders,* ed. Kelly, 312–19.

———. *Thief-taker General: The Rise and Fall of Jonathan Wild*. New York: St. Martin's, 1970.

Janet, Pierre. *The Major Symptoms of Hysteria*. 1929. Rpt. New York: Hafner, 1965.

Johnstone, R. W. *William Smellie: The Master of British Midwifery*. Edinburgh: Livingstone, 1952.

Keevil, J. J. "The Bagnio in London, 1648–1725." *Journal of the History of Medicine* 7 (1952): 250–57.

Kierkegaard, Søren. *The Concept of Dread*, trans. Walter Lowrie. Princeton UP, 1957.

King, Lester S. *The Medical World of the Eighteenth Century*. Chicago: U of Chicago P, 1958.

Kittredge, G. L. *Witchcraft in Old and New England*. Cambridge, Mass.: Harvard UP, 1929.

Konigsberg, Ira. *Samuel Richardson and the Dramatic Novel*. Lexington: UP of Kentucky, 1968.

Landa, Louis. "The Shandean Homunculus: The Background of Sterne's 'Little Gentleman.' " *Restoration and Eighteenth-century Literature: Essays in Honour of Alan Dugald McKillop*. Ed. C. Carroll Camden. Chicago: U of Chicago P, 1963. 49–68.

Lanham, Richard A. Tristram Shandy *and the Games of Pleasure*. Berkeley: U of California P, 1973.

Laurence-Anderson, Judith. "Changing Affective Life in 18th-century England and Samuel Richardson's *Pamela*." *Studies in Eighteenth-Century Culture* 10 (1981): 445–56.

Leed, Jacob. "Richardson's Pamela and Sidney's." *AUMLA* no. 40 (1973): 240–45.

Lerenbaum, Miriam. "Moll Flanders: 'A Woman on her own Account.' " *The Authority of Experience: Essays in Feminist Criticism*. Ed. Arlyn Diamond and Lee R. Edwards. Amherst: U of Massachusetts P, 1977. 101–17.

McKillop, Alan Dugald. *The Early Masters of English Fiction*. Lawrence: U of Kansas P, 1956.

McMaster, Juliet. "The Equation of Love and Money in *Moll Flanders*." *Studies in the Novel* 2 (1970): 131–44.

Malcolm, Janet. *Psychoanalysis, the Impossible Profession*. New York: Knopf, 1981.

Martin, Terence. "The Unity of Moll Flanders." *MLQ* 22 (1961), 115–24. Rpt. *Moll Flanders*, ed. Kelly, 362–71.

Mead, Kate Campbell (Hurd). *A History of Women in Medicine: From the Earliest Times to the Beginning of the Nineteenth-Century*. Haddam, Conn., 1938. Rpt. New York: AMS Press, 1977.

The Memoirs of Martinus Scriblerus. Ed. Charles Kerby-Miller. 1950. Rpt. New York: Russell and Russell, 1966.

Miller, Nancy K. *The Heroine's Text: Readings in the French and English Novel, 1722–1782*. New York: Columbia UP, 1980.

Moglen, Helene. *The Philosophical Irony of Laurence Sterne*. Gainesville: U of Florida P, 1975.

Muecke, D. C. "Beauty and Mr. B." *SEL* 7 (1967): 467–74.

Neumann, Erich. *The Great Mother: An Analysis of the Archetype*. Trans. Ralph Manheim. Bollingen Series 47. Princeton: Princeton UP, 1955.

Notestein, Wallace. *A History of Witchcraft in England from 1558 to 1718*. Washington, D.C.: American Historical Association, 1911.

Novak, Maximillian E. "Defoe's 'Indifferent Monitor': The Complexity of *Moll Flanders*." *ECS* 3 (1970): 351–65. Rpt. *Moll Flanders*, ed. Kelly, 414–21.

Ong, Walter J. *Interfaces of the Word: Studies in the Evolution of Consciousness and Culture*. Ithaca: Cornell UP, 1977

Onians, Richard Brixton. *The Origins of European Thought About the Body, the Mind, the Soul, the World, Time and Fate*. Cambridge: Cambridge UP, 1951.

Palmer, William J. "Two Dramatists: Lovelace and Richardson in *Clarissa*." *Studies in the Novel* 5 (1973): 13–21.

Park, William. "Clarissa as Tragedy." *SEL* 16 (1976): 461–71.

Patch, Howard R. *The Goddess Fortuna in Medieval Literature*. Cambridge, Mass.: Harvard UP, 1927.

Preston, John. *The Created Self: the Reader's Role in Eighteenth-Century Fiction*. New York: Barnes and Noble, 1970.

Price, Martin. *To the Palace of Wisdom: Studies in Order and Energy from Dryden to Blake*. Garden City, N.Y.: Doubleday, 1964.

Radner, John B. " 'The Youthful Harlot's Curse': The Prostitute as Symbol of the City in 18th-Century Literature." *Eighteenth-Century Life* 2 (1976): 59–64.

Rank, Otto. *The Trauma of Birth*. London: Kegan Paul, 1929.

Richetti, John J. *Popular Fiction Before Richardson: Narrative Patterns 1700–1739*. Oxford: Clarendon, 1969.

Riley, Madeleine. *Brought to Bed*. London: Dent, 1968.

Rilke, Rainer Maria. *Letters to a Young Poet*. Trans. M. D. Herter Norton. Rev. ed. New York: Norton, 1962.

Rose, H. J. *A Handbook of Greek Mythology*. New York: Dutton, 1959.

Rothstein, Eric. *Systems of Order and Inquiry in Later Eighteenth-Century Fiction*. Berkeley: U of California P, 1975.

Rousseau, G. S. "Threshold and Explanation: the Social Anthropologist and the Critic of Eighteenth-Century Literature." *The Eighteenth Century: Theory and Interpretation* 22 (1981): 127–52.

Sacks, Elizabeth. *Shakespeare's Images of Pregnancy*. New York: St. Martin's, 1981.

Schnorrenberg, Barbara Brandon. "Is Childbirth Any Place for a Woman? The Decline of Midwifery in Eighteenth-Century England." *Studies in Eighteenth-Century Culture* 10 (1981): 393–408.

Shinagel, Michael. "The Maternal Paradox in *Moll Flanders*: Craft and Character." *Cornell Library Journal* 7 (1969): 3–23. Rpt. *Moll Flanders*, ed. Kelly, 404–14.

Short-Title Catalogue of Books Printed Before 1851 in the Library of the Royal College of Obstetricians and Gynaecologists. 2nd. ed. London: Royal College of Obstetricians and Gynaecologists, 1968.

Shuttle, Penelope, and Peter Redgrove. *The Wise Wound: Menstruation and Everywoman*. London: Gollancz, 1978.

Spencer, Herbert R. *The Renaissance of Midwifery*. London: Harrison, 1924.

———. *The History of British Midwifery from 1650 to 1800*. London: Bale, 1927. Rpt. New York: AMS Press, 1978.

Stone, Lawrence. *The Family, Sex, and Marriage in England 1500–1800*. London: Weidenfeld and Nicolson, 1977.

Thomas, Keith. *Religion and the Decline of Magic*. New York: Scribner's, 1971.

Thompson, Roger. *Unfit for Modest Ears: A Study of Pornographic, Obscene, and Bawdy Works Written or Published in England in the Second Half of the Seventeenth Century*. London: Macmillan, 1979.

Tillich, Paul. *The Courage to Be*. New Haven: Yale UP, 1952.

Todd, Janet. *Women's Friendship in Literature*. New York: Columbia UP, 1980.

Towers, A. R. "Sterne's Cock and Bull Story." *ELH* 24 (1957): 12–29.

Turner, Victor, *The Ritual Process: Structure and Anti-Structure*. Ithaca: Cornell UP, 1969.

Veith, Ilza. *Hysteria: The History of a Disease*. Chicago: U of Chicago P, 1965.

Warner, William Beatty. *Reading* Clarissa: *the Struggles of Interpretation*. New Haven: Yale UP, 1979.

Watt, Ian. *The Rise of the Novel: Studies in Defoe, Richardson and Fielding*. 1957. Berkeley: U of California P, 1965.

Weinstein, Arnold. *Fictions of the Self, 1500–1800*. Princeton: Princeton UP, 1981.

Whiting, J. R. S. *A Handful of History*. Dursley, Gloucs.: Sutton, 1978.

Wilson, Stuart. "Richardson's *Pamela*: An Interpretation." *PMLA* 88 (1973): 79–91.

Zimmerman, Everett. *Defoe and the Novel*. Berkeley: U of California P, 1975.

INDEX

46, 63; Moll Flanders (the character) x, 4–5, 10, 15, 18–19, 22, 30, 38, 40–42, 45–68 passim, 130, 252, 254–55; her "grand Secret," 46, 49, 55; her "true Name," 46, 49–50, 65, 67, 254, 269; as author, 250, 254, 257; and fate, ix, 45–46, 48, 51, 55, 57, 64–65, 67; and her mother, 48–50, 53–55, 67–68, 269; and Jemy, 49, 51, 60, 66–67; and Newgate, 41, 49, 62, 65–68, 168, 271; and Governess ("Mother Midnight"), 4, 10, 19, 22, 24, 26, 41, 45–68 passim, 213, 234, 241, 243, 252, 268–70, 279 (as midwife, 47, 53–55; as bawd, 52–53; as witch, 55; as Moll's fate, 47, 57; Moll's final relation to, 254–55); Robinson Crusoe, xi
Dekker, Thomas, 264–65
"delicacy" (female), 33
Desdemona, 3, 267
Diamond, Arlyn, 270
Dickens, Charles, xi, 230
Diogenes Laertius, 222
Dionis, Pierre, General Treatise of Midwifery, 221–22, 226, 266, 291
Discourse of Artificial Beauty, A, 275
Discourse of Women, A, 25
Donne, John, xi, 42, 217–18, 242, 267, 274, 286, 289
Donnison, Jean, 17, 21, 212, 264
Doody, Margaret, ix, 276, 279
Drake, James, 292
Draper, Mrs. Daniel ("Eliza"), 287
Drexelius (Jeremiah Drexel), 142
Dryden, John, xi, 109, 157, 261, 265, 277, 282–83
duenna, 265
Dunkirk, demolition of, 241–42
Dunton, John, The Night-Walker, 21, 30, 74, 265–66, 272, 274, 278, 293
Dussinger, John, 273, 276, 278, 282

Eagleton, Terry, xii
Earth (as mother), 7, 15
Easlea, Brian, xiii, 277, 287, 289–91
Eaves, T. C. Duncan, 272, 281
Eddy, W. A., 291
Edmund, 116
Edwards, Lee R., 270
Egyptians, ancient, 11

Eliot, T. S., 113, 261
embryology (18th-c.), 202
England, x, 204, 207, 214
English Midwife, The, 262
Ent, George, 289
Erasmus, Desiderius, 214
Erebus, 7
Erickson, Robert A., 286–87
Eve, 24, 33, 38, 57, 111, 120, 124, 129, 136, 213, 265
Everyman, 201

Fainall, xii
Fame, 9
Farrell, William J., 276
Fasbender, Heinrich, 261
Fate (fates, the Fates, destiny; see also "midwife," "bawd," "witch," "Mother Midnight" and entries under individual novels), 14, 41; role of in English fiction, ix; humanized, 4, 8, 252; as figure (in 17th- and 18th-c. literature), 88, 252; Greek Fates, 7–8, 40, 55, 71, 219, 251–52, 276; and Night, 7; with urn of names, 8–9; and the world, 8; androgynous nature of, 8; as oracle, 8; as a power, 8, 252; as fée, fairy, 11; as spinner of mankind, 7, 11, 13, 73, 251; as reader, 256, 259; defined, 4, 8, 249, 252; duality of, ix, 249, 252; and hand image, 252; linguistic nature of, ix, 4, 8–11 (as fatum, 8–9, 133, 178, 214; oral aspect of, 9; written aspect of, 10); and silence, 10; Book of, 9; fata scribunda, 9; and astrology, 9; and procreation, ix, 9; law of, 10; and binding nature of, 252; rhetoric of, 252–53
Festrop, Ann, 270–71
Fielding, Henry, 10, 22, 67, 218, 239, 250, 272, 281, 290
Fielding, Sarah, 276
Foley, Robert, 290
Folkenflik, Robert, 272
Folly, Dame, 214
Foote, Samuel, 31
Forbes, Thomas, 17, 263–64
Ford, John, 264
Fortune, 7, 14, 40, 211, 214, 231
France, 207
Francis Spira, 142
Fraser, Antonia, 279

320 INDEX

77; as her reader, 75–78, 99–102; as her author, 100–02; and her fate, 78, 81, 89, 100, 252; his rape of the text, 101–02, 164); and Mrs. Jewkes, xi, 4–5, 19, 22, 41, 80–98 *passim*, 131, 141, 151, 155, 167–68, 172, 184–85, 213, 229, 234, 241, 252, 272–74; (as cunning woman, 83, 85; as bawd, 82–83, 88; as witch, 83, 85–86, 88; as "torturing" midwife, 87–88; description of, 87–88; Pamela's final relation to, 255); *Sir Charles Grandison*, 124

Riley, Madeleine, 262
Rilke, Rainer Maria, 288–89
Rochester, Earl of, 21, 33
romance, medieval English, 272
Roman de la Rose, 265
Rose, H. J., 11, 262
Rösslin, Eucharius, 199, 263
Rothstein, Eric, 285
Rousseau, G. S., 293
Rowley, William, 264
Rueff, Jacob, 263–64
Rumour (as fate), 9

Sacks, Elizabeth, 285
sage femme, 264
Sawyer, Mother Elizabeth, 264
Scot, Reginald, 88
Scriblerians, the, 186, 196, 202, 277, 287, 291
secrets, women's, 6, 250
Serious Proposal to the Ladies, A, 293
Sermon, William, *The Ladies Companion*, ix, 5–7, 12, 19, 21, 53, 59–61, 94, 213, 261–62, 264, 269–70, 274, 286–87, 289; definition of midwife, 5–6
servant girls, 22, 30
sexual intercourse, 222–23, 225–26, 290
Shadwell, Thomas, 265
Shakespeare, William, 3, 5, 109, 116, 125, 132, 139, 162–63, 188
Sharp, Jane, ix, 12, 16–17, 51, 221–22, 262–64, 273–74, 288–89, 291; on sexual anatomy, 16
Shekinah, 206
Shinagel, Michael, 271
Shipton, Mother, 19–20, 88, 264
Shirley, John, 265
Shuttle, Penelope, 263

Sidney, Sir Philip, 273
Silenus, 187
Sin, iconography of, 282
Smart, Christopher, xi, 277
Smellie, William, 212, 230, 235–36, 245, 287; "Adrianus Smelvgot," 232, 234; on mechanism of labor, 205, 250; on retarded childbirth, 233, 293; on sexual act, 288; diction of, 292
Smith, Harriet, xi
Smollett, Tobias, 250, 290
Socrates, 19, 71, 250; son of a midwife, 6
Sodom, 195
Solomon, 25, 38, 172, 176
Some Considerations upon Streetwalkers, 267, 281
Sparsit, Mrs., xi
Spencer, Herbert R., 262
Spenser, Edmund, 3, 109
Spinners, the, 7
Starr, G. A., 268–71
stars, the (and fate), 9
Stedmond, John, 290
Sterne, Laurence, xii, 5, 9, 25, 30, 42, 195–259 *passim*, 284–85; and Dodsley, 195–96; as literary anatomist, 198, 241, 258; library of, 286; on "first causes," 199; and Swift, 200; and Old Testament, 200; and the feminine, 203, 287, 293; and women's secrets, 250; and Nature, 289; and Madam, 204; and use of birth metaphors, 284; and his reader, 259; and written word, 250; and fate, 246–47, 287; self-description of, 288, 290; and lack of carnality, 207; as quasi-libertine, 290; and "Eliza," 287; as "Yorick," 287, 289–90
WORKS:
Letters, 284, 287–89, 293; *A Sentimental Journey*, 284, 286; *Tristram Shandy*, ix, 4–5, 10, 96, 195–248, 252, 262, 284–93; printing of, 195–96; as book, 196–97, 201, 210, 217; as midwife book, 198–210; three main actions of, 230; Tristram Shandy (the character), 195–248 *passim*, 250, 252–53, 258–59; on fate (fatality, the Fates), 199, 204, 211, 214, 217, 219, 231, 241, 243–44, 252, 259; and "the whole secret," 200, 202, 289; and Yorick, 204, 217–18; and Jenny, 207,

witch, ix, 4, 40, *264,* defined, 17; white
witch, 5, 18; black witch, 5, 18; and
maleficium, 17; and fate, 11; and cauls,
264, 266; evil eye of, *274;* and midwife, 17, 22; and bawd, 18–20, *264;*
and whore, *264*
witchcraft, 12, 19, 45, 80, 85–86, 142, 164,
241, 275
Wodehouse, John, *288*
Woolley, Hannah, *266*
Wolveridge, James, *Speculum Matricis,* ix,
13, 200, 205–06, 231, 262, 286–87,
290–91
woman (women; see also "womb"), 3–42
passim; representation of in 17th–18th
c., 33, 95–97, 215, 253; as man's
house, 25, 34; and art of sewing, 29,
34; and art of language, 33–34, 173;
and arts of pleasing, 34; and books,
267; "delicacy" of, 33, 107; and reputation for chastity, 37, 39, 268–69; secret
knowledge of, 6, 41; and orgasm, *280;*
and "grandmother wisdom," 148; and
Wisdom tradition, 171–77, 182, 192,

257; and Nature, 213; and error, *290;*
and "Hysterick Passion" (hysteria), 95–
97; and witchcraft, 142; and 17th c.
praisers of, 25, 33, 128, 173; and
motherhood, 45, 113–14; and mother-
daughter relationships, 40; as own betrayer, 37–39, 256; and the early
novel, 253
womb, defined, 15; metaphors for, 15–16,
222; history of, *263;* child sewn in, 13–
16, 29, 73, 84, 99, 249; independent
existence of, 15–16, 221; influence of,
15–16, 253
word (logos), 8
Work, James A., *284*
Wycherley, William, *265*

York, 195–96
York Courant, The, 285
Young, Edward, *276, 281, 283*

Zimmerman, Everett, *270*
Zoroaster, 206

AMS Studies in the Eighteenth Century: No. 10
ISSN: 0196-6561

Other titles in this series:

No. 1. Paul J. Korshin, editor. *Modern Language Association of America. Proceedings of the 1967-68 Neoclassicism Conferences. With a Selected Bibliography 1920-68.* 1970.

No. 2. Francesco Cordasco. *Tobias George Smollett: A Bibliographical Guide.* 1978.

No. 3. Paula R. Backscheider, editor. *Probability, Time, and Space in Eighteenth-Century Literature.* 1979.

No. 4. Ruth Perry. *Women, Letters, and the Novel.* 1980.

No. 5. Paul J. Korshin, editor. *The American Revolution and Eighteenth-Century Literature.* 1986.

No. 6. G. S. Rousseau, editor. *The Letters and Papers of Sir John Hill (1714-1775).* 1984.

No. 7. Paula R. Bachscheider. *A Being More Intense. A Study of the Prose Works on Bunyan, Swift, and Defoe.* 1984.

No. 8. Christopher Fox, editor. *Psychology and Literature in the Eigthteenth Century.* With illustrations by Michael DePorte. 1986.

No. 9. John F. Sena. *The Best-Natured Man. Sir Samuel Garth, Physican and Poet.* 1986.